Jaegwon Kim is one of the most eminent and most influential contribu-
tors to the philosophy of mind and metaphysics. This collection of essays
presents the core of his work on supervenience and mind with two sets
of postscripts especially written for the book.

The essays focus on such issues as the nature of causation and events,
what dependency relations other than causal relations connect facts and
events, the analysis of supervenience, and the mind–body problem. A
central problem in the philosophy of mind is the problem of explaining
how the mind can causally influence bodily processes. Professor Kim explores this problem in detail, criticizes the nonreductionist solutions to it,
and offers a modified reductionist solution of his own.

Both professional philosophers and their graduate students will find
this an invaluable collection.

CAMBRIDGE STUDIES IN PHILOSOPHY

Supervenience and mind

CAMBRIDGE STUDIES IN PHILOSOPHY

General editor ERNEST SOSA

Advisory editors J. E. J. ALTHAM, SIMON BLACKBURN,
GILBERT HARMAN, MARTIN HOLLIS, FRANK JACKSON,
WILLIAM G. LYCAN, JOHN PERRY,
SYDNEY SHOEMAKER, BARRY STROUD

RECENT TITLES

Supervenience and mind

SELECTED PHILOSOPHICAL ESSAYS

Jaegwon Kim

CAMBRIDGE
UNIVERSITY PRESS

Published by the Press Syndicate of the University of Cambridge
The Pitt Building, Trumpington Street, Cambridge CB2 1RP
40 West 20th Street, New York, NY 10011-4211, USA
10 Stamford Road, Oakleigh, Melbourne 3166, Australia

© Cambridge University Press 1993

First published 1993

Printed in the United States of America

Library of Congress Cataloging-in-Publication Data
Kim, Jaegwon.
Supervenience and mind : selected philosophical essays / Jaegwon Kim.
p.   cm. – (Cambridge studies in philosophy)
Includes bibliographical references and index.
ISBN 0-521-43394-0. – ISBN 0-521-43996-5 (pbk.)
1. Philosophy of mind.   2. Metaphysics.   I. Title.   II. Series.
BD418.3.K56   1993
128' .2 – dc 20   93-361
                                   CIP

A catalog record for this book is available from the British Library.

ISBN 0-521-43394-0 hardback
ISBN 0-521-43996-5 paperback

For Sylvia

Contents

Preface

The essays selected for this volume have been written over a period of approximately twenty years since the early 1970s, and are reprinted here without changes except for typographical and minor stylistic corrections and the updating of footnotes. Part I consists of papers on the metaphysical issues of events, causation, and supervenience; Part II includes papers on issues in the metaphysics of mind – in particular, mind–body supervenience and mental causation. Each part ends with a set of postscripts indicating my current thoughts on some of the central problems discussed therein.

I wish I could say that I stand by everything I said in these papers; on some issues I do of course, but on others my views have changed, rather significantly in a few instances, and I expect them to continue to change and evolve. On some of the issues I am not even clear just what I am now prepared to defend. This is the case, for example, with the theory of events. In Essays 1 and 3, I formulated and argued for what is now standardly called the "property exemplification" account of events, and I still think that it is a viable approach. However, I am now inclined to think that ontological schemes are by and large optional, and that the main considerations that should govern the choice of an ontology are those of utility, simplicity, elegance, and the like. Concerning such questions as whether there "really are" events (over and beyond substances and their properties), whether substances are "ontologically prior to" events or vice versa, what the "metaphysical nature" of events is, along with many other similar questions about facts, properties, continuants, time-slices, and so forth, it just seems wrong-headed to think that there are "true" answers, answers that are true because they correctly depict some pre-existing metaphysical order of the world. I think that the heart of ontological inquiry lies in construction rather than description. That is, the primary job of ontology should be to work out and purvey ontological options, alternative schemes that will suit our varied activities and aims in science and philosophy. Carnap may have been exactly right with his distinction between "external" and "internal" questions. I should add, though, that I do not hold this view about metaphysics in general, or even about all ontological issues.

Part I begins with three essays on events, causation, and noncausal modes of determination between events. Essay 1 ("Causation, Nomic Subsumption, and the Concept of Event") explores some ontological issues concerning the relata of causal relations within the framework of a broadly Humean ("nomic-subsumptive") conception of causation. This requires me to sharpen and refine a conception of event that I had earlier proposed in "Events and Their Descriptions."[1] This approach to the metaphysics of events, usually considered one of the two main alternatives in event theory (along with Donald Davidson's), is further elaborated in Essay 3 ("Events as Property Exemplifications").[2] Essay 2 ("Noncausal Connections") explores ways in which some events can depend on, or be determined by, other events – in particular, ways that are not modes of causal determination or dependence.

The remaining essays in Part I are concerned with the concept of supervenience and its applications. I wrote Essay 4 ("Concepts of Supervenience") as a general study of the supervenience relation, a project that was begun several years earlier in my "Supervenience and Nomological Incommensurables."[3] The characterization of "weak," "strong," and "global" supervenience, which has become fairly standard, is worked out in some detail here (a new definition of "strong" supervenience is offered in Essay 5, however). Essay 5 ("'Strong' and 'Global' Supervenience Revisited") was written in response to an error discovered in my "proof" in Essay 4 to show that global supervenience implies strong supervenience. I point out certain peculiar properties of global supervenience, and argue that to the extent that global supervenience fails to imply strong supervenience, it falls short as a relation of dependence strong enough for the statement of a robust physicalist position on the mind–body problem. But the question whether global supervenience implies strong supervenience remains murky, and is taken up again in my postscripts to Part I. Essay 6

1 In *Essays in Honor of Carl G. Hempel,* ed. Nicholas Rescher (Dordrecht: Reidel, 1969).
2 Important recent works on events include Lawrence B. Lombard, *Events: A Metaphysical Study* (London: Routledge & Kegan Paul, 1986), and Jonathan Bennet, *Events and Their Names* (Indianapolis: Hackett Publishing Company, 1988).
3 *American Philosophical Quarterly* 15 (1978): 149–156.

("Epiphenomenal and Supervenient Causation") applies supervenience to an analysis of macrocausation – that is, causal relations involving macroevents – in terms of causal processes at a more fundamental level, suggesting that we view mental causation as a species of macrocausation supervenient on underlying physiological causal processes.

Supervenience is standardly explained as a relation between two sets of properties over a *single domain* of individuals (e.g., mental and physical properties over the domain of persons or organisms; moral and nonmoral properties over the domain consisting of agents, acts or states of affairs, etc.). In Essay 7 ("Supervenience for Multiple Domains") I take steps toward extending the supervenience relation to pairs of property families over two distinct domains of individuals. Some broader issues of general interest are seen to arise when such an extension is attempted – for example, issues that have a bearing on the characterization of global supervenience. An early version of Essay 8 ("Supervenience as a Philosophical Concept") was delivered as the third annual Metaphilosophy Address at the CUNY Graduate Center in May 1989. It was intended as an overview of the state of philosophical discussion on the supervenience concepts around then, but contains a fair amount of new material as well. It also includes a brief historical survey in which I call attention to the role of "supervenience" in the emergentist writings and its relation to the supervenience concepts currently used by some nonreductive materialists. I speculate in that paper that perhaps Hare and others picked up the term "supervenience" from the emergentists; I am now pretty well convinced of that, as I am that the emergentists were the first "nonreductive physicalists" (see Essay 17).

Part I ends with three postscripts on supervenience. Postscript 1 discusses some issues that arise when *relations* as well as properties are explicitly taken into account in defining supervenience. In Postscript 2, I present reasons for taking a somewhat deflationary view of the metaphysical significance of the supervenience relation, a view that represents a departure from the rather expansive perspective taken in Essay 4. Postscript 3 contains further reflections on the relation between global and strong supervenience.

The essays of Part I span a period of two decades, and I wrote them, "one at a time," with little concern for developing a larger and more comprehensive system. In retrospect, though, a certain unity of philosophical purpose seems to emerge: these essays all have something to do with the relationships of *determination* and *dependence* – both the causal and noncausal kinds – holding for properties, events, and states of the world.

I believe that my interest in this was kindled in part by the realist stance on explanation that I have always found appealing (briefly stated in the opening paragraph of Essay 4; it is also in the background of my arguments in Essay 13). According to "explanatory realism," when something is correctly invoked as an explanation of another thing, the explanatory relation must be grounded in some objective relation of dependence or determination holding for the explanans and the explanandum. It rejects the idea that explanation, or understanding, is only an internal fact about our psychology or cognition – say, a matter only of "intellectual satisfaction," or of the "unity" and "simplicity" of our hypotheses – and promotes the view that there must be an objective basis, outside our system of beliefs, that makes correct explanations correct, and that separates true understanding from the illusory kind.[4] I realize that to some philosophers this will sound too baldly and naively realist, although there are others to whom it is not much more than a truism. I realize, too, that realism about explanation in this sense contrasts with a broadly "constructivist" stance on ontology that I expounded above in connection with event theory. In any case, from this perspective of explanatory realism, a study of objective dependence and determination relations is an essential component of the metaphysics of explanation.

Part II consists of a group of essays on the mind–body problem; the single exception is Essay 12 ("What is 'Naturalized Epistemology'?"), which concerns the issues of normativity and naturalism in epistemology. The concept of supervenience, however, plays a critical role in the arguments of this paper, and this was the reason for its inclusion in this volume. Essay 10 ("Psychophysical Supervenience") is concerned with the problem of formulating the thesis that the mental supervenes on the physical and the question why we might think it true. This paper includes a discussion of the apparent failure of certain intentional states to supervene "locally" – that is, on the *internal* physical states of the subject. The position that I defend concerning the psychological import of this failure of supervenience is analogous, in some ways, to the "narrow content" approach to mental causation now favored by some philosophers.[5] I now believe that the arguments of this paper are limited, and that they must be supple-

---

4 I discuss this in greater detail in "Explanatory Realism, Causal Realism, and Explanatory Exclusion," *Midwest Studies in Philosophy* 12 (1988): 225–240. David-Hillel Ruben defends a realist position very much like mine in his interesting book *Explaining Explanation* (London: Routledge, 1990), ch. 7.
5 See, e.g., Jerry Fodor, *Psychosemantics* (Cambridge, Mass.: The MIT Press, 1987), ch. 2.

mented by considerations of mental causation. One way of doing so, perhaps, is to flesh out the following line of thought: Suppose that the model of "supervenient causation" is the most plausible account of mental causation (see, however, "Postscripts on Mental Causation," section 1). But this account requires mind–body supervenience, from which it follows that if we want mental causation, we had better accept mind–body supervenience, and that if mental causation is real, mind–body supervenience must also be real.

Essay 11 ("Psychophysical Laws") began as a set of lecture notes for a class in philosophy of mind, and it was intended as nothing more than an exercise in the analysis and reconstruction of Davidson's well-known but ill-understood argument for the thesis, which many found surprising and implausible when first published in 1970,[6] that there can be no laws relating mental and physical phenomena. But for better or worse the paper comes across, I think, as a defense of Davidson. I was, and still am, ambivalent about Davidson's argument (or my version of it, anyway); in fact, the considerations adduced in the argument are prima facie incompatible with the strong supervenience of the mental on the physical, a thesis that I accept, at least provisionally, in several essays included in this volume. I must say, though, that I have not yet come across a totally convincing refutation of Davidson's argument.

Essay 13 ("Mechanism, Purpose, and Explanatory Exclusion") revives an old issue concerning the relation between a "purposive" explanation of a human action in terms of the agent's "reasons" and a "mechanistic" (e.g., neurobiological) explanation of it in terms of physiological mechanism. I defend the view, which has not been popular among philosophers, that the two types of explanations must be regarded as incompatible and mutually exclusionary – *unless* we accept an appropriate reductive relationship between intentional states and underlying biological processes. Further, I formulate and defend a general principle of "explanatory exclusion," the thesis that there can be no more than one "complete" and "independent" explanation for any single explanandum. My argument for this claim, especially as it pertains to causal explanations, provides a metaphysical underpinning for some of my principal arguments concerning mental causation.

Essay 14, delivered as the Presidential Address before the Central Division meeting of the American Philosophical Association in April 1989, is

6 "Mental Events," in *Experience and Theory*, ed. Lawrence Foster and J. W. Swanson (Amherst, Mass.: University of Massachusetts Press, 1970).

a critique of the current orthodoxy on the mind–body problem, "nonreductive materialism," which attempts to combine a materialist ontology (variously called "token physicalism," "the token-identity thesis," "ontological physicalism," etc.) with a dualism of mental and physical properties. The gist of my argument is that there is no plausible way in which the nonreductive physicalist can explain the causal efficacy of the mental, and, in consequence, that the nonreductivist is unable to defend the reality of the mental. Because of the nature of the occasion for which it was prepared, the arguments of this paper are somewhat roughly formulated and briskly presented. Some of these arguments appear in a more detailed form, and are better defended, elsewhere in this volume (Essays 15, 16, and 17).[7] Essay 15 ("Dretske on How Reasons Explain Behavior") examines Fred Dretske's interesting recent attempt to vindicate the causal efficacy of intentional states,[8] and further develops my account of mental causation as supervenient causation.

Essay 16 ("Multiple Realization and the Metaphysics of Reduction") is an extended examination of the widely accepted view that the so-called "multiple realizability" of mental properties refutes mind–body reductionism. I advance new considerations concerning "disjunctive properties" as nomic properties (here I depart from the views defended in Essay 8), and draw some unexpected implications concerning the status of the mental and the nature of psychology as a special science. I expect to do further work along the lines indicated in this paper.

Finally, Essay 17 ("The Nonreductivist's Troubles with Mental Causation") is an elaboration and continuation of my arguments in Essay 14 concerning the difficulties besetting the nonreductivist in accounting for mental causation. I argue that nonreductive physicalism resembles emergentism in certain critical respects, and that, like emergentism, it faces the notorious (and, to the nonreductive physicalist, devastating) problem of "downward causation."

Two postscripts on mental causation are appended to Part II. In Postscript 1, I express some reservations about my account of mental causation as supervenient causation. Postscript 2 sketches, in broad outlines, an alternative account of mental causation on the basis of considerations on mental properties advanced in Essay 16. I also describe, and commend,

---

7 Some of my arguments in Essay 14 are criticized by Donald Davidson in his "Thinking Causes," in *Mental Causation,* ed. John Heil and Alfred Mele (Oxford: Oxford University Press, 1993); for my reply see "Can Supervenience and 'Nonstrict Laws' Save Anomalous Monism?" in the same volume.

8 Fred Dretske, *Explaining Behavior* (Cambridge, Mass.: The MIT Press, 1988).

"multiple-type physicalism," a position on the ontology of mind that is intermediate between token physicalism and classic type physicalism. This postscript represents the kind of approach to the issues of mind and mental causation that I am now inclined to favor; however, all of this is part of the work I am now doing, and the situation on mental causation looks to me still quite fluid.

In writing these essays on the mind–body problem, my primary preoccupation has been with the problem of delineating the place of mind in a physical world, a project shared by many others who have worked in the philosophy of mind over the past several decades. Two basic assumptions both define the problem and constrain its possible solutions. The first assumption is physicalism, the claim that the world is fundamentally a physical world governed by physical law; the second assumption is mental realism, the view that mentality is a real feature of our world. Mental realism, as I argue in Essay 17, requires that mentality have genuine causal powers, powers to affect other events and processes of this world, whether these are mental or physical. Mental realism seems fundamental to our conception of ourselves as cognizers and agents; its renouncement would render our moral and cognitive life wholly unintelligible to us, plunging us into a state of self-alienation in which we could no longer understand, or care, why we do what we do, or how our norms and beliefs regulate our deliberations and decisions, or whether our emotions are appropriate in light of our beliefs and values. Nor does physicalism seem an avoidable option: if we take our science seriously – that is, if we are concerned to base our beliefs and judgments on our best knowledge of the world – it is difficult to resist the view that what is physical determines all the facts of the world. Not for nothing do we think of physics as our basic science. The central issue of the mind–body debate, therefore, is to answer this question: How is mental causation possible in a physical world? That is, how can the mind exert its causal powers in a world constituted by physical stuff and governed by physical law? Many of the essays in Part II are concerned, directly or indirectly, with this question. Mental causation arguably is the central issue in the metaphysics of mind. I believe that this issue will be with us for some time – in fact, as long as we have the mind–body problem.

Many institutions at which I have taught over the years have generously supported my work; I want especially to mention, with gratitude and fondness, the University of Michigan and Brown University. In writing the papers collected here I had the benefit of comments and advice from many friends and colleagues, as acknowledged in individual papers, but I would like to mention here the following people who have been especially helpful and supportive over the years: David Benfield, Richard Brandt, Roderick Chisholm, Fred Feldman, Terry Horgan, Jerry Katz, Barry Loewer, Brian McLaughlin, Joe Mendola, Sydney Shoemaker, Larry Sklar, Ernest Sosa, Jim Van Cleve, and Nicholas White. Another person I wish to remember here is the late Herbert Heidelberger, a classmate in graduate school and former colleague at Brown, who was a mentor to me as well as a friend. I owe special thanks to Ernie Sosa, general editor of the Cambridge Studies in Philosophy series, for his advice and encouragement. Justin Broackes, Victor Caston, Ernie Sosa, and Jim Van Cleve have given me helpful comments and advice on the two sets of postscripts included in this volume. Maura Geisser, my editorial assistant, has ably and conscientiously assisted me with many tedious chores through the entire editorial process.

This book is dedicated to my wife, Sylvia, who has sustained me and my work all these years with her unconditioned support and affection.

June 1993
Providence, Rhode Island

Sources

"Causation, Nomic Subsumption and the Concept of Event," *Journal of Philosophy* 70 (1973): 217–236. Reprinted by permission of the *Journal of Philosophy*.

"Noncausal Connections," *Noûs* 8 (1974): 41–52. Reprinted by permission of Blackwell Publishers, Inc.

"Events as Property Exemplifications," in *Action Theory*, eds. Myles Brand and Douglas Walton (Dordrecht, Holland: D. Reidel Publishing Co., 1976), 159–177. Reprinted by permission of Kluwer Academic Publishers.

"Concepts of Supervenience," *Philosophy and Phenomenological Research* 45 (1984): 153–176. Reprinted by permission of *Philosophy and Phenomenological Research*.

"'Strong' and 'Global' Supervenience Revisited," *Philosophy and Phenomenological Research* 48 (1987): 315–326. Reprinted by permission of *Philosophy and Phenomenological Research*.

"Epiphenomenal and Supervenient Causation," *Midwest Studies in Philosophy* 9 (1984): 257–270. Reprinted by permission of *Midwest Studies in Philosophy*.

"Supervenience for Multiple Domains," *Philosophical Topics* 16 (1988): 129–150. Reprinted by permission of the editor of *Philosophical Topics*.

"Supervenience as a Philosophical Concept," *Metaphilosophy* 21 (1990): 1–27. Reprinted by permission of the editor of *Metaphilosophy*.

"Psychophysical Supervenience," *Philosophical Studies* 41 (1982): 51–70. Reprinted by permission of Kluwer Academic Publishers.

"Psychophysical Laws," in *Actions and Events: Perspectives on the Philosophy of Donald Davidson,* eds. Ernest LePore and Brian McLaughlin (Oxford: Basil Blackwell, 1985), 369–386. Reprinted by permission of Blackwell Publishers, Inc.

"What is 'Naturalized Epistemology'?" *Philosophical Perspectives* 2, *Epistemology* (1988): 381–405, ed. James E. Tomberlin (copyright by Ridgeview Publishing Co., Atascadero, Cal.). Reprinted by permission of Ridgeview Publishing Company.

"Mechanism, Purpose, and Explanatory Exclusion," *Philosophical Perspectives* 3, *Philosophy of Mind and Action Theory* (1989): 77–108, ed. James E. Tomberlin (copyright by Ridgeview Publishing Co., Atascadero, Cal.). Reprinted by permission of Ridgeview Publishing Company.

"The Myth of Nonreductive Materialism," *Proceedings and Addresses of the American Philosophical Association* 63 (1989): 31–47. Copyright © 1989 by the American Philosophical Association. Reprinted by permission of the American Philosophical Association.

"Dretske on How Reasons Explain Behavior," in *Dretske and His Critics,* ed. Brian McLaughlin (Oxford: Basil Blackwell, 1991), 52–72. Reprinted by permission of Blackwell Publishers, Inc.

"Multiple Realization and the Metaphysics of Reduction," *Philosophy and Phenomenological Research* 52 (1992): 1–26. Reprinted by permission of *Philosophy and Phenomenological Research.*

"The Nonreductivist's Troubles with Mental Causation," in *Mental Causation,* eds. John Heil and Alfred Mele (Oxford: Oxford University Press, 1993), 189–210. Reprinted by permission of Oxford University Press.

Part I

Events and supervenience

1

Causation, nomic subsumption, and the concept of event

In his celebrated discussion of causation Hume identified four prima facie constituents in the relation of causation. As everyone knows, they are constant conjunction, contiguity in space and time, temporal priority, and necessary connection. As ordinarily understood, the causal relation is a binary relation relating causes to their effects, and so presumably are the four relations Hume discerns in it. But what do these four relations tell us about the nature of the entities they relate?

Constant conjunction is a relation between generic events, that is, kinds or types of events; constant conjunction makes no clear or nontrivial sense when directly applied to spatiotemporally bounded individual events.[1] On the other hand, it is clear that the relation of temporal priority calls for individual, rather than generic, events as its relata; there appears to be no useful way of construing 'earlier than' as a relation between kinds of classes of events in a causal context.

What of the condition of contiguity? This condition has two parts, temporal and spatial. Temporal contiguity makes sense when applied to events; two events are contiguous in time if they temporally overlap. But spatial contiguity makes best sense when applied not to events but to objects, especially material bodies; intuitively at least, we surely understand what it is for two bodies to be in contact or to overlap. For events, however, the very notion of spatial location often becomes fuzzy and indeterminate. When Socrates expired in the prison, Xantippe became a widow and their three sons became fatherless. Exactly *where* did these latter events take place? When Hume's two billiard balls collide, what obviously are in spatial contact are the two balls. Are the *motions* of the balls also in spatial contact? Reflections on these and other cases suggest

---

I am indebted to Richard Brandt, Alvin and Holly Goldman, and Ernest Sosa for helpful suggestions.
1 By 'event' simpliciter I always mean individual events; when I mean generic events I shall say so.

that the locations of events, and hence their spatial contiguity relations, are parasitic in some intricate ways on the locations of objects.[2] As for the controversial idea of necessary connection, we are clearly more at home with this notion taken in the *de dicto* sense as applying to sentences, propositions, and the like, than when it is taken in the *de re* sense as applying directly to objects and events in the world.

Hume's four conditions, therefore, seem at first blush to call for apparently different categories of entities as relata of causal relations. We might say that the four conditions are jointly incongruous ontologically, thereby rendering the causal relation ontologically incoherent. I do not intend these remarks as criticisms of the historical Hume; I am merely pointing up the need for a greater sensitivity to ontological issues in the analysis of causation.

In this paper I want to examine some logical and ontological problems that arise when we try to give a precise characterization of Humean causation.[3] (I call "Humean" any concept of causation that includes the idea that causal relations between individual events somehow involve general regularities.) In fact, my chief concern will be focused not on the full-fledged concept of causation but rather on the concept of nomic subsumption, the idea of bringing individual events under a law, which is at the core of the Humean approach to causation. I begin with an examination of one popular modern formulation of Humean causation, "the nomic-implicational model."

I. "SUBSUMPTION UNDER A LAW"

When we try to explain the notion of subsuming events under a law, a notion of central importance to Humean causation, we immediately face a problem which turns out to be more intractable than it might at first appear: laws are sentences (or statements, propositions, etc.), but events are not. Exactly in what relation must a pair of events stand to a law if the law is to "subsume" the events? Given the categorial difference between laws and events, it would be quite senseless to say that one of the events must be "logically implied" by the other event taken together with the law. However, the temptation to use logico-linguistic constructions is

---

2 Zeno Vendler makes the claim that events are primarily temporal entities, whereas objects are primarily spatial, and that the attributions of temporal properties and relations to objects and of spatial properties and relations to events are derivative. See his *Linguistics in Philosophy* (Ithaca, N.Y.: Cornell, 1967), pp. 143–144.

3 For a general discussion of Humean causation see Bernard Berofsky, *Determinism* (Princeton, N.J.: Princeton University Press, 1971), esp. chs. IV, VI, and VII.

great, and one tries to bring events within the purview of logic by talking about their descriptions.

(1) Law *L* subsumes events *e* and *e'* (in that order) provided there are descriptions *D* and *D'* of *e* and *e'* respectively such that *L* and *D* jointly imply *D'* (without *D* alone implying it).[4]

Thus, according to this formulation, the law 'All copper expands upon heating' subsumes the events described by 'This piece of copper was heated at *t*' and 'This piece of copper expanded at *t*'. The basic idea is that nomic subsumption is nomic implication between appropriate event descriptions.

Here 'describe' is the key word. The crucial assumption of the nomic-implicational model as embodied in (1) is that *certain sentences describe events*. But how do we explain this notion? There are three important related problems here: (i) What types of sentences describe events? (ii) Given an event-describing sentence, what particular event does it describe? (iii) Under what conditions do two such sentences describe the same event?

Recent investigations[5] have shown that there are no simple answers to these questions and that the intuitive ideas we have about them are full of pitfalls, if not outright contradictions. Let us briefly see how a seemingly natural and promising line of approach runs quickly into a dead end.

Consider a sentence like 'This piece of copper was heated at *t*', which we would take as a typical event-describing sentence. We may think of the whole sentence as describing the event of this piece of copper being heated at *t*. An event-describing sentence in this sense has the form 'Object *x* has property *P* at time *t*' and affirms of a concrete object that it has a certain empirical property at a time (let us not worry about polyadic cases). Such a sentence, if true, is thought to describe the event of *x*'s having *P* at *t*. Now, once this approach is adopted, the following development is both natural and inescapable: if object *a* is the very same object as object *b*, then the event of *a*'s having *P* at *t* is the same event as the event

---

4 Compare Arthur Pap: "In the scientific sense of 'cause', an event *A* causes an event *B* in the sense that there is a law, *L*, such that from the conjunction of *L* and a description of *A* the occurrence of *B* is logically deducible." *An Introduction to the Philosophy of Science* (New York: Free Press, 1962), p. 271. We shall not consider here the difficulty that, according to (1), undescribed events are not subsumable under any law and as a result cannot enter into causal relations.

5 See, e.g., Donald Davidson, "The Individuation of Events," in Nicholas Rescher *et al.*, eds., *Essays in Honor of Carl G. Hempel* (Dordrecht: Reidel, 1969); and my "Events and Their Descriptions: Some Considerations," *ibid.*

of b's having P at t. Thus, if 'a' and 'b' are coreferential, the sentences 'a has P at t' and 'b has P at t' describe the same event.[6] But now see what happens to the nomic-implicational model (1).

Let the law '$(x)(Fx \rightarrow Gx)$' subsume the two events described by 'c has F' and 'c has G' (we drop 't' for simplicity). Then, if 'b has H' is any true event-describing sentence, the law subsumes the event described by 'b has H' and the event 'c has G'; for the former event is also described by '$(Ix)(x = b \ \& \ c$ has $F)$ has H',[7] which, together with the law '$(x)(Fx \rightarrow Gx)$', but not by itself, implies 'c has G'. In fact, it can be shown that any law that subsumes, in the sense of (1), at least one pair of events subsumes every pair.

The moral of these difficulties for the nomic-implicational model is this: once the description operator 'I' is available, we can pack as much "content" as we like into any singular sentence, and this can likely be done without changing the identity of the event described. Obviously, this is bound to cause trouble for any account of causation or nomic subsumption based on the relation of logical implication, since logical implication essentially depends on the content of sentences.[8]

So far we have examined the difficulties for (1) that arise from the notion of a sentential description of an event. Let us now go on to difficulties of another type arising from the other central idea of (1): that nomic subsumption of events can be linguistically mirrored by nomic implication between their descriptions.

The obvious similarity between the so-called "covering-law model" of explanation and what we have called "the nomic-implicational model" of causation will not have escaped notice. It should then come as no surprise that difficulties for one have counterparts in the difficulties for the other; however, this fact seems not to have been fully appreciated.

A valid argument having the following properties will be called a 'D-N argument' ('D-N' for 'deductive-nomological'): (i) its premises include both laws and singular sentences and its conclusion is singular, and (ii) the argument becomes invalid upon the deletion of the laws from the premises. The covering-law model of explanation, as a first approximation, can be formulated thus: an event is explained when a D-N argument

6 For more details see my "Events and Their Descriptions: Some Considerations," *ibid.*
7 We follow Dana Scott in the use of 'I' as definite description operator. See Scott, "Existence and Description in Formal Logic," in Ralph Schoenman, ed., *Bertrand Russell: Philosopher of the Century* (Boston: Little Brown, 1967).
8 Thus, the method favored by Davidson for handling event-describing sentences runs afoul of the same difficulties in connection with (1). See his "Causal Relations," *Journal of Philosophy*, LXIV, 21 (Nov. 9, 1967): 691–703, esp. p. 699.

is constructed whose conclusion describes that event. In terms of 'D-N argument', the nomic-implicational model of subsumption under a law comes to this: two events are subsumed under a law just in case there is a D-N argument whose premises are the law and a description of one of the events and whose conclusion is a description of the other event.

It is trivial to show that the notion of D-N argument as characterized cannot coincide with that of explanation, for the following is easily shown: for any law L and a true event-description D', there is a true singular sentence D such that 'L, D, therefore D'' is a D-N argument.[9] Thus, one law would suffice to explain any event you please. As an example: you want to explain why an object b has property F, for any b and F you choose. So you construct the following D-N argument: 'Copper is an electric conductor, b is F or b is nonconducting copper, therefore b is F'.

With regard to this and similar cases, the proponent of the nomic-implicational model might plead that the singular premise in such an argument (e.g., 'b is F, or b is nonconducting copper'), being a compound sentence of a rather artificial sort, cannot be thought of as an event-description.[10] Apart from the fact that this reply presupposes a satisfactory solution to the problem raised earlier of characterizing 'event-describing sentence', it seems to have a good deal less force against a pseudo-D-N argument like this: 'All crows are black, b is a crow, and c has the color of b. Therefore c is black'.

There is as yet no adequate formulation of the notion of 'D-N argument' that can successfully cope with these and other simple anomalous arguments; and it is unclear how examples of the second sort just described can be handled within the existing scheme of the theory of explanation. In any case, the unsettled state of the formal theory of deductive explanation implies a similar unsettled state for the nomic-implicational approach to Humean causation.

Enough has been said, I think, to justify at least a temporary shift of strategy away from the logico-descriptive approach underlying the nomic-implicational model. In the two sections to follow, we shall explore a direct "ontological approach" which dispenses with talk of descriptions and implications.

---

9 For further details see Carl G. Hempel and Paul Oppenheim, "Studies in the Logic of Explanation," reprinted in Hempel, *Aspects of Scientific Explanation* (New York: Free Press, 1965), and the references given in Hempel's "Postscript" to this article.

10 In fact, a clearer understanding of event-describing sentences is likely to help us with the problem of characterizing the structure of deductive explanation, since many counterexamples to the standard account contain singular premises which are intuitively not event-describing.

II. THE STRUCTURE OF EVENTS

Once we abandon the logico-descriptive approach, we must begin taking events seriously, since the only clear alternative to it is to define the causal relation directly for events without reliance on linguistic intermediaries. But what is an event? What sort of structures do we need as relata of causal relations? In this section I sketch an analysis of events[11] on the basis of which I shall formulate three versions of Humean causation in the next section.

We think of an event as a concrete object (or n-tuple of objects) exemplifying a property (or n-adic relation) at a time. In this sense of 'event', events include states, conditions, and the like, and not only events narrowly conceived as involving changes. Events, therefore, turn out to be complexes of objects and properties, and also time points and segments, and they have something like a propositional structure; the event that consists in the exemplification of property P by an object x at time t bears a structural similarity to the sentence 'x has P at t'. This structural isomorphism is related to the fact that we often take singular sentences of the form 'x has P at t' as referring to, describing, representing, or specifying an event; also we commonly and standardly use gerundial nominals of sentences to refer to events as in 'the sinking of the *Titanic*', 'this match's being struck', 'this match's lighting', and so forth.

We represent events by expressions of the form

$$`[(x_1, \ldots, x_n, t), P^n]'$$

An expression of this form refers to the event that consists in the ordered n-tuple of concrete objects $(x_1, \ldots, x_n)$ exemplifying the n-adic empirical attribute P^n at time t. Strictly speaking, P^n is $(n + 1)$-adic since we count 't' as an argument place; but we follow the usual practice of reckoning, for example, redness as a property rather than a relation even though objects are red, or not red, *at a time*. (In fact, there is no reason why time should be limited to a single argument place in an attribute, but let us minimize complexities not directly relevant to our central con-

---

11 This account was adumbrated in my "On the Psycho-Physical Identity Theory," *American Philosophical Quarterly*, III, 3 (July 1966): 227–235. It bears a resemblance to R. M. Martin's analysis in "Events and Descriptions of Events," in J. Margolis, ed., *Fact and Existence* (Oxford: Blackwell, 1969) and also to Alvin I. Goldman's account of action in *A Theory of Human Action* (Englewood Cliffs, N.J.: Prentice-Hall, 1970), ch. 1. Nancy Holmstrom develops a similar notion of event in her doctoral dissertation, *Identities, States, and the Mind–Body Problem*, The University of Michigan, 1970.

cerns.) We shall abbreviate '$(x_1, \ldots, x_n)$' as '(X_n)' and '$(x_1, \ldots, x_n, t)$' as '(X_n, t)' respectively, and drop the superscript from 'P^n'. The variable 't' ranges over time instants and intervals; when 't' denotes an interval, 'at t' is to be understood in the sense of 'throughout t'. We call P, (X_n), and t, respectively, "the constitutive attribute," "the constitutive objects," and "the constitutive time" of the event $[(X_n, t), P]$.

We adopt the following as the condition of event existence:

Existence condition: $[(X_n, t), P]$ exists if and only if the n-tuple of concrete objects (X_n) exemplifies the n-adic empirical attribute P at time t.

Linguistically, we can think of '$[(X_n, t), P]$' as the gerundive nominalization of the sentence '(X_n) has P at t'. Thus, '[(Socrates, t), drinks hemlock]' can be read "Socrates' drinking hemlock at t." Notice that $[(x, t), P]$ is not the ordered triple consisting of x, t, and P; the triple exists if x, t, and P exist; the event $[(x, t), P]$ exists only if x has P at t. As property designators we may use ordinary (untensed) predicative expressions; when the order of argument places has to be made explicit we use circled numerals;[12] e.g.,

$$[(a, b, c, t), ② \text{ stands between } ① \text{ and } ③]$$

corresponds, by the existence condition, to the sentence 'b stands between a and c at t'. The proviso that the constitutive attribute of an event be "empirical" is intended to exclude, if one so wishes, tautological, evaluative, and perhaps other kinds of properties; but we must in this paper largely leave open the question of exactly what sorts of attributes are admissible as constitutive attributes of events.

When P is a monadic attribute, that is, when only "monadic events" are considered, the following identity condition is immediate:

Identity condition I_1: $[(x, t), P] = [(y, t'), Q]$ if and only if $x = y$, $t = t'$, and $P = Q$.

Thus, Socrates' drinking hemlock at t is the same event as Xantippe's husband's drinking hemlock at t, and this liquid's turning blue at t is the same event as its turning the color of the sky at t.

12 Following W. V. Quine, *Methods of Logic* (New York: Holt, Rinehart & Winston, 1950), pp. 130ff. For formal development property abstracts could be used; see e.g., Richard Montague, "On the Nature of Certain Philosophical Entities," *Monist*, LIII, 2 (April 1969): 159–194.

Two objections might be voiced at this point. First, it might be contended that the event [(Brutus, t), stabs Caesar] is the very same event as [(Caesar, t), is stabbed by Brutus], although our identity condition pronounces them to be distinct. Our reply here is that what the critic might have in mind are the dyadic events [(Brutus, Caesar, t), stabs] and [(Caesar, Brutus, t), is stabbed by], and that, according to the identity condition for dyadic events below, these events are indeed one and the same. Generally, we do not allow "mixed universals"[13] such as stabbing Caesar as constitutive attributes of events; only "pure universals"[13] are allowed as such.

Second, it might be objected that the event [(Xantippe's husband, t), dies] is identical with the event [(Xantippe, t), becomes a widow], viz., Xantippe's husband dying at t is the same event as Xantippe's becoming a widow at t, although again I_1 is not satisfied. We answer that these are indeed different events. Consider, for example, their locations: the first obviously took place in the prison in which Socrates took the poison, but it is not clear exactly where the second event occurred. We might want to locate it where Xantippe was at the moment of Socrates' death (and this is the procedure we shall adopt), but clearly not in the prison. To be sure, the two events are connected; in fact, the biconditional '[(Xantippe's husband, t), dies] exists if and only if [(Xantippe, t), becomes a widow] exists' is demonstrable from the existence condition; one might wish to say that necessarily one exists if and only if the other does. But this has no tendency to show that we have one event here and not two. One could just as well argue that since 'The husband of Socrates' wife exists if and only if Socrates' wife exists' is necessarily true, the husband of Socrates' wife is the same as Socrates' wife.

Now for dyadic events: if we want the identity '[(Brutus, Caesar, t), stabs] = [(Caesar, Brutus, t), is stabbed by]', we obviously cannot simply repeat I_1 for dyadic events. But what we should say is equally obvious. For any dyadic relation R, let R^* be its converse. We then have:

Identity condition I_2: $[(x, y, t), R] = [(u, v, t'), Q]$ if and only if either (i) $(x, y) = (u, v)$, $t = t'$, and $R = Q$, or (ii) $(x, y) = (v, u)$, $t = t'$, and $R = Q^*$.

For the general case of n-adic events, we need to generalize the concept of converse to n-adic relations. Any n-termed sequence can be permuted in $n!$ different ways (including the identity permutation). If k is a permutation on n-termed sequences (note that k is a *scheme* of permutation, not

13 For a possible explanation of these terms, see Arthur W. Burks, "Ontological Categories and Language," *Visva-Bharati Journal of Philosophy*, III (1967): 25–46, esp. pp. 28–29.

a particular permuted sequence), then by 'k (X_n)' we denote the sequence resulting from permuting the sequence (X_n) by k. The $n!$ permutations on n-termed sequences form a group, and for each permutation k there exists an inverse k^{-1} such that $k^{-1}(k(X_n)) = (X_n)$. If k is a permutation on n-termed sequences and R is an n-adic relation, $k(R)$ is to be the n-adic relation such that, for every (X_n), (X_n) has $k(R)$ if and only if $k^{-1}(X_n)$ has R.[14] It follows that, for each k, $k(X_n)$ has $k(R)$ if and only if (X_n) has R. The $n!$ permutations of an n-adic relation R can be thought of as the converses of R. Just as the converse of a dyadic relation may be identical with the relation itself (that is, the relation is symmetric), some of the converses of an n-adic relation may in fact be identical.

We now state the identity condition for the general case:

Identity condition I_n: [(X_n, t), P] = [(Y_m, t'), Q] if and only if there exists a permutation k on m-termed sequences such that (X_n) = $k(Y_m)$, $t = t'$, and $P = k(Q)$.

Obviously, I_n entails I_1 and I_2 for $n = 1, 2$. We say, for example, that [(a, b, c, t), ① gives ② to ③] = [(c, b, a, t), ① receives ② from ③]. The permutation involved here is (13)(2), i.e., the permutation whereby the first element is replaced by the third, the second by itself, and the third by the first.

This completes the presentation of what is admittedly a sketchy account of events. And it is only a beginning; many interesting problems remain. First of all, there is the problem of characterizing more precisely the syntactical and semantical properties of the operator '[ ]'. According to our identity condition, Socrates' dying is a different event from Xantippe's becoming a widow. What then is the relationship between the two? What is the relationship between my firing the gun and my killing Jones?[15] How are such notions as "complex events," "compound events," "part–whole" (for events), etc., to be explained? And above all, there is the problem of how the notion of "property" (generally, that of "attribute") is best construed for the purposes of an event theory of this kind, and in particular how those properties which can be constitutive proper-

<hr>

14 This is not intended as a definition, but only an informal explanation, of '$k(R)$'. As a definition it would likely be construed as presupposing an extensional interpretation of attributes (whether in the possible-world semantics or in some other scheme), whereas I prefer to be silent on this issue here. It may be useful, however, to point out that we are as much entitled to this informal explanation of '$k(R)$' as we are to the usual informal explanation of the notion of 'converse' of a binary relation.

15 This problem is extensively discussed in Goldman, *A Theory of Human Action*. See also the APA Symposium on "The Individuation of Action" by Goldman, Judith Jarvis Thomson, and Irving Thalberg, *Journal of Philosophy*, LXVIII, 21 (Nov. 4, 1971); 761–787.

ties of events (these properties can be called "generic events") should be characterized. It seems to me that the resolution of these problems about events depends on a satisfactory general account of properties; in fact, many interesting problems about events are likely to remain unresolved until such an account is on hand. In any case, we shall be alluding below to some of these further problems.

III. CAUSATION REVISITED

There appears to be a general agreement that the requirement of constant conjunction for causal relations for individual events is best explained in terms of lawlike correlations between generic events. Constant conjunction obviously makes better sense for repeatedly instantiable universals than for spatiotemporally bounded particulars. But, given a particular causal relation between two individual events, precisely which generic events must be lawfully correlated in order to sustain it?

Our account of events gives a quick answer. Every event has a unique constitutive property (generally, attribute), namely the property an exemplification of which by an object at a time is that event. And, for us, these constitutive properties of events are generic events. It follows that each event falls under exactly one generic event, and that once a particular cause–effect pair is fixed, the generic events that must satisfy the constant conjunction requirement are uniquely fixed. It is important to notice the distinction drawn by our analysis between properties *constitutive* of events and properties *exemplified* by them. An example should make this clear: the property of dying is a constitutive property of the event [(Socrates, t), dying], i.e., Socrates' dying at t, but not a property exemplified by it; the property of occurring in a prison is a property this event exemplifies, but is not constitutive of it. Under our account, then, if Socrates' drinking hemlock (at t) was the cause of his dying (at t'), the two generic events, drinking hemlock and dying, must fulfill the requirement of lawlike constant conjunction.

This procedure, therefore, is in sharp contrast with the procedure in which the inner structure of events is not analyzed and which, as a result, does not associate with each event a unique constitutive property. On that approach no distinction is made between properties constitutive of events and properties exemplified by them; and an individual event is usually thought to fall under many, in fact an indefinite number of, generic events; for example, one and the same event can be the moving of a finger, the pressing of the trigger of a gun, a shooting, and a mercy killing.[16] How, on that view, might one answer the question raised at the outset of this section? Evidently, it would be too strong to require that every generic event under which the cause event falls be lawfully related to every generic event under which the effect event falls. A more reasonable proposal, which seems to be what many have in mind, would be to say that two causally related events are such that there are at least two lawfully correlated generic events under which they respectively fall. Thus, two events, e and e', satisfy the constant-conjunction requirement just in case there are generic events F and G such that e is an F-event, e' is a G-event, and F-events are constantly conjoined with G-events.

Given the considerable freedom permitted by this formula in the choice of the generic events to which the two events belong, the requirement of constant conjunction as stated turns out to be too easy to satisfy. If any grouping of events is allowed as a generic event – or if any property exemplifiable by events is taken as one – then the requirement thus interpreted becomes quite useless; it can be shown that every event satisfies this requirement with respect to any event that satisfies it with respect to at least one event. For let e_1 and e_2 satisfy the requirement in virtue of the constant conjunction between F-events and G-events; that is, e_1 is of kind F, e_2 is of kind G, and whenever an F-event occurs there occurs a corresponding G-event. Let e_3 be any arbitrary event and let R be any relation such that $R(e_3, e_1)$. We explain 'H' to be true of any event e just in case $(\exists f)(R(e, f) \ \& \ F(f))$. Then clearly e_3 belongs to the generic event H, and H-events are constantly conjoined with G-events, from which it follows that e_3 and e_2 satisfy the requirement of constant conjunction. This plainly is a result we want to avoid.[17]

In comparison, our procedure will make it a good deal more difficult – too difficult, some will say – to satisfy the constant-conjunction requirement because, as we noted, once cause and effect are fixed, the generic events that must lawfully correlate are also fixed. There may be a way of framing a reasonable condition of constant conjunction without associating a unique generic event with each event, but it is hard to see what it could be. In any case I do not wish to suggest that the foregoing considerations tilt the balance decisively in favor of our procedure; as we shall

16 Compare Donald Davidson: "I flip the switch, turn on the light, and illuminate the room. Unbeknownst to me I also alert a prowler to the fact that I am home. Here I do not do four things, but only one, of which four descriptions have been given." "Actions, Reasons, and Causes," *Journal of Philosophy*, LX, 23 (Nov. 7, 1963): 685–700, p. 686.
17 This has been adapted from an argument given by J. A. Foster in "Psychophysical Causal Relations," *American Philosophical Quarterly*, V, 1 (January 1968): 65–66.

shortly see, there is a difficulty of a somewhat similar nature for our procedure as well.

What does it mean to say that two generic events are constantly conjoined or lawfully correlated? It clearly is not enough to repeat the usual formula that the occurrence of an event of one kind is always followed by an event of the other kind. We need to make more specific the relation between the given event of the first kind and *the* event of the second kind that is to be associated with it. As an example, the heating of a metallic object and the expansion of a metallic object would be constantly conjoined, according to this formula, provided only that whenever a metallic object is heated, *some* metallic object *somewhere* expands. In this particular case, what we have in mind is that whenever a metallic object is heated *it* expands. But this cannot be made into a general requirement, since we must allow causal relations between events whose constitutive objects are different. A similar sort of indeterminacy besets the expression 'whenever' in the above formula; we do not want to say that a given event of kind F and the particular event of kind G that follows it must be simultaneous; but to leave this indefinite ("each F-event is followed by a G-event at some time or other") is to render the requirement vacuous.

What seems needed, then, is a way of relating a particular F-event to that particular G-event with which it is associated by the constant conjunction of F-events with G-events. Such a relation would also be useful for correctly pairing a cause with *its* effect and an effect with *its* cause. If two rifles are fired simultaneously, resulting in two simultaneous deaths, we need a relation of that kind to pair each rifle shot with the death it causes and not with the other.[18] Notice, by the way, that those who would allow for each event a multiplicity of generic events are faced with the same pairing problem.

If x's being F at t is causally related to y's being G at t', this must be so in virtue of some relation R holding for x, t, y, and t'. How else could the following two facts be explained? First, given that x is F at t, there are objects other than y that are not G at t'; and there are times other than t' at which the object y is not G. Second, again given that x is F at t and this event causes y's being G at t', there can be (and usually would be) other individual events of kind G occurring at t' that are causally unrelated to x's being F at t. Now it seems that there are three different

18 Haskell Fain raises a similar problem in "Some Problems of Causal Explanation," *Mind*, LXXII, 288 (October 1963): pp. 519–532.

ways in which such a relation could be worked into an analysis of Humean causation: (A) we look for a single "pairing relation" for all cases of constant conjunction (or Humean causal relations); (B) we let the choice of a suitable pairing relation depend on the specific generic events F and G to be correlated (and perhaps the choice may also depend on the specific individual events to be causally related); (C) we build such a pairing relation into the cause event so that the cause is not the event of x's being F at t, but rather the "complex event" of x's being F and also being in relation R to y at t.

In what follows we explore these three possibilities. In addition to their individual strengths and shortcomings, all three will be seen to be subject to one important difficulty. But a close examination and discussion of the comparative merits and faults of these three approaches cannot be attempted here, although of course I shall be making remarks relevant to a comparative evaluation of them. The order in which the three approaches will be considered is this: first (B), then (A), and finally (C).

An analysis of the causal relation that falls under (B) is the following definition of 'causal sufficiency' offered by J. A. Foster (*op. cit.*, p. 67):

a's being F is causally sufficient for b's being G if and only if there exists a relation R such that

(i) $F(a)$, $G(b)$, and $R(a,b)$
(ii) $(x)(F(x) \rightarrow (\exists y)(G(y) \,\&\, R(x,y)))$[19]
(iii) $(x)(F(x) \,\&\, R(x,b) \supset x = a) \,\&\, (x)(G(x) \,\&\, R(a,x) \supset x = b)$

The condition (ii) of course is the constant-conjunction requirement; and the condition (iii) states that the pairing relation R must be such that at most one thing that is F, namely a, bears R to b and that a bears R to at most one thing that is G, namely b. The choice of R depends not only on F and G but also on a and b.

It seems to me that Foster's (ii) is not the most useful way of stating the lawlike correlation of F and G; there appears to be no simple way of accommodating such mundane examples of causal relations as a's firing a rifle and b's dying, a's having such-and-such a mass and b's accelerating with such-and-such a rate of acceleration (toward a by gravitational attraction), and so on. The problem is simply that the laws in question do

19 We use the arrow '$\rightarrow$' to denote whatever type of implication the reader deems appropriate for stating laws in something like this form (this in effect is also Foster's practice). We do not consider here the question of precisely what sort of "nomic force" if any, should be carried by a statement of a constant conjunction. For various possible interpretations of causal or nomological implication, see Arthur W. Burks, *Cause, Chance, and Reason* (Chicago: University of Chicago Press, 1977).

not entail a statement of the form (ii) to the effect that if any object has property F *there exists at least one object* y fulfilling the consequent of (ii). (Foster restricts his definition so that a, b, and objects in the range of '*x*', '*y*', . . . , are "momentary particulars" without temporal duration, but this doesn't affect the problem.) It would seem that (ii) is more usefully stated thus: $(x)(y)(F(x) \ \& \ R(x,y) \to G(y))$.

In any case, let us turn to another problem. Let us assume, as Foster does, that, for any spatiotemporal objects a and b, their exact spatiotemporal relation R satisfies the condition (iii), regardless of what F and G may be; this assumption holds if the identity of spatiotemporal objects is determined completely by their spatiotemporal location. With this assumption at hand we can show the following: If a's being F is causally sufficient for b's being G, then for any object c there exists a property H such that c's being H is causally sufficient for b's being G. For let R_1 be the spatiotemporal relation between c and a, and let R_2 be the spatiotemporal relation between c and b. And we set H to be the property denoted by the expression '$(\exists y)(F(y) \ \& \ R_1(x,y))$'. Then, the law '$(x)(H(x) \to (\exists y)(G(y) \ \& \ R_2(x, y)))$' holds; and the other conditions are obviously satisfied. To make this more concrete, consider this case: the object b's being heated is causally sufficient for its expanding (here $a = b$ and the relation R can be taken as identity). Let c be an object exactly 50 miles due north of the object that is being heated. The property H in this case is the property an object has in virtue of there being another object 50 miles due south that is being heated. Moreover, given the law that all objects expand when heated, we have the law that for any object x if x has the property H, then there exists an object 50 miles due south which is expanding. From this it follows that c's having property H is causally sufficient for b's expanding.

Cases like this need not be regarded as necessarily objectionable for Foster's definition, which defines causal sufficiency, not causation. However, they would be clearly objectionable if the relation defined were that of causation. It would be absurd to say that object c's having H caused object a to expand, or that c causally influenced or interacted with a. Notice that Foster's definition can be directly mirrored in our framework of events, since the entities related by his causal sufficiency, a's being F, b's being G, etc., are close analogues of our $[(a, t), F]$, $[(b, t), G]$, etc. The implication of the above example then is that, under a definition of the causal relation similar to Foster's definition of 'causal sufficiency' (notice here that the possible alteration of the condition (ii) does not materially affect the difficulty), if an event is caused by another, then every object is the constituent object in some event which is a cause of the first; that is, there would be no object "causally independent" of that event.

As we shall see, the two remaining ways of handling the pairing problem are open to difficulties of a similar sort. The gist of the difficulties is this: when there is a constant conjunction between F and G, then, for any object you please, we can pick a property H such that the object has H, and H is constantly conjoined with G. Thus, this spurious constant conjunction rides piggyback, so to speak, on the genuine correlation between F and G; we may call this problem "the problem of parasitic constant conjunctions."

We may, I think, question whether the artificially concocted property H can in general be regarded as a constitutive property of an event. A negative answer seems plausible, although a persuasive defense of it would be a subtle and difficult matter. We feel that for an object to have this sort of property (recall the special case of H above) is not always for it to undergo, or be disposed to undergo, a "real change"; my being 50 miles east of a burning barn is hardly an event that happens to me.[20] But it would be a mistake to ban all such properties; my being in spatial contact with a burning barn is very much an event that happens to me. Whether a clear distinction between these two kinds of cases can be made that does not beg the question by using causal concepts is an interesting question to which I know of no completely satisfying answer. This is a special case of the more general problem alluded to earlier, namely that of characterizing the properties whose exemplification by an object at a time is an event, i.e., generic events.

We now turn to the approach (A) to the pairing problem. One feature of the event $[(c, t), H]$ which enters into an unwanted causal relation with the event $[(b, t), G]$ is the fact that its constitutive object c, need not be in spatial contact with the constitutive object b, of $[(b, t), G]$. In fact, Hume's condition of spatial contiguity is not mentioned at all in Foster's definition of 'causal sufficiency'. Thus, if we are willing to go along with Hume here, the contiguity relation presents itself as a natural candidate for the pairing relation. This way of handling the pairing problem differs from the one we have just considered in that there would be a single uniform relation doing the job for all causal relations independent of the particular cause and effect events.

As Hume was aware, however, direct contiguity cannot be generally

20 In this connection see Peter Geach's interesting remarks on "Cambridge changes" in *God and the Soul* (London: Routledge & Kegan Paul, 1969), pp. 71–72.

required for causal relations; following Hume's own suggestion,[21] we shall try first to explain 'direct contiguous causation' and then explain 'causation' as a "chain" of direct contiguous causal relations. Thus, the analysis of causation that follows is not only "Humean"; it is also Hume's.

We first need the contiguity relation for events. It would seem that this relation must be explained in terms of the contiguity relation for objects and times of events (an object is contiguous with another at a time). Thus, if $[(a, T), P]$ is contiguous with $[(b, T'), Q]$, this must be so in virtue of a contiguity relation holding for a, b, T, and T'; and the relevant aspect of the objects a and b is their spatial location at the indicated times. Let '$loc(x,t)$' denote the spatiotemporal location of x at time t (where x exists at t); where t is an interval, $loc(x,t)$ will be a spatiotemporal volume. In order not to complicate our problems excessively we consider here only monadic events.

We say that two events $[(a,T), P]$ and $[(b,T'), Q]$ are contiguous just in case $loc(a,T)$ is contiguous with $loc(b,T')$ – we assume of course that the two events exist. How contiguity of spatiotemporal location is to be explained is a question that depends on the properties of the space-time involved; since nothing in this paper hinges on the exact explanation of this notion, we leave it unanalyzed. We now define 'direct contiguous causation' as follows (we abbreviate 'contiguous with' as 'Ct'):

$[(a, T), P]$ is a *direct contiguous cause of* $[(b, T'), Q]$ provided:

(i) $[(a, T), P]$ is contiguous with $[(b, T'), Q]$.

(ii) If $a = b$: $(x)(t)(t')([(x, t), P]$ exists & $Ct(loc(x, t), loc(x, t')) \rightarrow [(x, t'), Q]$ exists).
If $a \neq b$: $(x)(y)(t)(t')([(x, t), P]$ exists & $Ct(loc(x, t), loc(y, t')) \rightarrow [(y, t'), Q]$ exists).

We define 'contiguous cause' in terms of the ancestral of direct contiguous causation:

e is a contiguous cause of e' if and only if $e \neq e'$ and e bears to e' the ancestral of the relation of direct contiguous causation – that is to say, $(S)(e' \ \varepsilon \ S \ \& \ (f)(g)(f \ \varepsilon \ S \ \& \ g$ is a direct contiguous cause of $f \supset g \ \varepsilon \ S) \supset e \ \varepsilon \ S)$.

Whether contiguity in this sense ought to be required of causal relations as a matter of definition is a debatable issue; in particular, the verifi-

21 Hume writes: "Tho' distant objects may sometimes seem productive of each other, they are commonly found upon examination to be link'd by a chain of causes, which are contiguous among themselves, and to the distant objects; and when in any particular instance we cannot discover this connexion, we still presume it to exist." *Treatise of Human Nature*, bk. I, pt. III, sec. II.

cation of the existence of a causal chain of the required sort may in practice be an impossible task in many areas of science in which causal attributions are regularly made; and the belief that such a chain must exist may be only metaphysical faith. But these are the questions we must leave aside.[22] Let us now turn to the last of the three ways of dealing with the pairing problem distinguished earlier.

Recall the example of two rifle shots causing two simultaneous deaths. We raised the question how each shot is to be paired with the death it causes. Causal chains will probably help us here, but there seems to be another, perhaps more natural and simpler, way of handling it. It may be said that the cause of a death here is not a rifle shot simpliciter, but rather the rifle shot *cum* the event (state) of the rifle's being in such-and-such a spatiotemporal relationship to the man whose death it causes. Thus, the cause of the man's death is the set of events: the rifle's being fired and its being in a certain relation R to the man (at the time it was fired); we could perhaps speak of a single "compound" or "composite event" of the rifle's being fired and being in relation R to the man. In either case, the man, who is the constitutive object in the effect event, figures in the cause as a constitutive object. Again restricting ourselves essentially to monadic cases, we may capture this idea as follows:

The set of events, $[(a, T), F]$ and $[(a, b, T), R]$, is a cause of the event $[(b, T'), G]$ provided:

(i) $[(a, T), F]$, $[(a, b, T), R]$, and $[(b, T'), G]$ exist, and
(ii) $(x)(y)(t)([(x, t), F]$ exists & $[(x, y, t), R]$ exists $\rightarrow [(y, t + \Delta t), G]$ exists), where $\Delta t = T' - T$.
(iii) The law in (ii) does not hold if one or the other of its antecedent clauses is deleted.

We should be wary of speaking of "composite events" before a precise characterization of them is on hand. But at least we can say this: If $[(a, T), P]$ and $[(a, b, T), R]$ exist, then, by the existence condition, the event $[(a, b, T), R^*]$ exists, where $R^*(x,y)$ at t just in case $P(x)$ at t & $R(x,y)$ at t, on the assumption that R^* is a generic event. Also, conversely, if this dyadic event exists, the two former events exist. This is the intuitive content of the concept of "conjunctive event" in a simple case of this kind; but a general formulation of this concept is yet to be worked out. In any case, if we allow ourselves conjunctive events of at least this simple sort, we can simplify the preceding formulation of Humean causation:

22 For a brief discussion of these problems see Patrick Suppes, *A Probabilistic Theory of Causality* (Amsterdam: North Holland, 1970), pp. 30–32, 82–91.

$[(a, b, T), P]$ is a cause of $[(b, T'), Q]$ provided:

(i) $[(a, b, T), P]$ and $[(b, T'), Q]$ exist, and

(ii) $(x)(y)(t)([(x, y, t), P]$ exists $\rightarrow [(y, t + \Delta t), Q]$ exists), where $\Delta t = T' - T$.

(There is of course no simple way of stating (iii) of the preceding formulation; but when the definition is stated for composite events, (iii) doesn't seem needed.) In special cases, $a = b$, and the cause event as well as the effect event would be monadic. But generally the cause event will be a dyadic or higher-place event involving, as one of its constitutive objects, the constitutive object of the effect event; and the first term of a constant conjunction will in general be a relational generic event rather than a monadic one.[23]

Let us briefly note here how the problem of parasitic constant conjunctions arises for direct contiguous causation as formulated above. What happens is this: suppose $[(a,t), F]$ is a direct contiguous cause of $[(b,t), G]$, where for simplicity we have assumed $t = t'$. Let c be any object such that b is the only object with which c is contiguous (for simplicity we drop t) and b is the only object with which both a and c are contiguous. We can then construct a property H such that c has H and $[(c,t), H]$ is a direct contiguous cause of $[(b,t), G]$; letting R be some relation such that $R(c,a)$, we can let H be the property that belongs to an object x just in case $(\exists w)(R(x,w) \;\&\; F(w) \;\&\; (\exists!z)(\mathrm{Cont}(x,z)) \;\&\; (\exists!z)(\mathrm{Cont}(x,z) \;\&\; \mathrm{Cont}(w,z)))$, where again for simplicity we have deleted reference to time and where 'Cont' is used as a contiguity predicate applicable to objects simpliciter. But notice that the conditions on the object c here are severer than for Foster's definition; and there seems to be no general argument to show that our definition of 'contiguous causation' succumbs always to this sort of difficulty. In this way, the difficulty of parasitic constant conjunctions is somewhat mitigated for the relation of contiguous causation.

It is easily seen that our last formulation of Humean causation is also open to the difficulty of parasitic constant conjunctions; however, we omit the details.

Apart from this difficulty of parasitic constant conjunctions, I find the preceding two accounts of Humean causation (contiguous causation and

23 The causal relation defined here is, in many respects, weaker than the relation of contiguous causation earlier defined, and is open to the following sort of difficulty. Jones has terminal cancer, and there is a law that any human being having cancer (of the kind and stage Jones has) is dead within two years. And in two years Jones is dead. However, Jones actually died in a traffic accident. The present definition of the causal relation will erroneously certify Jones's cancer as a cause of his being dead, whereas contiguous causation avoids cases of this sort in a natural way.

the account that takes cause as essentially a relational event) attractive; on the other hand, the first account borrowed from Foster is somewhat unintuitive, and, even with the suggested alteration of the condition (ii), the last condition (iii) on the pairing relation appears somewhat ad hoc. In any event, various refinements can be attempted on these definitions. In particular, there is the problem of building temporal asymmetry into them, if this is desired. Also, according to these definitions, all correlated properties in the same object, e.g., thermal and electrical conductivity in metals (at constant temperature), turn out to be symmetrically related by the causal relation. (I assume that we would not want to attribute a causal relation directly between electrical and thermal conductivity; the correlation is to be explained by reference to the microstructure of metals.) It seems likely that clues to a correct account of these cases will be found not at the level of analysis in this paper but at a deeper metaphysical level involving such concepts as substance, power, and accident, or at a pragmatic level involving the concept of controlling one parameter by controlling another.[24]

These refinements, as well as others which are necessary to account for some of the well-known difficulties for Humean causation,[25] are beyond the scope of the present paper and must await another occasion. It is best, therefore, to look upon the tentative accounts of Humean causation in this section not as full-fledged analyses of causation, but rather as approximations to the broader notion of subsumption of events under a law, an idea that forms the foundation of the Humean, or nomological, approach to causation. In any event, my aim here has been to outline a uniform and coherent ontological framework of events adequate for formulation of Humean causation rather than to resolve substantive issues traditionally associated with the Humean approach. These issues must of course ultimately be handled within the suggested framework if it is to prove its worth. It is hoped, however, that we have at least made a modest beginning and that we now have a clearer perception of the directions in which to explore and the problems and promises to be expected along the way.

24 Georg H. von Wright has recently worked out an account of causation on the basis of the concept of an agent's bringing about some state of affairs by doing a certain action, in *Explanation and Understanding* (Ithaca, N.Y.: Cornell, 1971).
25 One such refinement would consist in taking account of the common observation that what we ordinarily take as a cause is seldom by itself a necessary or sufficient condition for the event it is said to have caused. For a plausible treatment of this problem, see J. L. Mackie, "Causes and Conditions," *American Philosophical Quarterly*, II, 4 (October 1965): 245–264; and my "Causes and Events; Mackie on Causation," *Journal of Philosophy*, LXVIII, 14 (July 22, 1971): 426–441.

2

Noncausal connections

"If the match had not been struck, it would not have ignited." This counterfactual expresses a relationship of dependency between two events: the ignition of the match was dependent on the match's being struck. Here, the dependency is a causal one: the striking of the match caused it to light. We also say: the ignition was causally determined by the striking. The causal relation is a paradigmatic case of what I shall call relations of "dependency" or "determination" between events and states; in fact, it is the only relation of this sort that has been explicitly recognized and widely talked about.

The dominant place accorded to the causal relation is evident in the fact, for example, that the thesis of universal determinism is most often stated in some such form as "Every event has a cause." The implicit assumption in such a formulation is that being determined comes to the same thing as being caused. This, however, requires reconsideration. There appear to be dependency relations between events that are not causal, and, as I shall argue, universal determinism may be true even if not every event has a cause. These noncausal dependency relations are pervasively present in the web of events, and it is important to understand their nature, their interrelations, and their relation to the causal relation if we are to have a clear and complete picture of the ways in which events hang together in this world.

II

When Socrates expired in the Athenian prison, Xantippe became a widow. The onset of Xantippe's widowhood was determined by the death of Socrates. As we might say, Xantippe became a widow in consequence of, as a result of, or in virtue of Socrates' death. It might be objected that here there is one event, not two, that the death of Socrates is in fact identical with Xantippe's becoming a widow.

We shall not give an extended argument here for the view that these two events are not identical, except to mention two points. One concerns the spatial locations of these events: the death of Socrates occurred in the prison, whereas it isn't at all plausible to locate Xantippe's becoming a widow there. The latter event, if it had a location at all, took place where Xantippe was when Socrates died. Second, I find much to recommend in an account of events according to which an event is a structure consisting of a concrete object, a property exemplified by it, and the time at which it is exemplified.[1] It is a consequence of this view that Socrates' dying at a time t is not the same event as Xantippe's becoming a widow at t. Apart from these two points, some of the remarks below concerning the asymmetric relationships between the two events should reinforce the duality view with respect to them.

Given that these are distinct events, what is their relationship to each other? I think that part of the resistance against the account of events just alluded to stems from the feeling that the duality of these events is unacceptable in view of the obvious intimate relationship between the two. The answer is of course that their being different events does not preclude their being intimately related. The top of this table is not the same thing as the table; that doesn't mean that the two are not intimately related: one is part of the other. Once one adopts the duality position, however, the relation between the two events must be clarified: if identity is not the relation between them, what is it?

Is it the causal relation? Is the death of Socrates a cause of Xantippe's becoming a widow? There are difficulties with this causal view. First of all, the two events occur with absolute simultaneity. (If it is thought that death is a process not an instantaneous event, we could take the termination of the process of death as our example.) Thus, if it is plausible to locate these events at different spatial positions, we would have to accept this case as one in which causal action is propagated instantaneously through spatial distance. Moreover, under the regularity account of causation – the view associated with Hume that individual causal relations instantiate nomic regularities – it is difficult to think of any sort of contingent empirical law to support a causal relation between the two events.

In fact, the relation strikes us as more intimate than one that is mediated by contingent causal laws. Given that Socrates is the husband of Xantippe,

1 See Essays 1 and 3 of this volume.

his death is sufficient, logically, for the widowing of Xantippe: under the condition of their monogamous marriage it is necessary that if the death of Socrates occurs at a time, Xantippe becomes a widow at the same time. As we might say, in all possible worlds in which Socrates is the husband of Xantippe at time t and in which Socrates dies at t, Xantippe becomes a widow at t.

III

Thus, one might say that the proposition that the death of Socrates occurred at t, taken in conjunction with the standing condition that Socrates was the husband of Xantippe at t, entails the proposition that the onset of Xantippe's widowhood occurred at t. Notice, however, that as far as entailment goes, the death of Socrates and the widowing of Xantippe are symmetrically related: it is necessarily true that, given their marital state, Socrates dies at a time if and only if Xantippe becomes a widow at that time. So the entailment relation is reversible. However, the dependency of Xantippe's widowhood on Socrates' death is not reversible. Whether or not Xantippe becomes a widow at a time depends on whether or not her husband dies at that time, in a sense of "dependence" in which the converse of that isn't true: whether or not Socrates dies at a time does not depend on whether or not Xantippe becomes a widow at that time. This asymmetry is reflected in our attitude toward the following two counterfactuals:

If Socrates had not died at t, Xantippe would not have become a widow at t.

If Xantippe had not become a widow at t, Socrates would not have died at t.

We would take the first of these as evidently true. Under the counterfactual supposition of the second that Xantippe did not become a widow at t, we would more likely alter the marital condition of Socrates than tamper with the fact of his death at t. The precise mechanics of all this remains to be explained – and there have been important contributions in this area in the last several years – but there is little doubt that the counterfactual dependency, to use a term of David Lewis',[2] between the two events is irreversible.

Another aspect of the asymmetric dependency between the two events involves agency. We would presumably accept the first but reject the second of the following two statements:

2 In his "Causation", *Journal of Philosophy* 70 (1973): 556–67.

By bringing about the death of Socrates, we could bring about Xantippe's widowhood.

By bringing about Xantippe's widowhood, we could bring about the death of Socrates.

A common sort of case in which the relation of bringing about a state or event q by bringing about a state or event p is asymmetric is where p and q are causally related. For example, by bringing about an increase in the length of a pendulum, we can bring about a change in its period of swing, but we don't think we can bring about an increase in its length by changing its period of swing. In this case, the asymmetry of the agency relation, as we shall call it, lies in the causal asymmetry between states or events brought about by the actions:[3] the change in the length is the cause of the change in the period, and the change in the period is not the cause of the change in the length. (This is so even though the lawlike correlation between them is completely symmetric.) By bringing about the cause, you bring about the effect; you cannot bring about the cause by bringing about the effect. In the same way, the asymmetry of the agency relation in "We could bring about Xantippe's widowhood by bringing about Socrates' death" points to the asymmetry of the dependency relation between Xantippe's widowhood and Socrates' death. As in the causal case, the asymmetry of the former appears to be rooted in the asymmetry of the latter.

IV

We do one thing *by* doing another, and this "by-relation", as it is sometimes called, generates chainlike (or, as Goldman claims,[4] treelike) structures of actions. Thus, I move my hand, thereby turning the knob, thereby opening the window, thereby letting in fresh air, and so on. The relationship between any two adjacent actions in such a chain seems to exhibit many of the features, lately noted, characteristic of noncausal event determination.

Consider the two actions, my turning the knob and my opening the window. (1) The counterfactual "If I had not turned the knob, I would

---

3 Some philosophers want to explain causal asymmetry in terms of the asymmetry of the agency relation; see Douglas Gasking, "Causation and Recipes", *Mind* 64 (1955): 479–87; Georg H. von Wright, *Explanation and Understanding* (Ithaca, N.Y.: Cornell University Press, 1971).

4 Alvin I. Goldman, *A Theory of Human Action* (Englewood Cliffs, N.J.: Prentice-Hall, 1970), ch. 2.

not have opened the window" seems to be true. (2) The converse counterfactual "If I had not opened the window, I would not have turned the knob" appears either false or at best dubious. (3) There is a definite feeling that the action of opening the window is dependent on, determined by, the action of turning the knob, which gives substantial intuitive content to the term "generation" used by Goldman to characterize the dependency relations of this sort between actions. (4) The relation between the actions, however, is not causal – my turning the knob does not cause my opening the window.

An interesting feature of such an action pair is this: it is not only the actions that exhibit an asymmetric dependency relationship; the states or events brought about by them also exhibit such a relationship. Let us think of actions as cases of bringing about a state of affairs or event;[5] thus, an action can be given a canonical description "S brings about p", where p is an individual state or event. Thus, my turning the knob is my bringing about the knob's turning, and my opening the window is my bringing about the window's being open. Following von Wright,[6] we may call the state or event brought about by an action the "result" of that action. Evidently, then, the result of the first action, namely the knob's turning, is a cause of the result of the second, namely the window's being open. So we have a two-tier dependency structure: the action of bringing about q is dependent on the action of bringing about p, and q is dependent (causally, in this case) on p. It is plausible to think that the former dependency is to be explained in terms of the latter, and that the asymmetry of the latter relation is what generates the asymmetry of the former.

The action pair just considered is an instance of what Goldman calls "causal generation". But the dual structure of dependency is not limited to this variety of action generation. Consider my signaling for a turn by extending my left arm, which is a case of Goldman's "conventional generation": the two actions exhibit the features (1)–(4) noted above, and the results of these actions, a turn signal being made and my left arm's being extended, exhibit a similar dependency relation. Here, the determinative relation between the results isn't causal; it involves conventions and rules

5 See Roderick M. Chisholm, "Freedom and Action", in *Freedom and Determination*, ed. Keith Lehrer (New York: Random House, 1966); also von Wright, *Explanation and Understanding*. Not all actions are happily viewed as cases of bringing about an event or state; see Donald Davidson, "The Logical Form of Action Sentences", reprinted in his *Essays on Actions and Events* (Oxford: Oxford University Press, 1980).

6 *Explanation and Understanding*, pp. 66ff.

rather than laws and regularities. If we go back to the case of Socrates' death and Xantippe's becoming a widow, we have a case of Goldman's "simple generation": according to his scheme, my bringing about Socrates' death would simply generate my bringing about Xantippe's widowhood. We have already noted the dependency relation between the two actions and also between their respective results.[7]

The following conjecture, I think, is in order: the hierarchical structure of actions generated by the agency relation is ultimately grounded in a parallel hierarchical structure of events and states that are the results of these actions in von Wright's sense. And this suggests an account of the agency relation and action structures generated by it within a broader theory of events, states, and the determinative dependency relations that hold for them. This line of approach derives support from the fact that certain features of an action structure appear to be explainable in terms of the features of the determinative structure of events and states underlying it. For example, the asymmetry and transitivity of the agency relation, the two properties that are essential for generating the treelike structures of Goldman, are perhaps rooted in the asymmetric and transitive nature of the determinative dependency relations, causal and noncausal, that hold for the underlying network of events and states. A central problem in carrying out such a project would be to characterize a relation R for events and states such that if an agent brings about p, then, for any q, p is related by R to q if and only if the agent brings about q by bringing about p. It is likely that such an R will be a broad relation of event dependency that subsumes as special cases the causal relation and other dependency relations noted in this paper.

These larger speculations aside, there are more specific problems of interest concerning actions and dependency relations, of which we mention some below without comment.

(i) Is the following generally true: if p causes q, and a person S brings about p, then S brings about q by bringing about p? Is the foregoing generally true when p noncausally determines q, say, in the manner of the death of Socrates and the widowing of Xantippe?

7 Goldman recognizes a fourth type of action generation which he calls "augmentation generation"; for example, my extending my arm augmentatively generates my extending my arm out the car window. This type of case, too, seems analyzable in a similar way: here the relation between the events or states brought about by the two actions would be one of *inclusion* (my arm's being extended out the car window *includes* its being extended). It is of course a further problem to explain an appropriate notion of "inclusion".

(ii) If S brings about p, and p causes q, is it correct or useful to say that S's bringing about p is a *cause* of q? What of the case in which p noncausally determines q?

(iii) Are there iterative cases of bringing about (e.g., my bringing about your bringing about p), and if there are, what principles govern them? For example, if S brings about W's bringing about p, does S bring about p?

(iv) Let us say, following what has become a standard usage, that S's bringing about p is a *basic action* in case there is no q such that S brings about p by bringing about q. If S's bringing about p is a basic action, can p be determined causally or noncausally by another event q?

V

An object is being heated, and as a result it is expanding. Let us assume there is a lawlike regularity for heating and expansion instantiated by this causal relation. We define a property expression "F" to be true of any object just in case there is an object 50 miles due south which is being heated. Then the following regularity obtains: whenever an object has property F, another object 50 miles due south is expanding. This regularity is completely general, and appears to be capable of sustaining a counterfactual of the form "If this object had F, there would be an object 50 miles due south which is expanding." Under the standard regularity account of laws a statement expressing this derived correlation between F and expansion would qualify as a law, and under some version of the regularity account of causation an object's having F would be certified as a cause of another object's expanding.[8]

Apart from the obvious difficulties this presents for the regularity account of causation (and, we may add, the covering-law account of explanation), we are inclined to be dubious about the status of F as a *constitutive property* of events, that is, a property an exemplification of which by an object at a time is an event, and dubious also about the "law" connecting F with expanding. That there is an unexceptional, law-based regularity between them cannot be denied; however, this "law" seems incapable of providing causal or explanatory connections: we cannot say that a given object is expanding *because* another has the property F. And the reason for this seems to lie in F. Although it is a well-defined property, an exemplifying of F by an object is not, we feel, a "real event" or "real change". The real change in this situation occurs to the object that is being heated,

8 For further discussion of cases of this kind in connection with Humean causation, see Essay 1 of this volume.

and an object has *F* solely in virtue of that event. The trouble has nothing to do with the way the term *"F"* is explained; this is evident from the fact that there is nothing untoward about *F**-events, where *"F*"* is true of an object in case there is an object 50 miles due north which has property *F.* Notice, further, that an event like an *F*-event is not what C. J. Ducasse and others have called an "unchange" – a static condition persisting through a period of time, e.g., the temperature of an object remaining constant over a period of time. An unchange can be as "real" as real changes, and can be a cause of other events in a full-blooded sense. What distinguishes events like *F*-events is their parasitic, derivative nature; *F* does not represent a condition *in* the object to which it is attributed, whether or not the condition involves a change.

Our *F*-event is a typical case of what Peter Geach has called, somewhat sardonically, a "mere Cambridge change".[9] A "Cambridge change" is said to occur to an object if there is a predicate true of it at a time but false of it at a later time. (According to Geach, this was the criterion of "change" advocated by such illustrious Cambridge philosophers as Russell and McTaggart.) So all real changes are Cambridge changes – at least those that are representable by predicates – but the converse clearly is not true. Let us borrow the term "Cambridge" with a slight modification: we shall say "Cambridge change" or "Cambridge event" where Geach would say "*mere* Cambridge change", etc. We shall also speak of "Cambridge dependence" and "Cambridge determination" to refer to the manner in which *F*-events are determined by, and are dependent on, heating events, and in which, as we shall shortly see, the widowing of Xantippe is determined by, and is dependent on, the death of Socrates.

Someone's becoming a widow is much like an *F*-event: in each case, an object undergoes a change in a property in virtue of its being related in a prescribed way to another wholly distinct object undergoing a change. And the manner in which the event of becoming a widow depends on a death is much like the way an *F*-event depends on an event of heating, as one can verify by checking the asymmetric and noncausal character of the latter dependence. We may say, therefore, that Xantippe's becoming a widow is a Cambridge event, Cambridge-dependent on the death of Socrates.

We earlier argued that Socrates' death is not a cause of Xantippe's widowhood. What then is its cause? The death was caused by Socrates' drinking of hemlock. Could this event be a cause of Xantippe's widowhood?

9 In his *God and the Soul* (London: Routledge & Kegan Paul, 1969), p. 71.

As in the case of F and expansion, we can even provide a nice Humean law to subsume Socrates' hemlock drinking and Xantippe's becoming a widow. For, given the law, let us assume, that anyone who drinks hemlock dies, we have the law – at least a Humean regularity – that anyone whose husband drinks hemlock becomes a widow. But this "law", though completely general and counterfactual-sustaining, does not appear to sanction a causal judgment connecting the antecedent and the consequent. For by what causal mechanism does the ingestion of hemlock lead to the widowhood? We can trace the causal chain from the hemlock drinking to the death, but no farther; the connection between the death and Xantippe's becoming a widow isn't causal. And it seems that the only way a causal chain could reach the widowhood is through the death. Also, the time interval between the hemlock ingestion and the onset of widowhood has no relationship at all to their spatial distance or any other significant feature of the widowhood; her widowhood commences when and precisely when Socrates expires as a result of the hemlock poisoning.

To rule out Socrates' drinking as a cause of Xantippe's widowhood is to rule out, by implication, any other event that is a cause of the death as a cause of the widowhood. And if neither Socrates' death nor any of its causes is a cause of Xantippe's widowhood, we can only conclude, I think, that this event has no cause. We can tell a story about how it came about that Xantippe became a widow, but this isn't to specify its cause, nor is it to give a causal explanation of it. Events like that are determined by other events; their occurrence is completely dependent on the occurrence of others, but this is not to say that they are causally determined by them. Acknowledging such events is not to give up universal determinism; it only means that determinism should not be understood as a thesis asserting that every event is causally determined.

VI

We have so far identified two sorts of ways in which an event is noncausally determined by other events: one is "Cambridge dependence", exemplified by an event pair such as the death of Socrates and the widowing of Xantippe, and the other is agency dependence, exemplified by a pair of actions of which one is done by doing the other. Are there other modes of noncausal event determination? I believe that event composition is one important way in which events are determined by others. By "event composition" I have in mind the way in which an event is composed of other events as its constituents. There are various distinguishable

30

ways in which an event can be said to be a composite event; the following are some of the more obvious ones:

(1) Fred makes a jumpshot. He jumps, and he shoots the basketball at the same time. The event of Fred's making a jumpshot is a composite event having as its constituents the jumping and the shooting.

(2) The surface of a liquid is turning from yellow to orange. This event can be thought of as consisting of two events, the left half of the surface turning from yellow to orange and the right half doing the same. These constituent events are spatial parts of the composite event.

(3) Analogously, an event can have other events as temporal parts.

The counterfactual dependency between a composite event and its constituents, taken severally, appears to exhibit the sort of asymmetry we noted in connection with Cambridge dependence. A counterfactual like "If Fred had not jumped at t, he would not have made a jumpshot at t" appears generally true, whereas the truth of its converse appears either dubious or dependent on some special features of individual cases. As for the asymmetry of the agency relation, the situation is a bit more compli- cated. Let e be a composite event having e_1 and e_2 as its sole constituents. Is it always true to say "We can bring about e by bringing about e_1 and e_2"? If "bring about e_1 and e_2" means "bring about $e_1 + e_2$" where "$+$" denotes the particular mode of event composition involved, then the statement appears uninterestingly true − or uninterestingly false; for e is $e_1 + e_2$. On the other hand, if "bring about e_1 and e_2" means "bring about e_1 and bring about e_2", the statement is again true − unless "bring about e_1 and bring about e_2" is taken to imply that the two events can be brought about independently of each other. It is not difficult to find cases of composite events in which we can bring about the constituent events only by bringing about the composite event as a whole, for example, a complex learned motion which we can execute only as a whole. Such a case provides an example in which one can bring about a constituent event by − perhaps only by − bringing about the composite event.

What this brief discussion shows is that, unlike Cambridge depen- dence, compositional dependence does not show a clear asymmetry with respect to the agency relation. Some such divergence is only to be ex- pected, for a composite event, unlike a Cambridge event, is not a mere shadowy epiphenomenon of events that go on elsewhere; it is literally a composite of these events. Another point of difference is that composi- tional dependence, unlike Cambridge dependence, transmits causal rela- tions: any event which is a causal condition of a constituent event is also a causal condition of the composite event of which it is a constituent.

31

Agency dependence, too, appears to transmit causal relations: if an action is done by doing another, a causal condition of the latter is also a causal condition of the former (this is noted by Goldman),[10] and in this respect agency dependence, too, differs from Cambridge dependence.

On the other hand, all these noncausal modes of event determination transmit determinative relations: if an event is dependent on another in any one of these ways, any determinative condition of the second is also a determinative condition of the former. There is nothing surprising about that; it's something one would expect from dependence and determination relations.

A close study of compositional dependence will repay us in two ways. First, a clear understanding of it is likely to shed light on the notion of "real change". For a change in the composition of an object is as clear a case of a change being *in* the object as we can think of. (Recall the ancients' idea that the soul is immortal because it is indivisible, that is, has no parts.) Second, the micro–macro relation between states and events appears to be a special case of compositional dependence, and it is likely that a systematic treatment of the latter will help us with understanding the former. Needless to say, the micro–macro relation plays a crucial role in many philosophical problems.

VII

What we have said so far generates a host of questions. Just to mention a few: Why isn't the death of Socrates itself a Cambridge event dependent on other "more basic" events? Are there events that might be called "basic" (compare with "basic actions")? Is it really necessary or useful to treat things like someone's becoming a widow as events, and if not, what sort of thing are they? What is a "real event"? Do Cambridge events enter into causal relations?

Events in this world are interrelated in a variety of ways. Among them, the ones we have called dependence or determination relations are of great importance. Broadly speaking, it is these relations, along with temporal and spatial ones, that give significant structure to the world of events. The chief aim of the present paper has been to show that causation, though important and in many ways fundamental, is not the only such relation, and that there are other determinative relations that deserve recognition and careful scrutiny.

10 *A Theory of Human Action*, p. 75.

3

Events as property exemplifications

The term 'event' ordinarily implies change, and most changes are changes in a substance. Whether coming into being and passing away can be construed as changes in substances is a question we shall not consider here. A change in a substance occurs when that substance acquires a property it did not previously have, or loses a property it previously had. Whether fissions and fusions of substances can be considered as cases of losing or acquiring properties is, again, a question we shall not discuss in this paper. By 'substance' I mean things like tables, chairs, atoms, living creatures, bits of stuff like water and bronze, and the like; there is no need here to associate this notion with a particular philosophical doctrine about substance.

Besides events, we also speak of "states". If "events" signal changes, "states" seem to be static things, "unchanges", to use a term of C. J. Ducasse's;[1] some examples of states would be my body's weighing 140 pounds, the earth's being nearly spherical in shape, and the presence of oxygen in this room. There are, however, good reasons for not taking this dichotomy of changes and unchanges, or of events and states, too seriously at the initial stage of developing a theory of events. For one thing, there are cases that are hard to classify; e.g., the whirring of my typewriter, having a throbbing pain in the right elbow. Then there are "conditions", which, it seems, can be either events or states depending on essentially pragmatic contextual factors. And what of "processes"? A deeper analysis may reveal subtle and important differences among these entities, but I think that can wait until we have a good enough grasp of

I have benefited from discussions with, or unpublished materials furnished by, the following persons: David Benfield, Richard Cartwright, Roderick Chisholm, Donald Davidson, Fred Feldman, Michael A. Slote, Ernest Sosa, and Ed Wierenga.
1 In Ducasse, C. J., *Causation and the Type of Necessity,* Univ. of Washington Press, Seattle, 1924.

them as a distinct ontological category. Of course, this may turn out to be a wrong move; there may not be a single, unitary ontological category of interest comprising all, or even most, of them. But if we are wrong here, it would be philosophically profitable to find out that we are.

Moreover, it is a philosophical commonplace to use the term 'event' in a broad sense, not only to refer to changes but also to refer to states, conditions, and the like. When universal determinism is formulated as "Every event has a cause" or "the aim of science" is said to be the explanation and prediction of events in nature, it surely is not intended that states, narrowly so-called, escape the net of causal relations or that it is not the business of science to explain why certain states obtain, e.g., why the sky looks blue or why the earth is pear-shaped. To give one more reason for playing down the differences between events and states: some properties already imply changes in the substance that has them; for example, fading in color, falling, and freezing. This means that a change need not necessarily be characterized as a losing or acquiring of some property; it may simply be the *having* of some property at a time.

Just as changes are changes of properties in substances – again leaving aside such difficult cases as coming into being, passing away, fusion and fission – states and conditions are states and conditions *of* or *in* substances or systems of substances. Add this to our earlier reasons for underplaying the differences between changes and unchanges, and we naturally arrive at a conception of events and states as *exemplifications by substances of properties at a time*. This account can be called 'the property-exemplification account' of events; it has also been called a theory of events as "structured complexes", since it attributes to an event a complex structure: an event (or state) is a structure consisting of a substance (an n-tuple of substances), a property (an n-adic relational attribute), and a time. This in essence is the view of events I have advocated in several earlier papers.[2]

This view of events has been criticized from many quarters, notably by Donald Davidson. The present paper aims at providing further clarifications of the theory, in part in light of some of these criticisms, and also

2 'On the Psycho-Physical Identity Theory', *American Philosophical Quarterly* 3 (1966), 231–32; 'Events and Their Descriptions: Some Considerations', N. Rescher *et al.* (eds.), *Essays in Honor of Carl G. Hempel,* Reidel, Dordrecht-Holland, 1969; 'Causation, Nomic Subsumption, and the Concept of Event', Essay 1 of this volume. A similar account of action was given by Alvin Goldman in *A Theory of Human Action,* Prentice-Hall, Englewood Cliffs, N.J., 1970; an account of events very much like mine is found in R. M. Martin's 'On Events and Event-Descriptions', J. Margolis (ed). *Fact and Existence.* See also N. L. Wilson, 'Facts, Events and Their Identity Conditions', *Philosophical Studies* 25 (1974), 303–21.

raises some further issues concerning events and actions. In order to do this we need to state a few more details of the property-exemplification account. According to this account, each individual event has three unique constituents: a substance (the "constitutive object" of the event), a property it exemplifies (the "constitutive property" or "generic event"), and a time. An event is a complex of these three, and I have used the notation $[x, P, t]$, or variants thereof, as a canonical notation for events in general. There are two basic principles in the theory, one stating the conditions under which an event exists (occurs, if you like) and the other stating the conditions under which events are identical.

Existence condition: Event $[x, P, t]$ exists just in case substance x has property P at time t.

Identity condition: $[x, P, t] = [y, Q, t']$ just in case $x = y$, $P = Q$, and $t = t'$.

(For simplicity's sake we won't bother with dyadic and higher-place events, although these will show up later as examples. For details see my 'Causation, Nomic Subsumption, and the Concept of Events', Essay 1 of this volume.) We shall sometimes use the expression 'event structure'[3] when we want to refer specifically to entities satisfying these conditions, i.e., events under the property-exemplification account.

As far as monadic events are concerned, i.e., events involving nonrelational, one-place attributes as constitutive properties, the theory can easily be developed along a different line: dispense with the existence condition and define the *predicate* 'is an event' over ordered triples of substances, properties, and times. An ordered triple $\langle x, P, t \rangle$ would be an event just in case the substance x has the property P at time t. The existence of the triple would be guaranteed by the principles of set theory, provided x, P, and t exist, whether or not x has P at t. And the identity condition for events would merely be a special case of the identity condition governing n-tuples. For dyadic and higher-place events, this approach of defining an event predicate within set theory introduces some complexities in regard to the identity condition, complexities which are by no means insuperable. In any case this approach has the advantage of using the familiar set-theoretic apparatus and of doing away with a special operator '[, ,]', which some people seem to find mysterious (but given the identity condition, '[, ,]', may be taken as a special case of the familiar definite description operator, and in this regard it is not different from the set-abstraction operator '{v| . . . v . . . }'). It would also allow us to speak of

3 This expression was suggested by Richard Cartwright.

"possible events", i.e., the ordered triples $\langle x, P, t \rangle$, whether or not x has P at t, which might be useful for certain philosophical purposes.[4]

What is essential is that we are assuming as primitives the three functors on events: 'is the constitutive property of', 'is the constitutive object of', and 'is the time of the occurrence of'. The theory states that just in case a substance x has property P at t, there is an event whose constitutive object is x, whose constitutive property is P, and whose time of occurrence is t (the existence condition), and that events are identical just in case they have the same constitutive property, object, and time (the identity condition). This is the core of the account of events under discussion. The introduction of the notation '[, ,]' is merely abbreviatory; the use of the set-theoretic machinery *may* have certain metaphysical consequences, depending on one's metaphysical views of sets, as regards, for example, the essential properties of events. But I regard these as peripheral issues pertaining largely to the mode of presentation of the theory; the basic elements of the account are not essentially altered thereby.

The account so far presented is not an "eliminative" or "reductive" theory of events; that is, it does not attempt to show that events are in some eliminative sense "reducible" to substances, properties, and times. (It may be remarked, though, that a better case for the elimination or reduction of events might be made if we take the ordered triple approach sketched above.) I do not know exactly when a metaphysical theory is "reductive"; the account, however, attempts to tell us something about the metaphysical nature of events by relating them to such other ontological categories as substances, properties, and times. And I have tried to show, in several earlier papers, how this view of events can provide a useful framework within which to develop and discuss theories of causation and explanation, and the mind–body problem; I believe it also provides a framework in which an account of the relation between micro-events and macro-events can be developed.[5]

I have said little about what properties are allowable as constitutive properties of events; namely, what "generic events" are. It clearly will not do to count as an event the exemplification of any arbitrary property by an object. This becomes obvious if one thinks, as many do, that there is a property expressed by any open sentence, or if one thinks of properties

4 For a treatment of "possible facts" somewhat along these lines see Bas van Fraassen, 'Facts and Tautological Entailments', *Journal of Philosophy* 66 (1969), 477–87.

5 Interesting results have been obtained along these lines by Terence Horgan in his doctoral dissertation. *Microreduction and the Mind–Body Problem*, at The University of Michigan, 1974.

in the way modal logicians do nowadays, namely as functions from possible worlds to sets of individuals. There is also the problem, a difficult and important one, of properties ordinarily considered generic events, e.g., becoming a widow, which give rise to "Cambridge events".[6] It will only beg the issue to try to explain 'generic event' in terms of such notions as 'change' and 'alteration'. And it may be tempting, but no less question-begging, to try to define it in terms of overtly causal concepts, for "real changes" or "real events" seem to be just those that make a causal difference, and generic events seem to be just those properties whose possession by an object bestows upon it a causal power or potency, or whose possession by an object indicates its being subjected to such powers.

This causal approach, I think, may turn out to be the correct one – but in a roundabout way: the basic generic events may be best picked out relative to a scientific theory, whether the theory is a common-sense theory of the behavior of middle-sized objects or a highly sophisticated physical theory. They are among the important properties, relative to the theory, in terms of which lawful regularities can be discovered, described, and explained. The basic parameters in terms of which the laws of the theory are formulated would, on this view, give us our basic generic events, and the usual logical, mathematical, and perhaps other types of operations on them would yield complex, defined generic events. We commonly recognize such properties as motion, colors, temperatures, weights, pushing, and breaking, as generic events and states, but we must view this against the background of our common-sense explanatory and predictive scheme of the world around us. I think it highly likely that we cannot pick out generic events completely a priori. If generic events are understood along these lines, not all of the Boolean combinations of generic events can be relied on to yield generic events; for example, if two generic events are from different theories or rival theories about the same subject matter. It isn't even clear that if F is a generic event, non-F is also a generic event in every case.

There is also the following problem: generic events are often picked out by verbs and predicates. Now there is a group of words that modify them – adverbs and, generally, predicate modifiers. The question arises: If 'F' is a predicate or verb designating a generic event and α is a predicate modifier, under what conditions does '$\alpha(F)$' designate a generic event?

6 See my 'Noncausal Connections', Essay 2 of this volume. The term 'Cambridge change' comes from Peter Geach, *God and the Soul*, Routledge & Kegan Paul, London, 1969, p. 71.

The answer will of course depend on the particular properties of 'α' and of 'F'. If walking is a generic event, walking slowly seems to be one also. What about walking while chewing gum, walking toward the Eiffel Tower, and walking exactly two thousand years after the death of Socrates? Are they *kinds of events*? Or should we treat the modifiers as indicating properties *of* the individual events arising from the generic event of walking – e.g., treat '(being done) while chewing gum' as designating a property of the event of my walking at a particular time *t*? We shall briefly recur to this problem below.

II

A metaphysical theory of events of the sort just sketched must be distinguished from a theory of the "logical form" of event and action sentences – a theory that attempts to exhibit the relevant logical and semantical structures of sentences about events – of the sort initiated essentially by Donald Davidson in an influential series of papers.[7] To call attention to this distinction is not to say there are no important connections between the two. Davidson has made ontological claims based on his work on the logical form of event and action sentences; most notably, he has claimed that his investigations have shown that events and actions must be admitted into our ontology as values of bound variables, and that they are "particulars" that can be described and referred to in various nonequivalent ways. However, Davidson has also emphasized a distinction between a logical and semantical theory of event discourse and a metaphysical theory of events:[8]

> On the score of ontology, too, the study of logical form can carry us only a certain distance. . . . Given this much, a study of event sentences will show a great deal about what we assume to be true concerning events. But deep metaphysical problems will remain as to the nature of these entities, their mode of individuation, their relation to other categories.

Davidson did go beyond a theory of event sentences: in his paper 'The Individuation of Events'[9] he has given us a principle of individuation for events. It is this: events are the same just in case they have the same causes and the same effects. This criterion has been criticized as covertly circular,

---

7 To cite a few: 'The Logical Form of Action Sentences'. N. Rescher (ed.), *The Logic of Decision and Action*, Univ. of Pittsburgh Press, Pittsburgh, 1967; 'Causal Relations', *Journal of Philosophy* 64 (1967), 691–703; 'Truth and Meaning', *Synthese* 17 (1967), 304–23.

8 'Action and Reaction', *Inquiry* 13 (1970), 140–48.

9 In N. Rescher (ed.), *Essays in Honor of Carl G. Hempel*.

since causes and effects themselves are events.[10] If the criticisms are correct, it may be unsound as a "criterion" of individuation; nonetheless, it may be true that events having the same causes and same effects are in fact one and the same, although one wonders how the criterion would fare in an indeterministic, causally irregular world (this world could be such a world). Further, it may in fact turn out that my criterion of event identity is coextensive with Davidson's: that is, for events x and y, $x=y$ under the identity condition of the property-exemplification account of events if and only if $x=y$ under Davidson's criterion.[11]

Let us now look into the question whether the property-exemplification account of events is incompatible with Davidson's theory of event sentences and his metaphysical claims based on that theory. The two are often considered as competing theories,[12] and it is a matter of some interest to see what differences, if any, exist between them.[13]

Central to Davidson's theory of event sentences is the point that a sentence like

(1) Flora dried herself with a towel on the beach at noon,

which is just the sort of sentence often said to "describe" or "represent" an event, contains a covert existential quantification over concrete events, and its logical form should be brought out thus:

(2) There is an event e such that e is a drying of Flora by Flora, e was done with a towel, e occurred on the beach, and e occurred at noon.

Now there seems to be no reason why the variable 'e' cannot take as its values the event structures of the property-exemplification account: in fact, no reason why the particular event structure [(Flora, Flora), ① dries ②, noon] isn't just the value of 'e' that makes (2) true. As (2) affirms, this event − an action, as it happens − has the property of being done with a towel, the property of occurring on the beach, and so on. Notice, by the

---

10 E.g. by N. L. Wilson in 'Facts, Events and Their Identity Conditions'; and by George Sher in 'On Event-Identity", *Australasian Journal of Philosophy* 52 (1974), 39–47.

11 In 'On Kim's Account of Events and Event-Identity', *Journal of Philosophy* 71 (1974), 327–36, Alexander Rosenberg claims that, with a slight revision in my account of events, Davidson's criterion and my criterion are equivalent under the Humean constant-conjunction view of causation.

12 Davidson himself refers to my account as a "rival" account, in his 'Events as Particulars', *Noûs* 4 (1970), 25–32, p. 26, footnote 4.

13 I shall not discuss here Roderick M. Chisholm's very different theory of events as "states of affairs" in his sense of abstract intensional entities, developed in his *Person and Object*, Open Court Publishing Co., 1976. See also his 'Events and Propositions', *Noûs* 4 (1970), 15–24.

way, that the first clause in the matrix of (2) says '*e is a drying* of . . .'; this
'is a (verb)-ing' construction and other verb nominalizations are good
clues for identifying the generic events involved in Davidsonian para-
phrases of event sentences. To cite two of his own examples:[14]

(3a) The boiler exploded in the cellar.
(3b) There exists an x such that x was an explosion and x was in the cellar and x
     was of the boiler
(4a) Jack fell down . . .
(4b) There is an event e such that e is a falling down of Jack . . .

On my account exploding, falling, and the like are generic events in the
intended sense; the boiler and Jack, in the above examples, are the constitutive substances of the two events respectively.

Obviously, my events can be quantified over; and there is no problem
about quantifying *into* the event structures unless of course there happen
to be other barriers to quantification such as psychological modalities. My
events are "particulars" and "dated". That they are dated is obvious. I am
not clear what "particulars" are; but events in my sense have locations
in space, namely the locations of their constitutive substances (if mental
substances have no spatial location, then mental events would have no
spatial location either, which presumably is what some dualists want to
claim). And my events are not "eternal" objects; they do not exist in all
possible worlds; they exist only if the existence condition is met, which
is a contingent matter of fact. If this doesn't show that something is "concrete" or "particular", what does?[15]

Davidson has considered it an important mistake to regard a sentence
like

(5) Doris capsized the canoe yesterday

as picking out a unique event, for she may have capsized the canoe more
than once yesterday. Generally speaking, it is a mistake, according to him,
to think of such sentences as playing the role of singular terms for events.
Now my account does not compel us to render (5) into

(6) The event [Doris, capsized the canoe, yesterday] occurs.

(Here we disregard the fact that a dyadic event may be involved; we also
disregard the tense.) For we may put (5) thus:

14 The first pair comes from his 'Eternal vs. Ephemeral Events', *Noûs* 5 (1971), 335–49,
   p. 337; the second from 'Causal Relations', 696.
15 Chisholm refers to both Davidson's account and mine as variants of "the concrete event
   theory" in *Person and Object*.

(7) $(\exists t)([\text{Doris, capsizes the canoe, } t]$ exists and t belongs to yesterday).

But we are not quite through with Davidson on this point. According to the existence condition, as I intended it, if an object x exemplifies P at t in the sense of *throughout t*, then the existence of a *unique* $[x, P, t]$ is guaranteed by the identity condition. Davidson writes:[16]

> Some actions are difficult or unusual to perform more than once in a short stretch of time, and this may provide a specious reason in some cases for holding that action sentences refer uniquely to actions. Thus with 'Jones got married last Saturday', 'Doris wrote a check at noon', 'Mary kissed an admirer at the stroke of midnight'. It is merely illegal to get married twice on the same day, merely unusual to write checks simultaneously, and merely good fortune to get to kiss two admirers at once.

Let us assume that kissing some admirer or other is a generic event. My two conditions, then, imply that there is the unique event of Mary's kissing an admirer at the specified time. From the existence of this event, however, nothing follows as to how many persons she kissed at the time, although ordinarily, it would be safe enough to assume she kissed one person. Suppose she in fact kissed two admirers, Steve and Larry. If we take the dyadic kissing, x's kissing admirer y, as the generic event involved, the two conditions entail the existence of two unique dyadic kissings, Mary's kissing Steve and her kissing Larry. Thus, there are three kissings here, which some might find a bit disconcerting; but once it is realized that they are one monadic kissing and two dyadic kissings, the situation need no longer strike us as implausible or incoherent. In fact, it seems to me that that is what we should say to describe Mary's kissings.[17]

Another point of some importance, though obvious, is this: there is nothing in my account that implies that from any sentence about an event we can read off what the event's constitutive components are. From the sentence 'A momentous event occurred yesterday' we can only approximately locate the time of the event; we can tell nothing about its constitutive property or substance. From the sentence 'The momentous event that occurred yesterday caused the event now under discussion by the regents of the university' we can say nothing about the constituents of these events, except, again, the time of the first event. This is as it should be. The situation is quite similar with sentences about physical objects. In a sense knowing what the constitutive object, property, and time of an

---

16 'The Individuation of Events', 220.
17 Especially if we keep in mind the fact that there being three different kissings does not entail that there can be no intimate and significant relations between them.

event are *is* to *know what that event is*. Although we are here treading on uncertain grounds, my canonical description of an event, I believe, gives an "intrinsic description" of an event (assuming that the three components are given "intrinsic descriptions"), in the sense in which such descriptions as 'the momentous event yesterday' and 'the event now under discussion' are "extrinsic". I am not here prepared to explain, much less define, what is to be meant by 'intrinsic' and 'extrinsic'; perhaps they are explainable in terms of a combination of modal and epistemic concepts.

There are other points of apparent disagreement between Davidson's views and mine, some of which will be taken up in succeeding sections. But overall it seems to me that there are no irreconcilable *doctrinal* differences between Davidson's theory of event discourse as a semantical theory and the property-exemplification account of events as a metaphysical theory. True enough, Davidson and I disagree about particular cases of individuation of events; for example, whether Brutus's stabbing Caesar is the same event as Brutus's killing Caesar. But most of these differences about particular cases seem traceable to possible differences in our views about causation, explanation, and intensionality. Where Davidson says, with regard to a sentence like

(8) The collapse was caused, not by the bolt's giving way, but the bolt's giving way so suddenly,

that here 'was caused' should be understood in the sense of 'is causally explained', and that explanations "typically relate statements, not events",[18] I would take (8) more literally and be inclined to take it as evidence for saying that in virtue of their different causal properties, the bolt's giving way and the bolt's giving way suddenly are different events, though one is "included" in the other. But here we are coming dangerously close to some difficult problems about the relationship between causation and explanation, and the intensionality of causal and explanatory relations, problems well beyond the scope of the present paper.

III

One of the most frequently voiced objections to the theory of events as property exemplifications is the point that this theory multiplies events beyond necessity. Not only is Brutus's stabbing Caesar distinct from his

18 'Causal Relations', 703. (8) is a slightly altered version of Davidson's own example.

killing Caesar and also from his assassinating Caesar; but in fact no stabbings are killings, and no killings are assassinations.[19] What seems worse, Brutus's stabbing Caesar is also a different event from Brutus's stabbing Caesar with a knife, since stabbing and stabbing with a knife presumably are different properties; and neither of these events is the same as Brutus's stabbing Caesar in the heart; and so on. These considerations seem to have led some philosophers to think that the property-exemplification account does not permit redescriptions of events,[20] since any addition or deletion from a given description would alter the constitutive property of the event in question.

Let us first examine the problem of redescribing an event. It is true that if an event description is altered so that a different generic event is picked out, then the resulting description, on my view, would pick out a different event. That much is clear enough. And the same applies to the names and descriptions of the constitutive objects and times of events. On the other hand, it is not part of the account in question that the use of different predicates − nonsynonymous, logically inequivalent predicates − invariably leads to a multiplicity of properties. 'Is blue' and 'has the color of the sky' pick out the same property, namely the color blue.[21] Moreover, as noted earlier, events themselves *have* (exemplify) properties; Brutus's stabbing Caesar has the property of occurring in Rome, it was intentional, it led to the death of Caesar and caused Calpurnia to grieve, and so on. Needless to say, the properties an event exemplifies must be sharply distinguished from its constitutive property (which is exemplified, not by the event, but by the constitutive substance of the event). It is also a property of Brutus's stabbing Caesar that its constitutive property is stabbing. Thus, events can be redescribed by the use of different predicates expressing the properties *of* (exemplified by) them; what cannot be done is to redescribe them by tampering with their constitutive properties. The point I am making should be obvious if we consider such "extrinsic" descriptions of events as 'the event we are talking about' and 'the most unforgettable event in David's life'. What the theory implies is that if 'the most unforgettable event in David's life' refers, then the event thus

19 Davidson in his 'Comments' on Martin's 'On Events and Event-Descriptions', Margolis (ed.,), *Fact and Existence,* 81. Also Rosenberg in 'On Kim's Account of Events and Event-Identity'.
20 E.g. Carl G. Hedman claims this in his 'On When There Must Be a Time-Difference Between Cause and Effect', *Philosophy of Science* 39 (1972), 507–11.
21 On property identity, see Peter Achinstein, 'The Identity of Properties', *American Philosophical Quarterly* 11, 1974, 257–75.

referred to must have a structure of the sort the theory attributes to events; for example, the event could have been David's falling off a horse at age five.

But the foregoing isn't likely to satisfy the critics as allowing us a full range of describing and redescribing events. 'Brutus stabbing Caesar' and 'Brutus killing Caesar', they insist, *are* redescriptions of the same event; and what may seem even more obvious, 'Brutus's stabbing Caesar' and 'Brutus's stabbing Caesar with a knife' are two descriptions of the same event, one being somewhat more detailed and more informative than the other. Similarly, for such examples as 'Sebastian's stroll', 'Sebastian's leisurely stroll', and 'Sebastian's limping stroll'. Here we return to the initial objections mentioned at the outset of this section.

I do not want to discuss here the question of whether Brutus's stabbing Caesar is the same event as Brutus's killing Caesar; for I have little to add to the existing arguments in favor of their distinctness.[22] Also, intuitively, it is more plausible to deny identity in cases like it than in cases like Sebastian's stroll and Sebastian's leisurely stroll (where, we suppose, Sebastian did stroll leisurely).

So what of Sebastian's stroll and Sebastian's leisurely stroll? First of all, there is the question whether being leisurely is to be taken as a property exemplified by the event of Sebastian's stroll, or as modifying the generic event of strolling, thereby issuing in another generic event, namely strolling leisurely. If the former line is taken, there is no special problem – no more problem here than there is in the case of 'this red rose on the table' and 'this withered red rose on the table' where there is one unique red rose on the designated table which is withered. So on this approach Sebastian's stroll, after all, turns out to be the very same event as Sebastian's leisurely stroll, i.e., Sebastian's stroll, which, as it happens, was leisurely.

Thus, the general strategy is this: we deny that strolling leisurely or stabbing with a knife are generic events, although strolling and stabbing are. The modifiers 'leisurely' and 'with a knife' are taken, not as modifying 'strolling' and 'stabbing', but rather as indicating properties of the individual events which arise from the exemplifications of the generic events designated by 'strolling' and 'stabbing'. We could say, somewhat more generally, that predicate modifiers indicating means-manners-

22 I have in mind: Lawrence H. Davis, 'Individuation of Actions', *Journal of Philosophy* 67 (1970), 520–30; Judith Jarvis Thomson, 'The Time of a Killing', *Journal of Philosophy* 68 (1971), 115–32; Alvin I. Goldman, 'The Individuation of Action', *Journal of Philosophy* 68 (1971), 761–74.

methods, may be construed in this way.[23] Taking this way out, however, is not entirely appealing, for at least two reasons: first, it would place a very severe and urgent burden on us to produce an account of generic events and of the modifiers of expressions designating them, although this is a problem that one has ultimately to face in any case. Second, this approach neutralizes one of the initial motivations for developing the structured complex view of events. Whatever else events might be, they were intended to be entities that enter into causal relations with one another, and that can be objects of explanations. But it is clear that we may want to explain not only why Sebastian strolled, i.e., Sebastian's stroll, but also why he strolled leisurely, i.e., his leisurely stroll. Under the approach being considered, the second explanation would be of why Sebastian's stroll was leisurely; we would be explaining why a certain event had a certain property, not why a certain event occurred. But perhaps it was a mistake to bring very broad and general considerations about explanations into a theory of events, to begin with. The desire to have events as the relata of causal relations could, I believe, be accommodated within this approach, although some of the specific things I have said in earlier articles about causation would have to be retracted (especially, the claim that for Humean causation there must be a lawlike connection between the generic events of any two causally connected individual events).

The other strategy for dealing with Sebastian's stroll and his leisurely stroll, which one might call "the official line" of the property-exemplification account, is to affirm that these are different, if not entirely distinct, events. Not entirely distinct since the latter *includes* the former.[24] I will not try to give a characterization of 'inclusion' for events here; a completely general characterization gets, as far as I know, to be very complicated without being philosophically interesting; also, various different kinds of "inclusion" have to be distinguished (obviously, the sense in which an assassination *includes* a killing or strolling leisurely *includes* strolling is very different from the sense in which, say, my walking to the door *includes* my moving my left foot to take the first step, or the burning of the barn *includes* the burning of the roof of the barn). But I assume that it's intuitively plausible to say there is some relation here that can be called "inclusion". Difference need not be total distinctness or

23 Such a view is suggested by Judith Jarvis Thomson in her 'Individuating Actions', *Journal of Philosophy* 68 (1971), 774–81.
24 Goldman would say that the former 'level-generates' the latter; see *A Theory of Human Action,* Chapter 2.

absence of any significant relation whatever. Once this is granted, there being two events (actions) here, and not one, impresses us as not such an extravagant claim after all. Take this table: the top of the table is not the same thing as the table. So there are two things, but of course one table – in fact, there are lots of things here if you include the legs, the molecules, the atoms, etc., making up the table.

Unfortunately, we are not through with the proliferating events. The new difficulty I have in mind is this: Granted there are two events here, of which one is included in the other. Now, Sebastian's strolling is a strolling – a stroll event, if you like – and Sebastian's strolling leisurely is also a stroll event. You say they are two events, not one; so it follows that there are two stroll events, both strolled by Sebastian on that memorable night through the streets of Bologna. In fact, given such generic events as strolling with a cane in hand, strolling with a limp, and so on, there were indefinitely many strolls strolled by Sebastian that night! And of course indefinitely many stabbings administered by Brutus on Caesar!

The analogy with tables and other sundry physical objects may still help us here. We normally count this as *one* table; and there are just so many (a fixed number of) tables in this room. However, if you believe in the calculus of individuals,[25] you will see that included in this table is another table – in fact, there are indefinitely many tables each of which is a proper part of this table. For consider the table with one micrometer of its top removed; that is a table different from this table; and so on.

It would be absurd to say that for this reason we must say there are in fact indefinitely many tables in this room. What I am suggesting is merely that the sense in which, under the structured complex view of events, there are indefinitely many strolls strolled by Sebastian may be just as harmless as the sense in which there are indefinitely many tables in this room. The proliferation of events with which my account of events is often charged is not in itself serious; for "the number of *events*" is very much like "the number of *things*" or "the number of *facts*"; 'event' isn't an ordinary run-of-the-mill count noun. What is bothersome is the seeming fact that the number of stabbings or strollings seems to go beyond any bound. 'Stabbing' and 'stroll' seem to be as good count nouns as 'table' and 'apple'. In any case I hope that I have succeeded in mitigating this difficulty. If I have not, the earlier strategy of handling the proliferation problem would merit more serious consideration.

25 In the sense of Nelson Goodman, *The Structure of Appearance*, Harvard University Press, Cambridge, 1951.

IV

The question has been raised whether my account of events has implausible consequences concerning the essential properties of events.[26] Take Sebastian's leisurely stroll at midnight. According to the structured complex account, it may be thought, there are three essential properties of that event: one, that the stroll was strolled by Sebastian; two, that it was a leisurely stroll; and three, that it occurred at midnight. More generally, it is alleged that the account is committed to the thesis that the three constituents of an event constitute the essential properties of the event. It is then argued that, at least, the time of the occurrence of an event is not an essential property of it. Sebastian's stroll could have taken place five minutes before or after midnight. And perhaps its being a leisurely stroll isn't an essential property of the stroll either; if Sebastian had been pressed for time, the stroll would have been a brisk one. Similarly, the stroll could have been taken by someone else. Suppose that the midnight stroll was done as some sort of ritual by a member of a secret society chosen by lottery, and that it so happened that Sebastian was so chosen. If Mario, Sebastian's friend, had been chosen, then Mario would have strolled that stroll.[27]

It isn't clear to me what, if anything, an analysis or metaphysical theory of something implies about the essential properties of that thing. There is a metaphysical theory of physical objects, which is of respectable vintage and tradition, that asserts that a physical object is a "congeries of properties" or something like that. So this table is a "congeries" of such properties as brown color, the mass it has, and so on. But presumably it is not a consequence of the theory that the table has essentially the properties it actually has, that the brown color of the table is an essential property of it. Why should it be thought, then, that the structured complex view of events is saddled with the essentialist consequences mentioned above?

But perhaps it is my identity condition for event structures that is the chief focus of the objections. Here, too, analogy with other cases makes it difficult to see how any essentialist consequences necessarily follow from identity criteria. It is at least a respectable identity criterion for physical

---

26 Ed Wierenga has raised this question in his doctoral dissertation, *Three Theories of Events*, University of Massachusetts at Amherst, 1974.

27 This is substantially what Davidson says in 'Eternal vs. Ephemeral Events' to answer a question raised by Chisholm.

objects that they are the same just in case they are completely coincident in space and time. From this it does not follow that a physical object is essentially where and when it in fact is. To give another, possibly controversial, example, the extensionality criterion of set identity does not entail that a given set has its members essentially. It seems at least arguable that the set of the planets could have comprised eight planets rather than nine; even if this is wrong, it's not easy to see how the extensionality criterion (or any part of the usual mathematical theories of sets) shows it; we would need an independent metaphysical argument.

On the other hand, I don't want to claim that the essentialist consequences attributed to my account are in themselves false. At least, I find it plausible to think of the constitutive substance of an event as essential to the identity of that event. The fact that someone other than Sebastian could have taken a stroll in his place does not make it the case that the very stroll that Sebastian took could have been taken by someone else. If Mario had been chosen to stroll that night, then there would have been another stroll, namely Mario's. It has been remarked by some philosophers that, although you could have a pain that is qualitatively identical with the pain I am now having, you could not, logically or metaphysically, have the very same, numerically identical pain that I have.[28] The event of my strolling could not, logically or metaphysically, occur to anyone else any more than the event of my being in pain could. Only Socrates could have died *his* death. It seems not implausible to think that events and states are essentially individuated with respect to their constitutive substances.

The essentiality of the constitutive property to the identity of an event is less certain. For one thing, the question seems to depend on some of the issues earlier raised concerning generic events. If strolling leisurely is a generic event, there seems to be a case for saying that the generic event is not essential to the identity of an event which involves it. But it is highly dubious that Sebastian's leisurely stroll could have been a run or a crawl, and it certainly could not have been a coughing or dozing, although Sebastian could have stayed home that night with a cold, coughing and dozing. The case seems still weaker for the essentiality of the time of occurrence: it seems correct to say that the stroll could have occurred a little earlier or later than it actually did. The stroll, we suppose, could have taken place five minutes later than it actually did, but could it – the very same stroll – have occurred five months later? Five years? In

28 Jerome Shaffer in 'Persons and Their Bodies', *Philosophical Review* 75 (1966), 59–77.

any case, caution is required: we should not infer, from the mere fact that Sebastian could have strolled at a different time, the conclusion that this very stroll Sebastian took could have occurred at that different time.

Some of these issues may have important bearings on other philosophical problems, such as the identity theory of mind; also, what we want to say about the bearing of generic events on the essential properties of events may in turn constrain what we want to pick as generic events. And what I said earlier about "knowing what a given event is" and an "intrinsic description of an event" is likely to have a bearing on these issues. There is at present only a mass of intuitions, some conflicting with others, which need to be sorted out by a theory. We don't have such a theory, and in any case, events don't seem to be much worse off than anything else with respect to these problems about essences.

There is an essentialist consequence I am willing to accept: events are, essentially, structured complexes of the sort the theory says they are. Thus, events could not be substances, properties, and so on. But this should not be confused with the assertion that *each* event structure has *its* constituents essentially. This assertion is at least partially true, as I argued; but the general problem is still open.

V

Actions are usually taken as a subclass of events. How to characterize this subclass is a problem considered very important, but we shall not be concerned with it here. Killings are actions – at least, those that involve agents (I assume falling rocks and lightnings can also kill) – and thus events as well. But what is a killing? As has frequently been observed of late, 'kill' is a near synonym of 'cause to die'. Since killing presumably isn't a basic action, not for humans at any rate, it must involve two events, one an action performed by the killer and the other the death caused by the action. Thus, Brutus's killing Caesar seems to be nothing other than some action of Brutus causing the death of Caesar. The action event of Brutus's killing Caesar thus threatens to turn into a *relation,* a *causal* relation, between two events. And Brutus's stabbing Caesar, the cause event in this causal relation, itself may turn into a causal relation between two events, in the same way. Thus, killings so analyzed don't seem to fit the model of events under the property-exemplification account; they do not seem to have the complex event structure it attributes to events; instead, they seem to be relations between events.

This feature isn't limited to action events. As noted some time ago by

C. J. Ducasse, many transitive verbs are implicitly causal; e.g., 'pull', 'push', 'break', 'shatter'. When the wind blows the door open, this involves a causal relation: the pressure of the wind on the door causes the opening of the door. So the event of the wind's blowing open the door appears to turn into a causal relation between two events, the wind's pressure on the door and the door's opening. The question arises: Are we to accept these causal relations themselves, i.e., one event's causing another, as events?[29] Or should we fit them into some other ontological category, say, facts?

One argument for treating, say, killings as events may be this: they are just the sort of thing that can have causes and effects, and just the sort of thing that can be given causal explanations. Brutus's killing Caesar may have been caused by Brutus's political ambitions and personal jealousies; it in turn caused Calpurnia's grief and caused Caesar to be absent from the Roman Senate the next day. It is of the essence of events that they can enter into causal relations. So why not treat killings and other actions as events?

This argument isn't decisive, however. As earlier noted, there are two events involved in Brutus's killing Caesar: Brutus's action, which was his stabbing Caesar, and Caesar's death. When we cite Brutus's motives and beliefs as causes of the killing, we do not seem to be saying that they are the causes of the stabbing's causing the death; rather, we seem to be saying that they are causes – or among the causes – of Brutus's undertaking the action, namely the stabbing of Caesar, which he believed would result in Caesar's death. I would venture the hypothesis that what we normally take to be a cause of the killing will ultimately turn out to be a cause – or among the causal conditions – of the basic action which was undertaken by Brutus in the endeavor that Caesar be dead and which in fact did cause the death.

What of the effects of the killing? Calpurnia's grief may very well have been caused by her *belief* that Caesar was dead, or that Caesar was so brutally murdered, or that it was Brutus who killed him. As for Caesar's absence from the Senate the following day, we can attribute it to his death as one of its effects. I think that what we normally take as an effect of a killing is often attributable to the death of the person killed or someone's cognitive attitude, such as belief, toward some aspects of the killing.

I believe similar things can be said of events that do not involve agents.

---

29 From similar considerations N. L. Wilson concludes ". . . 'alerting', 'killing' and all the other causative verbs do not refer to events" in 'Facts, Events and Their Identity Conditions', 318.

The rock shatters the window. This we normally call an event. But it involves a causal relation: the rock's impact on the window caused it to shatter. What is the cause of the rock's shattering the window? Well, Johnny threw the rock. But we can take Johnny's throwing the rock as the cause of the rock's impact on the window, namely the first of the two events in the causal relation. The rock's shattering the window caused a cut on my hand. Again, the cut can be construed as an effect of the shattering of the window, namely the second of the two events in the causal relation, and not as the effect of the rock's shattering the window. One might object: But what of the fragility of the window glass? Why isn't that a cause of the rock's impact's causing the shattering? We do say: If the glass in the window had not been so fragile, the rock's impact would not have caused the window to shatter. Furthermore, the fragility of the window glass is not a cause of the rock's impact on the window. My reply is this: we still need not say that the fragility is a cause of one event's causing another; it is a cause, along with the rock's impact and perhaps other things, making up the complete cause of the window's shattering.

So the thesis I am suggesting is this: the causes and effects of actions and events exhibiting the causal features under discussion are attributable to the events in the causal relation that constitute such an action or event. (I leave aside here effects like Calpurnia's grief that may be caused by beliefs about such actions and events.) The thesis has two interpretations, one stronger than the other: (1) all causes of, say, a killing are among the causes of the action that caused the death, and all effects of the killing are among the effects of the death; and (2) all causes of the killing are among the causes of the action that caused the death or of the death, and all effects of the killing, too, are among the effects of the action or of the death. The stronger thesis, (1), appears to be false; suppose that as a result of the vigorous wielding of the knife, Brutus dislocated his right shoulder. It would be correct to say that Brutus's dislocating his right shoulder was caused by his killing Caesar, but clearly it is not caused by Caesar's death. The weaker interpretation (2) of course accommodates this sort of example. In any case, if the thesis is correct in either interpretation, we can block the argument that killings must be treated as events since they enter into causal relations.

If we decide not to regard killings and such as events, then it would be open to us to regard them as *facts* (which should not preclude us from taking events simpliciter as a special subclass of facts): Brutus's killing Caesar is the fact that some action of Brutus caused Caesar to die, and the rock's shattering the window is the fact that the rock's impact caused the

51

window to shatter. Such events and actions turn out to be causal facts. Treating them in this way may affect the ontology of action theory, theory of explanation, and the analysis of causation. And it may lead us to the talk of "basic events", namely those events not involving causal and other relations among events.

But the above is not the only course open to us. If we are prepared to accept causal properties as generic events, that is, if we are prepared to allow causal relations between events to appear in generic events, then we could accommodate killings and their ilk within our scheme. For we can render

(9) Brutus's doing some action which caused Caesar's death

into

(10) [(Brutus, Caesar), for some generic action event P and times t^* and $t'[(\text{①}, \text{②}), P^{\text{①②}}, t^*]$ caused $[\text{②}, \text{dies}, t'], t].$[30]

Which way is better? I think that the second way leads to a messy situation with regard to the problem of characterizing generic events, and creates complications in the theory of causation, explanation, and so forth. The first way is largely unexplored at this stage, but I would look upon it more favorably; I think it presents us with interesting possibilities to explore.[31]

30 The question of the relationship between t^*, t', and t is discussed by Judith Jarvis Thomson in 'The Time of a Killing'.
31 The problem of generic events that contain causal relations is related to Bernard Berofsky's problem of characterizing "R-sentences" in his *Determinism,* Princeton Univ. Press, Princeton, 1971, Chapter V, esp. 157ff.

4

Concepts of supervenience

For Herbert Heidelberger

I. INTRODUCTION

We think of the world around us not as a mere assemblage of unrelated objects, events, and facts, but as constituting a system, something that shows *structure,* and whose constituents are connected with one another in significant ways. This view of the world seems fundamental to our scheme of things; it is reflected in the commonplace assumption that things that happen in one place can make a difference to things that happen in another in a way that enables us to make sense of one thing in terms of another, infer information about one thing from information about another, or affect one thing by affecting another. Central to this idea of interconnectedness of things is a notion of *dependence* (or, its converse, *determination*): things are connected with one another in that whether something exists, or what properties it has, is *dependent on,* or *determined by,* what other things exist and what kinds of things they are. It is in virtue of these dependency or determinative relationships that the world can be made intelligible; and by exploiting them we are able to intervene in the course of events and alter it to suit our wishes. Activities like explanation, prediction, and control would make little sense for a world devoid of such connections. The idea that "real connections" exist and the idea that the world is intelligible and controllable are arguably equivalent ideas.

Causation is a preeminent example of what I am calling determinative or dependency relations; apart from those that are logically based, such as entailment, it is the only explicitly recognized and widely discussed relation of this kind. Causes determine their effects, and effects are dependent, for their existence and properties, on their causes. It is not for noth-

---

An earlier version of this paper was presented at the Herbert Heidelberger Memorial Conference at University of Massachusetts and Smith College in April, 1983. I dedicate this paper to Herb's memory.

ing that Hume called causation "the cement of the universe";[1] causation is the cosmic glue that binds discrete objects and events together, making them mutually significant – even in Hume's atomistic world – and thereby helping to provide a necessary basis for the prediction and control of natural phenomena. It is congenial to the broadly realist view of the world that most of us accept to think of the network of causal relations in the world as underlying, and supporting, the network of explanatory and other epistemic relations represented in our knowledge of it.

The part–whole relation is also important; however, its importance seems to derive largely from the belief that many crucial aspects of a whole including its existence and nature are dependent on those of its parts. That is, mereological relations are significant because mereological determination, or "mereological supervenience,"[2] is, or is thought to be, a pervasive fact.

There has lately been an increasing interest in the concept of *supervenience,* especially for its possible applications to the mind–body problem, microreduction, and physicalism. It is useful to think of supervenience as belonging in that class of relations, including causation, that have philosophical importance because they represent ways in which objects, properties, facts, events, and the like enter into dependency relationships with one another, creating a system of interconnections that give structure to the world and our experience of it. Modes of dependency or determination may differ from one another in various ways; if supervenience is thought of as such a mode, questions arise as to exactly how it differs from others, whether it is a single homogeneous relation or represents in reality two or more distinguishable relationships, and whether supervenient determination presents a philosophically significant alternative to other determinative relations.

The idea of supervenience seems to have originated in moral philosophy. In the following well-known passage G. E. Moore describes a certain dependency relationship between moral and nonmoral properties that has later come to be called "supervenience":

> . . . if a given thing possesses any kind of intrinsic value in a certain degree, then not only must that same thing possess it, under all circumstances, in the same degree, but also anything *exactly like it,* must, under all circumstances, possess it in exactly the same degree.[3]

1 In *An Abstract of A Treatise of Human Nature.*
2 See Jaegwon Kim, "Supervenience and Nomological Incommensurables," *American Philosophical Quarterly* 15 (1978): 149–56.
3 *Philosophical Studies* (London, 1922), p. 261.

Moore himself, however, seems not to have used the term "supervenience"; it was R. M. Hare, I believe, who, writing many years later, gave it the philosophical currency it now enjoys. The following passage from Hare is now generally recognized as a classic source that helped to shape the initial contours of the concept:

> First, let us take that characteristic of "good" which has been called its supervenience. Suppose that we say "St. Francis was a good man." It is logically impossible to say this and to maintain at the same time that there might have been another man placed exactly in the same circumstances as St. Francis, and who behaved in exactly the same way, but who differed from St. Francis in this respect only, that he was not a good man.[4]

Here, Hare speaks of supervenience as a "characteristic" of the term "good." However, it is clear that it is more usefully construed as a *relation*, a relation between "good" and terms that denote such things as patterns of behavior and traits of character. What Hare is saying is that it is "logically impossible" for there to be two persons who are exactly alike in these latter respects and yet differ in respect of being a good man. It is also clear that supervenience is better thought of as a relation not between properties or terms taken singly but between *sets* or *families* of them. Thus, we can say that all valuational properties (that is, the set of all valuational properties) are supervenient upon the set of all natural or descriptive properties. We shall in this paper discuss supervenience chiefly for properties rather than predicates; the choice here is indifferent to an extent, but, as we shall see, not wholly so. One could also speak of supervenience for sentences, facts, events, propositions, and languages; I shall argue below that fact supervenience can be understood in terms of property supervenience. It will become plausible, I believe, that property supervenience is fundamental, and that supervenience for most other entities can be explained in terms of it.

It is this evident generalizability beyond the sphere of ethics that makes supervenience an attractive and promising concept worthy of closer attention. Perhaps because of this, one now sees an increasing use of the term "supervenience" in a variety of areas, indicating the presence of substantial shared intuitive content. Thus, the aesthetic properties of a work of art have been claimed to be supervenient on its physical properties.[5] Some

---

4 *The Language of Morals* (London, 1952), p. 145.
5 Frank Sibley, "Aesthetic Concepts," *Philosophical Review* 68 (1959): 421–50; Jerrold Levinson, "Aesthetic Supervenience," *Southern Journal of Philosophy* 22, Supplement (1984): 93–110.

philosophers have found in psychophysical supervenience an attractive alternative to reductionist physicalism; it is thought that the supervenience thesis acknowledges the primacy of the physical without committing us to the stronger claims of physical reductionism.[6] The idea that valuational terms in general supervene on nonvaluational ones has been extended to epistemic terms, terms used for making epistemic appraisals, such as "evident," "certain," and "justified." The view that criteria of epistemic justification must be stated in nonepistemic terms can be thought of as an expression of the thesis that epistemic properties are supervenient on nonepistemic characteristics and relationships (e.g., causal properties and logical relations).[7] Leibniz's obscure doctrine of the dispensability of relational judgments is perhaps interpretable as the thesis that relations are supervenient on properties.[8] Quine's thesis of translational indeterminacy is usefully construed as the denial of the claim that meaning supervenes on the totality of physical fact.[9] Mereological supervenience has already been mentioned. There are other interesting questions we might formulate in terms of supervenience: Are causal relations supervenient on particular matters of noncausal fact? Are laws supervenient on their instances? Do theories supervene on data? Often the belief that there is a supervenience relation in a given domain, for example in the domain of the mental vis-à-vis the physical, forms an implicit premise of great importance that motivates and shapes the specific theories concerning that domain. Acceptance or rejection of the supervenience of the mental on the physical leads to the most basic division between theories of the mind–body relation: theories that accept psychophysical supervenience are fundamentally materialist, and those that reject it are fundamentally antimaterialist. This difference seems philosophically more basic and more

6 See note 11; also Kim, "Psychophysical Supervenience," Essay 10 of this volume, and "Psychophysical Supervenience as a Mind–Body Theory," *Brain and Cognition Theory* 5 (1982); Stephen P. Stich, "Autonomous Psychology and the Belief-Desire Thesis," *The Monist* 61 (1978): 573–91; John Haugeland, "Weak Supervenience," *American Philosophical Quarterly* 19 (1982): 93–103.

7 See Ernest Sosa, "The Foundations of Foundationalism," *Noûs* 14 (1980): 547–64, esp. p. 551. Also Alvin I. Goldman, "What is Justified Belief?" in *Justification and Knowledge,* ed. G. S. Pappas (Dordrecht, 1979), in which Goldman says he is looking for *nonepistemic conditions* for justified belief.

8 See, e.g., Hide Ishiguro, *Leibniz's Philosophy of Logic and Language* (Ithaca, 1972). It seems that Leibniz used the Latin word "supervenire" in stating his theory; see the quotation in footnote 3 on p. 71 of Ishiguro, op. cit.

9 This is especially clear in Quine's reply to Chomsky in *Words and Objections,* ed. D. Davidson and J. Hintikka (Dordrecht, 1969), esp. pp. 302 f.

significant than the usual classification of mind–body theories as "monist" or "dualist." [10]

This paper is intended as a general discussion of supervenience as a relation of dependency or determination. I shall be claiming that there are two separable concepts of supervenience, one stronger than the other, and that often what is offered in a philosophical discussion is the weaker of the two whereas what is needed is the stronger one. I shall also argue that the stronger relation is equivalent to "global supervenience," [11] an alternative conception favored by some writers. One issue that will receive attention is what supervenience between two domains entails about the existence of kind-to-kind connections between them, and what this means for such relations as definability and reducibility between the two domains.

II. WEAK SUPERVENIENCE

The passage quoted above from Hare suggests this initial conception of the supervenience relation: the moral is supervenient on the natural in the sense that if two objects (persons, acts, states of affairs, and the like) are alike in all natural respects they must of necessity be alike in all moral respects. That is to say, things cannot differ with respect to some moral characteristic unless there is some natural property with respect to which they differ. Much the same idea is present in Donald Davidson's formulation of psychophysical supervenience:

> Although the position I describe denies there are psychophysical laws, it is consistent with the view that mental characteristics are in some sense dependent, or supervenient, on physical characteristics. Such supervenience might be taken to mean that there cannot be two events alike in all physical respects but differing in some mental respects, or that an object cannot alter in some mental respects without altering in some physical respects. [12]

Here Davidson gives two explanations of supervenience, the first stated for events and the second for objects. I am not focusing on the fact that one is for events and the other is for objects; I am only interested in the

10 For more details on this point, see Kim, "Psychophysical Supervenience as a Mind–Body Theory," op. cit.
11 (Added 1993.) This claim is controversial; see Essay 5 and "Postscripts on Supervenience," section 3, in this volume.
12 "Mental Events" in *Experience and Theory*, ed. L. Foster and J. W. Swanson (Amherst, 1979), p. 88.

general forms of the two explanations, and want to point to the fact that the first conforms to the pattern indicated in Hare's statement: mental characteristics supervene on physical ones in that no two things (objects, events, and the like) could differ with respect to some mental characteristic unless they differed also in some physical characteristic – that is, coincidence in the physical entails coincidence in the mental. If we were to create an exact physical replica of you, it and you would be psychologically indistinguishable. (Davidson's second explanation, as I shall suggest later, indicates a stronger relation of supervenience.)

A general analysis of supervenience that captures these ideas is straightforwardly developed. Let A and B be two nonempty families of properties (for simplicity we exclude relations) closed under the usual Boolean property-forming operations, complementation, conjunction, and disjunction (and perhaps others such as infinite conjunction and disjunction). This then is a definition of "weak supervenience" (the reason for calling it "weak" will be made clear below):

A *weakly supervenes* on B if and only if necessarily for any x and y if x and y share all properties in B then x and y share all properties in A – that is, indiscernibility with respect to B entails indiscernibility with respect to A.

We shall call A the *supervenient family* and B the *supervenience base (family)*; properties in A are *supervenient properties,* and those in B are the *base properties.*

As an example: consider the set, A, containing the property of being a good man (G) and having the Boolean closure property; and let B be the set containing the property of being courageous (C), that of being benevolent (V), and that of being honest (H), and closed under the Boolean operations. A contains only two properties, G and $-G$, besides the tautological one (G v $-G$) and the impossible one (G & $-G$). Suppose A weakly supervenes on B. This means that if two men share the same properties in B, say, both are honest and benevolent but lack courage (this will insure they share all other properties in B), then they must both be good men or neither is (they of course cannot differ in regard to the tautological or impossible property). Or, what is the same, if one is a good man but the other is not, there must be some property in B with respect to which they differ (say, the first is courageous but the second is not). Any differences in A must be accounted for by some difference in B.

To fix this further in mind: consider what we may call *B-maximal properties:* these are the strongest consistent properties constructible in B, and for our present example there are eight of these: C & V & H, C & V &

−H, C & −V & H, . . . , −C & −V & −H. These properties are mutu- ally exclusive, and every object must have just one of these. Clearly, two objects are indiscernible in B just in case they have the same B-maximal property. Weak supervenience of A on B therefore comes to this: any two objects with the same B-maximal property must have the same properties in A − they are both G, or both −G. Or, using the terminology of "pos- sible world," we may say: there is no possible world in which two objects have the same B-maximal property and yet differ in respect of G.

Given weak supervenience of A and B, therefore, within each possible world generalizations of the following form will hold:

(1) $(\forall x)[B_i(x) \rightarrow G^*(x)]$,

where, for each i, B_i is a B-maximal property and G^* is either G or −G. Whether G or −G is to be associated with a given B-maximal property is a feature of the specific possible world; but within each world these exceptionless universal conditionals between the property of being a good man on the one hand and the virtues of courage, benevolence, and hon- esty on the other must hold. Within each world, in fact, the following biconditionals hold:

(2) $(\forall x)[B^*(x) \leftrightarrow G(x)]$
     $(\forall x)[B\#(x) \leftrightarrow -G(x)]$

where B^* and $B\#$ are each a disjunction of B-maximal properties.

All of these points remain valid for weak supervenience generally, when B is finite; if B is not finite, these results will depend on the form- ability of B-maximal properties, which requires infinite conjunction, and their infinite disjunctions. I shall argue later that these operations are ac- ceptable for properties (as distinguished from predicates), and they will be assumed in some of the formal arguments below (it will be clear ex- actly where they are used).

I dwell on these details in order to make the point that, although the definition of "weak supervenience" follows very closely the bench-mark explanations of supervenience in the literature, as witness the quotations from Hare and Davidson, the relation it defines is considerably weaker than one might have expected − indeed, too weak for some of its typical intended applications. The key to seeing this is that in a generalization of the form (1) above, which associates a supervenient property for each maximal property in the base family, whether G^* is G or −G depends on the particular world under consideration, and is not a feature invariant across possible worlds. This means that weak supervenience of A and B (returning to our example) permits the following:

(a) In this world anyone who is courageous, benevolent, and honest is a good man, but in another possible world no such man is good; in fact, every such man is evil in this other world.
(b) Again, in this world anyone who has courage, benevolence, and honesty is good; in another world exactly like this one in respect of the distribution of these virtues, no man is good.
(c) In another possible world just like this one in respect of who has, or lacks, these traits of character, every man is good.

It is plain that weak supervenience permits these possibilities, for it only requires that *within* any possible world there not be two things agreeing in B but diverging in A, and this condition is met in each of these cases. It does not require that if in another world an object has the same B-properties that it has in this world, it must also have the same A-properties it has in this one. The particular associations between A-properties and B-properties in a given world cannot be counted on to carry over into other worlds.

Thus, weak supervenience falls short of the following condition: fixing the base properties of an object fixes its supervenient properties. This condition expresses a presumptive desideratum on the explication of supervenience: base properties must *determine* supervenient properties in the sense that once the former are fixed for an object, there is no freedom to vary the latter for that object. Weak supervenience goes some way toward this idea of determination: if you fix the base properties of two objects in the same way in a given world then you must fix their supervenient properties in the same way in that world. But under weak supervenience that is as far as the base properties constrain the attribution of the supervenient properties. That this is less than what we might expect of a relation of determination or dependence can be seen in various ways. Determination or dependence is naturally thought of as carrying a certain modal force: if being a good man is dependent on, or is determined by, certain traits of character, then having these traits must *insure* or *guarantee* being a good man (or lacking certain of these traits must insure that one not be a good man). The connection between these traits and being a good man must be more than a *de facto* coincidence that varies from world to world. We should be able to say: although Charles is not a good man, he *would* be one if only he *had* some benevolence in his nature as well as being honest and courageous. We should also be able to say: anyone who has these three virtues *would* be a good man although it is unfortunate that no

60

one has them all. Claims like these seem integral to what we mean when we speak of "good-making characteristics": any "X-making characteristic" must be such that if anything had it, it must of necessity have X (at least, it must necessarily be of positive relevance to its having X). Weak supervenience of moral upon nonmoral properties does not entail that there are nonmoral "conditions" or "criteria" for moral properties.

Another idea that is often associated with the idea of supervenience is this: if the moral supervenes on the nonmoral, any two worlds exactly alike in all nonmoral respects must be alike in all moral respects (in fact, they must be one and the same world). But this does not obtain under weak supervenience, as we have already seen. Similar points can be made about psychophysical supervenience: weak psychophysical supervenience is consistent with the existence of a world that is just like the actual one in every physical detail but in which no mentality, no consciousness, is manifested, and also a world that is just like ours except that a low-grade pain permeates every object everywhere. Thus, if we were to look, with Davidson, to supervenience for a relation of dependency for the mental vis-à-vis the physical, we would likely not find it in weak supervenience.

I find the following remarks by Moore instructive as well as surprising:

> I should never have thought of suggesting that goodness was "non-natural," unless I had supposed that it was "derivative" in the sense that, whenever a thing is good (in the sense in question) its goodness (in Mr. Broad's words) "depends on the presence of certain non-ethical characteristics" possessed by the thing in question: I have always supposed that it did so "depend," in the sense that, if a thing is good (in my sense), then that it is so *follows* from the fact that it possesses certain natural intrinsic properties, which are such that from the fact that it is good it does *not* follow conversely that it has those properties.[13]

We need not know exactly what Moore meant here by the term "follow" or "depend" to know that its force exceeds weak supervenience. For weak supervenience, as we have seen, only requires that any two things having the same natural properties must be either both good or both not good. This surely is not enough for saying that a thing's being good "follows" from its having the natural properties it has; weak supervenience, therefore, cannot explicate the notion of "dependence" Moore had in mind.

Does weak supervenience then have any useful philosophical applications? Although it is evidently not strong enough to serve as an analysis

13 In Moore's "A Reply to My Critics" in *The Philosophy of G. E. Moore,* ed. P. A. Schilpp (Chicago and Evanston, Illinois, 1942), p. 588.

of a full relation of dependence or determination, I believe it marks an interesting and significant relation of *partial* dependence or determination. Consider the case of moral supervenience again: perhaps all Hare wanted was weak supervenience.[14] Under weak supervenience there would be an inconsistency in one's commending an object (saying that it is good) but failing to commend another that is, or is believed to be, exactly like it in all descriptive details; however, there is nothing inconsistent, or incoherent, in failing to commend either while acknowledging the same descriptive properties of the two objects. This, in essence, is the prescription "Treat like cases alike" in ethical contexts. Weak supervenience, therefore, gives us the much discussed *Principle of Universalizability* of ethical judgments understood as a *consistency requirement*.[15] There is, however, a stronger sense in which the universalizability of ethical judgments has been understood: every singular ethical judgment must be supportable by a fully *general covering principle*. This stronger requirement goes beyond weak supervenience, corresponding rather to the notion of "strong supervenience" to be explained in the following section. That these two versions of the Universalizability Principle turn out to correspond nicely with the two concepts of supervenience distinguished in this paper speaks well for the naturalness as well as philosophical interest of the two concepts. These remarks about two Principles of Universalizability obviously apply to other cases involving valuational judgments (e.g., in aesthetics and epistemology).

Davidson has likened the relationship between the semantic notion of truth and syntactical concepts to psychophysical supervenience: in spite of the fact that truth is not definable or reducible in terms of syntax there is a sense in which the truth of a sentence depends on its syntactic properties.[16] This can, I think, be taken as something like weak supervenience: any two sentences that are syntactically indiscernible are in fact the same

14 According to Haugeland's report of a conversation with Hare (in Haugeland, op. cit.), it seems likely that what Hare had in mind is only my weak supervenience. This impression is confirmed by Professor Hare's inaugural address to the Aristotelian Society entitled "Supervenience," *Aristotelian Society*, Supplementary Volume 58 (1984): 1–16. The notions of "supervenience" and "entailment" as Hare explains them in his address turn out to correspond, roughly, to my weak and strong supervenience, respectively.

15 The distinction between two versions of the universalizability requirement is borrowed from J. Howard Sobel's unpublished notes on "Dependent Properties"; I also owe to Sobel the quotation from Moore's "Reply" (see note 13). Also useful in this connection are Monroe C. Beardsley, "On the Generality of Critical Reasons," *Journal of Philosophy* 59 (1962): 477–86; and Robert L. Holmes, "Descriptivism, Supervenience, and Universalizability," *Journal of Philosophy* 63 (1966): 113–19.

16 "Mental Events," p. 88.

sentence and must therefore have the same truth value. But obviously the truth value of a sentence cannot in general be relied on to be stable from world to world. Davidson's use of this example to explain supervenience points to the possibility that weak supervenience is also what he had in mind in speaking of psychophysical supervenience. This interpretation fits in neatly with Davidson's doctrine of psychophysical anomalism to the effect that there are no lawlike connections between mental and physical kinds. Lawlike connections must be stable over possible worlds (at least relative to some accessibility condition), and such connections between the mental and the physical are exactly what weak psychophysical supervenience does not require. On the other hand, this interpretation has a weakness: any robust materialist position should affirm, I think, that what is material determines all that there is in the world,[17] and this weak supervenience cannot give us. Although I am not sure whether Davidson would accept a full materialist position in my sense it seems that he wants more than weak supervenience.

Although it falls short of full-fledged materialism, weak psychophysical supervenience may be a possible thesis worth pondering: one might argue, for example, that although no physical fact about an organism, whether its behavior or its physiology, compels us to attribute to it some particular mental state, or any mental state at all, consistency requires that if two organisms manifest the same behavior and physiology, the same mental state must be attributed to each, and that this is the only constraint on the ascription of mental states. I think some such view may be held by those who take the attribution of mental states as just another case of positing theoretical explanatory states (relative to, say, behavior), and who take the possibility of the "inverted spectrum" seriously.

Another related case is this: even if, as many philosophers believe, theories are "underdetermined" by all possible data, they may be weakly supervenient on data in the following sense: although no set of data compels the choice of a particular explanatory theory, "relevantly similar data" must be explained by "relevantly similar theories." Weak supervenience as applied here thus yields a consistency requirement on theory construction in the same way that weak moral supervenience yields a consistency

17 For formulations of materialism see Terence Horgan, "Supervenience and Microphysics," *Pacific Philosophical Quarterly* 63 (1982): 29–43; Horgan, "Supervenience and Cosmic Hermeneutics," *Southern Journal of Philosophy* 22, Supplement (1984): 19–38. David Lewis, "New Work for a Theory of Universals," *Australasian Journal of Philosophy* 61 (1983): 343–77; for a related approach see Geoffrey Hellman and Frank Thompson, "Physicalism: Ontology, Determination and Reduction," *Journal of Philosophy* 72 (1975): 551–64, and "Physicalist Materialism," *Noûs* 11 (1977): 309–45.

requirement on ethical judgments, clarifying one precise way in which data constrain theory. There may be other interesting applications of weak supervenience; I hope, though, that what we have seen is enough to persuade us of its potential interest as a philosophical concept.

III. STRONG SUPERVENIENCE

A clue to an appropriate way of strengthening weak supervenience to obtain a stronger relation is seen when we consider the following equivalent formulation of weak supervenience:

A *weakly supervenes* on B if and only if necessarily for any property F in A, if an object x has F, then there exists a property G in B such that x has G, and if any y has G it has F.

Let us first see that the two definitions are equivalent. First, we show weak supervenience given by the earlier definition entails that newly defined. Assume that for some F in A, x has F. We need to show, for some G in B, that x has G, and that anything y with G has F. Let G be the B-maximal property of x (in any given world under consideration). Then trivially x has G. To show that anything y with G has B: suppose some y has G. Since both x and y have G and G is a B-maximal property, x and y share all properties in B. So by weak supervenience as first defined, x and y must share all properties in A. But F is in A and x has F. So y, too, must have F.

Second, to show that the second definition entails the first: assume x and y share all properties in B, and suppose they do not share all properties in A – that is, for some F in A, x has F but y does not. Since x has F, weak supervenience as defined in the second definition entails that for some G in B, x has G, and anything with G has F. By assumption, x and y share all properties in B; so y, too, has G, whence y has F, yielding a contradiction.

The key aspect of the second definition is its last clause, the requirement that any object having G also has F. The force of this clause is that *within* each world this G-F generalization must hold; it does not require that the G-F connection be stable across worlds. This suggests that in order to get a stronger supervenience relation that will insure the stability of connections between supervenient properties and their base properties,

64

we should try prefixing this clause with a suitable modal operator. It turns out that this yields what we want.[18]

This approach is also suggested by the second explanation of supervenience offered by Davidson in the passage quoted earlier; as will be recalled, the explanation was this: "an object cannot alter in some mental respect without altering in some physical respect." The modal force of "cannot" and reference to mental and physical "respects" strongly suggest that a proper way to understand what Davidson has in mind here is in terms of a connection between mental and physical characteristics that is constant over possible worlds. The last quoted passage from Moore on the "dependence" of goodness on natural properties, too, suggests a similar approach.

So let A and B be families of properties closed under Boolean operations as before:

A *strongly supervenes* on B just in case, necessarily, for each x and each property F in A, if x has F, then there is a property G in B such that x has G, and *necessarily* if any y has G, it has F.

To illustrate this, let us return to the example of being a good man and the three character traits of courage, benevolence, and honesty. The idea of strong supervenience comes to this: if St. Francis is a good man, there must be some combination of these virtues (say, honesty and benevolence) such that St. Francis has it, and anyone who has it *must* be a good man. This particular combination of the traits, however, need not be the only one in the base family that can "ground" being a good man; Socrates, too, is a good man, but the virtues that he has are courage and honesty rather than honesty and benevolence. Socrates is a good man in virtue of being courageous and honest while St. Francis is a good man in virtue of being honest and benevolent. Generally speaking, a supervenient property will have *alternative supervenience bases* – base properties that are each sufficient for the supervening property. If A strongly supervenes

18 In an earlier paper, "Supervenience and Nomological Incommensurables," op. cit., I said, incorrectly, that weak supervenience as defined by the first definition in this paper could be "equivalently defined" by a definition that in effect defines "strong supervenience" below. David Sanford's careful comments led me to see that this was a mistake, and that there in fact were two concepts of interest here. I was also helped by Barry Loewer who sent me his unpublished material on supervenience in which an essentially identical distinction is made. Others who have pointed out to me the failure of the claimed equivalence include Anthony Anderson and James Van Cleve (in his unpublished "Defining Supervenience"). I first made use of this distinction in "Psychophysical Supervenience as a Mind–Body Theory," op. cit.

on B, the B-maximal property of an object is a supervenience base for every A-property the object has. But a B-maximal property will often be stronger than is needed to serve as a base for a given A-property, and what is of interest would be a *minimal base* in the sense that any property weaker than it is not a supervenience base. (In contrast, B-maximal properties can be called "maximal bases.") If being a good man strongly supervenes on natural properties, any good man's maximal natural property (perhaps, a long conjunction of all his natural properties) would be a supervenience base for being a good man; however, this is obviously more than what we need (it would include the person's height, weight, date of birth, etc.) and would be less than perspicuous. On the other hand, the conjunctive property of being honest and benevolent may constitute a minimal base – a substantially more informative and more useful notion that justifies us in saying that this man is good *in virtue of* his honesty and benevolence, that his being good *consists in* in his having these traits of character, or that he is good *because* he is honest and benevolent.[19]

The modal term "necessarily" occurs twice in the definition of strong supervenience. It is neither possible nor desirable to specify in advance how necessity is to be understood here; an appropriate specification must depend on the particular supervenience thesis under consideration, and different readings of "necessarily" will yield different supervenience theses to consider. For example, if one is interested in the supervenience of moral upon natural characteristics, both occurrences of the term are perhaps best taken to signal logical or metaphysical necessity. For psychophysical supervenience it is possible to interpret the first occurrence as metaphysical necessity and the second as nomological necessity; it is also possible to interpret both as metaphysical, or both as nomological. In the case of mereological supervenience the most plausible construal may be that the first occurrence signifies metaphysical necessity and the second nomological or physical necessity. The main point is that different readings of the modal terms will generate different supervenience theses, and that this flexibility is a desirable feature of the definition as stated. We should, therefore, leave an exact interpretation of "necessarily" as a parameter to be fixed for particular cases of application.

The following relationship between the two concepts of supervenience is obvious:

19 Similar problems arise for the notion of a causal condition; often what is of interest is a minimal set of conditions sufficient for the effect, not just any sufficient set.

(3) Strong supervenience entails weak supervenience; weak supervenience does not entail strong supervenience.

The following is also obvious:

(4) Both supervenience relations are transitive, reflexive, and neither symmetric nor asymmetric.

In most cases of interest supervenience seems in fact asymmetric; for example, although many have claimed the supervenience of valuational on nonvaluational properties, it is apparent that the converse does not hold. Similarly, although psychophysical supervenience is an arguable view, it would be manifestly implausible to hold that the physical supervenes on the psychological. This asymmetry of supervenience may well be the core of the idea of asymmetric dependence we associate with the supervenience relation. For when we look at the relationship as specified in the definition between a strongly supervenient property and its base property, all that we have is that the base property entails the supervenient property. This alone does not warrant us to say that the supervening property is *dependent on,* or *determined by,* the base, or that an object has the supervening property *in virtue of* having the base property. These latter relations strongly hint at an asymmetric relation. We have learned from work on causation and causal modal logic the hard lesson that the idea of causal dependence or determination is not so easily or directly obtained from straightforward modal notions alone; the same in all likelihood is true of the idea of supervenient determination and dependence. Ideas of dependence and determination, whether causal, supervenient, or of other sorts, stubbornly resist capture in simpler and more transparent terms. The only possibly helpful suggestion I have is this: the asymmetric dependence of a supervenient property upon its base property may well derive from the asymmetric dependence of a comprehensive and integrated system of properties, of which it is an element, upon a similarly comprehensive and systematic family of base properties. Thus, the supposed dependence of, say, pain as a mental occurrence on some electrochemical processes of the nervous system may well be due to the asymmetric supervenient dependence of the whole family of mental phenomena on physical processes. This latter asymmetry, according to the present account, is simply the fact (if it is a fact) that the mental strongly supervenes, in the sense defined here, on the physical but not conversely. So what I am suggesting is a kind of holism: individual dependencies are grounded in the dependency between systems, not the other way around.

67

IV. GLOBAL SUPERVENIENCE AND KIND-TO-KIND
CONNECTIONS

We now turn to another approach to analyzing supervenience, an approach favored by some writers on psychophysical supervenience and materialism.[20] This alternative approach speaks globally of "worlds" and "languages," and yields what may be called a concept of "global" or "world supervenience."[21] Thus, psychophysical supervenience has been explained by saying that worlds that are physically indiscernible are psychologically indiscernible (in fact, such worlds are one and the same). The supervenience of the moral on the nonmoral too could be explained in a similar way: there could not be two worlds that are indistinguishable in every nonmoral detail and yet differ in some moral respect. As will be recalled, we used such formulations in our discussion of the weakness of weak supervenience. Some might prefer this global approach to our own with the thought that by making explicit references to property-to-property connections between the supervenient family and its base (as in our second definition of weak supervenience and that of strong supervenience), our definitions beg an important question against those who invoke supervenience precisely because of its promise as a dependency relation free of commitment to property-to-property connections that smacks of discredited reductionism of various sorts.

Now, whether two worlds are discernible or indiscernible psychologically (or physically, etc.) is essentially a matter of how psychological properties are distributed over the individuals of the two worlds. If the worlds differ in respect of some *general* psychological fact, this must be reflected in some difference in the *singular* psychological facts they contain. Thus, to say that two worlds are psychologically discernible is tantamount to saying that for some psychological property P and an individual x, x has P in one but not in the other; to say that two worlds are psychologically indiscernible is to say that for every psychological property P and every individual x, x has P in one just in case x has P in the other.

Let A and B be sets of properties as before, and consider:

A *globally supervenes* on B just in case worlds that are indiscernible with respect to B ("B-indiscernible," for short) are also A-indiscernible.

20 See the papers by Horgan, Haugeland, and Lewis cited in notes 6 and 17.
21 I borrow the term "global supervenience" from Paul Teller in his "Relational Holism and Quantum Mechanics," *British Journal for the Philosophy of Science* 37 (1986): 71–81.

Discussion in section II has already shown that global supervenience is stronger than weak supervenience. Here is an argument to show that global supervenience is equivalent to strong supervenience. To show strong supervenience entails global supervenience: assume w_1 and w_2 are B-indiscernible but A-discernible. Then for some F in A and some x, $F(x)$ in w_1 but $-F(x)$ in w_2. Let B* be the B-maximal property of x in w_1; then, by the strong supervenience of A on B, necessarily $(\forall y)[B^*(y) \to F(y)]$. Since w_2 is B-indiscernible from w_1, $B^*(x)$ in w_2. Hence, $F(x)$ in w_2, yielding a contradiction. Next, to show the converse: suppose strong supervenience fails. Then, for some object x and property F in A such that $F(x)$, if any G is in B and x has G, G fails to entail F. ("G entails F" is short for "Necessarily anything having G has F.") This is equivalent to saying that for this x and F, the B-maximal property of x does not entail F. Let w* be the actual world: in w* we have $F(x)$ and $B^*(x)$. Consider another world w# that is just like w* in the distribution of B-properties over individuals; in particular, $B^*(x)$ in w#. However, since B* does not entail F, we can consistently suppose that $-F(x)$ in w#.[22] Thus, w* and w# are B-indiscernible but A-discernible; that is, A does not globally supervene on B. This completes the argument.

Global supervenience, therefore, is nothing but strong supervenience. The equivalence of these two concepts has a mutually reinforcing effect: the fact that two independently conceived notions turn out to be equivalent testifies to their naturalness and intuitive philosophical content. Moreover, it shows that in terms of commitment to kind-to-kind correlations there is no difference at all between global and strong supervenience; the thought that global supervenience is free from such commitments is a mistake.

What if we defined global supervenience for "facts"? We might have something like this: "Facts of kind P supervene on facts of kind Q just in case worlds that are identical in regard to facts of kind Q are identical in regard to facts of kind P." This formulation does not explicitly mention properties of individuals in either the analysandum or the analysans; however, it seems essentially equivalent to our formulation above in terms of properties. For what is it for two worlds to be "identical in regard to facts of kind P"? Think of worlds as certain maximal classes of facts; then for two worlds to be identical in regard to facts of kind P is for them to contain the same facts of kind P. The maximality condition on worlds as

---

22 (Added 1993.) This is an error. For further discussion of this issue, see Essay 5, section 2, and "Postscripts on Supervenience," section 3, in this volume.

classes of facts would presumably entail that two worlds contain the same facts of kind P if and only if they contain the same *singular facts* of kind P. A singular fact, I take it, is something of the form *a is F,* where a is an individual and F a property; and to say that the fact that a is F is a fact of kind P (say, a psychological fact) amounts, arguably, to saying that F is a property of kind P (say, a psychological property). It follows then that for two worlds to be identical in regard to facts of kind P is for the following to hold: for any property F of kind P and any x, x has F in one world if and only if x has F in the other. Thus, the notion of identity of worlds in regard to facts of kind P comes to the notion earlier explained of indiscernibility of worlds with respect to a set of properties of kind P. Moreover, it is by now evident that on the present construal of "facts" and of what it is for a fact to be "of kind P," talk of "properties of kind P" can in general replace talk of "facts of kind P" in discussions of supervenience, and, in particular, that supervenience of facts is reducible to supervenience of properties.[23]

What does the supervenience of A and B imply about the existence of correlations between the properties in the two families? Part of the answer is already clear from the definitions of weak and strong supervenience:

(4) If A weakly supervenes on B, then for every F in A there is a property G in B such that $(\forall x)[G(x) \rightarrow F(x)]$.

(5) If A strongly supervenes on B, then for every F in A there is a property G in B such that *necessarily* $(\forall x)[G(x) \rightarrow F(x)]$.

Our earlier discussion showed that if infinite conjunction and disjunction are assumed, (4) can be strengthened to:

(4a) If A weakly supervenes on B, then for each property F in A there is a property G in B such that $(\forall x)[G(x) \leftrightarrow F(x)]$, that is, each A-property has a coextension in B.

Under the same assumption, a companion result can be shown for (5) as well:

(5a) If A strongly supervenes on B, then for each property F in A there is a property G in B such that necessarily $(\forall x)[G(x) \leftrightarrow F(x)]$, that is, every A-property has a *necessary coextension* in B.

23 Supervenience for states and events, too, is reducible to property supervenience if they are construed as property exemplifications; for such a conception of states and events see "Events as Property Exemplifications," Essay 3 of this volume. If the alternative conception of events associated with Davidson (see, e.g., "The Individuation of Events" in Davidson, *Essays on Actions and Events* (Oxford, 1980)) is adopted, events could simply be treated as individuals, that is, as values of the variables "x," "y," etc., in the definitions of supervenience, again making a special notion of event supervenience unnecessary.

The following proves (5a): Let F be a property in A. We may assume F to be contingent; i.e., some x has F in some possible world w. ((5a) is trivially true for noncontingent F.) By the definition of strong supervenience there is a property G in B such that x has G (in w) and necessarily $(\forall y)[G(y) \rightarrow F(y)]$. Let $B_{x,w}$ be the B-maximal property x has in w. We have then:

$$\text{Necessarily } (\forall y)[B_{x,w}(y) \rightarrow G(y)],$$

whence:

$$\text{Necessarily } (\forall y)[B_{x,w}(y) \rightarrow F(y)].$$

And for each v that has F in a world u, we will have:

$$\text{Necessarily } (\forall y)[B_{v,u}(y) \rightarrow F(y)].$$

Let B* be the infinite disjunction of these B-maximal properties; then

$$\text{Necessarily } (\forall y)[B*(y) \rightarrow F(y)].$$

It is easy to see we also have the converse:

$$\text{Necessarily } (\forall y)[F(y) \rightarrow B*(y)].$$

For suppose not; then in some world w#, there is an object x such that F(x), but not B*(x). But by strong supervenience there is some property K in B such that K(x) in w# and necessarily $(\forall y)[K(y) \rightarrow F(y)]$. Let B# be the B-maximal property of x in w#. Then, as before, necessarily $(\forall y)[B\#(y) \rightarrow F(y)]$, and it follows that B# is one of the disjuncts in B*. Hence, x must have B*, yielding a contradiction. We thus have:

$$\text{Necessarily } (\forall y)[B*(y) \leftrightarrow F(y)].$$

Note that the force of "necessarily" in this biconditional is that of the inner modal term (that is, the second occurrence of "necessarily") in the definition of strong supervenience. Depending on whether in a given case of supervenience we have logical, metaphysical, or nomological necessity for this term, we have in that sense of necessity a necessarily coextensive property in the base family for every supervenient property. In the case of nomological necessity, some might question this; we will take up this issue in the following section.

V. SOME PHILOSOPHICAL CONSIDERATIONS

The principal conclusions of the preceding section are, first, that strong supervenience is committed to the existence of a necessary coextension in the base family for each supervenient property; and, second, that this commitment cannot be avoided by embracing global supervenience. For the two supervenience relations are in fact one. This should be found prima facie disturbing by some philosophers who have used supervenience to formulate certain philosophical claims. As we saw earlier, a full sense of dependency cannot be captured by weak supervenience; strong or global supervenience is needed. But to have this degree of dependency is *ipso facto* to be committed to the existence of a pervasive system of necessary property-to-property entailments, as is evident from the very definition of strong supervenience. And (5a) strengthens this: each supervenient property has a necessarily *coextensive* property in the base family. This may be more than what some philosophers thought they had bargained for.

We have already noted a possible dilemma in which Davidson may find himself: weak psychophysical supervenience appears too weak to yield materialism, but strong supervenience seems too strong in entailing the existence of a pervasive system of psychophysical equivalences. But Davidson's prime motive for advocating psychophysical supervenience is precisely to acknowledge the dependence of the mental on the physical but at the same time deny that there are laws connecting psychological and physical properties. What our results seem to show is this: if you want psychophysical dependence, you had better be prepared for psychophysical laws – or, at any rate, necessary psychophysical entailments. Some might dispute this line of thought on the ground that "nomological properties," i.e., those that are admissible in laws, are not closed under Boolean operations – that is, these operations, when applied to such properties, do not always yield properties fit to appear in laws.[24] B-maximal properties, their infinite disjunctions, and the like are "too complex," "too artificial and unnatural," and "too heterogeneous," it is argued, to be "natural kinds."

This raises various complex issues about the ontology and epistemology of laws, reduction, definition, and the like. I can, however, only indicate here the general approach I think we ought to take. First, we need to be sensitive to the distinction between *predicates* and *properties,* and beware that complexity or artificiality attaching to predicates (or linguistic

24 For interesting considerations along these lines see Paul Teller's "Comments on Kim's Paper," *Southern Journal of Philosophy* 22, Supplement (1984): 57–61. My remarks here, which include reactions to some of Teller's critical points, represent a modification and elaboration of the views I defended earlier, especially in "Supervenience and Nomological Incommensurables," op. cit.

constructions in general) need not attach to the properties they express. A long Boolean combination of predicates would normally be complex *qua* predicate; on the other hand, the property it expresses need not inherit that complexity (the Boolean expression may be equivalent to a short and simple one). The definitions in this paper have been framed for properties, not predicates; such operations as infinite conjunctions and infinite disjunctions would be highly questionable for predicates, but not necessarily for properties – any more than infinite unions and intersections are for classes. The property of being less than one meter long can be thought of as an infinite disjunction (e.g., of all properties of the form, being less than $n/n + 1$ meters long, for every natural number n). In fact, we could do with *sets* of properties, dispensing with infinite conjunctions and disjunctions. The main point is that there is no direct inference from the constructional details of properties to their complexity or artificiality, whatever these things may mean for properties.

When we speak of laws, we may have in mind either sentences or some nonlinguistic, nonconceptual, objective connections between properties. If laws are taken to be sentences, our results do not show that psychophysical supervenience entails the existence of biconditional laws. For we are given no guarantee that there are predicates, especially reasonably simple and perspicuous ones, to represent the constructed properties. Reformulating our basic definitions in terms of *predicates* rather than properties will not help; for that would make infinitary procedures highly dubious, perhaps unacceptable. Moreover, strong psychophysical supervenience stated for psychological and physical predicates seems considerably less plausible than when stated for properties: it asserts that for each psychological predicate there is a physical predicate that (logically or nomologically) entails it. What is the physical predicate that entails, say, "being bored"? It seems that we would at least need to appeal to "ideal physical languages" and the like to get started, and this might bring us right back to talk of properties.

If, on the other hand, laws are construed as objective connections between properties, which can be expressed by sentences or statements ("nomological" or "lawlike statements"), then (5a) must be accepted as stating that there are biconditional laws – if laws are "only" nomologically necessary, then equivalences that are at least as strong as laws – between supervenient and base properties. But what are the implications of this? Does it mean that the supervenient properties (or theories formulated in terms of them) are necessarily "reducible" to their bases? That moral properties are definable in naturalistic terms, that psychology is reducible to physical theory, and so on? It might seem that these biconditional laws, or necessary equivalences, supply the "bridge laws" required by the classical conception of intertheoretic reduction. But this conclusion would be premature. Reduction, explanation, and the like are epistemic activities, and the mere fact that such equivalences or biconditionals "exist" is no guarantee that they are, or will ever become, *available* for reductive or explanatory uses. "Availability" here is best understood, I think, in terms of representation in a well-confirmed explanatory theory, and this in turn will depend on, among other things, our own cognitive powers, and our proclivities and idiosyncrasies in matters of what we find comfortable and satisfying as explanations. So the existence of a necessary physical coextension for every psychological property would have no direct bearing on our ability to carry out a physical reduction of psychology.

What we could more reasonably expect is this: as science makes progress, it will succeed in identifying an increasing number of *local* physical coextensions for psychological properties, that is, physical coextensions *restricted to specific domains* (e.g., particular biological species); and a sufficiently broad system of such local coextensions can serve as a base for "local reductions" of psychological theories. As many have pointed out, any given mental state is likely to have "multiple physical realizations" over distinct physical structures or biological species; however, for any given species or kind of structure, there may well be a uniform base, and if a comprehensive array of such bases is identified for, say, human psychological states, then human psychology could be "locally reduced" to physical theory.[25] If Martian psychological states, because of the different Martian anatomy and physiology, have different physical bases, Martian psychology would have to receive a different local physical reduction, even if the Martians and humans instantiate the same psychology.

Moore held the view that goodness is a "simple nonnatural" property, where by "simple" he meant indefinability and by "nonnatural" inaccessibility through normal sensory experience. Given this, it is somewhat remarkable that he was entirely unperturbed by the supervenience of goodness on natural properties. In fact, in the passage last quoted he says that *unless* he had thought that the goodness of an object "followed" from its natural properties he would "never have thought of suggesting that

25 On "local reductions" see Kim, "Psychophysical Supervenience as a Mind–Body Theory," op. cit.; also Robert C. Richardson, "Functionalism and Reductionism," *Philosophy of Science* 46 (1979): 533–58.

goodness was 'non-natural'." If the goodness of a thing "follows" from its natural properties which, we may assume, are accessible through normal sense-experience, why then isn't goodness itself so accessible? Perhaps, it might be replied that accessibility in this sense isn't the issue; what is crucial is that goodness has no direct or immediate "presentation" in sensory experience. But if goodness does follow from natural properties, why isn't this enough as a basis for a naturalistic epistemology of goodness, and why doesn't this make the intuitionist moral epistemology at best otiose?

It is interesting to note Moore's observation that, although the goodness of a thing follows from certain of its natural properties, from the fact that it is good it does *not* follow that it has these natural properties. Would our (5a) have discomfited Moore? Probably not, for the term "follow" as used by Moore, and perhaps also in its general philosophical usage, appears to have an unmistakable epistemological dimension: if goodness "follows" from certain natural properties, we should be able to "see" or "infer" that a thing is good by seeing that it has these natural properties. The necessary naturalistic coextension of goodness, as far as the arguments of this paper go, has no such epistemological status: we know it must exist, if strong supervenience obtains, but may never know "what it is." Nor can such a coextension be expected to provide a definitional basis for the term "good"; in fact, its existence does not suffice even to show the "in principle" definability of "good" in naturalistic terms. For the notion of definition carries certain semantic and epistemological associations, and even if we could identify the underlying naturalistic coextension of goodness we cannot expect these associations to hold for it.

We seem to have reached the conclusion that supervenience relations by themselves imply nothing directly about such relationships as definability and reducibility, if the possibility involved in "definability" or "reducibility" is construed in a fairly strong and realistic sense. However, as I shall argue later, there is a critical tension between acceptance of a supervenience thesis with regard to a pair of domains and rejection of all significant epistemic or conceptual relationships between the domains. But let us first briefly turn to the issue of *autonomy*.

What does supervenience imply about the autonomy of what supervenes in relation to its base? Although a thorough discussion would require a more precise understanding of the relevant concept of autonomy, it seems that weak supervenience can be entirely consistent with autonomy; that, in fact, may be one of its chief attractions. However, the case

75

is different with strong supervenience: under strong supervenience, the base wholly determines the supervening properties. If strong psychophysical supervenience holds, what happens in the realm of the mind is determined in every detail by what happens in the physical realm. This determinative relation is an objective matter; it does not depend on whether anyone knows anything about it, or what expressions are used to talk about mind and body. Unlike in the case of reduction and definition, epistemological considerations do not intrude here. That is perhaps why global supervenience is often used to state the doctrine of materialism. Likewise, strong supervenience of moral upon natural properties may signal a form of "moral naturalism" – not the definitional thesis of ethical naturalism, but a metaphysical thesis that recognizes the ontological primacy of the natural over the moral.[26]

Thinking about causal determination will, I believe, give us a useful point of analogy in thinking about supervenient determination. If causal determinism ("Every event has a cause") holds, every occurrence has a temporally earlier determinative condition. However, this says nothing about how successful we shall be in identifying causes and framing causal explanations; it is also silent on how successful we shall be in discovering causal laws. Explanation is an epistemological affair, and the claim that all events are causally explainable is an epistemological thesis, or a methodological doctrine, not entailed by the metaphysical thesis of universal causation alone (unless the former is expressly read so as to mean the latter). Similarly, the thesis that a given domain supervenes on another is a metaphysical thesis about an objectively existent dependency relation between the two domains; it says nothing about whether or how the details of the dependency relation will become known so as to enable us to formulate explanations, reductions, or definitions.

Having sundered the metaphysical thesis of causal determinism from its associated epistemological thesis about the possibility of causal explanation, we are now in a position to bring them together and appreciate their mutual relevance. There is, first, this much direct relationship: where there is no causal relation, there can be no correct causal explanation. When an event causes another, that constitutes the objective fact that makes a corresponding causal explanation "correct" or "true." More generally, we can think of the thesis of causal determinism as providing a

26 For a discussion of moral supervenience in relation to the problem of moral realism see S. W. Blackburn, "Moral Realism" in *Morality and Moral Reasoning*, ed. J. Casey (London, 1971).

metaphysical basis for the methodological strategy or principle enjoining us to search for explanations of natural events in terms of their causal antecedents, and also providing an explanation of why this strategy works as well as it does. Acceptance of causal determinism, therefore, can be viewed as an expression of a commitment to the method of causal explanation as an epistemological strategy. Conversely, it is our success, limited though it may be, in discovering causal connections and formulating causal explanations that forms an essential basis of our belief in causal determinism.

Similarly, the belief that a supervenience relation obtains for a pair of domains can motivate our search for specific property-to-property connections in terms of which illuminating reductions and edifying definitions might be formulated. Where strong supervenience obtains, (5a) gives us the assurance that such connections in the form of necessary equivalences are there to be discovered, without of course the further assurance that we shall succeed in discovering them or that they will be representable in an explanatory theory. A case in point is mereological supervenience, the doctrine that the macro-properties of material things are supervenient on their micro-properties. It is this metaphysical doctrine of atomism that seems to underlie and support the enormously productive research strategy of micro-reduction in modern theoretical science. And, conversely, the success of this research strategy reinforces our belief in mereological supervenience. Perhaps, similar remarks apply to moral supervenience: the belief that the moral supervenes on the nonmoral may have shaped some of the major assumptions and tasks of moral philosophy, such as the search for naturalistic definitions of ethical terms, the belief that there must be nonmoral "criteria" for moral ascriptions, the belief that there are such things as "good-making" or "right-making characteristics," and the perennial attempts to state conditions for the rationality of acts or justness of institutions in naturalistic and descriptive terms.

I think these remarks explain the point of (5a): it helps us to see the connection between the thesis of supervenience concerning a pair of domains and a certain epistemological strategy we may adopt in regard to them. It explains how the belief in the supervenience thesis can lead to, and in turn be supported by, the expectation that one domain can be understood – reduced, defined, explained, etc. – in terms of the other through the discovery of necessary equivalences that (5a) assures us must exist. The tension I alluded to earlier, several paragraphs back, arises precisely because this connection is contravened in embracing supervenience but rejecting at the same time all significant conceptual or epistemic relationships. That is to say, there is a sense, though a weak one, of possibility in which (5a) shows that strong supervenience entails the possibility of reduction or definition across the domains involved.[27]

27 In addition to the persons whose help has already been cited, I am indebted to David Benfield, Earl Conee, Fred Feldman, John Heil, Terence Horgan, Arnold Koslow, Brian McLaughlin, Robert Richardson, Ernest Sosa, and Paul Teller.

5

"Strong" and "global" supervenience revisited

In an earlier paper, "Concepts of Supervenience,"[1] I characterized two distinct concepts of supervenience, "strong" and "weak," and compared them with each other and with a third concept, "global supervenience." In this paper I wish to correct an error in the earlier paper and present further material on supervenience, including a new characterization of strong supervenience, which I believe is particularly perspicuous, and a discussion of the adequacy of global supervenience as a determination relation. I shall also present a strengthened relation of global supervenience based on *similarity* rather than *indiscernibility* between worlds, which may well be a more useful concept than the currently popular conception of global supervenience.

1. A NEW CHARACTERIZATION OF "STRONG SUPERVENIENCE"

Let A and B be two sets of properties (closed under complementation, conjunction, disjunction, and perhaps other property-forming operations).[2] A is said to *weakly supervene* on B just in case:

(I) Necessarily, for any x and y, if x and y share all properties in B, then x and y share all properties in A – that is, indiscernibility in B entails indiscernibility in A.

This corresponds in a straightforward way to the informal characterization of supervenience commonly found in the literature.[3] As was shown in the

---

I have received helpful comments on topics discussed here from David Lewis, Barry Loewer, Joe Mendola, Brad Petrie, Ernest Sosa, Paul Teller, Nicholas White, and Stephen Yablo.

1 Essay 4 of this volume.
2 Infinite conjunction and disjunction are needed for some of the arguments in "Concepts of Supervenience."
3 See, e.g., R. M. Hare, *The Language of Morals* (London: Oxford University Press, 1952), p. 145.

earlier paper, weak supervenience can be equivalently explained as follows:

(II) Necessarily, for any object x and any property F in A, if x has F, then there exists a property G in B such that x has G, and if any y has G, it has F.

As I argued, although supervenience thus characterized (especially by (I)) corresponds, essentially word for word, to the notion that many philosophers profess to have in mind, it yields only a fairly weak relationship seemingly inadequate for many of the uses to which it has been put; in particular, it seems too weak to fully capture the intuitive relation of "determination" or "dependency" between sets of properties (or facts, states, and the like). The following stronger relation of supervenience, therefore, was introduced: A is said to *strongly supervene* on B just in case:

(III) Necessarily, for any object x and any property F in A, if x has F, then there exists a property G in B such that x has G, and *necessarily* if any y has G, it has F.

This definition closely parallels the second characterization above, (II), of weak supervenience, the only difference being the presence of the modal expression "necessarily" governing the general conditional "if any y has G, it has F." The insertion of this modal qualifier guarantees world-to-world stability for the correlations between supervenient properties and their "base properties," a feature conspicuously lacking in weak supervenience.

One question not addressed in "Concepts of Supervenience" is whether there is an alternative definition of strong supervenience which formally parallels the first characterization (I) of weak supervenience in the same way that the definition (III) of strong supervenience parallels the second definition (II) of weak supervenience. Such a definition would be useful and instructive since (I) is the most common ("canonical," one might say) way of explaining supervenience, perhaps because of its appealingly intuitive and perspicuous form. A characterization of strong supervenience with a similar form would have similar virtues, wearing on its sleeve the nature of its relationship to weak supervenience. Of course the definition, (III), helps in a limited way, when contrasted with the second definition, (II), of weak supervenience. The limitation stems from the fact that the second definition of weak supervenience, although formally equivalent to the first, lacks its familiarity and intuitive clarity.

In a forthcoming paper,[4] Brian McLaughlin introduces a relation of supervenience (of A on B) characterized thus:

(IV) For any worlds w_j and w_k, and for any objects x and y, if x has in w_j the same B-properties that y has in w_k, then x has in w_j the same A-properties that y has in w_k.

McLaughlin's definition, as it turns out, is what we are looking for: the relation it characterizes is equivalent to strong supervenience as given by (III) and it is obvious that McLaughlin's definition formally parallels definition (I) of weak supervenience. It differs from (I) only in that indiscernibility in A or B can be "cross-world" as well as within a single world. Thus, we might put McLaughlin's definition like this: A *strongly supervenes* on B just in case *cross-world indiscernibility in B entails cross-world indiscernibility in A*.

Another virtue of the new definition is this: What makes weak supervenience weak is, as noted, the fact that it does not guarantee stability across worlds for the correlations between supervenient properties and their base properties – that is to say, these correlations have no modal force. However, the earlier definition, (III), introduces this guarantee through an explicit clause, an easy but, for that reason, somewhat uninstructive way of doing things. A better way would have been to construct a definition of strong supervenience that has a certain intuitive rightness in its own right and from which one could show, by an argument, that supervenience under this conception turns out to have the desired characteristics. McLaughlin's definition clearly fills the bill.

McLaughlin's supervenience is easily seen to be equivalent to strong supervenience as defined by (III). To show, first, that McLaughlin's supervenience entails strong supervenience: Assume, for any property F in A, x has F at w_i. Let B_i be the B-maximal property of x at w_i (the B-maximal property of an object at a world is the strongest B-property the object has in that world; it entails every B-property of the object; see "Concepts of Supervenience," Essay 4, section II). Let B_i be the G in the definition of strong supervenience; we need to show that necessarily if any y has it, it has F. Suppose otherwise – that is, at some w_j there is a y such that y has B_i but not F. Thus, x has B_i at w_i and y has B_i at w_j; that is, x and y have the same B-properties in these worlds respectively, and by McLaughlin's supervenience, they must have the same A-properties in the respective

4 "Why Try to Bake an Intentional Cake With Physical Yeast and Flour?" (unpublished manuscript).

worlds. Since x has F in w_i, y must have F in w_j, contradicting the supposition. Hence, A strongly supervenes on B.

To show the converse: Assume x at w_i and y at w_j share the same B-properties. Let F be any A-property that x has at w_i; we need to show that y has F at w_j. By strong supervenience there is a property G in B such that x has G at w_i, and necessarily (that is, at every world) anything with G has F. Ex hypothesi, y at w_j has all the B-properties x has at w_i. So y has G at w_j, from which it follows that y has F at w_j. Hence, A supervenes on B in the sense of McLaughlin.

2. GLOBAL SUPERVENIENCE DOES NOT ENTAIL STRONG SUPERVENIENCE

In "Concepts of Supervenience," I claimed that strong supervenience is equivalent to "global supervenience" explained as follows:

> Any two worlds indiscernible with respect to B-properties are indiscernible with respect to A-properties.[5]

But this was an error, as Geoffrey Hellman, John Bacon, Bradford Petrie, and others[6] have pointed out. Strong supervenience does entail global supervenience; however, the converse does not hold, as Petrie shows with the following simple example:

> Consider the two worlds, w_1 and w_2, each with two individuals a and b. In w_1, a has G and F, and b has G. In w_2, a has G but not F, and b lacks G.[7]

It is clear that this pair of worlds is a counterexample to the strong supervenience of F on G (or, more verbosely, the unit set of F on that of G). However, the example leaves open the possibility that F globally supervenes on G: since the two worlds are not G-indiscernible they cannot be

---

5 Before this can be taken as a precise definition it must be sharpened in various respects; e.g., how indiscernibility with respect to a set of properties is to be understood for worlds not sharing the same domain of individuals, and whether or not "haecceitism" is accepted for individuals. These issues, however, will not affect the present discussion.

6 Hellman in personal communication and in "Determination and Logical Truth," *Journal of Philosophy* 82 (1985): 607–16 (see footnote 3, pp. 608–09); Bacon, "Supervenience, Necessary Coextensions, and Reducibility," *Philosophical Studies* 49 (1986): 163–76; Petrie, "Global Supervenience and Reduction," *Philosophy and Phenomenological Research* 48 (1987): 119–30. Paul Teller and Neil Tennant also called this to my attention.

7 "Global Supervenience and Reduction." Petrie first presented this counterexample in his doctoral dissertation, *Semantics and Physicalism,* The University of Michigan, 1985.

a counterexample to the global supervenience of F on G. Therefore, global supervenience cannot entail strong supervenience.[8]

3. IS GLOBAL SUPERVENIENCE STRONG ENOUGH?

But what is the metaphysical significance of the failure of global supervenience to entail strong supervenience?[9] To see Petrie's example as showing this failure is to see, I think, the limitation of global supervenience as a relation of determination or dependence. Given the existence of worlds like w_1 and w_2, which is permitted by global supervenience of F on G, does it make sense to think of F as being "dependent on," or "determined by," G? In w_1 a has G and also F; in w_2, however, a has G but lacks F; and the only fact in this world that might account for this failure of the G-F connection in a is the fact that another object b, which, we may assume,[10] is totally unrelated to a, has non-G, although it has G in w_1. Clearly it is possible to think of other bizarre pairs of worlds that violate strong supervenience but are compatible with global supervenience.

It is difficult to see how, given worlds like these, F's global supervenience on G could support G-F subjunctives or counterfactuals; and it is equally difficult to see how in the face of these facts one could claim that F is *dependent* on G, or that all the F-facts are *determined* by the G-facts. I doubt that many will find such a claim persuasive.

This conclusion gains further support from the following fact: *global supervenience does not even entail weak supervenience*. For consider a world in which an object has both G and F and another has G but not F. Such a world is excluded by the claim that F weakly supervenes on G, since in

---

8 John Pollock pointed out to me another problem with my claim that global supervenience entails strong supervenience: the definition of strong supervenience makes use of two modal operators, which are allowed to be different ("Concepts of Supervenience," Essay 4, section III), whereas that of global supervenience uses only one, and special assumptions about the properties of these operators (e.g., that the single modal operator in global supervenience is an S5 operator) are needed to get the argument going.

9 I shall not discuss here possible ways of modifying the concepts involved or introducing additional metaphysical premises to force strong supervenience out of global supervenience. Ernest Sosa and Barry Loewer have suggested to me the possibility of adding quantification and identity to the apparatus of property construction; David Lewis and Joseph Mendola have raised the possibility of using metaphysical considerations to disarm the Petrie-style examples. (For further discussion see "Postscripts on Supervenience," section 3, in this volume.)

10 Notice that this assumption does not beg the question: all we need is one such pair of worlds for some F and G for which we can agree that G determines F.

it there are two objects indiscernible with respect to G and yet discernible with respect to F. However, the existence of such a world is entirely consistent with F's global supervenience on G. Given that two objects have G in a world, weak supervenience of F on G requires that they both have, or lack, F in that world. Global supervenience requires no such thing; it only requires that there not be *another* possible world in which G is distributed over the same individuals as in the first world but in which F is distributed differently. Since weak supervenience does not entail global supervenience,[11] these two relations are independent of each other.

Perhaps this is not the sort of thing that can be proved or disproved, but I think it highly plausible to regard weak supervenience as minimally necessary for any claim of determination or dependency between sets of properties. Never mind world-to-world stability of connections between two sets of properties; if these connections don't hold even within a single world – that is, there are objects entirely indiscernible in regard to a given set of properties and yet differing in the properties alleged to be determined by, or dependent on, those properties – it is difficult to see any merit in the claim that there is a genuine relation of determination or dependency here. How is it possible to advance a claim of physical dependency of the mental if, as permitted by the global supervenience of the mental on the physical, there should exist a human being physically indistinguishable from you in every respect who has a mental life entirely different from yours or who has no mental life at all?

I think that we have seen all possible cases in which global supervenience without strong supervenience can obtain, for the simple case involving two properties F and G. To defeat the strong supervenience of F on G, we need a world w and an object a such that although a has F in w, for every property G* constructible from G that a has in w (that is, G or non-G) the conditional "Necessarily if anything has G* it has F" fails. We may suppose that G* is G (that is, a has G in w). "Necessarily if G then F" can fail in two ways: (i) the nonmodal conditional "If G then F" fails in w (in w there exists another object which has G but not F), or (ii) the nonmodal conditional fails in another world (containing an object with G but not F). In either case global supervenience of F on G can be saved, as we have seen: (i) is a situation in which even weak supervenience fails, and Petrie's example is a minimal case of type (ii) in which global supervenience is preserved. In neither of these two situations in which global supervenience can be had without strong supervenience does it

11 "Concepts of Supervenience."

seem at all reasonable to regard F as being determined by, or dependent on, G. It seems to me that cases of global supervenience without strong supervenience involving richer sets of properties follow the same pattern.

A. MATERIALISM AND GLOBAL SUPERVENIENCE

These considerations put in jeopardy the expectation many philosophers have held of global supervenience. They have looked to it as a mode of "determination without reduction," a way in which one set of properties (or facts, sentences, events, etc.) can determine another even in the absence of property-to-property connections between them. We might put their slogan thus: "Global determination without local determinations!"

For example, some philosophers have characterized materialism in the following way: There are no two worlds indiscernible in physical respects (facts, etc.) and yet discernible in some psychological respects (facts, etc.).[12] It is often claimed that this is materialism enough, despite the fact that it says nothing, at least overtly, about the existence of specific psychophysical correlations of the sort that would underwrite reductionism. In fact, the distinctive virtue of global supervenience is sometimes thought to be precisely its failure to entail something like strong supervenience with its psychophysical type-type correlations, which threaten to breathe new life into the unwanted psychophysical reductionism. But before we accept global psychophysical supervenience as a significant form of materialism we should consider this: it is consistent with this version of materialism for there to be a world which differs physically from this world in some most trifling respect (say, Saturn's rings in that world contain one more ammonia molecule) but which is entirely devoid of consciousness, or has a radically different, perhaps totally irregular, distribution of mental characteristics over its inhabitants (say, creatures with brains have no mentality while rocks are conscious). As long as that world differs from this one in some physical respect, however minuscule or seemingly irrelevant, it could be as different as you please in any psychological respect you

12 See, e.g., John Haugeland, "Weak Supervenience," *American Philosophical Quarterly* 19 (1982): 93–103; Terence Horgan, "Supervenience and Microphysics," *Pacific Philosophical Quarterly* 63 (1982): 29–43; David Lewis, "New Work for a Theory of Universals," *Australasian Journal of Philosophy* 61 (1983): 343–77; Paul Teller, "Relational Holism and Quantum Mechanics," *British Journal for Philosophy of Science* 37 (1986): 71–81; Petrie, "Global Supervenience and Reduction." I am not suggesting that all these philosophers had an anti-reductionist motive in formulating materialism in the form of global supervenience (Lewis in particular must be excluded; see, e.g., "New Work for a Theory of Universals," p. 358).

choose. Moreover, as we saw, global psychophysical supervenience is consistent with there being within a given world, perhaps this one, two physically indistinguishable organisms with radically different psychological attributes. It is doubtful that many materialists would regard these consequences as compatible with their materialist tenets; it seems clear that they are not compatible with the claim that the mental is determined wholly by the physical.

Moreover, global supervenience without strong supervenience is difficult to understand. If the mental globally supervenes on the physical, that cannot be a brute and unexplainable fact, something we would want to accept as a fundamental, primitive fact about the world. We would feel, I think, that there should be an explanation of it. If, as strong supervenience affirms, there should exist appropriate connections between specific psychological properties of objects and their physical properties, that would give us a basis for an explanation. When we ponder the kinds of situations in which strong supervenience but not global supervenience fails, the failure of strong supervenience seems to make global supervenience unexplainable and incomprehensible. All this makes one wonder if there could ever be *evidence* of the sort we could reasonably expect to obtain that would support the global physical supervenience of the mental while ruling out its strong supervenience.[13] There is a strong inclination, I think, to look for an explanation of "global determination" in terms of specific "local determinations"; we would find global determination without local determination mysterious and difficult to understand. Perhaps, this is a manifestation of our micro-reductive proclivities. But then so much the worse for global supervenience without strong supervenience.

Is there anything positive to say in favor of global supervenience? In "Global Supervenience and Reduction," Petrie argues that it is especially well suited for the formulation of materialism in view of the well-known examples of Hilary Putnam and Tyler Burge[14] which appear to show that the contents of certain propositional attitudes can depend on factors external to the subjects to whom the attitudes are attributed. To adapt an example of Putnam's, consider Oscar and Oscar's counterpart on Twin

13 This point is recognized by Petrie, though apparently for somewhat different reasons, in "Global Supervenience and Reduction," Section 4. I believe he underestimates its seriousness.
14 Putnam, "The Meaning of 'Meaning,'" in his *Philosophical Papers,* Volume 2 (Cambridge: Cambridge University Press, 1975); Burge, "Individualism and the Mental," *Midwest Studies in Philosophy* 4 (1979): 73–121.

earth, which is just like the earth except only that on Twin Earth water is replaced everywhere by an observationally indistinguishable compound XYZ. We may assume Oscar and T. E. Oscar are molecule-for-molecule duplicates of each other.[15] It seems plausible to think that Oscar and T. E. Oscar, despite their physical indistinguishability, can have different beliefs: for example, Oscar believes that oil and water don't mix, while T. E. Oscar believes that oil and XYZ don't mix. This seems to show that beliefs do not in general strongly supervene on the physical states of the persons to whom they are attributed. Thus, it may be thought, we need a form of physicalism that is consistent with the failure of local determination of the mental by the physical, and global psychophysical supervenience seems precisely what we want. For it affirms that the psychological states of the world, taken as a whole, are determined by its physical states taken as a whole, without requiring every psychological state of an individual to be determined by *its* physical states.

How plausible is this argument? Without getting ourselves entangled in the dispute about "wide" and "narrow" content and related issues, we can see, I think, that this argument does not go as far as it might appear at first blush. Consider those causal–historical *relations* Oscar has had with respect to water, and more generally to his environment, *in virtue of* which his belief, but not T. E. Oscar's belief, has the content "oil and water don't mix," and similarly the causal–historical relations characterizing T. E. Oscar with respect to XYZ that account for *his* belief content. These relational properties, some of which are highlighted in Putnam's discussion, are the key to seeing how local determination can work here. That is, it is perfectly possible to construe these belief contents to be determined by, and strongly supervenient on, the physical properties, *including relational historical properties,* of Oscar and T. E. Oscar.[16] Further, it is *necessary* to construe the matter this way; for otherwise it would be entirely inexplicable why Oscar's belief has the content it has and not the content that T. E. Oscar's belief has, and vice versa. It is no accident that Oscar has beliefs about water, not about XYZ, and T. E. Oscar has beliefs about XYZ, not about water; we expect this difference to be grounded in certain further specifiable relevant differences between them – differences that are generalizable. And our expectation is, on the whole, not disappointed. Imagine what our reaction would be if we were not able to find

15 I think we can ignore the difficulty with this example that if water is everywhere replaced by XYZ the two Oscars could not be molecule-for-molecule indiscernible.
16 For other similar examples see my "Psychophysical Supervenience," Essay 10 of this volume.

any such difference because, we are told, *there was none*. That would be a situation in which we were asked to believe that there just was no intelligible basis for our ascribing different belief contents to Oscar and T. E. Oscar – that is, a situation in which belief attributions would become wholly mysterious and lose their sense. It is possible, of course, that the differences that ground the difference in content ascriptions include psychological features; but this would only mean that they, too, must in turn physically supervene in an appropriate sense if psychophysical supervenience is to hold.

Petrie also mentions the economic value of a coin as a property that is plausibly determined by the physical features of the world but not by those of the coin itself. That seems right, but only if we limit ourselves to the "intrinsic" physical properties of the coin. For the value of a coin is best taken as a relational property of the coin regarded as a physical object, a property something has only in its relation to a specific economic community. Under physicalism it would be plausible to regard this property as being determined by, and strongly supervenient on, the physical properties, again including relational ones, of the coin. Or consider the property of being the tallest man.[17] Whether I have this property depends not only on my height but on who else exists in this world. The property of being taller than any other man is a relational property, a property that an object has in virtue of its relationship to other individuals, and we of course expect its supervenience base to include the relational properties of individuals. If you have this property, it will strongly supervene on your other properties including relational ones (say, your height being eight feet and everyone else's height being less than that).

Examples like these, therefore, do not call for global supervenience. What they call for is an explicit recognition of relations and relational properties. The lesson we learn from the Putman and Burge-style cases that is relevant to the topic of supervenience is that contrary to what used to be taken for granted, many intentional states turn out not to be "intrinsic" or "internal"[18] to the subjects to whom they are attributed. Rather, they turn out to be "extrinsic" and "noninternal," dependent in complex ways on physical and social factors outside the subjects. It is no surprise then that we must seek a wider physical supervenience base for them, including relations and relational properties, if they are thought to be

17 Both Petrie and Teller have suggested examples of this kind.
18 For discussions of "internal" or "intrinsic properties" see my "Psychophysical Supervenience," Essay 10 of this volume; Lewis, "New Work for a Theory of Universals," and "Extrinsic Properties," *Philosophical Studies* 44 (1983): 197–200.

supervenient on the physical. A full account of these cases will be facilitated by a generalization of "strong" and "weak" supervenience to accommodate relations as well as properties.[19]

5. GLOBAL SUPERVENIENCE STRENGTHENED: SIMILARITY VS. INDISCERNIBILITY

There seems to be a natural way of strengthening the concept of global supervenience to blunt, at least to a degree, the thrust of the observations in the preceding section which, as we saw, appear to undermine the claim of global supervenience as a dependency relation. It makes sense to think that if the mental is dependent on the physical, then not only must any two worlds that are *physically indiscernible* be *psychologically indiscernible,* but also any two worlds that are *physically pretty much the same* must be *pretty much the same psychologically* as well – that is, worlds that are highly similar in physical respects must not show large psychological differences. This idea suggests the following concept of *similarity-based* global supervenience (of A on B):

(V) The degree to which any two worlds are similar in respect of B-properties is matched by the degree to which they are similar in respect of A-properties.

This definition is perhaps too strong: we may not want to require that two worlds that are B-*dissimilar* must also be equally A-*dissimilar.* For example, we may want to allow, under global psychophysical supervenience, the possibility that two worlds that are quite dissimilar in physical respects could display similar psychological characteristics (consider the "multiple physical realizability" of psychological states often invoked in discussions of the mind–body problem).[20] I think this is a debatable issue, but there is also the following weaker relation which will suffice for the present:

(VI) Worlds that are pretty much alike in B-properties are pretty much alike in A-properties.

If we understand indiscernibility as a limiting case of similarity where the degree of similarity is maximal, similarity-based global supervenience, under either of the two conceptions above, can be considered to entail the usual indiscernibility-based global supervenience as a special case.[21]

19 See "Postscripts on Supervenience," section 1, in this volume.
20 See Hilary Putnam, "Psychological Predicates," in *Art, Mind, and Religion,* ed. W. H. Capitan and D. D. Merrill (Pittsburgh: University of Pittsburgh Press, 1967).
21 Note that the similarity approach can be applied also to weak and strong supervenience, especially as these relations are characterized by (I) and (IV) in section I above.

It would be difficult to formulate general criteria for measurement of similarity in the sense intended here. Similarity in this sense can, and must, be evaluated along many seemingly incommensurable dimensions, and judgments of similarity are certain to be highly sensitive to a variety of contextual factors, giving rise to unresolvable disagreements. But these difficulties do not negate the substantial intuitive content this notion has for us; for it is only a generalization of the familiar notion of similarity with respect to a single property or determinable (e.g.; color, shape, etc.). It seems in any case at least as clear and robust as the related, and more general, notion of "comparative overall similarity" for worlds that David Lewis and others have exploited in developing the semantics of counterfactuals.[22] It surely is not more vague or problematic than the latter.

In any event, the strengthened relation of global supervenience requires that two worlds that are pretty much alike in the base properties must be pretty much alike in the supervenient properties. Thus, if the mental globally supervenes in this sense on the physical, a world that differs only minimally from this world in physical respects (in it Saturn's rings have one more ammonia molecule) cannot show large psychological differences (plants, but no creatures with brains, are conscious); perhaps it shouldn't show any psychological difference at all.

Consider again Petrie's two worlds which, while defeating the strong supervenience of F on G, were seen to be consistent with F's global supervenience on G. It is not obvious, however, that they are consistent with F's similarity-based supervenience on G. As may be recalled, in w_1 a has G and also F, and b has G; in w_2, a has G but not F, and b has non-G. Given these two worlds, does F globally supervene, in the new strengthened sense, on G? The answer depends on two things: How similar are the two worlds in regard to G, and how similar are they in regard to F? Clearly it is not possible to answer these questions for schematic examples; we would need to know, first of all, what properties F and G actually are, and if we are to make meaningful comparisons we would need to look at richer worlds, with more individuals and properties, and have some idea of what laws and regularities hold in them.

It is clear, however, that examples can be constructed that are consistent with similarity-based global supervenience, under either of the two definitions above, but not with strong supervenience; all we need to do is to think of two worlds that, while differing minimally from each other both

22 See Lewis, *Counterfactuals* (Cambridge: Harvard University Press, 1973), especially chap. 4.

in physical and in psychological respects, contains an object which, although it has identical physical properties in the two worlds, has negligibly different psychological properties. This will yield similarity-based psychophysical global supervenience. However, for any psychological property M the object has in one world but lacks in the other, there are no world-invariant general conditionals of the form "Anything with P has M," where P is a physical property of the object. So similarity-based global supervenience does not entail strong supervenience. And, unlike indiscernibility-based global supervenience, it is not entailed by strong supervenience either;[23] for we can imagine that mental characteristics, though strictly correlated with neural states, are in general critically sensitive to minuscule physical differences.

23 As Barry Loewer pointed out to me.

6

Epiphenomenal and supervenient causation

1. EPIPHENOMENAL CAUSATION

Jonathan Edwards held the doctrine that ordinary material things do not persist through time but are at each moment created, and recreated, by God ex nihilo. He writes:

> If the existence of created *substance,* in each successive moment, be wholly the effect of God's immediate power, in *that* moment, without any dependence on prior existence, as much as the first creation out of *nothing,* then what exists at this moment, by this power, is a *new effect,* and simply and absolutely considered, not the same with any past existence, though it be like it, and follows it according to a certain established method.[1]

Thus, the present "time slice" of this table, although it is very much like the one preceding it, has no causal connection with it; for each slice is a wholly distinct creation by God. The temporal parts of this table are successive effects of an underlying persisting cause, God's creative activity. In arguing for this doctrine, Edwards offers the following striking analogy:

> The *images* of things in a glass, as we keep our eye upon them, seem to remain precisely the same, with a continuing, perfect identity. But it is known to be otherwise. Philosophers well know that these images are constantly *renewed,* by the impression and reflection of *new* rays of light; so that the image impressed by the former rays is constantly vanishing, and a *new* image impressed by *new* rays every moment, both on the glass and on the eye. . . . And the new images being put on *immediately* or *instantly,* do not make them the same, any more than if it were done with the intermission of an *hour* or a *day.* The image that exists at this moment is not at all *derived* from the image which existed at the last preceding moment. As may be seen, because if the succession of new *rays* be intercepted, by something

---

1 Jonathan Edwards, *Doctrine of Original Sin Defended* (1758), Part IV, Chap. II. The quotation is taken from *Jonathan Edwards,* edited by C. H. Faust and T. H. Johnson (New York, 1935), 335. I owe this interesting reference to Roderick M. Chisholm's discussion of Edwards's views in connection with the "Doctrine of Temporal Parts," in *Person and Object* (La Salle, Ill., 1976), 138ff.

interposed between the object and the glass, the image immediately ceases; the *past existence* of the image has no influence to uphold it, so much as for a moment.[2]

Two successive mirror reflections of an object are not directly causally linked to each other; in particular, the earlier one is not a cause of the later one, even though the usual requirements of "Humean causation," including that of spatiotemporal contiguity, may be met. If all we ever observed were mirror images, like the shadows in Plato's cave, we might very well be misled into ascribing a cause–effect relation to the two images; but we know better, as Edwards says. The succession of images is only a reflection of the real causal process at the level of the objects reflected.

Edwards's example anticipates one that Wesley Salmon has recently used to illustrate the difference between "causal processes" and "pseudoprocesses":[3] consider a rotating spotlight, located at the center of a circular room, casting a spot of light on the wall. According to Salmon, a light ray traveling from the spotlight to the wall is a *causal process,* whereas the motion of the spot of light on the wall is only a *pseudoprocess.* Each spot of light on the wall is caused by a light ray traveling from the spotlight; however, it is not the cause of the spot of light appearing on the wall an instant later. Two successive spots of light on the wall are related to each other as two successive mirror images are related. Both pairs mimic causal processes and are apt to be mistaken for such. Neither, however, is a process involving a real causal chain.

By "epiphenomenal causation" I have in mind *roughly* the sort of apparent causal relation in the examples of Edwards and Salmon. I say "roughly" because, as will become clear later, they are somewhat less central cases of epiphenomenal causation, as this notion will be used in this paper; these examples are helpful, however, in the initial fixing of the concept that I have in mind. In any event, Edwards's contention was that *all* causal relations holding for material bodies, events, and processes are cases of epiphenomenal causation, the only true causation being limited to God's own creative actions. The world is constantly created anew by God; we may think that fire causes smoke, but it is only that God creates fire at one instant and then smoke an instant later. There is no direct causal connection between the fire and the smoke. The relation between them is one of epiphenomenal causation.

2 Faust and Johnson, *Jonathan Edwards,* 336.
3 Wesley C. Salmon, "An 'At-At' Theory of Causal Influence," *Philosophy of Science* 44 (1977): 215–24.

Another case of epiphenomenal causation, familiar in daily life, is the succession of symptoms associated with a disease: the symptoms are not mutually related in the cause–effect relationship, although to the medically naive they may appear to be so related. The appearance of a causal connection here merely points to the real causal process underlying the symptoms.

It should be clear that by saying that two events are related in an epiphenomenal causal relation I do not mean to suggest that the events themselves are "epiphenomena." The standard current use of this term comes from discussions of epiphenomenalism as a theory of the mind–body relation, and to call an event an "epiphenomenon" in this context is taken to mean that though it is a causal effect of other events, it has no causal potency of its own: it can be the cause of no other event, being the absolute terminal link of a causal chain. It is dubious that this notion of an epiphenomenon makes sense – for example, it is doubtful how such events could be known to exist.[4] In this paper I use the modifier "epiphenomenal" in "epiphenomenal causation" to qualify the causal relation, not the events standing in that relation.

One might object at this point that these examples of the so-called epiphenomenal causation are not cases of causation at all and that it is misleading to label them as such, because "epiphenomenal causation" sounds as though it is a *kind* of causal relation. In reply, I shall say two things: first, even though it is true that an earlier mirror image is not a cause of a later one, it is also true that there *is* a causal relation between the two – the two are successive effects of the same underlying causal process. To leave the matter where we have simply denied that the first is the cause of the second would be to ignore an important causal fact about the relation between the two events. Second, I shall argue that the central cases of epiphenomenal causation that will interest us will be seen to involve "real" causal relations and that epiphenomenal causal relations of this kind are pervasively present all around us.

What is common to these cases and the earlier examples, such as Edwards's mirror images, which do not seem to involve real causal relations, is just this: they all involve at least *apparent* causal relations that are *grounded* in some underlying causal processes. These causal relations, whether only apparent or real, *are reducible to more fundamental causal relations*. If one takes the view that reducibility entails eliminability, there perhaps is no signifi-

4 For a discussion of the issues see John Lachs, "Epiphenomenalism and the Notion of Cause," *Journal of Philosophy* 60 (1963): 141–45.

cant difference between the two types of cases. But then there also is the apparently opposed view: to be reduced is to be legitimized. I believe in any case that my use of the term "epiphenomenon" is entirely consistent with the standard dictionary definition of "epiphenomenon" as "secondary symptom," "secondary phenomenon," or "something that happens in addition"; the idea that an epiphenomenon is causally inert is best taken as a philosophical doctrine of epiphenomenalism as a theory about the nature of the mental, not as something that merely arises out of the meaning of the term "epiphenomenon."

The principal claims that I want to defend in this paper are the following: that macrocausation should be viewed as a kind of epiphenomenal causation in the broad sense sketched above; that macrocausation as epiphenomenal causation should be explained as "supervenient causation" in the sense to be explained below; and that psychological causation, that is, causation involving psychological events, is plausibly assimilated to macrocausation – that is, it is to be construed as supervenient epiphenomenal causation.

2. MACROCAUSATION AS SUPERVENIENT CAUSATION

By "macrocausation" I have in mind causal relations involving macroevents and states, where a macroevent or state is understood as the exemplification of a macroproperty by an object at a time (this characterization can be generalized to macrorelations in obvious ways). The micro–macro distinction is of course relative: temperature is macro relative to molecular motion; properties of molecules are macro relative to properties and relationships characterizing atoms and more basic particles, and so on. For our present discussion, however, the paradigmatic examples of macroobjects and properties are medium-sized material bodies around us and their observable properties. Thus, fire causing smoke would be a case of macrocausation; so is the rising temperature causing a metallic object to expand. All observable phenomena are macrophenomena in relation to the familiar theoretical objects of physics; hence, our first claim entails that all causal relations involving observable phenomena – all causal relations familiar from daily experience – are cases of epiphenomenal causation.

My defense of this claim is two-pronged. The first prong consists in a general argument to the effect that a certain familiar and plausible reductionist perspective requires us to view macrocausation as epiphenomenal causation. The second prong consists in the observation that modern theoretical science treats macrocausation as reducible epiphenomenal causation and that this has proved to be an extremely successful explanatory and predictive research strategy.

First, the general argument: philosophers have observed, in connection with the mind–body problem, that a thoroughgoing physicalism can no more readily tolerate the existence of irreducible psychological features or properties than irreducible psychological objects (e.g., Cartesian souls, visual images).[5] The thought behind this may be something like this: if F is an irreducible psychical feature, then its existence implies that something is F. (If F is never exemplified, being a mere "concept" of something psychical, the physicalist has nothing to worry about.) This means that there would be a physically irreducible event or state of this thing's being F, or a physically irreducible fact, namely the fact that the thing is F. So the world remains bifurcated: the physical domain and a distinct, irreducible psychical domain; and physical theory fails as a complete and comprehensive theory of the world. Moreover, we might want to inquire into the *cause* of something's being F. This gives rise to three possibilities, none of them palatable to the physicalist: first, the cause of the psychical event is a mystery not accessible to scientific inquiry; second, an autonomous psychical science emerges; third, physical theory provides a causal account of the psychical phenomena. The last possibility may be the worst, from the physicalist point of view: given the irreducibility of the psychical phenomena, this could only mean that physical theory would lose its *closed* character, by countenancing within its domain irreducibly nonphysical events and properties.

Parallel considerations should motivate the rejection of macrocausation as an irreducible feature of the world. It seems to be a fundamental methodological precept of theoretical physical science that we ought to formulate *microstructural theories* of objects and their properties – that is, to try to understand the behavior and properties of objects and processes in terms of the properties and relationships characterizing their microconstituents. The philosophical supposition that grounds this research strategy seems to be the belief that macroproperties are determined by, or supervenient upon, microproperties. This Democritean doctrine of mereological supervenience, or microdeterminism, forms the metaphysical backbone of the method of microreduction,[6] somewhat in the same way that the prin-

5 For example, see J. J. C. Smart, "Sensations and Brain Processes," *Philosophical Review* 68 (1958): 141–56.
6 The thesis of mereological supervenience itself need not carry a commitment to atomism.

96

ciple of causal determinism constitutes the objective basis of the method of causal explanation. (I shall return to these themes below.)

In this global microdeterministic picture there is no place for irreducible macrocausal relations. We expect any causal relation between two macroevents (x's being F and y's being G, where F and G are macroproperties) to be microreductively explainable in terms of more fundamental causal processes, like any other facts involving macroproperties and events. If the causal relation is backed up by a law relating F and G, we would expect this macrolaw to be microreducible. A standard example: the rising temperature of a gas confined within a rigid chamber causes its pressure to rise. This macrocausal relation is subsumed under a macrolaw (the gas law), which in turn is microreduced by the kinetic theory of gases. This explains, and reduces, the macrocausal relation. If the causal relation is at bottom just some sort of counterfactual dependency, then the macrocounterfactual "If x had not been F, y would not have been G" should be grounded in some lawlike connection involving microproperties associated with x and y in relation to F and G; or else, there should be some more basic counterfactual dependencies involving microconstituents of x and y that can explain the counterfactual dependency between F and G. It would be difficult to believe that this macrocounterfactual is a fundamental and irreducible fact about the world. At least, that should be our attitude if we accept the universal thesis of mereological supervenience and the validity of microreductive research strategy.

What is the general form of the reduction of a macrocausal relation to a microcausal process? The following model is attractively simple: if the macrocausal relation to be reduced is one from an instance of property F to an instance of property G, we need to correlate F with some microproperty m(F), and also G with m(G), and then show that m(F) and m(G) are appropriately causally connected. Showing the latter may take the form of exhibiting a precise law that connects the two microproperties, or a causal mechanism whereby an instance of F leads to an instance of G. How is the correlation between F and m(F) to be understood? The strongest claim defended by some philosophers is that F and m(F) are one and the same property.[7] The thought is that such property identities are necessary for the required microreduction to go through. Taking this identity approach, however, would force a reconstrual of the notions of microproperty and macroproperty; how could one and the same property

7 There is a large literature on this and related issues concerning microreduction; see, e.g., Lawrence Sklar, "Types of Inter-Theoretic Reduction," *British Journal for the Philosophy of Science* 18 (1967): 109–24; Robert L. Causey, *Unity of Science* (Dordrecht, 1977).

be both a microproperty and a macroproperty? But a more serious problem is this: in the given instance under consideration, the macroproperty may be "realized" or "grounded" in m(F), but in another instance F may be realized or grounded in a different microproperty m*(F), and there may be many other microproperties that can realize F, in that if anything has one of them, then necessarily it also exhibits F as a result. And it may well be that from the explanatory-causal point of view, the possibly infinite disjunction of these underlying microproperties could hardly be considered as a unitary property suitable as a reductive base.

The foregoing is a point often made in connection with the mind–body problem and used sometimes to support the "functionalist" view of the mental.[8] The multiple realizability of a state relative to a more basic level of analysis, or a richer descriptive vocabulary, appears to hold, with equal plausibility, for macrophysical characteristics in relation to microphysical properties and processes; perhaps this is a pervasive feature of mereological reduction. For these reasons, among others, I suggest the use of the concept of *supervenience*, which allows for the possibility of *alternative supervenience bases* for a given supervenient property, as particularly well suited for the purposes on hand. The core idea of supervenience as a relation between two families of properties is that the supervenient properties are in some sense *determined by*, or *dependent on*, the properties on which they supervene. More formally, *the supervenience of a family A of properties on another family B* can be explained as follows: necessarily, for any property F in A, if any object x has F, then there exists a property G in B such that x has G, and necessarily anything having G has F.[9] When properties F and G are related as specified in the definition, we may say that F is *supervenient* on G, and that G is a *supervenience base* of F. On this account, it is clear that a property in the supervenient family can have multiple supervenience bases: an object x has F, and for x the supervenience base of F is G; however, another object y that also has F does not have G, but rather has G*, as *its* supervenience base for F; and so on. Thus, if we think of macroproperties as supervenient on microproperties, the account allows for a given macroproperty F to be supervenient on a number of distinct microproperties; that is, an object has a certain macro-

---

8 See, e.g., Hilary Putnam, "The Nature of Mental States," and Ned Block and J. A. Fodor, "What Psychological States Are Not," both in *Readings in Philosophy of Psychology*, vol. 1, edited by Ned Block (Cambridge, Mass., 1980).

9 This corresponds to "strong supervenience" as characterized in my "Concepts of Supervenience," Essay 4 of this volume; for a general discussion of supervenience see also my "Supervenience and Nomological Incommensurables," *American Philosophical Quarterly* 15 (1978): 149–56, and Essay 8 of this volume.

property (e.g., fragility) in virtue of having a certain microproperty (e.g., a certain crystalline structure) on which the macroproperty supervenes; another object has the same macroproperty in virtue of having a different microproperty (another kind of crystalline structure); and so on.

The notion of *event supervenience* is easily explained on the basis of property supervenience: an event, x's having F, supervenes on the event, x's having G, just in case x has G and G is a supervenience base of F.

So the general schema for reducing a macrocausal relation between two events, x's having F and y's having G, where F and G are macroproperties, is this: x's having F supervenes on x's having m(F), y's having G supervenes on y's having m(G), where m(F) and m(G) are microproperties relative to F and G, and there is an appropriate causal connection between x's having m(F) and y's having m(G).

Any causal relation conforming to the pattern set forth above will be called a "supervenient causal relation." For the pattern can be taken to show the causal relation itself to be supervenient upon an underlying causal process through the supervenience of its relata upon the events involved in the underlying process.

I have left the causal relation between the two microevents unspecified; for it is not part of my present aim to advocate a particular analysis of causation. Generally, however, we would expect it to be mediated by laws, whether deterministic or statistical, and in favorable cases we may even have an account in terms of a mechanism by which one microstate evolves into another. But the kind of position I want to advocate here concerning macrocausation is largely independent of the particular views concerning the analysis of causation. Moreover, I do not wish to tie the fate of my general views about macrocausation too closely to the fate of my proposal regarding a proper construal of the relation between macroproperties and the microproperties on which they "depend." Although the use of mereological supervenience is an integral part of the total account being sketched here, the main points of the general picture of macrocausation I am advancing are independent of the question of what particular account is to be accepted for the macro–micro relation. What are these points? There are two: (1) macrocausal relations should be viewed as in general reducible to microcausal relations, and (2) the mechanism of the reduction involves identifying the microstates on which the macrostates in question depend, or with which they are correlated, and showing that a proper causal relation obtains for these microstates. Thus, to affirm (1) is to accept the view that macrocausation is to be viewed as epiphenomenal causation. To affirm that macrocausation is supervenient causation is to accept a particular account of the mechanism of reduction referred to in (2).

The sort of account I have given should be found attractive by those philosophers who believe that precise laws are rare – perhaps nonexistent – for macroproperties and states, at least those that are routinely referred to in ordinary causal talk, and that they must be "redescribed" at a more basic level before precise laws could be brought to bear on them.[10] My account in essence adds two things to this view: first, that *whether or not* there are macro-lawlike connections, macrocausal relations ought to be viewed as reducible to microcausal relations, and second, that what sanctions a given microredescription of a macrostate can be taken as a supervenience relation – that is to say, the relation between a macrodescription and a corresponding microredescription can be understood in terms of supervenience.

The broad metaphysical conviction that underlies these proposals is the belief that ultimately the world – at least, the physical world – is the way it is because the microworld is the way it is – because there are so many of just these sorts of microentities (elementary particles, atoms, or what not), and they behave in accordance with just these laws. As Terence Horgan has put it, worlds that are microphysically identical are one and the same world.[11] Even those who would reject this universal thesis of microdeterminism might find the following more restricted thesis plausible: worlds that are microphysically identical are one world from the physical point of view. This doctrine urges us to see macrocausal relations as emerging out of properties and relations holding for microentities, and this naturally leads to a search of microreductive accounts of macrocausal relations as well as other macroproperties, states, and facts. In fact, causal relations pervade our very conceptions of physical properties, states, and events (consider, for example, "heat," "magnetic," "gene"), and the reduction of causal relations, which often takes the form of exhibiting the micromechanisms underlying macrocausal relations, is probably the most important part of microreductive research. Causal relations that resist microreduction must be considered "causal danglers," which, like the notorious "nomological danglers," are an acute embarrassment to the physicalist view of the world.

10 For an influential view of this kind see Donald Davidson, "Causal Relations," *Journal of Philosophy* 64 (1967): 691–703.
11 See Terence Horgan, "Supervenience and Microphysics," *Pacific Philosophical Quarterly* 63 (1982): 29–43; see also David Lewis, "New Work for a Theory of Universals," *Australasian Journal of Philosophy* 61 (1983): 343–77.

There is ample evidence that the method of microreduction has been extremely successful in modern science, and it seems evident that much of the reduction that has been accomplished involves the reduction of macrocausal laws and relations.[12] The reduction of gas laws within the kinetic theory of gases is of course a case in point; such examples are legion. Given our interest in identifying and understanding causal connections, it is not surprising that a predominant part of the reductive efforts in scientific research is directed toward the microreduction of macrocausal laws and relations. These last few remarks constitute the promised second prong of my defense of the claim that macrocausation ought to be viewed as epiphenomenal causation – and, more specifically, as supervenient causation.

3. MEREOLOGICAL SUPERVENIENCE AND MICRODETERMINISM

The foregoing discussion moved fairly freely among such doctrines and concepts as microreduction, microexplanation, mereological supervenience, and microdeterminism, and I think it may be helpful to set forth their relationships more precisely. First of all, I am taking mereological supervenience and microdeterminism as a thesis concerning the objective features of the world – a metaphysical doctrine – roughly, as I said, to the effect that the macroworld is the way it is because the microworld is the way it is. The two doctrines can of course be sharpened and separated from each other. Mereological supervenience is usefully taken to be a general thesis affirming the supervenience of the characteristics of wholes on the properties and relationships characterizing their proper parts. Here, "characteristics" is understood to include relations, such as causal relations, among wholes. Mereological supervenience (in the sense of supervenience explained in the preceding section) requires that each macrocharacteristic be grounded in some specific microcharacteristics, and in this way it goes beyond the less specific thesis, earlier mentioned, that worlds that are microphysically identical are one and the same (physical) world. It may be convenient to reserve the term "microdeterminism" for this less specific thesis. It is plausible to think that under some reasonable assumptions, mereological supervenience as applied to the physical world

12 See the somewhat dated but still useful "Unity of Science as a Working Hypothesis" by Paul Oppenheim and Hilary Putnam, in *Minnesota Studies in the Philosophy of Science*, vol. 2, edited by Herbert Feigl et al. (Minneapolis, 1958).

entails microdeterminism; I am inclined to believe that, again under some reasonable assumptions, the converse entailment also holds.

In any event, it is useful to think of mereological supervenience and microdeterminism as constituting the metaphysical basis of the method of microreduction and microexplanation. By this I mean that the metaphysical doctrine rationalizes our microreductive proclivities by legitimatizing microreduction as a paradigm of scientific understanding and helping to explain why the microreductive method works as well as it does. Underlying this remark is the view that explanatory or reductive connections, as essentially epistemological connections, must themselves be grounded in the objective determinative connections holding for the events in the world. The root idea of causal determinism is the belief that the existence and properties of an event are determined by its temporally antecedent conditions. The metaphysical thesis of causal determinism can be thought of as the objective basis of the method of causal explanation – the method of seeking "laws of succession" and formulating explanations of events in terms of their antecedent conditions. Mereological supervenience views the world as determined along the part–whole dimension, whereas the causal determinism views it as determined along the temporal dimension; they respectively provide a metaphysical basis for the method of microreduction and that of causal explanation.

These are rather speculative and bald remarks; they are intended only to give a rough picture of the metaphysical terrain within which my more specific remarks concerning macrocausal relations can be located.

4. MENTAL CAUSATION AS SUPERVENIENT CAUSATION

To say that the causal relation between two macroevents is a case of epiphenomenal causation is not to be understood to mean that the relation is illusory or unreal. In this respect, Jonathan Edwards's case of mirror images, Salmon's moving spot of light, and the case of successive symptoms of a disease differ from our central cases of macrocausal relations. For in those cases, the causal relations are indeed only apparent: although the events are causally *related* in a broad sense, there is no direct causal relation *from* one event *to* the other – that is to say, one event is not the cause of the other. On the other hand, the causal relation between rising temperatures and increasing pressures of gases is no less "real" for being microreducible. To take microreducibility as impugning the reality of what is being reduced would make all of our observable world unreal.

However, one reason for bundling the two types of cases together under "epiphenomenal causation" is the existence of another sense of "real" in which reduction does make what is reduced "less real," a sense in which modern physics is sometimes thought to have shown the unreality of ordinary material objects or a sense in which secondary qualities are sometimes thought to be "less real" than primary qualities. As I mentioned earlier, reducibility is often taken to imply eliminability; but this is a complex and unfruitful question to pursue here. There is, however, another more concrete reason for viewing these two kinds of cases under the same rubric; in both there is present an *apparent* causal relation that is explained, or explained away, at a more fundamental level. The difference between the two cases is this: macrocausal relations are *supervenient causal relations* – supervenient upon microcausal relations – whereas cases like Edwards's mirror images are not. This can be seen by reflecting on the fact that in a perfectly straightforward sense, mirror images, symptoms of a disease, and so on are causal effects of the underlying processes – they are not mereologically supervenient upon those processes. This is the theoretical difference between the two cases: some epiphenomenal causal relations are supervenient causal relations, and these are among the ones that are "real"; there are also cases of epiphenomenal causation that do not involve direct causal connections, and these include ones in which the events involved are successive causal effects of some underlying process.

What of causal relations involving mental events? Consider a typical case in which we would say a mental event causes a physical event: a sharp pain in my thumb causes a jerky withdrawal of my hand. It is hardly conceivable that the pain sensation qua mental event acts directly on the muscles of my arm, causing them to contract. I assume we have by now a fairly detailed story of what goes on at the physiological level when a limb movement takes place, and no amount of intuitive conviction or philosophical argument about the reality of psychophysical causation is going to preempt that story. If the pain is to play a causal role in the withdrawal of my hand, it must do so by somehow *making use of* the usual physiological causal path to this bodily event; it looks as though the causal path from the pain to the limb motion must *merge* with the physiological path at a certain point. There cannot be two independent, separate causal paths to the limb motion. But at what point does the mental causal path from the pain "merge" with the physiological path? If there is such a point, that must be where psychophysical causal action takes place. The trouble, of course, is that it is difficult to conceive the possibility of some nonphysical event causally influencing the course of physical processes.[13] Apart from the sheer impossibility of coherently imagining the details of what might have to be the case if some nonphysical agent is going to affect the course of purely physical events, there is a deeper problem that any such nonphysical intervention in a physical system would jeopardize the closed character of physical theory. It would force us to accept a conception of the physical in which to give a causal account of, say, the motion of a physical particle, it is sometimes necessary to go outside the physical system and appeal to some nonphysical agency and invoke some irreducible psychophysical law. Many will find this just not credible.

The difficulty of accounting for the possibility of psychophysical causation is simply resolved if one is willing to accept psychophysical identity: the pain *is* in fact a certain neural state, and the problem of accounting for the psychophysical causal relation is nothing but that of accounting for the causal relation between two physical states. On the other hand, if, for various reasons, one is averse to accepting a straightforward identity thesis, as many philosophers are, then the problem of accounting for psychophysical causation confronts us as a difficult problem, indeed.[14] The classical form of epiphenomenalism fails to provide a satisfactory solution, for it denies that mental-to-physical causal action ever takes place: mental phenomena are totally causally inert. And this is what many thinkers find so difficult to accept. If our reasons and desires have no causal efficacy at all in influencing our bodily actions, then perhaps no one has ever performed a single intentional action![15]

It seems to me that what is being advocated as "new" epiphenomenalism is not much help either. According to Keith Campbell, mental states are in fact brain states, but they have residual irreducible phenomenal properties as well; however, these phenomenal properties are causally impotent.[16] This position is akin to one of the two characterizations of epiphenomenalism offered by C. D. Broad some decades ago:

13 For an effective description of the difficulty see Richard Taylor, *Metaphysics,* 3d ed. (Englewood Cliffs, N.J., 1983), chap. 3.
14 For some arguments against the identity thesis see Putnam, "The Nature of Mental States"; Saul Kripke, *Naming and Necessity* (Cambridge, Mass., 1980), 144–55. For discussions of the problem of psychophysical causation see, e.g., J. L. Mackie, "Mind, Brain, and Causation," *Midwest Studies in Philosophy* 4 (1979): 19–30; and my "Causality, Identity and Supervenience in the Mind–Body Problem," *Midwest Studies in Philosophy* 4 (1979): 31–49.
15 See, e.g., Norman Malcolm, "The Conceivability of Mechanism," *Philosophical Review* 77 (1968): 45–72.
16 *Body and Mind* (New York, 1970), chap. 6.

Epiphenomenalism may be taken to assert one of two things. (a) That certain events which have physiological characteristics have *also* mental characteristics, and that no events which lack physiological characteristics have mental characteristics. That many events which have physiological characteristics are not known to have mental characteristics. And that an event which has mental characteristics never causes another event in virtue of its mental characteristics, but only in virtue of its physiological characteristics. Or (b) that no event has both mental and physiological characteristics; but that the complete cause of any event which has mental characteristics is an event or set of events which has physiological characteristics. And that no event which has mental characteristics is a cause-factor in the causation of any other event whatever, whether mental or physiological.[17]

The only significant difference between Broad's (a) and Campbell's epiphenomenalism seems to be that Broad's epiphenomenalism is formulated for all *mental* characteristics, presumably including intentional states such as belief and desire as well as phenomenal states, whereas Campbell is happy to take a straight physicalist approach with regard to mental states not involving phenomenal qualia. It is interesting to note that some versions of the currently popular "token identity" thesis are also strikingly similar to Broad's epiphenomenalism. Consider, for example, the influential "anomalous monism" of Donald Davidson.[18] According to this account, there are no type–type correlations between the mental and the physical; however, each individual mental event is in fact a physical event in the following sense: any event that has a mental description has also a physical description. Further, it is only under its physical description that a mental event can be seen to enter into a causal relation with a physical event (or any other event) by being subsumed under a causal law. If we read "mental characteristic" for "mental description" and "physiological characteristic" for "physical description," then something very much like Broad's (a) above emerges from Davidson's anomalous monism.

Broad's epiphenomenalism, however, did not satisfy philosophers who looked for a place for our commonsense conviction in the reality of psychophysical causation. Thus, William Kneale refers to "the great paradox of epiphenomenalism," which arises from "the suggestion that we are necessarily mistaken in all our ordinary thought about human action."[19]

---

17 *The Mind and Its Place in Nature* (London, 1925), 472.
18 In "Mental Events," reprinted in Davidson, *Essays on Actions and Events* (New York, 1980).
19 William Kneale, "Broad on Mental Events and Epiphenomenalism," in *The Philosophy of C. D. Broad,* edited by P. A. Schlipp (New York, 1959), 453. See also Jerome A. Shaffer, *Philosophy of Mind* (Englewood Cliffs, N.J., 1968), 68–71; Taylor, *Metaphysics,* chap. 4.

It seems to me that, for similar reasons, Davidson's anomalous monism fails to do full justice to psychophysical causation – that is, it fails to provide an account of psychophysical causation in which the mental *qua mental* has any real causal role to play. Consider Davidson's account: whether or not a given event has a mental description (optional reading: whether it has a mental characteristic) seems entirely irrelevant to what causal relations it enters into. Its causal powers are wholly determined by the physical description or characteristic that holds for it; for it is under its physical description that it may be subsumed under a causal law. And Davidson explicitly denies any possibility of a nomological connection between an event's mental description and its physical description that could bring the mental into the causal picture.[20]

The delicate task is to find an account that will give the mental a substantial enough causal role to let us avoid "the great paradox of epiphenomenalism" without infringing upon the closedness of physical causal systems. I suggest that we view psychophysical causal relations – in fact, all causal relations involving psychological events – as epiphenomenal supervenient causal relations. More specifically, when a mental event M causes a physical event P, this is so because M is supervenient upon a physical event, P*, and P* causes P. This latter may itself be a supervenient causal relation, but that is no matter: what is important is that, at some point, purely physical causal processes take over. Similarly, when mental event M causes another mental event M*, this is so because M supervenes on a physical state P, and similarly M* on P*, and P causes P*.

Thus, if a pain causes the sensation of fear an instant later, this account tells the following story: the pain is supervenient on a brain state, this brain state causes another appropriate brain state, and given this second brain state, the fear sensation must occur, for it is supervenient upon that brain state. I think this is a plausible picture that, among other things, nicely accounts for the temporal gaps and discontinuities in the series of causally related mental events. Returning to the case of a pain causing a hand to withdraw, we should note that, on the present account, no causal path from the pain "merges" with the physiological causal chain at any point. For there is no separate path from the pain to the limb withdrawal; there is only one causal path in this situation, namely the one from the neural state upon which the pain supervenes to the movement of the hand.

20 See his "Mental Events" for an extended argument against psychophysical lawlike connections. I give an analysis, and a partial defense, of Davidson's arguments in "Psychophysical Laws," Essay 11 of this volume.

Does this proposal satisfy the desiderata we set for an adequate account of psychophysical causation? It would be foolish to pretend that the proposed account accords to the mental the full causal potency we accord to fundamental physical processes. On the other hand, it does not treat mental phenomena as causally inert epiphenomena; nor does it reduce mental causation to the status of a mere chimera. Mental causation does take place; it is only that it is epiphenomenal causation, that is, a causal relation that is reducible to, or explainable by, the causal processes taking place at a more basic physical level. And this, according to the present account, is also precisely what happens with macrophysical causation relations. *Epiphenomenal causal relations involving psychological events, therefore, are no less real or substantial than those involving macrophysical events. They are both supervenient causal relations.* It seems to me that this is sufficient to redeem the causal powers we ordinarily attribute to mental events. Does the account meet the other desideratum of respecting the closed character of physical theory? It evidently does; for supervenient epiphenomenal causation does not place the supervenient events at the level of the underlying causal processes to which it is reduced. Mental events do not become part of the fundamental physical causal chains any more than macrophysical events become part of the microphysical causal chains that underlie them.

One remaining question is whether psychological events do supervene on physical events and processes. If psychological states are conceived as some sort of inner theoretical states posited to explain the observable behavior of organisms, there is little doubt that they will be supervenient on physical states.[21] However, there are serious questions as to whether that is a satisfactory conception of the mental; and I believe these questions lead to a serious doubt as to whether *intentional* mental states, namely those with propositional content such as beliefs and desires, are determined wholly by the physical details of the organism or even by the total physical environment that includes the organism. However, this need not be taken as casting doubt on the account of psychological causation offered here; I think we may more appropriately take it as an occasion for reconsidering whether, and in what way, intentional psychological states enter into causal relations – especially with physical events. I think that the two questions, whether intentional psychological states are supervenient on the physical and whether they enter into *law-based* causal relations with physical processes, are arguably equivalent questions. Psycho-

21 For details see my "Psychophysical Supervenience," Essay 10 of this volume.

physical supervenience is a good deal more plausible, I believe, with regard to phenomenal mental states, and I am prepared to let the account of psychological causation proposed here stand for all psychological events and states that are physically supervenient.

7

Supervenience for multiple domains

1. INTRODUCTION

The leading idea in the notion of "supervenience" is commonly explained this way: things that are indiscernible in respect of properties of
one kind (the "base" or "subvenient" properties) are indiscernible in respect of properties of another kind (the "supervenient" properties).[1] If
moral properties are taken as supervenient properties and descriptive or
naturalistic properties are taken as base properties, we have the doctrine
of moral supervenience: the moral properties of persons, acts, and other
objects supervene on their descriptive or naturalistic properties. Similarly,
by taking mental properties as supervenient properties and physical properties as the base, we can formulate the doctrine of psychophysical supervenience: the psychological features of persons, organisms, etc., supervene on their physical characteristics.

Another familiar explanation of the idea goes like this: no difference in
properties of one kind without a difference in properties of a second
kind.[2] Thus, as we say, there can be no difference in moral properties
unless there is some difference in descriptive, or nonmoral, properties. In
both these initial characterizations, the things that have the supervenient
properties are assumed to be also the things that have the base properties.
If St. Francis is a good person, we say, then anyone who has all the naturalistic properties that St. Francis has must also be a good person; this
makes St. Francis and others the subjects of both moral and naturalistic
properties. Again, when we say that you and your "physical duplicate"

My thanks to Ernest Sosa and James Van Cleve for helpful comments.
1 For general discussions of supervenience and further references see, e.g., Paul Teller, "A
  Poor Man's Guide to Supervenience and Determination," *Southern Journal of Philosophy* 22
  (1984). The Spindel Conference Supplement: pp. 137–62; and my "Concepts of Supervenience," Essay 4 of this volume.
2 See David Lewis, "New Work for a Theory of Universals," *Australasian Journal of Philosophy* 61 (1983): 343–77, esp. 361–64.

would also be "psychological duplicates" of each other, we are assuming that you and your duplicate are the subjects of both physical and psychological properties. "Things" can of course be of many different sorts: you and St. Francis are persons, or biological organisms. But they could be objects of any kind, events, states, or even "worlds." For example, Donald Davidson explains psychophysical supervenience this way: "such supervenience might be taken to mean that there cannot be two *events* alike in all physical respects but differing in some mental respects. . . ."[3] This characterization assumes that events can have both physical and psychological characteristics. Some philosophers have chosen to explain a physicalist supervenience thesis in terms of *worlds,* like this: No two worlds can be exactly alike in all physical features and yet be different in some nonphysical feature.[4] And there is no reason why the "things" involved in a claim of supervenience cannot be abstract objects: numbers, properties, and the like.

In any case, the point to note is that our rough characterization of supervenience posits a *single fixed domain* of individuals, of whatever kind, with respect to which one set of properties is said to be supervenient on another set of properties. This is a feature preserved in some formal accounts of supervenience that have been offered. For example, what I have called "weak supervenience" is explained as follows (here and elsewhere A and B are nonempty sets of properties and D is a nonempty set of individuals):

(WS) A *weakly supervenes* on B with respect to domain D just in case, for any x and y in D and for any possible world w, if x and y are B-indiscernible (that is, indiscernible in respect of properties in B) in w, they are A-indiscernible in w.

"Strong supervenience," a stronger relation as its name suggests, is similarly explained, the difference being that it permits comparison of individuals as they are in different worlds. It will be useful to set down this definition as well, since these two supervenience relations will provide points of reference for others to be discussed.

---

3 "Mental Events," in his *Essays on Actions and Events* (Oxford and New York: Oxford University Press, 1980), p. 214. Italics added. Davidson goes on to give a second characterization of supervenience, this time in terms of "objects": ". . . or that an object cannot alter in some mental respect without altering in some physical respect." Ibid.

4 See, e.g., Terence Horgan, "Supervenience and Microphysics," *Pacific Philosophical Quarterly* 63 (1982): 29–43; John Haugeland, "Weak Supervenience," *American Philosophical Quarterly* 19 (1982): 93–103; Lewis, "New Work for a Theory of Universals."

(SS) A *strongly supervenes* on B with respect to domain D just in case for any x and y in D, and any worlds w and w*, if x in w is B-indiscernible from y in w*, then x in w is A-indiscernible from y in w*.

Often the reference to a domain is omitted, either for simplicity or because a universal domain is tacitly assumed; I have here explicitly framed the definitions relative to a domain to highlight this common feature: both supervenient and base properties are had by the same individuals.

John Haugeland has complained about just this aspect of these conceptions of supervenience: he says of Davidson's account of supervenience quoted above that "the problem with this passage as it stands is that, in characterizing supervenience, it takes the token–identity thesis for granted. Thus, it says, if two events are alike physically, then *they* (the *very same* two events) cannot differ mentally."[5] And with respect to my (WS) above, Haugeland says: "The properties M [supervenient properties] and N [base properties] are understood to be properties of the *same individual,* from the same domain D – which is all the token-identity thesis requires."[6] Haugeland's thought is this: if something like (WS) is understood as a statement of psychophysical supervenience with A as the set of psychological properties, B as a set of physical properties, and domain D as consisting of *events,* then the "token–identity" of psychological events with physical events has already been presupposed, quite independently of any special relationships between A and B. For, presumably, an event is a "psychological event" just in case it has some psychological property (or some psychological description is true of it), and similarly for a "physical event." And this, we must grant, is a fair reading of "mental event" and "physical event," at least for Davidson.[7]

Haugeland is right about this,[8] at least as far as the point pertains to Davidson's statement, quoted above, of psychophysical supervenience; he is also right about my (WS) *if* the domain is taken as a domain of *concrete events*. But there is no need for this construal of the domain; it is not only possible but more natural to think of the domain as consisting of persons or biological organisms (or material objects in general) and construe psychological and physical properties as properties of these substantival objects rather than of events. This will yield a significant thesis of psychophysical supervenience which does not presuppose token-identities between psychological and physical events. Moreover, even about David-

5 "Weak Supervenience," p. 96.   6 Ibid.   7 "Mental Events," pp. 211, 224.
8 With some minor provisos not worth worrying about, such as that there are at least two mental events differing in some mental respects.

son there is the following to be said: the token-identity presupposed by Davidson's formulation of supervenience is a thesis of no great importance or interest, a by-product of an optional ontological scheme assumed for formulating the supervenience thesis.[9] And Davidson's supervenience does involve a substantive thesis of psychophysical dependence, namely that psychological properties of events are determined by, or dependent on, their physical properties. The bare token-identity of the "subjects" of these properties, namely, events, is in itself not a significant physicalist thesis about the psychophysical relation.[10]

Be that as it may, Haugeland's point raises an interesting and, I think, important question, which is the main topic of this paper. This is the question of how supervenience can be understood as a relation between two families of properties *each applicable to a distinct domain of individuals.* Consider the radical dual-substance Cartesians: they are likely to take exception to the reading I gave above of (WS) or (SS) in which persons, or human bodies or organisms, are taken to instantiate both physical and psychological characteristics; they will contend that these two classes of properties call for disjoint sets of exemplifiers, that is, material and mental substances. For the Cartesians, my reading begs at least a significant part of the question about the mind–body relation, just as for Haugeland, Davidson begs the question of token-identity of mental and physical events. But, in spite of their dual-substance ontology, some of these Cartesians may be prepared to hold that what happens in the realm of souls is entirely dependent on what happens in the realm of bodies. We thus face the task of making sense of a supervenience relation involving two domains of individuals, something that could suit the needs of these improbable but not unintelligible Cartesians (although, as we shall see below, at a deeper level there is reason to question whether such a position ultimately makes sense).

The interest of multiple-domain supervenience can be seen in another

9 As was noted in note 3, Davidson gives a second characterization of supervenience in terms of "objects" rather than events.

10 I elaborate on this point in "Psychophysical Laws," Essay 11 of this volume. Haugeland, at any rate, is interested in finding a physicalism that is even weaker than the token-identity of mental with physical events ("Weak Supervenience," p. 96). Indeed, as he argues, his favored supervenience thesis, which he calls "weak supervenience" (this corresponds to our (GS2) below), does not entail the token-identity thesis. However, it is not clear that it is *strictly weaker* than token-identity, since the latter (in the sense of Davidson's anomalous monism) doesn't seem to entail Haugeland's weak supervenience either. It seems to me that as a doctrine about the mind–body relation Haugeland's "weak supervenience" is a good deal more substantive, and stronger, than mere anomalous monism.

area. One interesting application of the supervenience concept is mereological supervenience, the doctrine that the character of a whole is supervenient on the properties and relationships holding for its parts.[11] This apparently calls for two distinct domains: one domain consisting of wholes and another consisting of their parts. It would be of interest to know how a dependency relation can be formulated across two domains.

To accommodate these and similar cases we will develop two basic schemes of supervenience for multiple domains, along what seem intuitive and natural lines, and consider their relationships to some already familiar supervenience relations. Along the way and in the final section, we will explore some possible applications of the new concepts.

2. SUPERVENIENCE FOR MULTIPLE DOMAINS

Let us consider then two families of properties, A and B, and two domains, D_1 and D_2, over which they are respectively defined. How should we explain the idea that A supervenes on B, relative to the two domains? We can begin, I think, with something like the following as a leading idea: for a supervenience relation to hold in a situation of this kind, the way the supervenient properties are distributed over the members of their domain gets fixed by the way the base (subvenient) properties are distributed over the members of their domain. Let us set this out:

(MS1) $\langle A, D_1 \rangle$ supervenes on $\langle B, D_2 \rangle$ iff every complete distribution of B over D_2 entails a unique complete distribution of A over D_1.

Here and elsewhere D_1 and D_2 are nonempty sets of individuals, and A and B are nonempty sets of properties.[12] By a "complete distribution" of a set of properties over a domain we mean a complete specification, for each individual in the domain and each property in the set, of whether or not the individual has that property. It is of course assumed that the distribution is consistently made; e.g., no object is assigned both red and green.[13] By one distribution "entailing" another we mean that the first necessitates the second – that is, there is no world in which the first distri-

11 See my "Supervenience and Nomological Incommensurables," and Ernest Sosa, "Persons and Other Beings," *Philosophical Perspectives* 1 (1987): 155–88.
12 For some results to be mentioned below these sets must be assumed to be closed under Boolean operations (i.e., conjunction, disjunction, negation, and infinite conjunction and disjunction). See my "Concepts of Supervenience" for more details. For the bulk of this paper the closure property of property sets is not an issue.
13 For simplicity relations are not considered here, but if they are present, we must exclude distributions in which, e.g., R(a,b) and R(b,a) where R is necessarily asymmetric.

bution holds but the second distribution does not. There is a stronger interpretation of "necessitation," which would be appropriate for characterizing the supervenience of the domain D_1 itself – that is, if we want to say, in addition, that the existence of individuals in the supervenient domain is dependent on the existence of the individuals in the base domain. For this stronger notion, we should add something like this: There is no world in which individuals of D_1 exist but in which individuals of D_2 do not.[14] In this paper, we shall work with the weaker notion, assuming that D_1 and D_2 are given at the outset. Thus, the supervenience relation being defined obtains just in case there are no two worlds in which the base properties are distributed over their domain in the same way but in which the supervenient properties are distributed differently over their domain.

Consider again our improbable Cartesian who combines his belief in a realm of souls disjoint from material bodies with the belief that, in spite of their ontological separateness, what goes on with the souls is wholly determined once what goes on in the realm of matter is fixed. This is equivalent to saying that once the distribution of physical properties over the material objects of this world is fixed, that permits but one distribution of mental properties over the souls. Notice, though, that the determination here is holistic; the Cartesian is not saying that how things stand with a given soul is fixed by how things stand with a particular material body, or a particular set of material bodies short of the whole material domain; indeed, we may assume that he is making no assumption whatever as to whether souls are in some way associated, or "coordinated" as we shall be saying, with specific material bodies. Nonetheless, he believes that how things are in the mental realm is wholly fixed by how things stand in the material realm. (We may call this "Cartesian psychophysical supervenience.") I am not saying that this is a plausible position for anyone to hold; it is enough if it is a possible doctrine of psychophysical dependence and (MS1) captures its form. Note that although we have represented our Cartesian as believing that the two domains of individuals are disjoint, and also that the two families of properties are largely disjoint,[15] that is not a requirement of (MS1). That is, (MS1) does not in general require D_1 and D_2 to be distinct, much less disjoint; nor does it require

---

14 I am leaving appropriate quantifications of "individuals of D_1 (D_2)" deliberately vague here.

15 Even the most extreme Cartesian would allow some shared attributes for mental and material substances, e.g., temporal properties and relations; and also there is the technical point that Boolean closure may introduce trivial common properties, e.g., tautological ones.

A and B, the property families, to be distinct. Thus, a more cautious dualist may simply affirm a dependency thesis in the form of (MS1), without assuming that D_1 and D_2 are distinct; he may in fact want to leave open the possibility that D_1 is included in D_2. I think (MS1) as it stands has the level of generality we want in our broad initial characterization of multiple-domain supervenience.

But before we can move on, one aspect of (MS1) requires further clarification; as we shall see, the point to be discussed has implications for other formulations of supervenience. It concerns the question what it is for a set of properties to be distributed in "the same way" over a set of individuals. Consider two properties, F and G, and two individuals, a and b. To make the situation concrete, think of a and b as two Cartesian souls, F as thinking and G as hoping (you can supply propositional content if you wish). Are we to take the following distributions as one or two?

$$d_1: Fa, -Ga, -Fb, Gb$$
$$d_2: -Fa, Ga, Fb, -Gb$$

Thus, in d_1, a thinks but does not hope, and b does not think but hopes; in d_2, things are reversed – a does not think but hopes, and b thinks but does not hope. Both distributions have this common feature: there are two Cartesian souls, one of which thinks but does not hope and the other of which hopes but does not think.

If we consider d_1 and d_2 to be two different distributions, the subvenient distributions (for the illustrative example, distributions of physical properties over physical individuals) must be sensitive to their difference. Thus, suppose there are three physical individuals, x, y, and z, and a set of physical properties $p_1, \ldots, p_n$. Consider the following physical distribution:

$$e_1: P_j x, P_k y, P_l z,$$

where the P's are maximal consistent properties constructible from the $p_1, \ldots, p_n$. Let us suppose that e_1 entails neither d_1 nor d_2, but does entail their disjunction; that is to say, in every world in which e_1 is realized, either d_1 or d_2 is realized, and in some worlds e_1 and d_1 are realized together and in others e_1 and d_2 are realized together. If this were the case, would it defeat – should it be allowed to defeat – the supervenience, on the model of (MS1), of F and G on physical properties $p_1, \ldots, p_n$? If d_1 and d_2 are counted as two different distributions, this would be a defeater for the supervenience claim.

Before we can consider that question, we need to see what the alterna-

115

tive is. Notice that d_1 and d_2 are each obtainable from the other by a permutation of individuals a and b; in this sense, they can be said to be "isomorphic" to each other, and the principle of distribution individuation according to which d_1 and d_2 count as a single distribution can be called "structure-specific." In contrast, the individuation principle that counts d_1 and d_2 as distinct may be called "individual-specific."

It is clear that under structure-specific individuation we no longer have here a defeater for supervenience in the manner of (MS1). Of course under the coarser structure-specific individuation, e_1 counts as the same physical distribution as, e.g.:

$$e_2: P_k x, P_j y, P_l z,$$

and supervenience requires that whenever e_2 and others that are isomorphic to it are realized, d_1 or d_2 must be realized. But the fact remains that what is a counterexample against (MS1) under individual-specific individuation of distributions is not one against (MS1) under isomorphic individuation. Generally, the more finely we individuate distributions for the supervenient domain the more difficult it is for supervenience to obtain; and, correlatively, the more finely we individuate distributions for the base domain the easier it is for supervenience to obtain. However, the effects of the finer individuation under the individual-specific principle for the supervenient domain are not exactly offset by the application of the same individuation principle to the base domain. The two individuation principles give us inequivalent readings of (MS1). As we just saw, (MS1) under isomorphic individuation of distribution does not imply (MS1) under individual-specific individuation.

Does the converse implication obtain? That is, if (MS1) holds under individual-specific distribution individuation, does it hold also under isomorphic individuation? The answer is again in the negative. Consider again physical distributions e_1 and e_2 above: we can suppose that:

e_1 entails d_3: Fa, Ga, Fb, Gb
e_2 entails d_4: Fa, Ga, $-$Fb, $-$Gb

This supposition is consistent with the supervenience relation defined by (MS1) under individual-specific individuation of distributions, but not under structure-specific individuation. For, under the structural individuation principle, e_1 and e_2 are isomorphic and so count as a single distribution, whereas d_3 and d_4 are not isomorphic and therefore count as distinct. So the structure-specific distribution to which e_1 and e_2 correspond does not entail a unique structure-specific distribution for the supervenient

116

domain, and therefore, this is a counterexample to (MS1) under structure-specific individuation of distributions.

Hence, the converse entailment does not hold either: (MS1) under individual-specific individuation of distributions does not entail (MS1) under the structure-specific individuation. So we face the obvious question: Which individuation principle is the appropriate one for a supervenience relation like (MS1)?

This question gives rise to some quite complex issues that go beyond the scope of this paper; for now it will suffice to view the two modes of individuation as yielding two supervenience relations under (MS1), perhaps each appropriate to different cases of application. As we shall see below, similar questions arise in other contexts as well.

3. REMARKS ON GLOBAL SUPERVENIENCE

It will not have escaped notice that multiple-domain supervenience looks much like what has been called "global" supervenience, popular with some writers in philosophy of mind, understood as follows:

(GS1) Set A of properties *globally supervenes* on set B of properties just in case there are no two worlds indiscernible in B and yet discernible in A.

For suppose that mental and material substances are all the individuals, and that this domain of individuals is fixed for all possible worlds; assume further that mental and material properties are all the properties relevant to discriminating one world from another – that is, they are all the descriptive properties.[16] It is clear then that what we called "Cartesian supervenience" can also be expressed in the form of "global supervenience," since, given the fixed domain, the discernibility of worlds will depend solely on how the given properties are distributed over the individuals.

Some formulations of global psychophysical supervenience do not specifically speak of supervenience of *properties,* but instead speak broadly of the supervenience of "the mental" on "the physical," and advert to indiscernibility in physical or psychological "respects" or "features." But in most cases the talk of features or respects seems straightforwardly equivalent to, or explainable in terms of, talk of properties, and (GS1) as stated seems adequate to capture the form of these supervenience theses.

16 We need not suppose mental and physical properties in this context are mutually exclusive; mental properties must include all the properties attributable to mental entities, including those that can belong to physical entities as well, e.g., temporal properties and relations.

117

Some writers individuate worlds in terms of what *truths* (or *states of affairs*) hold in them, explaining supervenience something like this:

(GS2) A *globally supervenes* on B just in case there are no two worlds indiscernible in respect of *truths* of kind B and yet discernible in respect of *truths* of kind A.[17]

But this is an equivalent idea since we may assume that all the truths holding in a world are fixed, in the standard ways, by the "singular truths" that hold in it, that is, the distribution of the available properties over the individuals.[18]

Our earlier discussion of the individuation of distributions is obviously relevant to global supervenience, whether it is understood in terms of indiscernibility with respect to properties of a certain sort or with respect to "truths" of a certain sort. For example, what Haugeland calls "weak supervenience" of the mental on the physical comes to this: There are no two worlds in which the same physical sentences, but not the same psychological sentences, are true. We now see that singular sentences may have to be excluded from consideration – especially in view of the fact that general global supervenience permits variable domains of individuals so that a pair of worlds may have no individuals in common.[19] In any event, let us note the following about the relationship between multiple-domain and global supervenience: multiple-domain supervenience as defined by (MS1) is, in essence, equivalent to global supervenience with a fixed domain of individuals which is the union of the two domains involved. Thus, multiple-domain supervenience in the form of (MS1) is subsumable under global supervenience in the form of (GS1), though it is, I think, a structurally interesting special case worth recognition.

As we just noted, indiscernibility for worlds is more difficult to characterize if we take global supervenience in full generality, allowing domains of individuals to vary from world to world. Consider for example two worlds with disjoint domains of individuals. What is it to say that two

17 This corresponds to Haugeland's "weak supervenience" (not to be confused with weak supervenience defined by (WS)) in his "Weak Supervenience," p. 97.

18 We disregard modal truths which would require attending to truths in other worlds. Philosophers who favor something like (GS2) appear in general not to include modal truths among the truths considered.

19 Haugeland thinks that the source of the trouble with Davidson's supervenience and my (SS) and (WS) is their "reference to individuals"; but that doesn't seem right in view of the fact that something like (MS1), which does refer to individuals in Haugeland's sense, takes care of his worries about presupposing token-identity. In his own characterization of supervenience, however, he simply speaks sentences in general, without excluding singular sentences.

such worlds are indiscernible in respect of a certain set of properties, say, physical properties? Clearly, in evaluating these worlds for indiscernibility we must consider only general truths, disregarding singular truths altogether; for otherwise, no two such worlds would be indiscernible, and this means that the existence of the following two worlds would not violate psychophysical supervenience: worlds w and v, with disjoint domains of individuals, agree completely in point of generalized physical truths (we may suppose that there is a one–one function f from the domain of w to that of v such that x in the former has physical property P just in case f(x) in the latter has P, and similarly for relations) but the two worlds are radically different psychologically – say, w is much like our world whereas v is wholly lacking in mentality. Common references these days to "Twin Earth," which is "just like this earth in all physical respects," make sense only if singular truths are excluded from the basis of comparison. Also, common talk of "overall similarity" between worlds, familiar from semantics of counterfactuals, tacitly assumes the meaningfulness of similarity judgments for worlds with disjoint domains of individuals.[20]

There is a second problem: how are we to compare worlds with domains with different cardinalities? Even for worlds with domains of different sizes it should be meaningful, and sometimes true, to say that they are "alike" in physical, or psychological, respects, in a sense of "alike" that is relevant to claims of supervenience. For example, even if Socrates had never existed, this world would not have been altered in any significant psychological or physical respect. There must be a sense of "indiscernibility" relevant to claims of supervenience, we may feel, in which this world and this world *sans* Socrates must count as physically and psychologically indiscernible.

These questions arise for the definition of supervenience framed in terms of "regions" of worlds, as in a formulation by Terence Horgan. For Horgan, psychophysical supervenience obtains just in case there exist no two "regions," within one or more worlds, that are alike in all physical features but different in some psychological feature.[21] Horgan's regions are spatiotemporal zones that include objects, e.g., material bodies and persons, and the "features" in terms of which regions are compared for "likeness" are states of affairs involving objects (e.g., this desk's having

20 See David Lewis, *Counterfactuals* (Cambridge: Harvard University Press, 1973). Lewis's "counterpart theory" assumes no two worlds share any individuals.
21 Terence Horgan, "Supervenience and Microphysics," *Pacific Philosophical Quarterly* 63 (1982): 29–43. Horgan considers only regions of what he calls "P-worlds," which are, roughly, physically possible worlds (relative to the actual world).

such-and-such a mass). Evidently, the problems we have reviewed concerning individuation of distributions and worlds arise for Horgan as well, for different regions will, as a rule though not always, have disjoint domains of objects. Horgan is aware of this; that is why he explicitly excludes "nonqualitative features" (states of affairs involving specific individuals, e.g., Socrates being in pain) from the comparison base, and this corresponds to our exclusion of singular truths. However, Horgan's procedure leaves the general problem unresolved. In particular, it does not address the problem of domains with different cardinalities raised above: for example, should a region which contains one more hydrogen atom than another be counted, for that reason alone, as physically different? Perhaps not; however, there being so many atoms is, arguably, a qualitative feature of a region.[22]

Although I must set aside these general problems for another occasion, let me briefly describe the approach I find attractive. This approach takes *similarity* rather than *indiscernibility* as the central notion in terms of which global supervenience (and perhaps other supervenience relations as well) should be defined. We should grant that the world *sans* Socrates, for example, *is* indeed discernible in psychological respects from this world, for, among other things, it has one fewer creature with mentality. There remains, however, an important and relevant fact about these two worlds, and it is this: the worlds are *quite similar* to each other *in psychological respects*. And in the same way this world and this world *sans* Socrates are *quite similar in physical respects* as well. Now we can think of supervenience as requiring that similarity in the base properties must be matched by similarity in the supervenient properties. This leads to a new conception of global supervenience as follows:

(Similarity-based GS)   A *globally supervenes* on B iff any two worlds that are pretty much similar in respect of B are pretty much similar in respect of A.

If one wishes, indiscernibility-based supervenience, on the model of (GS1), can be retained as a special case of similarity-based supervenience, since indiscernibility can be taken as the maximum degree of similarity. The same idea can be applied to Horgan's "regions"; we can state Horgan's "regional" supervenience in terms of similarity between regions rather than indiscernibility (perhaps "being alike" can be taken as something falling short of total indiscernibility anyway). There is of course the

22 There is also the question whether singular truths should always be excluded: a general exclusion may not yield the intended result when a region is compared with itself across two worlds.

further difficult problem of "criteria of similarity." But the concept of similarity, though multi-dimensioned and evidently more complex than that of indiscernibility, is a richer concept that is in some ways more tractable and easier to handle. For unlike indiscernibility similarity is not an all-or-nothing affair, and for that reason, it is more flexible and can tolerate ambiguities and uncertainties to a degree, without losing its intuitive content. There are other reasons for preferring similarity over indiscernibility in formulating supervenience relations, but we cannot discuss them here.[23]

As we saw, (MS1) is equivalent to global supervenience with fixed domains. In consequence, it shares with global supervenience not only the latter's intuitive appeal but also its problematic features, as an explication of the determination or dependency relation.[24] As an example consider this: Cartesian psychophysical supervenience is compatible with the existence of a world in which some physical individuals have physically indistinguishable twins, and yet in which every mental individual is psychologically distinguishable from every other. That is to say, there can be a world in which physical duplicates, but no mental duplicates, exist. For the only thing that Cartesian supervenience of the mental upon the physical prohibits is the existence of another world in which physical properties, but not psychological properties, are similarly distributed.

These observations point to the *holistic* character of multiple-domain supervenience as defined by (MS1), and of Cartesian supervenience, which is an instance of it. There are two related aspects to this holism. First, the supervenience relation does not call for specific property-to-property correlations between supervenient and subvenient properties. That is, multiple-domain supervenience does not entail dependency relationships between specific A-properties and B-properties. In fact, there are no expressive resources here for formulating interesting A–B correlations; the best we can do to formulate specific "local" correlations would have to be something like this: "Whenever F (in A) is realized G (in B) is realized." Second, it does not permit us to say, of any particular individual in D_1, that *its* A-properties are dependent on the B-properties of any specific individual or individuals in D_2, short of all the individuals in D_2.

The second aspect of this holism arises from the fact that the supervenience relation requires no coordination between the entities of the two

23 For more details on this issue see my "'Strong' and 'Global' Supervenience Revisited," Essay 5 of this volume.
24 For more details on the problematic features of global supervenience see "'Strong' and 'Global' Supervenience Revisited."

domains. We shall consider below a supervenience relation with *coordinated* multiple domains. The first holistic aspect, namely the absence of specific property-to-property connections, is an inevitable consequence of the second aspect. For "local connections" between supervenient and base properties presuppose the possibility of some coordinating relation between the two domains of individuals so that it makes sense to speak, for any supervenient property instantiated by a given individual in the supervenient domain, of the base properties instantiated by those individuals in the base domain with which the given individual is coordinated. Unless there is such a possibility, there is no way of talking about specific property-to-property connections between the two families of properties.

The holistic character of this form of multiple-domain supervenience prompts an epistemological question: What evidence might we have for thinking that a supervenience thesis of this form holds in a given case? For example, what could be our ground for thinking that something like Cartesian supervenience holds? (Notice that the very same question arises for the claim of global supervenience of the mental on the physical.) It does not seem to be within our epistemic power to look at the global patterns of distribution of psychological and physical properties over total worlds and come to a reasoned conclusion as to whether dependencies exist between such worldwide patterns. It is considerably more plausible to think that what evidence we have for the supervenience thesis comes from the observation of mind–body correlations between specific minds and specific bodies coordinated with them.[25] How the coordinating process goes will depend heavily on what correlations are found to obtain under various schemes of coordination, and the scheme which maximizes correlations will be pronounced as the "right" one. In any event, evidence based on local dependencies can gain further strength from general metaphysical considerations about ontological priorities and dependencies between kinds of existents. However, it is doubtful that in the absence of evidence concerning specific correlations such metaphysical evidence alone could ever be sufficient to support supervenience claims. It is no accident that it isn't easy to think of cases of supervenience of this

25 It might be thought that Horgan's "regions" can play a role here: since his regions could be of any size, we could perhaps inductively confirm global supervenience claims on the basis of evidence about "smaller worlds," namely regions, which we could handle. But this only shows the epistemic priority of local dependencies; and, in particular, we should note this fact: spatiotemporal zones containing a single individual must count as "regions" for Horgan (call them "atomic regions"), and it seems that these atomic regions are in effect individuals. This means we might as well begin with something like my strong supervenience (SS), and dispense with talk of regions.

form that we could find plausibly true independently of the corresponding cases of stronger and more structured supervenience relations that are based on local correlations of properties, such as coordinated multiple-domain supervenience to be discussed in the next section and single-domain supervenience.

From a metaphysical point of view, too, supervenience claims having the form of uncoordinated multiple-domain supervenience seem perched on a rather unstable position, crying out for reformulation in terms of a more structured supervenience relation. For what could possibly explain why there is this kind of dependency relation between two domains – unless the individuals of one domain were related in significant ways to those of the other? If, for example, souls were substances wholly distinct from material substances, how is it possible for Cartesian supervenience on the model of (MS1) to hold? If we thought that such a relation held we would naturally assume, and look for, a coordinating relation between souls and bodies that would yield an explanation of how the holistic patterns of dependency arise out of the local dependencies between specific souls and bodies. (The classic Cartesian doctrine of course posits a serviceable coordinating relation for this job.) Such a coordinating relation may also make it possible for us to understand how the properties of a supervenient individual are determined by the properties of the subvenient individual with which it is coordinated (although of course at some point we must be prepared to count some dependency relations among the brute facts of the world). It seems that uncoordinated multiple-domain supervenience has a natural tendency to strengthen itself, gravitating toward the more structured supervenience relation with coordinated domains, and that its chief interest may lie in providing us with a way of formulating provisional dependency theses without a commitment to a specific coordinating relation. Again, these comments apply, mutatis mutantis, to global supervenience.

4. SUPERVENIENCE FOR COORDINATED MULTIPLE DOMAINS

Earlier I mentioned mereological supervenience as an example of supervenience with multiple domains, since the supervenient domain is made up of wholes and the base domain of their parts. But here the situation is different from the general case of multiple-domain supervenience we have just discussed, because the two domains are coordinated by a specific relation, the part–whole relation.[26] Because of this, single-domain supervenience can be pressed into service here. For we can take the domain of wholes as our only domain, and then take as our base properties not the set of properties and relations belonging to parts of these wholes but rather a set of what we may call "micro-based properties" or "micro-structural properties" which belong to the wholes. A simple but representative schematic example of such properties would be this: being made up of two parts x and y such that x is F and y is G and x is related by R to y. A property of this kind belongs to a whole in virtue of facts about its parts; whence the name "micro-based" or "micro-structural" property.[27] An example of micro-based property is having such-and-such mean translational kinetic energy, a stock example in the discussion of microreduction: this is a property that belongs to the wholes (gases), not to their parts (individual molecules). And we can consider how such properties of the wholes as temperatures supervene on their micro-based properties.[28]

Alternatively we can develop a supervenience relation with "coordinated multiple domains" in a simple and intuitive way, although as we shall see, an unresolved problem we saw earlier emerges again. Let D_1 and D_2 be two nonempty domains as before, and let R be a relation whose domain is D_1 and whose range is a subset of D_2. For any member x of D_1, R|x is the "image" of x under R (that is, the set of all objects in D_2 to which x is related by R). We can then define the following analogues of weak and strong supervenience:

(MWS) $\langle A, D_1 \rangle$ *weakly supervenes* on $\langle B, D_2 \rangle$ relative to relation R just in case necessarily for any x and y in D_1 if R|x and R|y are B-indiscernible, then x and y are A-indiscernible.

(MSS) $\langle A, D_1 \rangle$ *strongly supervenes* on $\langle B, D_2 \rangle$ relative to relation R just in case for any x and y in D_1 and any worlds w_1 and w_2, if R|x in w_1 is B-indiscernible from R|y in w_2, x in w_1 is A-indiscernible from y in w_2.

The expression "R|z in w" designates the image R picks out in w of z; to say "u in w_i is A-indiscernible from v in w_j," where A is a set of proper-

---

26 Note that mereological supervenience could begin life as a form of uncoordinated multiple-domain supervenience: e.g., as the claim that when the properties and relations of all the atoms of the world are fixed, that fixes the properties of all other objects.

27 David Armstrong calls such properties "structural properties"; see his *A Theory of Universals*, vol. II (Cambridge: Cambridge University Press, 1978), p. 69; and "A Combinatorial Theory of Possibility," *Canadian Journal of Philosophy* 16 (1986): 575–94.

28 An interesting question we cannot consider here is what in general would be involved in reducing all cases of supervenience with coordinated multiple domains to single-domain supervenience in this way.

ties, means that u has in w_i exactly those A-properties that v has in w_j. But what is it for R|x, which is a set, to be indiscernible, in respect of a certain family of properties, from R|y, another set? This problem is essentially the problem we considered above, in connection with Horgan, of defining indiscernibility for "regions." Consider the following strong criterion: there is a one–one function f from R|x to R|y such that for any property P in the set an object u in R|x has P if and only if f(u) has P. According to this, indiscernibility between x and y requires that R|x and R|y have the same cardinality, which seems stronger than what we want; we would want to say that a large and a small cube of sugar are both water-soluble in virtue of the fact that their respective parts (molecules) are in "the same micro-state." A weaker criterion would insist only that property distributions over the two sets agree on general truths (that is, existentially or universally quantified truths). This seems too weak, although the impression of weakness is somewhat mitigated when we see that relations may be included in the property set (for simplicity relations are not used in our constructions in this paper). What has to be done to formulate a workable standard is, again, to define appropriate *patterns* of distribution of properties over sets of individuals and then explain indiscernibility by comparing and matching these patterns. When the problem is looked at this way, it becomes increasingly clear that similarity makes better sense than indiscernibility. By replacing the latter with the former we can keep the theory itself simple and elegant, relegating the complications (the "dirty work") to its applications. This is possible because similarity has enough intuitive content to keep us going at least for some distance; indiscernibility on the other hand cries out for immediate clarification in precise terms – it does not tolerate vagueness or ambiguity very well. Notice that the single-domain approach to mereological supervenience sketched earlier does not really avoid this problem; it only hides it in the construction of "micro-based" properties.

When the coordinating relation R is many–one, each individual in the supervenient domain is associated with one unique individual in the base domain, and the thorny problem of defining indiscernibility for sets does not arise. However, there is a fact we should notice about this case. Let us focus on (MSS): consider two objects in D_1, a and b, each correlated by R with the same individual, u, in D_2. Trivially, for any w and any B, u in w is B-indiscernible from u in w. Thus, the supervenience claim requires that a in w be A-indiscernible from b in w. When the supervenient properties constitute a comprehensive and global set, like the set of mental properties, this would be highly unlikely if a and b are indeed distinct individuals. For example, if a and b are two souls that share all their psychological properties, what is there to prevent us from identifying them? Thus, R may turn out to be best construed as one–one rather than many–one.

Let us turn to the case in which the coordinating relation is one–one. Such may be what some dual-substance Cartesians might envisage for souls and human bodies: each human soul "animates" one unique human body, and each living human body is animated by one unique soul. For them, (MWS) and (MSS), especially the latter, can provide useful vehicles for formulating doctrines of supervenience: the character of a soul supervenes on the physical nature of its body.[29] I said earlier that a position of this sort is intelligible if not plausible. We now know, it might seem, how to be a physicalist – that is, recognize the primacy of the physical – and keep Cartesian souls, too. The position is at least logically consistent, and our multiple-domain supervenience (with a one–one R) displays its metaphysical structure. But does it have any plausibility at all? This is not the place to argue the merits of mind–body theories, but it seems evident that the usual simplicity considerations may strongly incline us against it, leading us to do away with a separate domain of souls altogether (that is, identifying them with their one–one correlated human bodies).[30] This move does not lead to the elimination of mentality from the world; psychological properties would now be attributed to human bodies and other appropriate organisms.

Let us pause briefly here and recount where we have been: we got started with a desire to accommodate Haugeland's complaint that something like my weak or strong supervenience begs the question of token identity – that is, it assumes that the subjects of psychological attributes are also the subjects of physical properties. We asked how a thesis of psychophysical supervenience could be formulated for those who deny that assumption, that is, those who accept (or wish to remain noncommittal about) a separate domain of souls, objects that have psychological but no physical attributes. This led to the formulation of (MS1), "supervenience for uncoordinated multiple domains," which we saw was equivalent to global supervenience (GS1) with a fixed dichotomous domain. But there

---

29 The relationship between (MWS) and (MSS) parallels that between weak supervenience (WS) and strong supervenience (SS). For details on the latter relation see my "Concepts of Supervenience."

30 There are some complex questions involving supervenience and separate existence. For a discussion of some of them, especially in connection with persons and bodies, see Ernest Sosa, "Persons and Other Beings," *Philosophical Perspectives* 1 (1987): 155–88.

were epistemological and metaphysical pressures on (MS1), pressures that moved us to posit a coordinating relation between the two domains and formulate "coordinated multiple-domain supervenience." We then saw that for the mind–body case the coordinating relation arguably had to be considered one–one; and we just saw how obvious simplicity considerations could force us to construe that relation as identity. So we are back where we began, by a circuitous and plausible, if not mandatory, route: a combination of logical, epistemological, and metaphysical considerations seems to show that the possibility for which Haugeland wants us to make provisions may not be a serious possibility after all. If you are a physicalist in the sense that you are prepared to accept the dependency of the mental on the physical, you may lose nothing of philosophical significance by working with single-domain supervenience. This tentative conclusion, which I cannot argue in detail here, is of some interest, although the mind–body problem is only a side issue for us in this paper, serving chiefly as a convenient source of examples.

When the coordinating relation R is identity, D_1 is a subset of D_2, and (MSS) and (MWS) will in effect collapse to their single-domained counterparts, (SS) and (WS), respectively.

In "Concepts of Supervenience" I argued that, on certain assumptions, each weakly supervening property has, in every world, a coextensive property in the base properties; and that, on the same assumptions, each strongly supervening property has a necessary coextension in the base properties, that is, a coextensive base property invariant from world to world. Similar results should hold for the special case of coordinated multiple-domain weak and strong supervenience in which the coordinating relation is one–one. The notion of coextensive properties must of course be reconstrued in obvious ways so that it may be applied across two domains relative to a one–one coordinating relation.

I believe that similar results can be stated for the general case as well, but it is obviously more complicated. The complication comes from the fact that we must define, for a family of properties F, the notion of a property (call it an "F*-property") applicable to *sets* of objects in such a way that an F*-property belongs to a set in virtue of its members having the F-properties that they have.[31] Suppose such a notion is on hand: If $\langle A, D_1 \rangle$ supervenes on $\langle B, D_2 \rangle$ relative to R, then for each property in A

31 The problem of constructing F*-properties is essentially the problem of defining the "sameness" or "likeness" of distributions of a set of properties over individuals, a problem from which we don't seem to be able to escape. I should also point out that the problem arises in connection with defining "micro-based properties" of wholes.

127

we would look for its coextension in those B*-properties which belong to the images in D_2 of objects of D_1 under R.

5. AN APPLICATION: VAN CLEVE'S NEW "BUNDLE THEORY"

Thus far we have mainly used theories of the mind–body relation to illustrate multiple-domain supervenience. Let us now look at another possible application, to the "bundle theory" of material objects. This theory holds that material objects are "bundles of (appropriately related) properties." In "Three Versions of the Bundle Theory"[32] James Van Cleve introduces, without endorsing it, a new version of the theory which is thought to be immune to some of the serious objections to the more standard formulations of the theory. This "third version," which Van Cleve likens to the translation version of phenomenalism, maintains that every statement about ordinary material objects can be translated, without loss of content, into statements solely about "bundles" of properties, *even though no object is identified with a specific bundle.* The analogy with translational phenomenalism comes from this: according to this version of phenomenalism, every statement about a material object is fully translatable into statements exclusively about sense-data (or other phenomenal objects or states), although no particular material object is identified with a class of actual or possible sense-data. Van Cleve associates the new version of the bundle theory with fictionalism about objects, but that arguably is an optional feature; the theory is prima facie consistent with a realist attitude about material objects, and to regard them as fictions is best taken as an additional philosophical step. There may well be good reason for taking this step, however, and I shall have a brief comment about this later.

Our multiple-domain supervenience, (MS1), provides us with a metaphysical structure that can be thought to underlie both the translational bundle theory and translational phenomenalism. Or, what is better, we can use multiple-domain supervenience as a scheme for formulating *metaphysical versions* of these translation theses. To see how this works, let us look at the bundle theory: take as the supervenient domain the class of material objects and as the base domain the class of property bundles of appropriate sorts. No member of the supervenient domain is identified with a member of the base domain; (MS1), as we know, requires no coordination between members of the two domains. Nevertheless, we may

32 *Philosophical Studies* 47 (1985): 95–107.

want to say, if we are sympathetic with Van Cleve's new bundle theory, that all truths about the supervening domain are fixed once the truths about the base domain are fixed. The supervenient and base properties can be chosen to suit the truths about material objects we want to accommodate. Thus, uncoordinated multiple-domain supervenience seems to give us a perspicuous general scheme that captures the metaphysical determinative relationship underlying the new bundle theory without the latter's implicit commitments to complex issues about meaning and translation. Freedom from such commitments is precisely what makes the metaphysical version more appealing than the translation version of the theory. Similar remarks hold for translational phenomenalism.

I argued earlier that uncoordinated multiple-domain supervenience is often epistemologically problematic and metaphysically insecure. It seems to me that Van Cleve's bundle theory, and its metaphysical version we have formulated, may well be subject to those symptoms. Consider the translational bundle theory: when a given material object statement is translated into a statement about property bundles, there must be some criteria for judging whether or not the purported translation is "correct" or "appropriate" in some sense, and the criteria invoked must be motivated and intelligible. It is difficult to see how such criteria could fail to be essentially "local" (e.g., they associate with each object a property bundle in the same space-time zone); how could we understand and apply criteria that are holistic through and through? And it seems to me that the best, perhaps the only, way to rationalize the basis of the criteria — that is, to see that the criteria are reasonable and make sense — is to see, or posit, some intelligible connections between the entities involved — that is, to have an intelligible metaphysics of the situation. But once such connections are established between objects and property bundles some of the crucial advantages of the new bundle theory may disappear. For example, one objection to the standard bundle theory is the claim that by identifying an object with a bundle of properties, it makes every property that an object has an essential property of it. If an object is in some way "coordinated" with a property bundle, a similar objection may arise; exactly how such an objection is to be formulated and how damaging it may turn out to be will depend on the nature of the specific coordinating relation.

Perhaps Van Cleve's association of the translational bundle theory with a fictionalism about material objects is explainable in terms of these metaphysical and epistemological pressures; it may be a way of dissipating them, or keeping them from arising, by reminding ourselves that material objects are fictions after all. On one widely held view, for example,[33] fictional objects have no properties, and hence no essential properties. Thus, the objection earlier mentioned to the bundle theory would prima facie not apply if objects were construed as fictions. It is not certain, however, that fictionalism can remove all of these pressures; we would still need motivated criteria for translation, and it is difficult to see how this need can be met without an appropriate coordination between the individuals of the two domains, whether or not one of the domains is thought to comprise only fictitious individuals.

33 See, e.g., Alvin Plantinga, "Two Concepts of Modality: Modal Realism and Modal Reductionism," *Philosophical Perspectives* 1 (1987): 189–232. Plantinga calls such a view "serious actualism," p. 197.

8

Supervenience as a philosophical concept

I. SUPERVENIENCE IN PHILOSOPHY

Supervenience is a philosophical concept in more ways than one. First of all, like such concepts as cause and rationality, it is often used in the formulation of philosophical doctrines and arguments. Thus, we have the claim that ethical predicates are "supervenient predicates", or that the characteristics of a whole supervene on those of its parts. And arguments have been advanced to show that the supervenience of moral properties undermines moral realism, or that, on the contrary, moral supervenience shows ethical judgments are "objective" after all. And, again like causality and rationality, the concept of supervenience itself has become an object of philosophical analysis and a matter of some controversy.

But unlike causality, supervenience is almost exclusively a philosopher's concept, one not likely to be encountered outside philosophical dissertations and disputations. The notion of cause, on the other hand, is an integral part of our workaday language, a concept without which we could hardly manage in describing our experiences and observations, framing explanations of natural events, and assessing blame and praise. Something similar can be said about the notion of being rational as well, although this concept is not as ubiquitous in ordinary discourse as that of cause. Supervenience of course is not unique in being a technical philosophical concept; there are many others, such as "haecceity" and "possible world" in metaphysics, "analyticity" in the theory of meaning, and the currently prominent concepts of "wide" and "narrow" content.

But this isn't to say that the word "supervenience" is a philosopher's neologism; on the contrary, it has been around for some time, and has had a respectable history. The O.E.D. lists 1594 for the first documented

This is the Third Metaphilosophy Address, delivered in May 1989 at the Graduate School of the City University of New York.

131

occurrence of the adjective "supervenient" and 1647–48 for the verb "supervene"; the noun "supervenience" occurred as early as 1664. In these uses, however, "supervene" and its derivatives were almost without exception applied to concrete events and occurrences in the sense of "coming upon" a given event as something additional and extraneous (perhaps as something unexpected), or coming shortly after another occurrence, as in "Upon a sudden supervened the death of the king" (1647–48) and "The king was bruised by the pommel of his saddle; fever supervened, and the injury proved fatal" (1867). There is also this entry from Charlotte Brontë's *Shirley* (1849): "A bad harvest supervened. Distress reached its climax". In common usage supervenience usually implies temporal order: the supervenient event occurs after the event upon which it supervenes, often as an effect. It is clear that even though the vernacular meaning of "supervenience" is not entirely unrelated to its current philosophical sense, the relationship is pretty tenuous, and unlikely to provide any helpful guide for the philosophical discussion of the concept.

I noted that supervenience is like haecceity and narrow content in that they are specifically philosophical concepts, concepts introduced by philosophers for philosophical purposes. But in one significant respect supervenience differs from them: haecceity and narrow content are notions used within a restricted area of philosophy, to formulate distinctions concerning a specific domain of phenomena, or for the purpose of formulating doctrines and arguments concerning a specific topic. Thus, the notion of haecceity arises in connection with the problem of identity and the essence of things; and the concepts of narrow and broad content emerge in the discussion of some problems about meaning and propositional attitudes. In contrast, supervenience is not subject-specific. Although the idea of supervenience appears to have originated in moral theory,[1] it is a general, methodological concept in that it is entirely topic-neutral, and its use is not restricted to any particular problem or area of philosophy. It is this subject-neutral character of supervenience that distinguishes it from the usual run of philosophical concepts and makes it an appropriate object of metaphilosophical inquiry. Supervenience is a topic of interest from the point of view of philosophical methodology.

In undertaking a philosophical study of supervenience we quickly run into the following difficulty. Because the term is rarely used outside philosophy, there is not a body of well-established usage in ordinary or scien-

---

1 However, see below on emergence and footnote 5.

tific language that could generate reliable linguistic intuitions to guide the inquiry; there are few linguistic or conceptual data against which to test one's speculations and hypotheses. This means that for supervenience there are not the usual constraints on the "analysis" of a concept; in a sense, there is no pre-existing concept to be analyzed. As we shall see, earlier philosophical uses of the concept do set some broad constraints on our discussion; however, when it comes to matters of detail supervenience is going to be pretty much what we say it is. That is, within limits we are free to define it to suit the purposes on hand, and the primary measure of success for our definitions is their philosophical usefulness. This, I believe, is the principal explanation of the multiplicity of supervenience concepts currently on the scene.

Perhaps, the concept of a possible world is also like this. If we want to use this concept in a serious way, we would need to explain what we mean, either by explicitly defining it or by providing appropriately chosen examples and applications. However this is done, we need not be bound, in any significant way, by previous usage; there is not a common body of philosophical usage to which one's conception of a possible world must answer. The only criterion of success here is pragmatic: how useful and fruitful the introduced concept is in clarifying modal concepts, systematizing our modal intuitions, and helping us sharpen our metaphysical opinions.

There is a long tradition of philosophical discussion of modal concepts, the notions of necessity and possibility, of essential and contingent properties, of essences and haecceities, and so on. In contrast, supervenience is a concept of a comparatively recent origin. R. M. Hare is usually credited with having introduced the term "supervenience" into contemporary discussion, and our present use of the term appears historically continuous with Hare's use of it in *The Language of Morals* (1952).[2] More than thirty years later, in his Inaugural Address, "Supervenience" (1984), to the Aristotelian Society,[3] Hare wonders who first used the term in its current philosophical sense, being quite sure that he was not that person. Hare says that he first used the term in an unpublished paper written in 1950, but is not able to name any particular philosopher who had used it before he did. In any case, Hare's introduction of the term didn't exactly start a stampede. There were, to be sure, isolated appearances of the concept in

2 London: Oxford University Press, 1952.
3 R. M. Hare, "Supervenience", *The Aristotelian Society,* Supplementary Volume 58 (1984): 1–16.

the ethical literature during the two decades following the publication of
The Language of Morals[4] but they were not marked by any real continuity,
or an awareness of its potential and significance as a general philosophical
concept. An idea related to supervenience, that of "universalizability" or
"generality" of moral judgments, was much discussed in moral philosophy during this period, but the debate remained pretty much one of local
concern within ethics.

It would be an error, however, to think that moral theorists had a mo-
nopoly on supervenience. On the contrary, early in this century, "supervenience" and its derivatives were used with some regularity by the emergentists, and their critics, in the formulation and discussion of the doctrine
of "emergent evolution", and it seems possible that Hare and others got
"supervenience", directly or indirectly, from the emergentist literature.
Many of the leading emergentists were British (for example, G. H.
Lewes, Samuel Alexander, C. Lloyd Morgan, C. D. Broad) and the emergence debate was robust and active in the 1930s and '40s. The doctrine
of emergence, in brief, is the claim that when basic physicochemical processes achieve a certain level of complexity of an appropriate kind, genuinely novel characteristics, such as mentality, appear as "emergent" qualities. Lloyd Morgan, a central theoretician of the emergence school,
appears to have used "supervenient" as an occasional stylistic variant of
"emergent", although the latter remained the official term associated with
the philosophical position, and the concept he intended with these terms
seems surprisingly close to the supervenience concept current today.[5]

The emergence debate, however, has by and large been forgotten, and
appears to have had negligible effects on the current debates in metaphysics, philosophy of mind, and philosophy of science, except perhaps in
some areas of philosophy of biology.[6] This is to be regretted because some

---

4 In *Moral Notions* (London: Routledge & Kegan Paul, 1967), pp. 158–159, Julius Kovesi
points to the same characteristic of "good" that Hare called supervenience, but without
using the supervenience terminology. Kovesi mentions that this characteristic is had by
many nonethical expressions as well, e.g., "tulip"; however, he does not develop this
point in any detail.
5 See especially Morgan's *Emergent Evolution* (London: Williams and Norgate, 1923). Others
who used "supervenience" in connection with the doctrine of emergence include Stephen C. Pepper, "Emergence", *Journal of Philosophy* 23 (1926): 241–45; and Paul Meehl
and Wilfrid Sellars, "The Concept of Emergence", *Minnesota Studies in the Philosophy of
Science,* vol. 1, ed. Herbert Feigl and Michael Scriven (Minneapolis: University of Minnesota Press, 1956).
6 See, e.g., Ernest Nagel, *The Structure of Science* (New York: Harcourt Brace & World,
1961); F. J. Ayala and T. Dobzhansky, eds., *Studies in the Philosophy of Biology: Reduction
and Related Problems* (Berkeley and Los Angeles: University of California Press, 1974).

of the issues that were then discussed concerning the status of emergent qualities are highly relevant to the current debate on mental causation and the status of psychology in relation to the biological and physical sciences.[7] In any case, the present interest in supervenience was kindled by Donald Davidson in the early 1970s when he used the term in his influential and much discussed paper "Mental Events"[8] to formulate a version of nonreductive physicalism. What is noteworthy is that the term has since gained quick currency, especially in discussions of the mind–body problem; and, more remarkably, the term seems by now to have acquired, among philosophers, a pretty substantial shared content. "Supervene" and its derivatives are now regularly encountered in philosophical writings, and often they are used without explanation, signaling an assumption on the part of the writers that their meaning is a matter of common knowledge.

And during the past decade or so attempts have been made to sharpen our understanding of the concept itself. Various supervenience relations have been distinguished, their mutual relationships worked out, and their suitability for specific philosophical purposes scrutinized. This has led David Lewis to complain about an "unlovely proliferation" of supervenience concepts, which he believes has weakened its core meaning.[9] I disagree with the "unlovely" part of Lewis's characterization, but he is certainly right about the proliferation. I think this is a good time to take stock of the current state of the supervenience concept, and reflect on its usefulness as a philosophical concept. That is my aim in this essay.

II. COVARIANCE, DEPENDENCE, AND NONREDUCIBILITY

The first use of the term "supervene" (actually, the Latin "supervenire") I have found in a philosophical text is by Leibniz. In connection with his celebrated doctrine concerning relations, Leibniz wrote:

> Relation is an accident which is in multiple subjects; it is what results without any change made in the subjects but supervenes from them; it is the

---

7 I discuss the doctrine of emergence in relation to the currently popular doctrine of nonreductive physicalism in "'Downward Causation' in Emergentism and Nonreductive Physicalism", in *Emergence or Reduction?*, ed. A. Beckermann, H. Flohr, and J. Kim (Berlin: De Gruyter, 1992).

8 Reprinted in Davidson, *Essays on Actions and Events* (Oxford: Oxford University Press, 1980); originally published in 1970.

9 *On the Plurality of Worlds* (Oxford & New York: Basil Blackwell, 1986), p. 14.

thinkability of objects together when we think of multiple things simultaneously.[10]

There has been much interpretive controversy concerning Leibniz's doctrine of relations – in particular, whether or not it was a reducibility thesis, to the effect that relations are reducible, in some sense, to "intrinsic denominations" of things. Leibniz's use of "supervene" in this context seems not inappropriate in our light: his thesis could be interpreted as the claim that relations supervene on the intrinsic properties of their relata. Such a claim would certainly be an interesting and important metaphysical thesis.

But Leibniz's use of "supervene" may well have been an isolated event; although I cannot say I have done anything like an exhaustive or systematic search, I have not found any other occurrence of the term since then, until we come well into the present century. However, the idea of supervenience, or something very close to it, if not the term "supervenience", was clearly present in the writings of the British Moralists. There is, for example, the following from Sidgwick:

> There seems, however, to be this difference between our conceptions of ethical and physical objectivity: that we commonly refuse to admit in the case of the former – what experience compels us to admit as regards the latter – variations for which we can discover no rational explanation. In the variety of coexistent physical facts we find an accidental or arbitrary element in which we have to acquiesce, . . . But within the range of our cognitions of right and wrong, it will generally be agreed that we cannot admit a similar unexplained variation. We cannot judge an action to be right for A and wrong for B, unless we can find in the nature or circumstances of the two some difference which we can regard as a reasonable ground for difference in their duties.[11]

Sidgwick is saying that moral characteristics must necessarily *covary* with certain (presumably nonmoral) characteristics, whereas there is no similar covariance requirement for physical properties. In terms of supervenience the idea comes to this: moral properties, in particular, the rightness or wrongness of an action, are supervenient on their nonmoral properties (which could provide reasons for the rightness or wrongness).

Concerning the concept of "intrinsic value", G. E. Moore said this:

10 *Die Leibniz-Handschriften der koenighlichen oeffentlichen Bibliothek zu Hannover,* ed. E. Bodemann, Hanover, 1895, VII, c, p. 74. Quoted by Hide Ishiguro in her *Leibniz's Philosophy of Logic and Language* (Ithaca: Cornell University Press, 1972), p. 71, fn. 3. The Latin text reads: "Relatio est accidens quod est in pluribus subjectis estque resultans tantum seu nulla mutatione facta ab iis supervenit, si plura simul cogitantur, est concogitabilitas".
11 *The Method of Ethics,* pp. 208–209. Quoted by Michael DePaul in his "Supervenience and Moral Dependence", *Philosophical Studies* 51 (1987): 425–439.

> . . . if a given thing possesses any kind of intrinsic value in a certain degree, then not only must that same thing possess it, under all circumstances, in the same degree, but also anything *exactly like it,* must, under all circumstances, possess it in exactly the same degree.[12]

Likeness of things is grounded, presumably, in their descriptive, or "naturalistic" properties – that is, their nonevaluative properties. Thus, Moore's point amounts to the statement that the intrinsic value of a thing supervenes on its descriptive, nonevaluative properties.

Hare, introducing the term "supervenience" into moral philosophy for the first time, said this:

> First, let us take that characteristic of "good" which has been called its supervenience. Suppose that we say, "St. Francis was a good man." It is logically impossible to say this and to maintain at the same time that there might have been another man placed exactly in the same circumstances as St. Francis, and who behaved in exactly the same way, but who differed from St. Francis in this respect only, that he was not a good man.[13]

It is clear that both Moore and Hare, like Sidgwick, focus on the characteristic of moral properties or ethical predicates that has to do with their *necessary covariation* with descriptive – nonmoral and nonevaluative – properties or predicates. The attribution of moral properties, or the ascription of ethical predicates, to an object is necessarily constrained, in a specific way, by the nonethical properties attributed to that object. For Moore the constraint has the modal force of "must"; for Hare, the violation of the constraint amounts to the contravention of logical consistency.

The basic idea of supervenience we find in Sidgwick, Moore, and Hare, therefore, has to do with property covariation: properties of one kind must covary with properties of another kind in a certain way. As Lewis put it, "no difference of one sort without differences of another sort";[14] and a change in respect of properties of one sort cannot occur unless accompanied by a change in respect of properties of another sort. If you have qualms about properties as entities, the same idea can be expressed in terms of predicates; if you think the predicates in question do not express properties, in something like the way ethical noncognitivists regard ethical predicates, you could express the idea in terms of "ascriptions" of predicates or the making of ethical judgments.[15]

---

12 *Philosophical Studies* (London, 1922), p. 261.
13 *The Language of Morals* (London, 1952), p. 145.
14 *On the Plurality of Worlds* (Oxford: Blackwell, 1986), p. 14.
15 See James Klagge, "Supervenience: Ontological and Ascriptive", *Australasian Journal of Philosophy* 66 (1988): 461–470.

Hare spoke of ethical and other evaluative predicates as "supervenient predicates", apparently taking supervenience as a *property* of expressions. But it is evident that the fundamental idea involves a *relation* between two sets of properties, or predicates, and that what Hare had in mind was the supervenience *of* ethical predicates *in relation to* nonethical, or naturalistic predicates. In fact, that was precisely the way Lloyd Morgan used the term, in the 1920s, some three decades before Hare; he used "supervenience" to denote a general relation, speaking of the supervenience of physical and chemical events "on spatiotemporal events",[16] and of deity as a quality that might be supervenient "on reflective consciousness".[17] As I said, Morgan used "supervene" and "emerge" as stylistic variants, and this means that supervenience is as much a general relation as emergence is.

Thus, Morgan and other emergentists were the first, as far as I know, to develop a generalized concept of supervenience as a relation, and their concept turns out to be strikingly similar to that in current use, especially in philosophy of mind. They held that the supervenient, or emergent, qualities necessarily manifest themselves when, and only when, appropriate conditions obtain at the more basic level; and some emergentists[18] took great pains to emphasize that the phenomenon of emergence is consistent with determinism. But in spite of that, the emergents are not reducible, or reductively explainable, in terms of their "basal" conditions. In formulating his emergentism, Morgan thought of himself as defending a reasonable naturalistic alternative to both mechanistic reductionism and such anti-naturalisms as vitalism and Cartesianism. Thus, Morgan's position bears an interesting similarity to the supervenience thesis Davidson has injected into philosophy of mind, and to many currently popular versions of nonreductive materialism which Davidson has helped inspire. In a passage that has become a bench mark to the writers on supervenience and nonreductive materialism, Davidson wrote:

> Although the position I describe denies there are psychophysical laws, it is consistent with the view that mental characteristics are in some sense dependent, or supervenient, on physical characteristics. Such supervenience might be taken to mean that there cannot be two events alike in all

16 Morgan, *Emergent Evolution*, p. 9.
17 Morgan, *Emergent Evolution*, p. 30. I should add that Morgan was here expounding Samuel Alexander's doctrine of emergence, and that he is skeptical about these two supervenience theses.
18 See Arthur O. Lovejoy's distinction between "indeterminist" and "determinist" theories of emergent evolution in his "The Meaning of 'Emergence' and Its Modes", *Proceedings of the Sixth International Congress of Philosophy* (New York, 1927): 20–33.

physical respects but differing in some mental respects, or that an object cannot alter in some mental respects without altering in some physical respects. Dependence or supervenience of this kind does not entail reducibility through law or definition: if it did, we could reduce moral properties to descriptive, and this there is good reason to *believe* cannot be done. . . . [19]

Both Morgan and Davidson seem to be saying that mental phenomena are supervenient on physical phenomena and yet not reducible to them.

What Davidson says about the supervenience relation between mental and physical characteristics is entirely consonant with the idea of property covariation we saw in Sidgwick, Moore, and Hare. But he did more than echo the idea of the earlier writers: in this paragraph Davidson explicitly introduced two crucial new ideas, earlier adumbrated in the emergence literature, that were to change the complexion of the subsequent philosophical thinking about supervenience. First, supervenience is to be a relation of *dependence:* that which is supervenient is dependent on that on which it supervenes. Second, it is to be a *nonreductive* relation: supervenient dependency is not to entail the reducibility of the supervenient to its subvenient base.[20]

Davidson had his own reasons for attaching these two ideas to supervenience. The quoted paragraph occurs in his "Mental Events" just after he has advanced his "anomalous monism", the doctrine that mental events are identical to physical events even though there are no laws connecting mental and physical properties. In writing this passage, he is trying to mitigate the likely impression that anomalous monism permits no significant relationships between mental and physical attributes, positing two isolated, autonomous domains. His psychophysical anomalism, the thesis that there are no laws connecting the mental with the physical, has sundered the two domains; with the supervenience thesis he is trying to bring them back together. But not so close as to revive the hope, or threat, of psychophysical reductionism.

In any event, these two ideas, dependency and nonreductiveness, have become closely associated with supervenience. In particular, the idea that supervenience is a dependency relation has become firmly entrenched, so firmly that it has by now acquired the status of virtual analyticity. But I think it is useful to keep these three ideas separate; so let us summarize the three putative components, or desiderata, of supervenience:

19 "Mental Events", p. 214.
20 Note that "nonreductive" is also consistent with reducibility. Thus, "nonreductive" is to be understood as indicting a neutral, noncommittal position with regard to reducibility, not as an affirmation of irreducibility.

139

Covariance: Supervenient properties covary with their subvenient, or base, properties. In particular, indiscernibility in respect of the base properties entails indiscernibility in respect of the supervenient properties.

Dependency: Supervenient properties are dependent on, or are determined by, their base properties.

Nonreducibility: Supervenience is to be consistent with the irreducibility of supervenient properties to their base properties.

Obviously, covariance is the crucial component; any supervenience concept must include this condition in some form. The main issue, then, concerns the relationship between covariance and the other two components, and here there are two principal questions. First, can covariance yield dependence, or must dependence be considered an independent component of supervenience? Second, is there an interpretation of covariance that is strong enough to sustain supervenience as a dependency relation but weak enough not to imply reducibility? More broadly, there is this question: In what ways can these three desiderata be combined to yield coherent and philosophically interesting concepts of supervenience? I will not be offering definitive answers to these questions here; for I don't have the answers. What follows is a kind of interim report on the ongoing work by myself and others on these and related issues.

III. TYPES OF COVARIANCE

In the quoted passage above, Davidson writes as though he held that property covariation of the sort he is specifying between mental and physical properties *generated* a dependency relation between them. That is, mental properties are dependent on physical properties *in virtue of* the fact that the two sets of properties covary as indicated. Is this idea sound? But what precisely is covariance, to begin with?

It turns out that the simple statement of covariance in terms of indiscernibility has at least two distinct interpretations, one stronger than the other, depending on whether things chosen for comparison in respect of indiscernibility come exclusively from one possible world, or may come from different worlds. We can call them "weak" and "strong" covariance. Let A and B be two sets of properties, where we think of A as supervenient and B as subvenient. I state two definitions for each type of covariance:

140

Weak covariance I: No possible world contains things, x and y, such that x and y are indiscernible in respect of properties in B ("B-indiscernible") and yet discernible in respect of properties in A ("A-discernible").

Weak covariance II: Necessarily, if anything has property F in A, there exists a property G in B such that the thing has G, and everything that has G has F.

Strong covariance I: For any objects x and y and any worlds w_i and w_j, if x in w_i is B-indiscernible from y in w_j (that is, x has in w_i precisely those B-properties that y has in w_j), then x in w_i is A-indiscernible from y in w_j.

Strong covariance II: Necessarily, if anything has property F in A, there exists a property G in B such that the thing has G, and *necessarily* everything with G has F.

For both weak and strong covariance, the two versions are equivalent under certain assumptions concerning property composition.[21] However, it will be convenient to have both versions. The sole difference between strong covariance II and weak covariance II lies in the presence of the second modal expression "necessarily" in the former; this ensures that the G–F correlation holds across possible worlds and is not restricted to the given world under consideration. I have elsewhere called the two types of covariance "weak supervenience" and "strong supervenience" respectively; I am using the "covariance" terminology here since I am trying to keep the idea of covariance and that of dependence separate. This is a purely terminological decision; if we liked, we could continue to use the supervenience terminology here, and then raise the question concerning the relationship between supervenience and dependence.

How should we understand the modal term "necessarily", or quantification over possible worlds, that occurs in the statements of covariance? I believe that a general characterization of covariance, or supervenience, should leave this term as an unfixed parameter to be interpreted to suit specific supervenience claims. The standard options in this area include metaphysical, logico-mathematical, analytic, and nomological necessity.

Hare's and Davidson's original statements of supervenience seem neutral with respect to weak and strong covariance. Interestingly, however, both have since come out in favor of weak covariance. Hare for moral supervenience and Davidson for psychophysical supervenience. In his Inaugural Address "Supervenience", Hare says that "what I have always had

21 See my "Concepts of Supervenience", Essay 4 of this volume, and "'Strong' and 'Global' Supervenience Revisited", Essay 5 of this volume.

in mind is not what Kim now calls 'strong' supervenience. It is nearer to his 'weak' supervenience. . . ."[22]

Davidson has recently given an explicit account of the notion of supervenience that he says he had earlier in mind:

> The notion of supervenience, as I have used it, is best thought of as a relation between a predicate and a set of predicates in a language: a predicate p is supervenient on a set of predicates s if for every pair of objects such that p is true of one and not of the other there is a predicate of s that is true of one and not of the other.[23]

We can easily verify that this is equivalent to weak covariance II, of the unit set consisting of p on the set s.

Hare and Davidson are not alone in their preference for weak covariance. Simon Blackburn, who has used normative supervenience as a premise in his argument against moral realism, opts for weak covariance as his favored form of supervenience, at least for the case of moral properties.[24] On his account, if property F supervenes on a set G of properties, the following holds: in every possible world, if something has F, its total or maximal G-property, G*, is such that anything with G* has F. Blackburn stresses that this last universal conditional, "Everything with G* has F", is to be taken as a material conditional with no modal force,[25] which makes his concept exactly fit our weak covariance II.

IV. COVARIANCE AND DEPENDENCE

As may be recalled, Davidson has said that the mental is "supervenient, or dependent" on the physical; here he seems to be using "supervenient"

22 "Supervenience", p. 4. Hare's actual definition of supervenience, pp. 4–5, is a little difficult to interpret in terms of our present scheme, in part because he still does not explicitly relativize supervenience, treating "supervenient" as a one-place predicate of properties. But there is little question that his definition of "F is a supervenient property" comes to "F is weakly covariant with respect to (G, not-G)" (it isn't wholly clear to me whether G is to be thought of as existentially quantified, or contextually indicated).

23 In his "Replies to Essays X–XII" in *Essays on Davidson: Actions and Events,* ed. Bruce Vermazen and Merrill B. Hintikka (Oxford: Clarendon Press, 1985), p. 242.

24 See "Supervenience Revisited", *Exercises in Analysis,* ed. Ian Hacking (Cambridge University Press, 1985). His (S), on p. 49, corresponds to weak covariance II; his (?), on p. 50, to strong covariance II. His argument against moral realism depends on accepting (S), not (?), as the appropriate form of moral supervenience. In "The Supervenience Argument Against Moral Realism", *Southern Journal of Philosophy* 30 (1992): 13–38, James Dreier urges a reading of Blackburn's argument on which it is committed to strong covariance.

25 Blackburn's (S), which he takes to characterize his notion of supervenience, is a little more complicated; it contains the relational predicate "x underlies y". However, I be-

and "dependent" interchangeably, or perhaps the former as specifying a sense of the latter. We have just seen that it is weak covariance that he says he had in mind when he spoke of supervenience. So there is the following substantive question: Can weak covariance give us a sense of dependence? Or equivalently: Can weak covariance be a form of supervenience if supervenience is to be a dependency relation?

Weak covariance does place a constraint on the distribution of supervenient properties relative to the distribution of their base properties. The question is whether this constraint is strong enough to warrant our considering it a form of dependence or determination. As I have argued elsewhere,[26] the answer must be in the negative. For concreteness consider the weak covariance of mental on physical properties; this covariance is consistent with each of the following situations:

(1) In a world that is just like this one in the distribution of physical properties, no mentality is present.
(2) In a world that is just like this one in all physical details, unicellular organisms are all fully conscious, while no humans or other primates exhibit mentality.
(3) In a world that is just like this one in all physical details, everything exhibits mentality in the same degree and kind.

These are all possible under weak covariance because its constraint works only *within* a single world at a time: *the fact that mentality is distributed in a certain way in one world has absolutely no effect on how it might be distributed in another world*. Intra-world consistency of the distribution of mental properties relative to the distribution of physical properties is the only constraint imposed by weak covariance.

This evidently makes weak covariance unsuitable for any dependency thesis with modal or subjunctive force. And modal force is arguably a necessary aspect of any significant dependency claim. Thus, when we say that the mental is dependent on the physical, we would, I think, want to exclude each of the possibilities, (1)–(3).[27]

Not so with strong covariance: property-to-property connections between supervenient and subvenient properties carry over to other worlds. That is obvious from both versions of strong covariance. Consider version

lieve what he has in mind with (S) is best read, and restated, as a definition of "underlie", that is, the converse of "supervene".

26 E.g., in "Concepts of Supervenience".
27 For some interesting considerations in defense of weak covariance in connection with materialism, see William Seager, "Weak Supervenience and Materialism", *Philosophy and Phenomenological Research* 48 (1988): 697–709.

II: When applied to the psychophysical case, it says that if anything has a mental property M, then there is some physical property P such that the "$P \rightarrow M$" conditional holds across all possible worlds. This supports in a straightforward way the assertion that the psychological character of a thing is entailed, or necessitated, by its physical nature. The strength of entailment, or necessitation, in this statement depends on how the modal term "necessarily" is interpreted, or alternatively, what possible worlds are involved in our quantification over them (e.g., whether we are talking about all possible worlds, or only physically or nomologically possible worlds, etc.).

But does strong covariance give us dependence or determination? If the mental strongly covaries with the physical, does this mean that the mental is dependent on, or determined by, the physical? As we saw, strong covariance is essentially a relation of entailment or necessitation. We notice this initial difference between necessitation and dependence: dependence, or determination, is usually understood to be asymmetric whereas entailment or necessitation is neither symmetric nor asymmetric. We sometimes speak of "mutual dependence" or "mutual determination"; however, when nonreductive physicalists appeal to supervenience as a way of expressing the dependence of the mental on the physical, they pretty clearly have in mind an asymmetric relation: they would say that their thesis automatically excludes the converse dependence of the physical on the mental. "Functional dependence", in the sense that the two state variables of a system are related by a mathematical function, may be neither symmetric nor asymmetric; however, what we want is *metaphysical* or *ontic* dependence or determination, not merely the fact that values of one variable are determined as a mathematical function of those of another variable.

It isn't difficult to think of cases in which strong covariance fails to be asymmetric: think of a domain of perfect spheres.[28] The surface area of each sphere strongly covaries with its volume, and conversely, the volume with the surface area. And we don't want to say either determines, or depends on, the other, in any sense of these terms that implies an asymmetry. There is only a functional determination, and dependence, both

28 This example is similar to the one used by Lawrence Lombard in his interesting and helpful discussion of covariance and dependence in *Events: A Metaphysical Study* (London: Routledge, Kegan Paul, 1986), pp. 225ff. My discussion here is indebted to Lombard, and also to Michael R. DePaul, "Supervenience and Moral Dependence", *Philosophical Studies* 51 (1987): 425–439; and Thomas R. Grimes, "The Myth of Supervenience", *Pacific Philosophical Quarterly* 69 (1988): 152–160.

ways; but we would hesitate to impute a metaphysical or ontological dependence either way.

Could we get a relation of dependency by requiring that the subvenient properties not also strongly covary with the supervenient properties? Let us consider the following proposal:[29]

A-properties depend on B-properties just in case A strongly covaries with B, but not conversely; that is, any B-indiscernible things are A-indiscernible but there are A-indiscernible things that are B-discernible.

In most cases of asymmetric dependence this condition appears to hold; for example, the mental strongly covaries with the physical, but the physical does not strongly covary with the mental; and similarly for the evaluative and the descriptive. Moreover, all of these examples involve large and comprehensive systems of properties. So the idea would be that when an asymmetric strong covariance obtains for two comprehensive systems of properties, a dependency relation may be imputed to them.

It isn't clear that this proposal states a necessary condition for dependence. For consider this: chemical kinds (e.g., water, gold, etc.) and their microphysical compositions (at least, at one level of description) seem to strongly covary with each other, and yet it is true, presumably, that natural kinds are asymmetrically dependent on microphysical structures. Here our mereological intuition, that macrophysical properties are asymmetrically dependent on microphysical structures, seems to be the major influence on our thinking, cancelling out the fact that the converse strong covariance may also be present. I admit that this is not a clear-cut example; for one thing, the converse strong covariance could perhaps be defeated by going to a deeper micro-level description; for another, one might argue that there is here no dependence either way, since being a certain chemical kind just *is* having a certain micro-structure.

It is even less clear whether the proposal states a sufficient condition for dependence. There is reason to think it does not. For what does the added second condition that B not covary with A really contribute? What is clear is this: the absence of strong covariance from B to A guarantees that B does not depend on A. For that means that there are objects with identical B-properties but with different A-properties. So the net effect of this added condition is just that B does not depend on A. The question

---

29 In "The Myth of Supervenience" Grimes considers a criterion of this form and rejects it as neither necessary nor sufficient. The possible counterexamples I consider below are consistent with Grimes's argument; however, only schematic examples are presented by Grimes.

then is this: Can we count on A to depend on B whenever A strongly covaries with B and B does not depend on A?

One might argue for an affirmative answer as follows: "Strong covariance between A and B requires an explanation, and it is highly likely that any explanation must appeal to an asymmetric relation of dependence. So either A depends on B or B depends on A; but the failure of strong covariance from B to A shows that B doesn't depend on A. Hence, A depends on B."

What this argument neglects, rather glaringly, is the possibility that an explanation of the covariance from A to B may be formulated in terms of a third set of properties. It seems clearly possible for there to be three sets of properties A, B, and C, such that A and B each depend on C, A covaries with B but B does not covary with A, and A does not depend on B.[30] Something like this could happen if, although both A and B covary with C, B makes finer discriminations than A, so that indiscernibility in regard to B-properties entails indiscernibility with respect to A, but not conversely.

As a possible example consider this: I've heard that there is a correlation between intelligence as measured by the IQ test and manual dexterity. It is possible that both manual dexterity and intelligence depend on certain genetic and developmental factors, and that intelligence strongly covaries with manual dexterity but not conversely. If such were the case, we would not consider intelligence to be dependent on, or determined by, manual dexterity.

Although the argument, therefore, has a serious flaw, it is not without value. Observed correlations of properties, especially between two comprehensive systems of properties, cry out for an explanation, and when no third set of properties is in the offing that might provide an appropriate ("common cause") explanation, it may be reasonable to posit a direct dependency relation between the two property families. The proposed criterion of dependent covariation says that if B fails to covary with A, that rules out the possibility that B depends on A, leaving A's dependency on B as the only remaining possibility. So the criterion may be of some use in certain situations; however, it cannot be regarded – at least, in its present form – as an "analysis" of supervenient dependence, since the needed further condition (i.e., that there not be a set C on which both A and B severally depend) itself makes use of the concept of dependence.

Trying to define dependence in terms of covariance is not likely to

30 Grimes makes a similar point in "The Myth of Supervenience", p. 157.

meet with complete and unambiguous success. Consider the case of causal dependence. Experience has taught us that we are not likely to succeed in defining an asymmetric relation of causal dependence, or causal directionality, in terms only of nomological covariations between properties or event kinds.[31] Unless, that is, we make a direct appeal to some relation that is explicitly asymmetric, like temporal precedence. We are not likely to do any better with supervenient dependence; the proposal above, with the further proviso that the strong covariation holds for two *comprehensive* sets of properties, may be close to the best that can be done to generate dependence out of covariation. All this points to the conclusion that the idea of dependence, whether causal or supervenient, is metaphysically deeper and richer than what can be captured by property covariance, even when the latter is supplemented with the usual modal notions.[32]

Much of the philosophical interest that supervenience has elicited lies in the hope that it is a relation of dependency; many philosophers saw in it the promise of a new type of dependency relation that seemed just right, neither too strong nor too weak, allowing us to navigate between reductionism and outright dualism. And it is the dependency aspect of supervenience, not the covariation component, that can sanction many of the usual philosophical implications drawn from, or associated with, supervenience theses concerning various subject matters. Often it is thought, and claimed, that a thing has a supervenient property *because,* or *in virtue of the fact that,* it has the corresponding base property, or that its having the relevant base property *explains* why it has the supervenient property. All these relations are essentially asymmetric, and are in the same generic family of relations that includes dependence and determination. Clearly, property covariation by itself does not warrant the use of "because", "in virtue of", etc., in describing the relationship any more than it warrants the attribution of dependence. Thus, if we want to promote the doctrine of psychophysical supervenience, intending it to include a claim of psychophysical dependence, we had better be prepared to produce an independent justification of the dependency claim which

---

31 For further discussion see J. L. Mackie, *The Cement of the Universe* (Oxford: Oxford University Press, 1974), ch. 7; David H. Sanford, "The Direction of Causation and the Direction of Conditionship", *Journal of Philosophy* 73 (1976): 193–207, and "The Direction of Causation and the Direction of Time", *Midwest Studies in Philosophy* 9 (1984): 53–75; Tom Beauchamp and Alexander Rosenberg, *Hume and the Problem of Causation* (New York and Oxford: Oxford University Press, 1981), ch. 6.
32 Could counterfactuals help? Perhaps; see, e.g., David Lewis, "Causation", *Journal of Philosophy* 70 (1973): 556–567; but also Grimes, "The Myth of Supervenience".

goes beyond the mere fact of covariance between mental and physical properties.

Property covariation *per se* is metaphysically neutral; dependence, and other such relations, suggest ontological and explanatory directionality – that upon which something depends is ontologically and explanatorily prior to, and more basic than, that which depends on it. In fact, we can think of the dependency relation as explaining or grounding property covariations: e.g., one might say that mental properties covary with physical properties because the former are dependent on the latter. Direct dependence, however, is not the only possible explanation; as we saw, two sets of properties may covary because each is dependent on a common third set.

The upshot, therefore, is this: it is best to separate the covariation element from the dependency element in the relation of supervenience. Our discussion shows that property covariation alone, even in the form of "strong asymmetric covariance", does not by itself give us dependency; in that sense, dependency is an additional component of supervenience. But the two components are not entirely independent; for it seems that the following is true: for there to be property dependence there must be property covariation. We can, therefore, distinguish between two forms of dependence, each based on one of the two covariation relations. Thus, "strong dependence" requires strong covariation, while "weak dependence" can do with weak covariation. What must be added to covariation to yield dependence is an interesting, and metaphysically deep, question. It's analogous, in certain ways, to J. L. Mackie's question as to what must be added to mere causal connectedness to generate "causal priority", or "causal directionality". Mackie and others have sought a single, uniform account of that in which causal priority consists; however, it isn't at all obvious that our question concerning dependence admits of a single answer. Evidently, dependency requires different explanations in different cases, and for any given case there can be competing accounts of why the dependency holds. Among the most important cases of supervenient dependence are instances of part–whole dependence ("mereological supervenience"), and these may constitute a special basic category of dependence. Concerning the supervenience of the moral on the naturalistic, the classic ethical naturalist will formulate an explanation in terms of meaning dependence or priority; the noncognitivist's account may involve considerations of the function of moral language and why its proper fulfillment requires consistency, in an appropriate sense, of moral avowals in relation to descriptive judgments. These cases seem fundamentally different from

148

one another metaphysically, and any "analysis" of dependence that applies to all varieties of dependence, I think, is unlikely to throw much light on the nature of dependence. We will briefly return to these issues in a later section.

V. COVARIANCE AND REDUCIBILITY

As previously noted, Davidson has been chiefly responsible for the close association of supervenience with both the idea of dependency and that of nonreducibility. Nonreducibility, however, has been less firmly associated with supervenience than dependency has been; and there has been some controversy as to whether supervenience is in fact a nonreductive relation. Also, it seems that the association of nonreducibility with supervenience has come about from the historical happenstance that Moore and Hare, who are well known for their supervenience thesis concerning the moral relative to the naturalistic, also formulated classic and influential arguments against ethical naturalism, the doctrine that the moral is definitionally reducible to the naturalistic.[33] So why not model a nonreductive psychophysical relation on supervenience? If the moral could be supervenient on the naturalistic without being reducible to it, couldn't the mental be supervenient on the physical without being reducible to it?[34] But it is possible that the sense of reduction Moore had in mind when he argued against the reducibility of the moral is very different from the concept of reducibility that is now current in philosophy of mind; and it is also possible that Moore was just mistaken in thinking that he could have supervenience without reducibility.

Moore's so-called "open question" argument suggests that the sort of naturalistic reduction he was trying to undermine is a *definitional* reductionism – the claim that ethical terms are analytically definable in naturalistic terms. Moreover, the argument is effective only against the claim that there is an *overt synonymy* relation between an ethical term and its purported naturalistic definition. For consider what the open question is intended to test: for any pair of expressions X and Y, we are supposed to determine whether "Is everything that is X also Y?" can be used to ask an intelligible and significant question. The idea is that if X is definable as Y (that is, if X and Y are synonymous), the question would not be an

---

33 There may also have been the influence of the emergentist doctrine that emergent properties are irreducible to their "basal" conditions.

34 For further discussion of supervenience in relation to nonreductive physicalism see my "The Myth of Nonreductive Materialism", Essay 14 of this volume.

intelligible one (consider: "Is everyone who is a bachelor also a male?" and "Does everything that is a cube also have twelve edges?"). It is clear that the logical equivalence of X and Y, or the fact that in some philosophical sense X can be "analyzed" as Y, etc., would not make the question necessarily unintelligible or lack significance. The nomological equivalence between X and Y probably was the furthest thing from Moore's mind; he pointedly says that even if we found a "physical equivalent" of the color yellow, certain "light-vibrations" as Moore puts it,[35] these light-vibrations are not what the term "yellow" *means*. So Moore's anti-naturalism was the denial of the definitional reducibility of ethical terms to naturalistic terms, where the notion of definition itself is extremely narrowly construed.

The kind of reduction Davidson had in mind in "Mental Events" is considerably wider than definitional reduction of the Moorean sort: the main focus of his antireductionist arguments is *nomological* reduction, reduction underwritten by contingent empirical laws correlating, and perhaps identifying, properties being reduced with those in the reduction base. Davidson's argument is two-pronged: the demise of logical behaviorism shows the unavailability of a definitional reduction of the mental, and his own psychophysical anomalism, the doctrine that there are no laws correlating mental with physical properties, shows that a nomological reduction isn't in the cards either.[36] Moore would have been unconcerned about nomological reducibility; his anti-naturalism apparently permitted strong, necessary synthetic a priori, relationships between the moral and the nonmoral.

I earlier noted that the issue of reducibility seemed less central to supervenience than that of dependence. It is somewhat ironic that covariance seems more intimately connected with reduction than it is with dependence. But before getting into the details we must know what we mean by reduction. Reduction is standardly understood as a relation between *theories*, where a theory is understood to consist of a distinctive theoretical vocabulary and a set of laws formulated in this vocabulary. The reduction of one theory to another is thought to be accomplished when the laws of the reduced theory are shown to be derivable from the laws of the reducer theory, with the help of "bridge principles" connecting terms of the reduced theory with those of the reducer.[37] Just what bridge laws are re-

---

35 *Principia Ethica*, p. 10.   36 For details see Davidson's "Mental Events".

37 This is the model of derivational reduction developed by Ernest Nagel in *The Structure of Science* (Harcourt, Brace & World, 1961). Whether this is the most appropriate model to be used in the present context could be debated; on this issue see William C. Wimsatt,

quired obviously depends on the strength of the two theories involved, and there seems very little that is both general and informative to say about this. The only requirement on the bridge laws that can be explicitly stated, independently of the particular theories involved, is the following, which I will call "the condition of strong connectibility":[38]

Each primitive predicate P of the theory being reduced is connected with a coextensive predicate Q of the reducer in a biconditional law of the form: "for all x, Px iff Qx"; and similarly for all relational predicates.

If this condition is met, then no matter what the content of the two theories may be, derivational reduction is guaranteed; for these biconditional laws would allow the rewriting of the laws of the theory being reduced as laws of the reducer, and if any of these rewrites is not derivable from the pre-existing laws of the reducer, it can be added as an additional law (assuming both theories to be true). In discussing reduction and covariance, therefore, we will focus on this condition of strong connectibility.[39]

To begin, weak covariance obviously does not entail strong connectibility. Weak covariance lacks an appropriate modal force to generate laws; as noted, the correlations entailed by weak covariance between supervenient and subvenient properties have no modal force, being restricted to particular worlds.

What then of strong covariance? Here the situation is different; for consider strong covariance II: it says that whenever a supervening property P is instantiated by an object, there is a subvenient property Q such that the instantiating object has it and the following conditional holds: necessarily if anything has Q, then it has P. So the picture we have is that for supervenient property P, there is a set of properties, Q_1, Q_2, . . . in the subvenient set such that each Q_i is necessarily sufficient for P. Assume that this list contains all the subvenient properties each of which is sufficient for P. Consider then their disjunction: Q_1 or Q_2 or . . . (or UQ_i, for short). This disjunction may be infinite; however, it

"Reductive Explanation: A Functional Account", in R. S. Cohen *et al.*, eds. *PSA 1974*, pp. 671–710.
38 Restricting ourselves to theories formulated in first-order languages.
39 There are various plausible considerations for thinking that derivational reduction as characterized isn't enough (and that it may not even be necessary). One line of consideration seems to show that we need *identities* of entities and properties rather than correlations; another line of consideration argues that the reduction must exhibit some underlying "mechanism", preferably at a micro-level, that explains how the higher processes work. We must bypass these issues here.

is a well-defined disjunction, as well-defined as the union of infinitely many sets. It is easy to see that this disjunction is necessarily coextensive with P.

First, it is clear enough that UQ_i entails P, since each disjunct does. Second, does P entail UQ_i? Suppose not: something then, say b, has P but not UQ_i. According to strong covariance, b has some property in the subvenient set, say S, such that necessarily whatever has S also has P. But then S must be one of the Q_i, and since b has S, b must have UQ_i. So P entails UQ_i. So P and UQ_i are necessarily coextensive, and whether the modality here is metaphysical, logical, or nomological, it should be strong enough to give us a serviceable "bridge law" for reduction.

So does this show that the strong connectibility is entailed by strong covariance, and hence that the supervenience relation incorporating strong covariance entails reducibility? Some philosophers will resist this inference.[40] Their concern will focus on the way the nomological coextension for P was constructed in the subvenient set – in particular, the fact that the constructional procedure made use of disjunction.[41] There are two questions, and only two as far as I can see, that can be raised here: (1) Is disjunction a proper way of forming properties out of properties? (2) Given that disjunction is a permissible property-forming operation, is it proper to form infinite disjunctions? I believe it is easy to answer (2): the answer has to be a yes. I don't see any special problem with an infinite procedure here, any more than in the case of forming infinite unions of sets or the addition of infinite series of numbers. We are not here talking about predicates, or linguistic expressions, but properties; I am not saying that we should accept predicates of infinite length, although I don't know if anything would go astray if we accepted infinite disjunctive predicates that are finitely specified (we could then introduce a simple predicate to abbreviate it). So the main question is (1).

Is disjunction a permissible mode of property composition? One might argue as follows for a negative answer, at least in the present context:

---

40 See Paul Teller, "Comments on Kim's Paper", and John Post, "Comment on Teller", both in *Southern Journal of Philosophy* 22 (1983), *The Spindel Conference Supplement* ("Supervenience"): 57–62, 163–167.

41 This in part meets an objection that John Post has raised (in his "Comment on Teller") against my earlier construction of these coextensions (in "Concepts of Supervenience") which made use of other property-forming operations. Post's specific objection was aimed at property complementation (or negation). On this issue see also William Seager, "Weak Supervenience and Materialism", and James Van Cleve, "Supervenience and Closure", *Philosophical Studies* 58 (1990): 225–238. Some remarks to follow in the main text are relevant to Post's point.

Bridge laws are laws and must connect nomological kinds or properties (so their predicates must be "lawlike", "projectible", and so on). However, from the fact that M and N are each nomic, it does not follow that their disjunction, M or N, is also nomic. Consequently, our constructional procedure fails to guarantee the nomologicality of the generated coextensions.

One might try to buttress this point by the following argument: the core concept of a property is *resemblance* – that is, the sharing of a property must ensure resemblance in some respect. We can now see that the disjunctive operation does not preserve this crucial feature of propertyhood (nor does complementation, one might add). Round objects resemble one another and so do red objects; but we cannot count on objects with the property of being *round or red* to resemble each other. This is why "conjunctive properties" present no difficulties, but "disjunctive properties", and also "negative properties", are problematic.

I do not find these arguments compelling. It isn't at all obvious that we must be bound by such a narrow and restrictive conception of what nomic properties, or properties in general, must be in the present context. When reduction is at issue, we are talking about theories, theories couched in their distinctive theoretical vocabularies. And it seems that we allow, and ought to allow, freedom to combine and recombine the basic theoretical predicates and functors by the usual logical and mathematical operations available in the underlying language, without checking each step with something like the resemblance criterion; that would work havoc with free and creative scientific theorizing. What, after all, is the point of having these logical operations on predicates? When we discuss the definitional reducibility of, say, ethical terms to naturalistic terms, it would be absurd to disallow definitions that make use of disjunctions, negations, and what have you; why should we deny ourselves the use of these operations in forming reductive bridges of other sorts? Moreover, it may well be that when an artificial-looking predicate proves useful, or essential, in a fecund and well-corroborated theory and gets entrenched, we will come to think of it as expressing a robust property, an important respect in which objects and events can resemble each other. In certain situations, that recognizing something as a genuine property would make reduction possible may itself be a compelling reason for doing so![42]

---

42 I wonder how "natural" the quantity $1/2 \ (mv^2)$ looked before it was identified as kinetic energy.

Let me make a final point about this. The fact that for each supervenient property, a coextension – a qualitative coextension if not a certifiably nomic one – exists in the subvenient base properties means that there is at least the possibility of our developing a theory that will give a perspicuous theoretical description of this coextension, thus providing us with strong reason for taking the coextension as a nomic property. At least in this somewhat attenuated sense, strong covariance can be said to entail the possibility of reducing the supervenient to the subvenient. And we should note this: if we knew strong covariance to fail, that would scotch the idea of reduction once and for all.

We should briefly look at "global supervenience", or "global covariance", as a nonreductive supervenience relation. For this idea has been touted by many philosophers as an appropriate dependence relation between the mental and the physical which is free of reductive implications.[43] The basic idea of global supervenience is to apply the indiscernibility considerations globally to "worlds" taken as units of comparison. Standardly the idea is expressed as follows:

Worlds that are indiscernible in respect of subvenient properties are indiscernible in respect of supervenient properties.

Worlds that coincide in respect of truths involving subvenient properties coincide in respect of truths involving supervenient properties.

For our present purposes we may think of indiscernibility of worlds in respect of a given set of properties (say, physical properties) as consisting in the fact that these properties are distributed over their individuals in the same way (for simplicity we may assume that the worlds have the same individuals).

It is known that this covariance relation does not imply property-to-property correlations between supervenient and subvenient properties; thus, it does not imply what I have called strong connectibility.[44] So global supervenience, along with weak supervenience, can qualify as a nonreductive relation. But this is a signal that global covariance may be quite

---

43 See, e.g., Terence Horgan, "Supervenience and Microphysics", *Pacific Philosophical Quarterly* 63 (1982): 29–43; David Lewis, "New Work for a Theory of Universals", *Australasian Journal of Philosophy* 61 (1983): 343–377. Also Geoffrey Hellman and Frank Thompson,"Physicalism: Ontology, Determination, and Reduction", *Journal of Philosophy* 73 (1975): 551–564.

44 See, e.g., Bradford Petrie, "Global Supervenience and Reduction", *Philosophy and Phenomenological Research* 48 (1987): 119–130. (Added 1993: for further discussion of this issue, see "Postscripts on Supervenience", section 3, in this volume.)

weak, perhaps too weak to sustain a dependency relation of significance.[45]

As I have argued elsewhere,[46] this can be seen in at least two ways. First, this form of covariance permits worlds that differ minutely in subvenient properties to differ drastically in respect of supervenient properties. Thus, global covariance of the mental with respect to the physical is consistent with there being a world that differs from this world in some insignificant physical detail (say, it contains one more hydrogen atom) but which differs radically in psychological respects (say, it is wholly void of mentality). Second, global covariance as explained fails to imply weak covariance; that is, it can hold where weak covariance fails. This means that psychophysical global covariance can be true in a world that contains exact physical duplicates with divergent psychological characteristics; it permits the existence in the actual world of an exact physical replica of you who, however, has the mentality of a fruit fly. There certainly is reason to wonder whether a supervenience relation whose property covariance requirement is this weak can qualify as a dependency relation. As I argued earlier, property covariance alone, even "strong covariance", does not yield dependence, and in that sense dependence must be considered an independent component of supervenience in any case. However, again as I argued, dependence does require an appropriate relation of property covariance. This raises the following question: Is global covariance strong enough to ground a respectable supervenience relation? We may well wonder whether a supervenience relation based on global covariance might not turn out to be incongruous in that, given this is what it requires of property covariance, the dependency component makes little sense.

I suggest, however, that we keep an open mind about this, and adopt an attitude of "Let one hundred supervenience concepts bloom!" Each may have its own sphere of application, serving as a useful tool for formulating and evaluating philosophical doctrines of interest. And this does not mean that we must discard the core idea of supervenience captured by the maxim "No difference of one kind without a difference of another kind". It's just that we now recognize that this core idea can be explained in distinct but interestingly related ways, and that what we want to say about a supervenience claim about a specific subject matter may depend on the interpretation of supervenience appropriate to the context. I think this is philosophical progress.

45 I believe this indeed is the case with psychophysical global supervenience; for details see my "'Strong' and 'Global' Supervenience Revisited" and "The Myth of Nonreductive Materialism".
46 "'Strong' and 'Global' Supervenience Revisited".

VI. GROUNDS OF SUPERVENIENCE

It has been argued that supervenience is a mysterious and unexplained relation, and hence that any philosophical argument couched in the vocabulary of supervenience is a retrogressive and obfuscating maneuver incapable of yielding any illumination for the issue on hand. For example, Stephen Schiffer takes a dim view of those who appeal to supervenience:

> How could being told that non-natural moral properties stood in the supervenience relation to physical properties make them any more palatable? On the contrary, invoking a special primitive metaphysical relation of supervenience to explain how non-natural moral properties were related to physical properties was just to add mystery to mystery, to cover one obscurantist move with another. I therefore find it more than a little ironic, and puzzling, that supervenience is nowadays being heralded as a way of making nonpleonastic, irreducibly non-natural properties cohere with an acceptably naturalistic solution to the mind–body problem. . . . the appeal to a special primitive relation of 'supervenience', as defined above, is obscurantist in the extreme.[47]

The supervenience relation Schiffer refers to "as defined above" is in effect our strong covariance II, with the further proviso that the relationship "necessarily everything with G has F" is an unexplainable "brute metaphysical fact".

There perhaps have been philosophers who deserve Schiffer's excoriations; however, we need to separate Schiffer's editorial comment that supervenience is a "brute metaphysical" fact from a mere claim of supervenience concerning a given topic. Schiffer's addition is a nontrivial further claim, which someone advocating a supervenience thesis might or might not wish to make, that goes beyond the claim of supervenient covariance or dependence. For there is nothing in the concept of covariance or dependence that forces us to view supervenience as invariably involving unexplainable relationships. In fact, when a supervenience claim is made, it makes perfectly good sense to ask for an *explanation* of why the supervenience relation holds. Why does the moral supervene on the nonmoral? Why do facts about wholes supervene, if they do, on facts about their parts? Why does the mental supervene on the physical?

It may well be that the only answer we can muster for some of these questions is that, as far as we can tell, it is a brute fact. But that need not be the only kind of answer; we should, and can, hope to do better. This

---

47 *Remnants of Meaning* (Cambridge: MIT Press, 1987), pp. 153–154.

is evident from the following fact alone: supervenience, whether in the sense of covariation or in the sense that includes dependence, is transitive. This means that it is possible, at least in certain situations, to answer the question "Why does X supervene on Y?" by saying that, as it turns out, X supervenes on Z, and Z in turn supervenes on Y. The interpolation of another supervenient tier may well explain why X-to-Y supervenience holds. (Compare: Why does X cause Y? Answer: X causes Z, and Z causes Y.) As Schiffer says, Moore gave a sort of "brute fact" account of moral supervenience, and given his metaethical theory he probably had no other choice: we "intuit" necessary synthetic a priori connections between nonnatural moral properties and certain natural properties. But it isn't just ethical intuitionists like Moore who accept moral supervenience; Hare, whose metaethics radically diverges from Moore's, too has championed moral supervenience. And we also have Blackburn, a "projectivist" moral antirealist, who professes belief in moral supervenience, not to mention John Post,[48] who is an objectivist about ethical judgments. As I take it, these philosophers would give different accounts of why moral supervenience obtains; as we noted in our earlier discussion of dependence as a component of supervenience, Hare would presumably give an account in terms of some consistency requirement on the use of language of prescription. And Blackburn has argued against "moral realism" on the ground that it, unlike his own projectivist "quasi-realism", is unable to give a satisfactory explanation of moral supervenience.[49]

We may distinguish between two kinds of request for a "ground" of a supervenience relation. One concerns *general* claims of supervenience: why a given family of properties, say mental properties, supervene on another family, say neurobiological properties. Why does the mental supervene on the physical, and why does the normative supervene on the nonnormative? These are perfectly good, intelligible questions, which may or may not have informative answers. The second type of request concerns the relationship between *specific* supervenient properties and their base properties: Why is it that pain supervenes on the activation of A-delta and C-fibers? Why doesn't, say, itch or tickle supervene on it? Why doesn't pain supervene on, say, the excitation of A- and B-fibers?

The potential for supplying explanations for specific supervenience re-

48 See his "On the Determinacy of Valuation", *Philosophical Studies* 45 (1984): 315–333.
49 See Blackburn, "Supervenience Revisited". For discussion of Blackburn's argument see James Klagge, "An Alleged Difficulty Concerning Moral Properties", *Mind* 93 (1984): 370–380; James Dreier, "The Supervenience Argument Against Moral Realism".

lationships varies for different mind–body theories. Both the behaviorist and the functionalist could formulate a plausible meaning-based explanation (I mean, plausible *given* their basic doctrines): pain, not itch, supervenes on physicalistic condition P because of an analytic, semantic connection between "pain" and the standard expression for P. For the behaviorist, the connection is a direct one of definability. The functionalist will appeal to an additional empirical fact, saying something like this: "pain", as a matter of meaning, designates a certain causal-functional role, and it turns out, as a contingent empirical fact, that condition P occupies this causal role (in organisms or structures of a given kind). The functionalist can push ahead with his search for explanations and ask: why does condition P occupy this causal role in these organisms? This question is an empirical scientific question, and may be given an evolution-based answer, or one based in engineering considerations (in the case of artifacts); and there may be answers of other types.

There are philosophers who have a fundamentally physicalist outlook on the mind–body problem and yet would reject any analytic, definitional relationships between mental and nonmental expressions. Many of them would accept a thoroughgoing dependence of the mental on the physical grounded in lawlike type–type correlations between the two domains. Epiphenomenalism is such a position; so is the classic nonfunctionalist type-identity theory based on the supposed existence of pervasive psychophysical correlations. It seems that someone holding a physicalist position like these has no choice but to view the relationship between, say, pain and C-fiber activation as a brute fact that is not further explainable, something like the way G. E. Moore viewed the relationship between the nonnatural property of goodness and the natural property on which it supervenes. In this respect, the position of a physicalist who accepts psychophysical supervenience, especially of the "strong covariance" sort, but rejects a physicalist rendering of mental expressions, is much like that of those emergentists who regarded the phenomena of emergence as not susceptible of further explanation; that is, it is not further explainable why mentality emerges just when these physicochemical conditions are present, but not otherwise. Samuel Alexander, a leading emergentist, recommended that we accept these emergence relationships "with natural piety"; Lloyd Morgan, referring to Alexander, announced, "I accept this phrase".[50]

Is this a serious blemish on nonfunctionalist physicalism? This is an

50 *Emergent Evolution*, p. 36.

interesting, and difficult, question. Its proponents might insist that all of us must accept certain brute facts about this world, and that it is necessary to count fundamental psychophysical correlations among them in order to develop a plausible theory of mind, all things considered. This is only an opening move in what is likely to be a protracted dialectic between them and the functionalists, something we must set aside.[51] I will conclude with some brief remarks concerning explanations of general supervenience claims.

I think that the only direct way of explaining why a general supervenience relation holds, e.g., why the mental supervenes on the physical, is to appeal to the presence of specific supervenience relations – that is, appropriate correlations between specific supervenient properties and their subvenient bases. If these specific correlations are themselves explainable, so much the better; but whether or not they are, invoking them would constitute the first necessary step. Moreover, such correlations seem to be the best, and the most natural, *evidential ground* for supervenience claims – often the only kind of solid evidence we could have for *empirical* supervenience claims. Even the nonfunctionalist physicalist has an explanation of sorts for psychophysical supervenience: it holds because a pervasive system of lawlike psychophysical correlations holds. These correlations are logically contingent and empirically discovered; though they are not further explainable, they constitute our ground, both evidential and explanatory, of the supervenience of the mental on the physical.

This shows why a global supervenience claim *unaccompanied by the corresponding strong supervenience (or covariance) claim* can be so unsatisfying: we are being asked, it seems to me, to accept a sweeping claim about *all possible worlds,* say, that no two worlds could differ mentally without differing physically, on faith as a brute fact. In the absence of specific psychophysical correlations, and some knowledge of them, such a supervenience claim should strike us as a mere article of faith seriously lacking in motivation both evidentially and explanatorily; it would assert as a fact something that is apparently unexplainable and whose evidential status, moreover, is unclear and problematic. The attitude of the friends of global psychophysical supervenience is not unlike that of Samuel Alexander and Lloyd Morgan toward emergence: we must accept it "with natural piety"!

---

51 See for further discussion Terence Horgan and Mark Timmons, "Troubles on Moral Twin Earth: Moral Queerness Revisited"; *Synthese* 92 (1992): 221–260. Ernest Sosa has pointed out to me that appeals to meaning and analyticity, too, might involve appeals to brute facts in the end.

But there is this difference: the emergentists could at least point to the observed lawful correlations between specific mental and biological processes as evidence for the presence of a general system of such correlations encompassing all mental processes, and point to the latter as the ground of the general thesis of mental emergence.

9

Postscripts on supervenience

1. RELATIONAL SUPERVENIENCE

Asked how badly he wanted to win the Super Bowl Washington Redskin left guard Russ Grimm replied, "I'd run over my mother to win it." The quote was repeated to Los Angeles Raider inside linebacker Matt Millen, who answered, "I'd run over her, too, – I mean Grimm's mother."

Sports Illustrated, January 30, 1984[1]

Accounts of supervenience to date have almost exclusively focused on properties (that is, monadic attributes), although relations are informally mentioned sometimes in connection with supervenience. What happens if relations are explicitly taken into consideration in characterizing supervenience?

Let A be the supervening set of attributes, and B the base set. Consider first the case in which A includes an n-adic relation R, but B includes only monadic properties. It is evident that for R to supervene on B, the following condition is necessary and sufficient:

For any n-tuples, $\langle x_1, \ldots, x_n \rangle$ and $\langle y_1, \ldots, y_n \rangle$ (to be abbreviated as X_n and Y_n respectively), if they are indiscernible in set B, then $R(X_n)$ iff $R(Y_n)$

Depending on whether the n-tuples compared are restricted to a single world or may be recruited from different worlds, this will yield either "weak" or "strong" supervenience (Essay 5). But what is it for two n-tuples, X_n and Y_n, to be indiscernible from each other with respect to B? Since B is assumed to include only properties and no relations, the answer is simple: X_n is indiscernible from Y_n in B just in case for each i $(1 \leq i \leq n)$ x_i is indiscernible from y_i in respect of B-properties.

Many sundry relations seem to supervene on properties in the sense explained. Take, for example, the relation of *being taller than.* If Mary and

---

1 Quoted in Jaakko Hintikka and Jack Kulas, *Anaphora and Definite Descriptions* (Dordrecht: D. Reidel, 1985), p. 220.

Jane share all monadic attributes and so do Larry and Fred, then Mary is going to be taller than Larry if and only if Jane is taller than Fred. For this case, the supervenience base needs only to include heights. Many other relations are similar, for example, *being as tall as, being heavier than, being warmer than,* and *being wealthier than.* These relations hold for pairs of objects because of their "intrinsic properties" alone.[2] Perhaps, for this reason, these relations do not represent "real connections"; for Mary to be taller than Larry is for Mary's height to exceed Larry's, which is merely a relationship between two magnitudes, namely, numbers representing their heights. The same goes for pseudo-relations like the one expressed by "x is tall and y is quick," which holds for a pair, $\langle a, b \rangle$, just in case a is tall and b is quick. In fact, it may be possible to define a useful notion of genuine "relatedness" or "connectedness" in terms of failure of supervenience on monadic attributes.[3]

Evidently, there are relations that prima facie do not supervene on properties; for example, causal relations and certain spatiotemporal relations (e.g., *being earlier than, being to the east of*).[4] It would seem, therefore, that any supervenience base of such relations must itself include relations. In any case, for generality we need to consider cases in which the base set, B, also includes relations. How should we explain "indiscernibility in B" for such a B? Suppose that the supervenient set A includes a property P. We want to say things like "x and y are either both P or both not-P if they are indiscernible in set B." But what does this mean when relations are present in B? For simplicity, let us suppose that B contains one dyadic relation R. Something like the following can serve as a natural starting point:

(I) x and y are indiscernible with respect to R iff for every z, $R(x,z)$ iff $R(y,z)$, and $R(z,x)$ iff $R(z,y)$

This raises a question. Suppose Charles loves his mother; for you to be indiscernible from Charles in respect of loving, (I) requires you to love Charles's mother, not your mother. Is this what we want?

2 However, there may be deep questions about whether mass, temperature, and other quantitative physical magnitudes are truly intrinsic or covertly relational. These questions are likely to involve complex issues about measurement theory and the epistemology and metaphysics of concepts and properties. It would seem that those who take a strong positivist (or verificationist) stance on properties might well insist that these magnitudes turn out, on final analysis, to be relational properties.

3 The Leibnizian doctrine of the unreality of relations could be viewed as the claim that all relations supervene on intrinsic properties of the relata.

4 For further discussion of this issue see Paul Teller, "Relational Holism and Quantum Mechanics," *British Journal for Philosophy of Science* 37 (1986): 71–81.

But actually this is no problem. Consider *loving one's own mother;* this is, strictly speaking, not a relation, but a *relational property* which, although it harbors a relation, is monadic, not dyadic. This relational property must be distinguished from another relational property, that of *loving some particular person,* say Elizabeth II (assuming that there are such properties). According to (I), x and y must both have or both lack the property of loving Elizabeth – that is, they must either both love, or not love, Elizabeth – if they are to be indiscernible in respect of the relation of loving. It may be that we want the relational property of loving one's own mother, not the relation of loving, in the base set; but as long as the base includes loving as a genuine relation, (I) may well be what we should require for indiscernibility.

The situation becomes a bit more complicated when we consider x and y as they are in two different worlds, since an individual existing in one world may not exist in the other. When (I) is applied to a single world (that is, when x and y are evaluated for indiscernibility as they are within a single world), the quantifier "every z" has a natural reading: "z" ranges over the individuals of that world. But when x and y are compared as they are in two distinct worlds, how should we interpret "every z"? Suppose that x loves Elizabeth in this world, w_1, but y in world w_2 does not love her – in fact, no one loves her in w_2, for she doesn't exist there. Suppose, however, that for every individual z which exists in both w_1 and w_2, the proposed condition holds; that is, x loves z in w_1 iff y loves z in w_2, and z loves x in w_1 iff z loves y in w_2. Should we say in this case that x in w_1 and y in w_2 are indiscernible in respect of loving? According to (I), they must be judged to be discernible. But we seem to have no clear "intuitions" about this, and it seems doubtful that there is a correct general answer here. For example, in a context in which we are discussing "universal love" as a virtue-making characteristic, it may well be appropriate to judge x and y to be indiscernible; on the other hand, in other contexts it may be relevant to consider just how many people one loves, in which case we may well take x and y to be discernible. But in these cases it may be that what we ought to include in the supervenience base are such relational properties as *loving everyone* and *loving n persons* (for some integer n) rather than the relation of loving.

Technically, we can set aside this issue by assuming the domain of individuals to be constant for all possible worlds. But that of course isn't to resolve it, since we must accept worlds in which some individuals of this world do not exist, although it may be a debatable question whether any world could have individuals that are not in this world. There is, however, a related issue. Consider the following situation: we want to discuss whether a certain property P of wholes supervenes on the properties and relations characterizing their parts. Let X and Y be two distinct wholes with no overlapping parts, and suppose X consists of parts, $x_1, \ldots, x_n$ and Y consists of $y_1, \ldots, y_m$. We would expect some properties of X and Y to depend on the relationships characterizing their parts – how these parts are organized and structured – as well as the properties of the parts. Thus, this seems like the kind of case to which relational supervenience, in particular one in which the supervenience base includes relations, is most usefully applied. What should we say about the conditions under which X and Y may be said to be "mereologically indiscernible" – that is, alike in respect of the way they are made up of parts?

In situations of this kind it would be absurd to enforce (I). For suppose that a dyadic relation, R, holds for two mereological parts of X, $\langle x_1, x_2 \rangle$; (I) would require for mereological indiscernibility of X and Y that some y_j be related by R to x_2! Obviously, what we want is that X and Y be characterized by *the same relational structure*. This means that what is important here is not *particularized relational properties* (like being R to x_2, loving Queen Elizabeth) but *generalized relational properties* (like being R to something or other, loving one's own mother, and loving at least one person). Thus, if x_1 has R to x_2, then some corresponding element, y_j, of Y must have R to an appropriate y_h, not to x_2. One way of making this precise would be to require that the two sets, $\{x_1, \ldots, x_n\}$ and $\{y_1, \ldots, y_m\}$, be *isomorphic* to each other under the properties and relations in base set B. That is:

There exists a one–one function f from $\{x_1, \ldots x_n\}$ to $\{y_1, \ldots, y_m\}$ such that for any r-adic attribute R in B, R holds for $\langle a_1, \ldots, a_r \rangle$ (where each $a_i \in \{x_1, \ldots, x_n\}$) iff R holds for $\langle f(a_1), \ldots, f(a_r) \rangle$.

This requires that $n = m$, and that is too strong. I believe we need mereological indiscernibility even when this condition doesn't hold; for certain purposes we would want to allow, say, two unequal masses of copper or two social groups with unequal numbers of members to be mereologically indiscernible. This issue is related to the one briefly discussed earlier that arises when two individuals from different worlds are compared for indiscernibility in respect of relations. What these cases suggest is that we may do well to work with *similarity* in the subvenient base set, rather than insist on indiscernibility, when relations are present. In particular, the supervenience of the properties of wholes might be more appropriately explained in terms of their *mereological similarity* rather than their *mereologi-*

cal indiscernibility. If this is not entirely off target, it has a moral for global supervenience as well: here, too, what we should be looking for may well be a high degree of *overall similarity between worlds* rather than strict indiscernibility, something that will be difficult to obtain for whole worlds (see Essay 5 for similarity-based global supervenience). In fact, it cannot obtain for worlds with different cardinalities, making global supervenience less useful than it should be. Another moral of these reflections is that strict relational supervenience – that is, relational supervenience satisfying a generalized version of (I) above – may not be such a useful concept after all; what is more useful may well be cases where the subvenient set contains relational properties, whether of the generalized or particularized sorts, rather than relations. And it may well be that most instances which we regard as cases of supervenience on relations are, in reality, not cases of relational supervenience, but cases of property supervenience in which the subvenient set includes relational properties.

In any case, many interesting issues arise when relations are explicitly brought into supervenience, and they are deserving of further study. I think that this will not only help clarify supervenience but also enhance our understanding of the nature of relations and relational properties.

2. MORE ON SUPERVENIENCE AND DEPENDENCE

In Essay 8, it was argued that the property covariation component of supervenience does not by itself entail the dependence of the supervenient properties on the subvenient base properties, and that the dependence relation involved in supervenience may differ from case to case. It was also suggested that a specific dependence relation might be invoked to *explain* why property covariation holds in a given case. I now want to draw some further consequences from these points.

I believe that these points, if correct, affect the possibility of using supervenience to build an *explanatory* account of something – say, of the mind–body relation. The thesis that the mental supervenes on the physical turns out to be a conjunction of the following two claims: *the covariance claim,* that there is a certain specified pattern of property covariation between the mental and the physical, and *the dependence claim,* that the mental depends on the physical.[5] But the thesis itself says nothing about the *nature* of the dependence involved: it tells us neither what kind of depen-

5 In Essay 8, nonreducibility was also considered; however, this is a controversial issue and the questions of reducibility are best left out of the concept of supervenience.

dency it is, nor how the dependency grounds or explains the property co-variation.

Moreover, unlike, for example, causal dependence, supervenient dependence does not represent a single, homogeneous type of dependence.[6] It is easily seen (Essay 8) that supervenience, or property covariation, holds in different cases for different reasons. Consider, for example, the supervenience of the moral on the nonmoral. Why do moral properties supervene on nonmoral ones? What might explain this? As we know, the proffered answers vary: the ethical naturalist tells us that it's because moral properties are definable in terms of nonmoral, "naturalistic" properties. For the noncognitivist, ethical predicates do not express real properties, and there are no such things as moral properties; she would try to derive the supervenience thesis from some kind of a consistency constraint on the language of prescription and evaluation.[7] The ethical intuitionist would take the supervenience relation as fundamental and unexplainable, something we can "intuit" through our "moral sense." A better answer, I think, is something along the following lines (Essay 12): moral supervenience – more generally, the supervenience of valuational properties or concepts on nonvaluational ones – derives from the very nature of valuation: all valuations require descriptive, nonvaluational criteria or grounds. That is, there cannot be an endless descending series of valuations, one depending on the next, ad infinitum; valuations must terminate in non-valuational grounds. These are at least possible accounts, and it is clear that no matter which of them, if any, is the correct one for valuational supervenience, we cannot expect the same explanation to hold for other cases of supervenience.

Consider mereological supervenience, the thesis that properties of wholes supervene on the properties and relations characterizing their parts. This supervenience relation does not seem explainable in terms of any of the candidate explanations we have just canvassed for valuational supervenience. It seems likely that mereological supervenience represents a metaphysically fundamental, *sui generis* form of dependence.

If this is right, there is no such thing as "supervenient dependence" as a *kind* of dependence. In this, it differs from causal dependence or mereological dependence. The latter do seem to be – at least, they have a better

6 It may of course turn out that causal dependence is no more homogeneous than is super-venience, in which case many of the comments to follow concerning supervenience may well apply to causation as well.

7 See James Klagge's helpful discussion of "ascriptive supervenience" in his "Supervenience: Ontological vs. Ascriptive," *Australasian Journal of Philosophy* 66 (1988): 461–470.

chance of turning out to be – types of dependence relation, dependencies grounded in the distinctive character of properties and relations involved. There is no harm in using the term "supervenient dependence" to refer, indifferently or disjunctively, to one or another of the many dependence relationships that can underlie the property covariance involved in instances of supervenience. But it now seems to me a mistake, or at least misleading, to think of supervenience itself as a special and distinctive type of dependence relation, alongside causal dependence, mereological dependence, dependence grounded in semantic connections, and others. It is worth noting that the present point is independent of the question whether property covariance entails dependence. Perhaps, property covariance could be suitably strengthened so as to yield dependence. But this still wouldn't tell us what kind of dependence is involved; and if the present considerations are correct, it couldn't, for there is no single kind of dependence that underlies all cases in which supervenience holds.

What kind of dependence relates mind and body? That is just what we should expect our theory of mind to tell us. It seems to me that any serious proposal that purports to address the mind–body problem must offer an account of why the mental–physical property covariation obtains, and it is natural to expect such an account to appeal to a dependence relation of some kind. Is it a matter of causal dependence? Is it in some way analogous to mereological supervenience? Is it after all a matter of meaning dependence, as logical behaviorists and some functionalists claim? Perhaps, a matter of divine intervention or plan as Malebranche and Leibniz thought? Or a brute and in principle unexplainable relationship which we must accept "with natural piety," as some emergentists used to insist? All these theories of mind seek to give an account, an explanation, of why there is a pervasive mental–physical property covariation, or why there can be no such account.

When we reflect on a mere claim of mind–body supervenience and compare it with these traditional options, we are struck by its failure to address this explanatory task. For it merely affirms a dependence relation of an unspecified sort and does nothing more to explain the nature of psychophysical covariance. But supervenience itself is not an explanatory relation. It is not a "deep" metaphysical relation; rather, it is a "surface" relation that reports a pattern of property covariation, suggesting the presence of an interesting dependency relation that might explain it. But we don't have a mind–body theory until we have something to say about the *ground* of mental–physical property covariation. I think the correct way of understanding the claim of psychophysical supervenience is this: it is not in itself an explanatory account of the mind–body relation; rather, it reports the data that such an account must make sense of. It is a "phenomenological" claim, not a theoretical explanation. Mind–body supervenience, therefore, does not state a solution to the mind–body problem; rather it states the problem itself.

But these reflections also tell us what needs to be done to upgrade a supervenience claim to the status of a substantive mind–body theory: you must specify the kind of dependence relation that underlies, and accounts for, the mind–body property covariation. A particularly important and promising approach to consider, I believe, is to explicate mind–body supervenience as an instance of mereological supervenience.[8] That is, we try to view mental properties as macroproperties of persons, or whole organisms, which are determined by, and dependent on, the character and organization of the appropriate parts, or subsystems, of organisms. As has been remarked, mereological supervenience seems to represent a metaphysically basic kind of dependence, and if psychological properties can be analyzed on the model of mereological supervenience,[9] that, I think, would be philosophical progress. Moreover, the mereological approach appears to gain support from considerations of scientific methodology: it fits in well with the research strategy of explaining psychological functions and capacities "by analysis" – that is, by showing how they result from the actions and interactions of subsystems.[10] Whether such microstructural explanations really "explain" mentality in the sense of making mentality, in particular consciousness, intelligible – something that the emergentists despaired of ever attaining – may be another question. Still, it may well be that mentality is best thought of as a special case of mereological dependence and determination.

In any case, these considerations do not invalidate the claim sometimes made that mind–body supervenience represents the minimal physicalist commitment. My suggestion is only that a bare claim of mind–body supervenience – especially, one stated in the form of global supervenience – does not constitute a *theory* of mind–body relation. This is consistent

8 This is the approach I suggested in my initial attempt to use supervenience for the mind–body problem, in "Supervenience and Nomological Incommensurables," *American Philosophical Quarterly* 15 (1978): 149–156.
9 The possibility of an analysis of this sort is consistent with a functionalist view of *psychological concepts,* just as a mereological analysis of, say, fragility (as a dispositional property) is consistent with the standard explanation of the *concept* of fragility in terms of a conditional about an object's response when subjected to stress or impact.
10 See Robert Cummins, *The Nature of Psychological Explanation* (Cambridge, Mass.: The MIT Press, 1983).

with the point, which I believe is true, that any physicalist who believes in the reality of the mental must at a minimum accept pervasive psycho-physical property covariance (in an appropriate form) *plus* the claim that a dependency relation underlies this covariance.

3. STRONG AND GLOBAL SUPERVENIENCE, ONCE AGAIN

As discussed in Essay 5, the following Petrie-style example of two worlds, shows that global supervenience does not *formally* imply strong superve-nience, since it formally rules out strong but not global supervenience:

$$w_1: Ga, Fa, Gb$$
$$w_2: Ga, \neg Fa, \neg Gb$$

Here, the supervenient set A is $\{F\}$, and the base set B is $\{G\}$, and we are supposing that the two sets are closed under Boolean operations. But what if we are allowed other operations to generate properties? Suppose that in addition to conjunction, disjunction, and negation (or comple-mentation), we also have on hand *identity* and *quantification* (see Essay 5, footnote 9). One property that can be obtained from G with these addi-tional procedures is this: $\exists y (x \neq y \ \& \ Gy)$. If this is admitted as a B-property, Petrie's example no longer works, for it is now consistent with the strong supervenience, as well as the global supervenience, of A on B. The reason of course is that a in w_1 is no longer indiscernible from a in w_2 with respect to the B-properties.

It seems that maneuvers of this kind could defeat all Petrie-style coun-terexamples. However, one might question whether properties like *there being another object that is G* should be considered a B-property. For exam-ple, it seems just wrong to consider the following a mental property: being such that there is another thing which is conscious (or "having a conscious world-mate").[11] But why are we unhappy with this as a mental property? It is fully definable in terms of properties whose mentality is not at issue *plus* logical expressions. The reason seems to be that although it "involves" a mental property in the sense that if it is exemplified, then necessarily mentality is exemplified,[12] the mental property involved re-mains wholly *extrinsic* to the things that have it. This rock, which has this

11 This is similar to the kind of reason for which some philosophers (for example, John Post) have been unhappy about closure under negation for the base properties.
12 This is analogous to Roderick Chisholm's sense of "imply" defined for properties in his *On Metaphysics* (Minneapolis: University of Minnesota Press, 1989), p. 101.

property, could exist, with all its intrinsic properties intact, in a world in which nothing conscious existed.

But if considerations of this kind are the reason for banning properties like $\exists y(x \neq y \ \& \ Gy)$, Petrie's example can be defeated another way: if w_1 and w_2 are possible worlds, the following worlds, w_3 and w_4, which are "restrictions" of w_1 and w_2 respectively, should also be possible worlds:

$$w_3\text{: } Ga, \ Fa$$
$$w_4\text{: } Ga, \ \neg Fa$$

But this defeats global supervenience as well as strong supervenience of $\{F\}$ on $\{G\}$.

But what if a and b are not distinct substances[13] – say, b is a proper part of a – so that there could not be a world with a but without b? Still, if $\exists y(x \neq y \ \& \ Gy)$ is truly an extrinsic property, and given that w_1 is a possible world, the following, too, should be a possible world:

$$w_5\text{: } Ga, \ Fa, \ \neg Gb$$

If so, the pair, w_2 and w_5, again defeats global as well as strong supervenience. To show this convincingly, we need more explicit characterizations of such notions as "extrinsic" and "intrinsic," and a better-articulated metaphysics of modalities and possible worlds.

In an interesting paper,[14] Cranston Paull and Theodore Sider attempt just that, and argue that, on their conception of "intrinsic property," global and strong supervenience are indeed equivalent when restricted to intrinsic properties. Correlatively, it seems a plausible conjecture that if extrinsic properties are included in both the supervenient and subvenient sets – in particular, if, along with the usual Boolean operations, identity and quantification are allowed for property composition – again the equivalence will obtain. Equivalence seems to fail, through the failure of implication from global to strong supervenience, only when extrinsic properties are present in the supervenient set but disallowed from the subvenient base.

It seems then that the question of the relationship between global and strong supervenience has not been fully settled. It is essentially a meta-

13 As may be recalled, the capacity for independent existence was traditionally associated with the concept of "substance."

14 "In Defense of Global Supervenience," *Philosophy and Phenomenological Research* 52 (1992): 833–854. This excellent paper contains other material of interest on supervenience; it is highly recommended.

physical question, rather than a purely formal one, as it is closely entwined with several metaphysical issues, and its full resolution does not seem possible until we are clearer about the larger metaphysical terrain that surrounds it.

Part II

Mind and mental causation

10

Psychophysical supervenience

Suppose we could create an exact physical replica of a living human being – exactly like him cell for cell, molecule for molecule, atom for atom. Such a replica would be indistinguishable, at least physically, from the original. For we are supposing that the replica is a perfect physical copy in every detail. The idea of such a replica, whether artificially created or naturally found, is a perfectly coherent one; in fact, it is consistent with all known laws of nature. The idea of course is a commonplace in science fiction.

Given that your replica and you are exactly alike physically, will you also share your psychological life with him? Will your replica have your psychological traits and dispositions, intellectual powers and artistic gifts, anxieties and depressions, likes and dislikes, and virtues and vices? Will it feel pain, remorse, joy and elation exactly in the way you do? That is, if two organisms have identical physical features, will they be identical in psychological characteristics as well?

According to many moral theorists, any two things sharing the same 'naturalistic' or 'descriptive' features cannot differ in respect of moral or evaluative properties. Thus, it has been said that if St. Francis is a good man, anyone who is just like him in all naturalistic respects – in this case, broadly psychological properties, such as traits of character and personality – must of necessity be a good man. This relationship between moral properties and nonmoral properties is often called 'supervenience': moral properties are said to be supervenient upon nonmoral properties in the sense that any two things that coincide in all nonmoral properties cannot diverge with respect to moral properties. The concept of supervenience is easily generalized so that we may speak of the supervenience relation

I have benefited from discussing with Terry Horgan many of the issues touched on in this paper.

for any two families of properties (or events, predicates, facts, etc.).[1] Briefly, a set F of properties is supervenient upon a set G of properties with respect to a domain D just in case any two things in D which are indiscernible with respect to G are necessarily indiscernible with respect to F (that is to say, any two things in D are such that necessarily if they differ with respect to F then they differ with respect to G).[2] We may call F 'the supervenient (or supervening) family' and G 'the supervenience base'.

The problem about the shared psychological life of persons and their physical duplicates can be given a perspicuous reformulation in terms of supervenience: Are psychological properties (events, processes, etc.) supervenient upon physical properties (events, processes, etc.)? Psychological supervenience, if it obtains, would give us one important sense in which the physical determines the mental: once the physical side of our being is completely fixed, our psychological life is also completely fixed. Since the physical obviously does not supervene upon the psychological, this determination is asymmetric: the physical determines the psychological, but the psychological does not determine the physical. Thus, psychophysical supervenience is one possible way in which the psychophysical relation can be characterized; and beyond this it has implications for various problems in the philosophy of mind such as the traditional mind–body problem, psychophysical reduction, and the possibility of psychophysical laws. We will touch on some of these issues below;[3] however, our chief concern will be the question what reason there might be for accepting the thesis of psychophysical supervenience.

Lest you think that an affirmative answer to the question of psychophysical supervenience automatically yields physicalism, let me remind you that G. E. Moore, to whom the thesis of moral supervenience is

1 See my "Supervenience and Nomological Incommensurables", *American Philosophical Quarterly* 15 (1978): 149–56; and "Concepts of Supervenience", Essay 4 of this volume. See also Terence Horgan, "Supervenience and Microphysics", *Pacific Philosophical Quarterly* 63 (1982: 29–43; and John Haugeland, "Weak Supervenience", *American Philosophical Quarterly* 19 (1982): 93–103.

2 This formulation, which closely follows the traditional wording used to explain 'supervenience', turns out to be the weaker of two distinguishable concepts of supervenience, and is in fact too weak to capture what seems to be intended by the use of this term in many contexts. These issues, however, do not substantively affect the present discussion. See my "Concepts of Supervenience".

3 See Horgan, "Supervenience and Microphysics"; Haugeland, "Weak Supervenience"; and my "Causality, Identity, and Supervenience in the Mind–Body Problem", *Midwest Studies in Philosophy* 4 (1979): 31–49; Harry A. Lewis, "Is the Mental Supervenient on the Physical?" in *Essays on Davidson: Actions and Events,* ed. Bruce Vermazen and Merrill B. Hintikka (Oxford: Clarendon Press, 1985).

often attributed, was a staunch and generally effective critic of ethical naturalism, the thesis that moral properties are definable by, or reducible to, naturalistic properties; in spite of his belief in the supervenience of the moral upon the naturalistic, he was an advocate of the autonomy of ethics and its irreducibility to natural science. It is possible that Moore was inconsistent in holding these positions, but the inconsistency is not obvious; it would need to be demonstrated. Similar comments apply to psychophysical supervenience and physicalism. If Moore was consistent, then by symmetry of reasoning the doctrine of psychophysical supervenience ought to be compatible with the denial of physicalism.[4]

II

I believe that most of us are strongly inclined to accept the doctrine of psychophysical supervenience in some form. Your replica is not only a person, but a person who is psychologically indistinguishable from you. He will share your beliefs, memories, likes and dislikes, wants and aversions, hopes and despairs; his internal life, as well as his external life, will be just like yours. As we shall see presently, there are psychological states you and your replica will not share, but the strong intuition prevails that some form of psychophysical supervenience must hold.

In a recent paper,[5] Stephen P. Stich considers a form of psychophysical supervenience. The thesis he considers, and which he endorses, is the following, called by him "the principle of psychological autonomy": "The properties and relations to be invoked in an explanatory psychological theory must be supervenient upon the *current, internal physical* properties and relations of organisms".[6] We can put this a bit more simply thus: Explanatory psychological properties and relations are supervenient upon the current internal physical properties of organisms. Stich, however, does not discuss in any detail reasons for or against this thesis of supervenience, his chief concern in the paper being the implication of this thesis for the belief-desire model for explanations of actions. We will later defend a thesis of psychophysical supervenience similar to Stich's, but let us begin by considering a broader and stronger form of the supervenience doctrine.

---

4 These questions of consistency are subtle and not easy to answer definitively. For further discussion, see Simon Blackburn, "Moral Realism", in *Morality and Moral Reasoning,* ed. J. Casey (London: Methuen, 1971); Lewis, "Is the Mental Supervenient on the Physical?"; and my "Supervenience and Nomological Incommensurables".
5 "Autonomous Psychology and the Belief-Desire Thesis", *The Monist* 61 (1978): 573–91.
6 Stich, "Autonomous Psychology and the Belief-Desire Thesis", p. 575.

(A) All psychological states and processes supervene on the contemporaneous physical states of the organism.

Two points of explanation: the qualification 'contemporaneous' is intended to indicate the requirement that if a certain psychological state occurs at a time, then that state is supervenient upon a physical state of the organism occurring *at the same time*. The point of this qualification will become clear when we examine some apparent counterexamples to the thesis as stated. Second, by 'physical state' we have in mind what may be called 'internal physical state'; that is, we want to exclude so-called 'relational properties' of the organism, such as its distance from the moon at a given time, its being larger than this typewriter, etc. It is not a simple matter to give a precise meaning to 'internal'; but the relative looseness of this and other notions we are making use of here will not affect our discussion. Third, when we speak of 'states' and 'events', we sometimes have in mind 'generic states' and 'generic events' – that is, *types* such as pain, itch, and belief that a stitch in time saves nine; at other times, we may be referring to concrete, dated instantiations of these generic events and states. In any particular case the context should make clear which sense is intended.

Why should anyone think (A) is true? At one point, many philosophers believed something like what Wolfgang Köhler and others called "psycho-physiological isomorphism",[7] which, for our present purposes, could be stated as follows:

The Psychophysical Correlation Thesis: For each psychological event M there is a physical event P such that, as a matter of law, an event of type M occurs to an organism at a time just in case an event of type P occurs to it at the same time.

The principle affirms the existence of a pervasive system of laws, of biconditional form, linking each mental event with some physical correlate, presumably some neurological state or process. Evidently, the Correlation Thesis implies the supervenience thesis (A) – if we assume that the modality involved in the concept of supervenience is satisfied by the nomological modality in the statement of the Correlation Thesis. Thus, anyone who accepts the Correlation Thesis would be committed to the doctrine of psychophysical supervenience.

7 See the selections by Köhler, Max Wertheimer, and others under "Psychophysiological Isomorphism", in *A Source Book in the History of Psychology,* ed. Richard J. Herrnstein and Edwin G. Boring (Cambridge: Harvard University Press, 1966). The isomorphism thesis defended by these psychologists is in fact a good deal stronger than the thesis that merely affirms the existence of a neural correlate for each mental state.

However, I think it would be wrong to think of the Correlation Thesis as providing *evidence* for the doctrine of psychophysical supervenience. For one thing, there are those who accept supervenience but not the Correlation Thesis, the latter being a stronger claim than the former.[8] Second, if there is an evidential relation here at all, the idea of psychophysical correlation should be seen as grounded in a belief in supervenience, and not the other way around; it seems to me that the belief that there must be laws connecting psychological events with physical events is derived from the general belief in the supervenience of the former on the latter, although a demonstration of this evidential priority would be a complex matter. In any event, the question of the possible support the Correlation Thesis might offer for psychophysical supervenience is made moot by the fact that most philosophers today would reject the Correlation Thesis.

There are various arguments in the recent literature in the philosophy of mind intended to refute the Correlation Thesis. One of the most influential of these, advanced by the proponents of 'functionalism', runs as follows: Any mental state, such as pain, can be 'physically realized' in many diverse types of organisms and physical structures (e.g., humans, mollusks, crustaceans, perhaps Martians and robots) so that, as a matter of empirical fact, it is extremely unlikely that some *uniform* physical state exists to serve as its physical correlate. Creatures whose physicochemical structures are entirely different from our own, or from anything we know on this earth, may yet be 'psychologically isomorphic' to us in the sense that the same psychological theory is true of them. Roughly speaking, this means that their observable behavior is best explained by imputing to them certain internal states which are connected among themselves, and to stimuli and behavior, in the way psychological states are so connected for humans. And yet the biochemistry of these creatures may be so different from ours that there is no sense in which we may speak of 'the same physical state' underlying, say, pain for both humans and these creatures. We may call this 'the multiple realization argument'.

This is not the place to discuss the merits of this argument; the only point I want to make here concerns the possibility of psychophysical laws, given the multiple realizability of psychological states. First of all, notice that the multiple realization argument implies nothing about the general impossibility of psychophysical laws; at best, it shows the impossibility of

8 For example, Donald Davidson, "Mental State", in *Experience and Theory*, ed. Lawrence Foster and J. W. Swanson (Amherst: University of Massachusetts Press, 1970).

psychophysical laws of a certain form (completely general biconditional laws of the form 'M iff P', where M is a mental state and P is a 'single' physical state). In fact, it is a tacit assumption of the argument that there are *species-specific* psychophysical laws, that is, laws connecting, say, pain with a certain neural correlate for each biological species. Indeed, the very notion of 'physical realization' of pain seems to presuppose the existence of nomological connections, *within each species,* between pain and some underlying neural process. If there were no such nomological link, in what sense does *this* neural state, and not some other one, 'realize' pain? And how would we know that it, and not some other state, is the physical realization of pain for this species? Similar comments apply to the talk of electronic-mechanical devices 'realizing' psychological states. Thus, the existence of species-specific psychophysical laws of the following form is not only consistent with the multiple realization argument but in fact presupposed by it:

Each human is such that it is in pain at a time if and only if it is in physical state P at the time.

Each mollusk is such that it is in pain at a time if and only if it is in physical state Q at the time, . . .

It is in virtue of these lawlike connections that P can be said to realize pain in humans, that Q realizes pain in mollusks, and so on.

The implications of these species-specific psychophysical laws for the question of psychophysical supervenience are clear. Even if the multiple realization argument refutes the unrestricted doctrine of psychophysical correlation it has no tendency to refute a more limited correlation thesis, one that asserts the existence of a physical correlate, within each species, for every psychological event. In fact, this thesis of species-restricted psychophysical correlation appears to be an implicit commitment of the multiple realization argument, and hence of the functionalist position. To derive psychophysical supervenience from the restricted psychophysical correlation thesis, the only additional assumption needed is the self-evident proposition that if two organisms or structures are physically indistinguishable from each other, then they belong to the same species. Replicas of humans are humans; replicas of felines are felines; and replicas of Martians are also Martians.

Thus, it is clear, in general, that various forms of the psychophysical correlation thesis logically entail the supervenience thesis. But this in itself is as one would expect, and provides little enlightenment concerning the question of evidence for psychophysical supervenience. For, as observed earlier, supervenience seems more fundamental, metaphysically and methodologically, than correlation, and although evidence for the Correlation Thesis is also likely to be evidence for supervenience, it would be pointless to argue to supervenience from correlation. A more interesting question is whether supervenience itself entails the Correlation Thesis, or if not then at least the existence of some psychophysical laws.[9] Let us now consider some specific putative counterexamples to the supervenience thesis (A), postponing till later more general evidential considerations.

III

Obviously, my replica and I do not share *all* properties in common. For example, we cannot be in the same place at the same time; I was born of natural parents, but he wasn't; I have siblings but he has none; I have lived in Ann Arbor for over ten years but he hasn't; I will be alive in 1984 but perhaps he won't be. These properties that we do not share may not strike us as very significant, but they are properties nonetheless. The philosophically interesting problem is whether the properties that I do not share with my replica include significant properties – significant in some clear and useful sense. That is, the interesting problem for us is whether all significant psychological properties are supervenient on physical properties. Let us consider some psychological properties that apparently are not supervenient.

(A) I *remember* being strafed by a jet fighter in a war over twenty years ago. My replica thinks he remembers this, too; in fact, he claims to have nightmares about this, and his mental imagery of the event is as vivid as mine. But of course he remembers no such thing, and the strafing is not part of his life experience. I also *know* and *truly believe* that I was strafed by a fighter plane, but my replica has no such knowledge, or true belief.[10]

(B) I am *thinking of* Vienna. We put my replica in the same brain state, and he has the visual imagery that I am having – say, that of an old church I was fond of visiting when I was in Vienna some years ago – and is thinking the same thoughts that I am thinking (how hot and humid that summer was in Vienna, . . .). And he shares my tendency to speak of

9 On this question, see Davidson, "Mental Events"; my "Supervenience and Nomological Incommensurables"; Lewis, "Is the Mental Supervenient on the Physical?"; Ted Honderich, "Psychophysical Lawlike Connections and Their Problem", *Inquiry* 24 (1981): 277–303.

10 There are some subtle questions about how the content of my replica's belief is to be specified, e.g., whether it refers to him or me. See Stich, "Autonomous Psychology and the Belief-Desire Thesis", for some of the complications.

Vienna (or at least to utter sentences containing the word 'Vienna') at dinner parties. Is he also thinking of Vienna? I do not think so. When I have a certain sort of visual imagery and am thinking certain thoughts, that counts as 'thinking of Vienna' because of a certain historical and cognitive relationship that I have with the city Vienna, a relationship that my replica lacks. To see this more clearly, think of a person who is having the very same phenomenological visual imagery that I am having, but who has never been to Vienna and has never heard of it, and whose visual image, which is qualitatively indistinguishable from mine, can be traced to a church in his hometown in Iowa. We would hardly say of this person that he is now thinking of Vienna. These points can be made with regard to other examples: *liking* or *disliking* some particular person; *wanting* some particular object; *fearing* some particular object or event. It is important to see that while wanting to eat *this particular hamburger* is similar to thinking of Vienna in the respect we are presently interested in, wanting to eat *some hamburger or other* is not. The latter may be supervenient upon brain states.

(C) I *am glad* that I was invited to the Dean's party last week, but am still *embarrassed* that I could not remember the first name of the Dean's wife. Notice that if I am glad that such-and-such is so-and-so, then not only must I believe that such-and-such is so-and-so, it must be the case that such-and-such is so-and-so; and similarly if I am embarrassed that such-and-such is so-and-so, then it must be true that such-and-such is so-and-so. If Jones falsely believes that he has won a fellowship we cannot truly say Jones is glad *that* he won a fellowship. My replica, therefore, cannot be said to be glad that he was invited to the party or embarrassed that he could not recall the hostess's name. Similar comments apply to many other states of feeling and emotion.

(D) *I see a tree.* My replica has not emerged from the laboratory, but his brain is put in the same state that obtains when I see a tree. So he is having a 'treeish sense-datum', just like mine. But he is not seeing a tree. Two persons or organisms can be in the same state – the same appropriate neural state – but one may be seeing, touching, etc., a tree, and the other not.

(E) Finally, let us consider *actions* – especially, actions that presuppose social contexts – networks of social practices, customs, and institutions. I am signing a check to pay off my mortgage. We put my replica in the same brain state and give him a blank check. He puts his (my?) signature on it, a signature that no expert from the bank could distinguish from mine. But is he paying off his mortgage? Is he even signing a check? He does not have a bank account, not to mention a mortgage. The answer, I think, is that he is not doing any of these things; he is not signing a check, and he is not paying off any mortgage. He cannot do these things because he is not as yet a full member of the social community whose institutions and practices make these actions possible. His being in appropriate internal physical states is not enough to enable him to engage in these acts.

IV

How shall we handle these cases? Some of these cases can be handled by removing the requirement that every mental state or event supervene on *contemporaneous* physical states; obvious examples include remembering. We could say that an instance of remembering occurring at a certain time does supervene on physical states but not on the synchronous ones, not on those occurring at the time the remembering takes place, but rather on a *longer temporal stretch of the physical history* of the organism that does the remembering. My Doppelgänger on Twin Earth does remember being strafed by a fighter plane, although my replica does not, and this is because the former, not the latter, has a life history similar to mine. Certain other cases discussed in the preceding section can be dealt with by enlarging the spatial scope of the supervenience base, by taking the trees seen, tables touched, and the person liked or disliked, in the supervenience base, but this is to go beyond the intended spirit of the thesis of psychophysical supervenience. I think it is important to be able to defend a form of the thesis that does not go outside the organism, a thesis that claims psychological states to be supervenient on the *internal* physical states of the organism.

I would suggest the following procedure. We first define the notion of an 'internal property' or 'internal state' of a thing, and then defend the following two theses:

The Supervenience Thesis: Every internal psychological state of an organism is supervenient on its synchronous internal physical state.

The Explanatory Thesis: Internal psychological states are the only psychological states that psychological theory needs to invoke in explaining human behavior – the only states needed for psychology.[11]

11 So my strategy in this paper can be thought of as splitting Stich's "principle of psychological autonomy" into two independent theses and considering the second thesis (the Explanatory Thesis) as providing a philosophical rationale for the first (the Supervenience Thesis).

The full defense of these theses would be a major task; however, I hope to be able to say enough about them to make them plausible.

First, what is 'an internal state' or 'internal property'? In *Person and Object*,[12] R. M. Chisholm introduces the notion of a property *rooted outside the time at which it is had:*

G is *rooted outside times at which it is had* = $_{def}$ Necessarily for any object x and for any time t, x has the property G at t only if x exists at some time before or after t.

The idea is straightforward: G is rooted outside the times at which it is had just in case the possession of G by an object implies the existence of the object at a time other than the time at which it has G. Thus, consider some examples: taking the second vacation in the Rockies, taking the first of the two walks today, being twenty years old, being divorced, being a future president, and so on. A psychological example is remembering: for you now to remember something you must have existed before. In analogy with this notion, we can define another:

G is *rooted outside the objects that have it* = $_{def}$ Necessarily any object x has G only if some contingent object wholly distinct from x exists.

The qualification 'contingent' is inserted because according to some philosophers there are 'necessary beings', beings that exist in all possible worlds. The qualification that the object other than x be *wholly distinct* from x is intended to exclude *proper parts* of x. If G is the property of being spherical, then if any object has G, then it follows necessarily that there is some object different from x, namely a spatial part of x. But this should not disqualify G from being an internal property. It will be seen that the notion we are after here corresponds, roughly, to the traditional notion of 'nonrelational property'.

We now define 'internal':

G is *internal* = $_{def}$ G is neither rooted outside times at which it is had nor outside the objects that have it.

We may say that an event or state is an *internal event* or *state* of an object just in case it is the object's having an internal property at a time. So if G is an internal property, an object's having G or being G at a time is an internal event or state. An *internal process* would be a causally connected or continuous series of internal events or states involving the same object or system of objects.

The Supervenience Thesis as stated concerns only internal psychologi-

12 (La Salle, Ill.: Open Court, 1976), p. 127.

cal states, namely those psychological states whose occurrence does not imply anything about the past or future, or anything existing other than the organism or structure to which the states occur. Brief reflection should convince us that these are the states we should be concerned with.[13] Let us look at the series of counterexamples we presented earlier against the broader, unrestricted thesis of psychophysical supervenience.

Consider the group (A). Remembering is not internal. If a person now remembers anything, that entails he existed before now; so remembering does not come under the purview of the Supervenience Thesis. Nor does knowing or believing truly: if I know, or believe truly, that the moon is round, it follows that a contingent object, namely the moon, exists.

What of believing? It is now customary to distinguish between belief *de re* and belief *de dicto,* although the precise import of the distinction is still controversial.[14] Roughly speaking, *de dicto* belief is believing a certain proposition, a dictum, to be true, while *de re* belief is believing *of* some *object,* a *res,* that it is thus and so. Belief *de dicto* will in general be internal states. The belief that the tallest man is a spy does not entail the existence of a tall man or a spy; the belief that ghosts are malevolent does not entail the existence of ghosts. On the other hand, belief *de re* is plausibly viewed as noninternal when the object of belief is other than oneself. If a given belief is *de re* with respect to a certain object, then this object must exist if that *de re* belief is to exist. You cannot have a belief about Mt. Everest unless Mt. Everest exists – and unless, furthermore, you are in a certain historical-cognitive relation to it.[15] However, belief *de se,* a special case of belief *de re,* is internal; my belief that I am now sitting entails the existence of no contingent object other than myself. I think the internal–noninternal split for beliefs corresponds to the division between those beliefs which we expect to supervene on bodily states and those for which we do not have such expectations.[16]

---

13 And not just when psychophysical supervenience is at issue; I think internal psychological states are just those states for which we should look for physical (neurophysiological) correlates, and which we would expect to enter into psychophysical laws. At least, we could say this: it would be absurd to look for neural correlates for noninternal psychological states, such as knowing (as distinguished from believing) and thinking of Vienna.

14 See, e.g., Tyler Burge, "Belief De Re", *Journal of Philosophy* 74 (1977): 338–62; John Pollock, "De Re Belief" (ms.).

15 I expand somewhat on this theme in "Perception and Reference Without Causality", *Journal of Philosophy* 74 (1977): 606–20.

16 This will be disputed by Stich, who takes the sameness of truth value as a necessary condition for two beliefs (that is, "belief tokens") to be the same belief ("belief type"). On this criterion, my replica's *de se* belief which he expressed by the sentence "I have

Group (B) is analogous to belief *de re*. If, as we argued, thinking of Vienna involves as an essential ingredient some historical-cognitive contact with the city Vienna, it fails to be internal as defined: my thinking of Vienna is 'rooted outside' in both of the senses that were considered. The same goes for other *de re* psychological attitudes, such as liking and disliking, fearing, admiring, and expecting, except when these attitudes are *de se*.

Some items in group (C) will be internal and some noninternal: my being pleased that Johnson has been elected to the city council will be noninternal, but my being pleased that I am now thinking will be internal. My being pleased that I did twenty pushups this morning is of course noninternal. I believe we would expect the internal states in this group to be supervenient.

Items in group (D), involving perceptual relations to external objects, will in general be noninternal: I cannot see or touch a tree unless a tree exists, and I cannot see or touch this particular tree unless this particular tree exists. Also, actions requiring societal contexts, the items in group (E), are noninternal; they presuppose the existence of persons in certain social relations, social institutions, and a history involving these things.

The Supervenience Thesis concerns only those psychological states or properties that are internal in our sense, and claims that they are supervenient upon the contemporaneous internal physical states of the organisms to which they occur. A moment's reflection should convince us that those who believe that our mental states are determined by the physical processes occurring in our bodies could not have noninternal states in mind. It is not that these noninternal states are not properly psychological, or

two brothers" is not the same belief as my belief which I would express by the use of the same sentence; for the former is false while the latter is true. From this it would follow, for Stich, that my replica does not share my belief that I have two brothers, from which it further follows that this *de se* belief is nonsupervenient. I reject Stich's criterion of belief identity as an appropriate one in the present context, and would hold that my replica and I share the same belief, in this case, in virtue of each of us exemplifying the property expressed by "x believes that x has two brothers" or "x believes himself to have two brothers". As an analogous case consider: it would be inappropriate to say that my replica and I have *different wants* when each of us wants to eat, on the ground that my replica wants it to be the case *he* eats, whereas I want it to be the case that *I* eat, and that these two desired states of affairs are different. My replica and I have the same want because each of us exemplifies the property expressed by "x wants it to be the case that x eats". There are many complex issues involved here, and we obviously cannot adequately deal with them here. Works relevant to these issues include Tyler Burge, "Individualism and the Mental", *Midwest Studies in Philosophy* 4 (1979): 73–121; Stephen L. White, "Partial Character and the Language of Thought", *Pacific Philosophical Quarterly* 63 (1982): 347–65.

that they have some nonpsychological mixtures;[17] my remembering that I had a severe headache yesterday is noninternal, although it presumably has no nonpsychological components. It is just that they go beyond what is *here* and *now* in the psychological space of the organism. The notion of a replica of a person as we have used here is a time-bound notion: something is a replica of me *now* but not a replica of me as I was ten years ago or as I will be ten years hence. On the other hand, some psychological states or events that occur to me now spill into other times and places, as it were. Remembering spills into the past; knowing into other places and times. In many cases, this is due to the so-called intentionality of the mental, although intentionality probably does not give us a general explanation of this phenomenon. So we cannot expect all my current psychological states to depend, or supervene, upon my current internal physical states.

There are two general ways of dealing with these apparently nonsupervenient psychological states: first, we can, as we have done, restrict the class of psychological states for which supervenience is to be claimed; second, we can broaden the supervenience base – in our case, the class of physical states – to accommodate the apparent exceptions. Thus, as previously noted, some instances of remembering could be handled by broadening the supervenience base to include a person's past physical history; in terms of the concept of a physical replica, this would amount to strengthening this concept so that a replica must match the original over a *stretch of time,* so that my replica must have qualitatively the same physical history that I have. To handle *de re* psychological states, we would need to broaden the supervenience base to include physical states of objects outside the organism; and ultimately we would need to speak of possible worlds, as Terence Horgan does, in formulating the thesis of psychophysical supervenience.[18] We could say, following Horgan, that any two possible worlds that are indistinguishable with respect to physical details are indistinguishable from the psychological point of view, or, more briefly, that any two worlds that are physically indistinguishable are in fact one and the same world. This form of generalized supervenience is of broad metaphysical interest, but its implications for specific problems concerning the mental are more difficult to gauge than is the case with a thesis that is formulated in terms of individual organisms and their psychological states.

17 As perhaps hinted at by Stich, "Autonomous Psychology and the Belief-Desire Thesis", p. 574.
18 Horgan, "Supervenience and Microphysics"; Haugeland, "Weak Supervenience".

This is one reason why the philosophical interest of the Supervenience Thesis needs to be shown, and this is the task of the Explanatory Thesis. As may be recalled, the Explanatory Thesis affirms that psychological theory needs only to invoke internal psychological states in formulating explanations of human behavior. We now turn to this claim.

V

In support of the Explanatory Thesis we shall try to make plausible the following claim: *the causal-explanatory role of any noninternal psychological state can be filled by some internal psychological state*. If this is true in general, then it will follow that no reference needs to be made in psychological theory to noninternal psychological states. Let us begin with knowing or believing truly. As we saw, these are noninternal. I know that if I turn this knob counterclockwise the burner will go on. Since I want the fire to go on, I turn the knob. My knowledge that turning the knob will cause the burner to go on plays a causal role in the explanation of my action of turning the knob. This is a simple and familiar sort of action explanation. It is clear, however, that knowledge is sufficient but not necessary to construct an action explanation: belief, or firm belief, is also sufficient. If I believe that the burner will go on if the knob is turned, then I will turn the knob if I have the desire to have the burner go on (assuming that there is no countervailing desire). In fact it is only the element of belief in knowing that is causally productive of the action. Similar comments apply to believing truly. My truly believing that something is so is not more efficacious in producing actions than my merely believing that something is so. As Stich says, "what knowledge adds to belief is psychologically irrelevant".[19]

It is true that whether or not my action succeeds in bringing about the intended result normally depends on whether the belief involved is true. Thus, whether my action results in the burner being turned on depends on whether my belief that it would go on if the knob is turned is correct. However, it is not part of the object of *psychological* explanation to explain why the burner went on; all it needs to explain is why I turned the knob. It might be objected that not only did I perform the action of turning the knob but I also performed that of *turning on the burner,* and that this latter action does involve – it logically entails – the burner's going on. This is correct; however, the action of turning on the burner, insofar as

---

19 "Autonomous Psychology and the Belief-Desire Thesis", p. 574.

this is thought to involve the burner going on, is not an action that it is the proper business of psychological theory to explain or predict. The job of psychological explanation is done once it has explained the bodily action of turning the knob; whether or not this action results in my also turning on the stove, my cooking the steak, my starting a house fire, and so on, is dependent on events and facts quite outside the province of psychology, and are not the proper concern of psychological theory. Only *basic actions,* not 'derivative' or 'generated' actions, need to be explained by psychological theory.[20]

We now turn to remembering. Memory turns out to be noninternal for two reasons: first, it implies something about the past, and second, in most cases, like knowing, it implies the existence of something other than the rememberer. When a person firmly believes that he remembers but fails to remember in virtue of the failure of one or the other of these two conditions, then we may assume there obtains in him some internal state which is just like a genuine case of remembering except for one of these conditions failing to obtain. This internal state may be some phenomenological experience, 'memory image' or belief about the past characterized by what Russell called the 'déjà-vu' quality; but depending on how remembering or memory is construed, it need not be any sort of conscious experience. This residual element of remembering, when remembering has been stripped down to an internal psychological state, may be called 'seeming to remember'. My claim would be that this seeming remembrance can do all of the explanatory work done by remembering. Thus, when I act in a certain way in part because of my remembering a certain thing, then under the same circumstances my replica will act in the same way because of his seeming to remember the same thing. Whether or not his seeming remembrance is a genuine case of remembering will not affect his behavior. This seems plausible when we reflect that remembering affects our behavior often as a source of belief, that seeming to remember is to remembering as believing is to knowing, and that, as we saw, insofar as behavior is concerned, belief is psychologically as efficacious as knowledge.

The foregoing exemplifies our strategy in defense of the Explanatory Thesis. The strategy is to argue that within each noninternal psychological state that enters into the explanation of some action or behavior

---

20 I have heard Richard Brandt defend this claim, although he has not done so in print. For a discussion of some relevant issues, see William P. Alston, "Conceptual Prolegomena to a Psychological Theory of Intentional Action", in *Philosophy of Psychology,* ed. S. C. Brown (New York: Harper & Row, 1974).

we can locate an 'internal core state' which can assume the causal-explanatory role of the noninternal state; we would in fact argue that this internal core is the causal and explanatory core of the noninternal state. It is in virtue of this core that the noninternal state has the psychological explanatory role that it has.

But why should we believe that there is such an internal core to every explanatory psychological state that is noninternal? Causal considerations of the following general sort make such an assumption both attractive and plausible. In constructing a psychological explanation of a piece of behavior, we are attempting to ascertain a psychological causal antecedent of that behavior. Considerations of causal contiguity and continuity lead to the belief that the proximate cause of the behavior must be located within the organism emitting the behavior – that is, there must be a proximate causal explanation of that behavior in terms of an *internal* state of the organism. Why should we think that there must be an internal *psychological* state which will serve as proximate cause of behavior? This is a difficult question, but part of an answer is contained in the observation that if this internal state has all the causal powers of the corresponding noninternal psychological state in the production of behavior, then there seems to be no reason not to think of it as psychological as well. And in many cases we can identify the internal psychological core of a given noninternal psychological state, as we have done above for knowing and remembering.

With this in mind, let us turn briefly to the remaining cases. When we see a tree, there is some internal phenomenal state going on; some internal representation of the tree will be present in us. In the language of the sense-datum theory, we are sensing a treeish sense-datum, or we are appeared to treeishly. The Explanatory Thesis would claim that whether there is an actual tree out there, or whether we are just having this internal presentation, makes no difference to the behavior emitted. In either case we may reach out for the real or imagined tree, answer 'Yes' when asked 'Do you see a tree?', and so forth. We finally come to actions. Let us return to the case of my replica's signing a check. The observable action he performs is the same as mine when I sign a check and pay off the mortgage, even though his observable physical action does not issue in signing a check and mine does. But it is clear that the success or failure of our undertaking here is not really up to us; once the appropriate physical action has been performed, it is not up to us whether that action issues in the signing of a check or the paying off of the mortgage. That depends on factors outside our immediate individual control. These nonbasic actions do not come within the purview of psychological theory; all a psychological theory of behavior needs to explain and predict are the basic actions individuals perform. Societal actions are generally nonbasic; they are produced by the basic actions that we perform, normally the basic bodily movements we can perform at will.

VI

In this final section we return to the question whether there are any positive reasons for thinking that psychological states – at least, the internal ones – supervene on physical states. I shall present one argument for psychophysical supervenience, and it runs as follows. First of all, I propose that we accept, in the present context, the functionalist conception of psychological states as those internal states which serve as intermediary states mediating between stimuli and behavior output.[21] This is the argument:

(1) My replica and I share all our current internal physical properties.

This premise is given *ex hypothesi,* namely, by the description of the situation to the effect that the replica is an exact physical copy of my body.

(2) But this does not mean that, at each and every instant, we share the same occurrent, physical properties.

This is evident. After the replica is created, he and I are going to have different sensory input, and engage in different activities; while I am typing, he is out playing tennis.

(3) We do share structural, dispositional properties. Our basic physical structure is identical – at least for now – and we share the same physical powers, capacities, and dispositions.

(4) One type of such dispositional properties would be the property of responding in certain characteristic ways to different types of internal or external stimuli. Thus, my replica and I share the same system of stable lawlike relationships of the following form:

$$\text{stimulus } S_1 \ \rightarrow \ \text{behavior output } O_1$$
$$\text{stimulus } S_2 \ \rightarrow \ \text{behavior output } O_2$$

.

.

.

---

21 This is somewhat simplified. See Hilary Putnam, "The Nature of Mental States", in his *Mind, Language and Reality* (London: Cambridge University Press, 1975); Ned Block, "Troubles with Functionalism", *Minnesota Studies in the Philosophy of Science* IX (Minneapolis: University of Minnesota Press, 1978).

(5) Now the question arises how we are to *explain* these particular input–output relationships. This question arises because these particular patterns of input–output connections are not necessarily shared by other human beings (although of course we expect there will be similarities).

Typically, such explanations will proceed by positing certain *internal states* to mediate the particular input with the particular output associated with that input. Different organisms differ in the output they emit when the same input is applied because their internal states at the time are different. We now come to perhaps the most controversial assumption of this argument, the functionalist interpretation of psychological states:

(6) These internal states posited to explain sensory input–behavior output relations *are* psychological states.

This is the functionalist conception of a psychological state: a psychological state is a 'functional state' that connects sensory inputs and behavior output in appropriate ways.

(7) If a series of psychological states, along with their mutual interconnections, are posited as the best explanation of the input–output connections in my case, then, in methodological consistency, the same psychological states must be posited in the case of my replica. For he and I share the same input–output connections.

This is something like a 'generalization argument' in moral theory. I think that there clearly is a similar consistency requirement in the case of scientific methodology, and (7) is well justified. Of course, (7) is what needs to be established, viz. that my replica and I share the same psychological properties. Thus, it follows:

(8) If two organisms or structures are physically identical, then their psychology is also identical. If two organisms coincide in the set of physical properties, they cannot diverge in the set of psychological properties. The psychological supervenes on the physical.

This completes the argument.

The leading idea of the argument is exceedingly simple; since my replica and I share the same input–output relations, and psychological states are just those states posited to explain these relations, the same psychological states must be posited for both of us. As was noted, the most obvious point of controversy in this argument is the functionalist interpretation of psychological state used at step (6). I hesitate to accept this conception of psychological state as a general characterization valid for all psychological states.[22] A fundamental question not touched by this argument is whether conscious (phenomenological) states, such as raw feels, visual images, and the like, are supervenient on bodily states, although this remark will be disputed by those who fully accept the functionalist account of psychological states. In any case, it is difficult to see what a general argument showing the supervenience of the phenomenological would look like. There may of course be broad metaphysical considerations in favor of physicalism from which the supervenience of phenomenological states could be derived. Also, the continuing discovery of lawlike connections, however rough and crude, between phenomenological experience and brain processes serves as limited but indispensable empirical evidence. The only reasonable thing to say at this point, I think, is the rather tame and unsurprising remark that the belief in psychophysical supervenience seems to be based on broad metaphysical and methodological considerations, which are yet to be spelled out, buttressed by what empirical evidence there is for specific psychophysical correlations.

22 See, e.g., Block, "Troubles with Functionalism"; Ned Block and J. A. Fodor, "What Psychological States Are Not", *Philosophical Review* 81 (1972): 159–81.

11

Psychophysical laws

I

The question whether there are, or can be, psychological laws is one of considerable interest. If it can be shown that there can be no such laws, a nomothetic science of psychology will have been shown to be impossible. The qualifier 'nomothetic' is redundant: science is supposed to be nomothetic. Discovery, or at least pursuit, of laws is thought to be constitutive of the very nature of science so that where there are no laws there can be no science, and where we have reason to believe there are none we have no business pretending to be doing science.

At least in one clear sense, therefore, the absence of psychological laws entails the impossibility of psychology as a science. This need not be taken to mean that there can be no scientists, called 'psychologists' or 'cognitive scientists', who study psychological topics and write useful tracts about them. It is to say that whatever else they may be doing that is useful and worthwhile, they will not be producing *psychological theories,* comprehensive and integrated systems of precise general laws, couched in a characteristic theoretical vocabulary, on the basis of which mental phenomena could be explained and predicted. If such theory-based explanatory and predictive activities are what we suppose psychologists *qua* psychologists to be engaged in, recognition of the impossibility of psychological laws would force us to reconsider the nature of psychology as an intellectual enterprise. In what follows we shall touch on this general issue, but our main topic here is the question of the possibility of laws about psychological phenomena.

It is no surprise, then, that Donald Davidson, who has vigorously ar-

I am indebted to Akeel Bilgrami, Reinaldo Elugardo, Fred Feldman, Adam Morton, Bruce Russell, Nicholas White, and the members of my seminars in philosophy of mind at Michigan in 1979 and 1982. Brian McLaughlin gave an interesting set of comments on this paper when it was presented at the Davidson Conference; however, they have not been taken into account in preparing the present draft.

gued against the possibility of psychological laws, titled one of his papers on this topic 'Psychology as Philosophy'.[1] The intended contrast of course is with 'psychology as a science', an unattainable goal if his striking arguments are sound. In advocating the lawlessness of the mental he joins a small but influential group of philosophers who have taken a dim view of the scientific prospects of psychology. Norman Malcolm, for example, has produced a set of arguments, inspired by broadly Wittgensteinian considerations, against scientific psychology.[2] There are also Quine's disdainful strictures on Brentano's 'science of intention'.[3] In this paper, however, we shall be concerned exclusively with Davidson's arguments contained in a series of three papers, 'Mental Events',[4] 'Psychology as Philosophy', and 'The Material Mind',[5] focusing especially on the first of these.

There are reasons for taking Davidson's arguments seriously and trying to get clear about them. The arguments are interesting and challenging, and have fascinated those interested in philosophy of mind; however, there is little agreement as to exactly how they are supposed to work.[6] Many philosophers have an opinion about how successful these arguments are (the published verdicts have been almost uniformly negative thus far), but most appear to feel uncertain about the accuracy of their interpretations, or think that the interpretations fail to make the arguments sufficiently interesting or plausible. Above all almost everyone seems to find Davidson's arguments extremely opaque; it is not difficult to discern the general drift of his thinking or pick out the basic considerations motivating the arguments; however, delineating their structure pre-

1 In *Philosophy of Psychology*, ed. S. C. Brown (Harper & Row, New York, 1974). Reprinted in D. Davidson, *Essays on Actions and Events* (Clarendon Press, Oxford, 1980).
2 *Memory and Mind* (Cornell University Press, Ithaca, N.Y., 1977). See also Bruce Goldberg, 'The Correspondence Hypothesis', *Philosophical Review,* 77 (1968), pp. 438–54.
3 W. V. Quine, *Word and Object* (The Technology Press of M.I.T., Cambridge, Mass., 1960).
4 In *Experience and Theory*, ed. Lawrence Foster and J. W. Swanson (University of Massachusetts Press, Amherst, 1970). Reprinted in Davidson, *Essays on Actions and Events.*
5 In *Logic, Methodology, and the Philosophy of Science*, vol. 4, ed. P. Suppes (North-Holland, Amsterdam, 1973). Reprinted in Davidson, *Essays on Actions and Events.*
6 The following, I believe, is a representative list of published discussions of Davidson's arguments (I am not including those that primarily focus on 'anomalous monism'): C. Z. Elgin, 'Indeterminacy, Underdetermination, and the Anomalous Monism', *Synthese,* 45 (1980), pp. 233–55; William Lycan, 'Psychological Laws', *Philosophical Topics,* 12 (1981), pp. 9–38; Ted Honderich, 'Psychophysical Lawlike Connections and Their Problem', *Inquiry,* 24 (1981), pp. 277–303; Brian Loar, *Mind and Meaning* (Cambridge University Press, Cambridge, 1981), pp. 20–5; Robert Van Gulick, 'Rationality and the Anomalous Nature of the Mental', *Philosophy Research Archives,* 1983; William Larry Stanton, 'Supervenience and Psychophysical Law in Anomalous Monism', *Pacific Philosophical Quarterly,* 64 (1983), pp. 72–9.

cisely enough for effective evaluation and criticism is another matter. In this paper I propose a way of looking at what I take to be Davidson's principal argument against nomological psychology. The suggested interpretation is based on a simple leading idea, and will help us piece together a coherent picture of Davidson's overall views of the mental and relate it to a wider context. My aim here is essentially to interpret and expound, not to evaluate or criticize. But obviously I am embarking on this project because I think the argument to be extracted from Davidson is plausible, at least at first blush, and philosophically important. As I hope will become clear, Davidson's argument has far-reaching implications regarding some basic issues about the nature of mind, such as mental autonomy, the possibility of free agency, and the status of commonsense explanations of human actions, and points to a conception of the mental that I find both intriguing and appealing.

Davidson's apparent strategy in 'Mental Events' is, first, to establish the following lemma:

> *Psychophysical Anomalism:*[7] There are no psychophysical laws, that is, laws connecting mental and physical phenomena. In fact, there *cannot* be such laws,

and then use it to argue for the desired general thesis of psychological anomaly:

> *Anomalism of the Mental:* 'There are no strict deterministic laws on the basis of which mental events can be predicted and explained.'[8]

The bulk of 'Mental Events' and 'Psychology as Philosophy' is devoted to establishing Psychophysical Anomalism, and much of the interest generated by these papers has been focused on Davidson's arguments for this thesis. In contrast the move from Psychophysical Anomalism to the full Anomalism of the Mental is made rather quickly and abruptly, within one short paragraph in 'Mental Events'; I shall make some suggestions about how this transition can be understood, but for the moment, and for much of this paper, we shall follow Davidson in concentrating on arguments for Psychophysical Anomalism.

7 The term 'psychophysical anomalism' is not Davidson's.
8 'Mental Events', p. 208 (page references to this article are to its reprinted version in Davidson, *Essays on Actions and Events*).

Davidson's conception of the psychological is based on *intentionality*. Expressions we use in attributing *propositional attitudes,* such as 'believe', 'fear', 'hope', and 'regret', are taken to constitute the basic psychological vocabulary; psychological laws then would be laws stated in terms of these intentional psychological expressions. Two questions may be raised about this way of understanding the psychological: first, whether it is broad enough to cover 'phenomenal states' or 'qualia', like pains and after-images, and second, whether it applies to the terms of trade of 'scientific psychology' or 'cognitive science' as it is practiced nowadays. These are large questions and cannot be taken up here; the second raises an issue about the relationship between 'commonsense psychology' and systematic psychology, a topic of much current interest,[9] and I shall make some remarks relevant to it below. In any event, the conception of the psychological as intentional does capture a large core of our commonsense psychological vocabulary, and a successful argument for the impossibility of psychological laws on this conception of the psychological would be of great interest and importance.[10] It would show, for example, that familiar explanations of actions in terms of an agent's beliefs and desires could not be nomological explanations backed by laws about beliefs, desires, and the like, as claimed by some writers (e.g., Carl Hempel[11]). And it would imply a significant general conclusion: law-based systematic psychology, if such a thing is possible, would have to make a radical break with the framework of our vernacular psychological idioms and truisms, which forms the basis of our shared ability to describe and make sense of our own motives and actions as well as those of our fellow humans, and without which communal human life would be unthinkable.

The initial impression one is likely to get from Davidson's discussion of Psychophysical Anomalism is something like this: we are first offered a long list of features that characterize the mental but not the physical and, conversely, features of the physical not shared by the mental. For example, the mental is intentional and rational but the physical is neither;

9 For a sustained recent treatment see Stephen P. Stich, *From Folk Psychology to Cognitive Science* (The M.I.T. Press, Cambridge, Mass., 1983). See also Adam Morton, *Frames of Mind* (Oxford University Press, Oxford, 1980).

10 Davidson explicitly limits his arguments to intentional mental states, e.g., 'Comments and Replies' following 'Psychology as Philosophy' in *Essays on Actions and Events,* p. 240.

11 In the title essay of *Aspects of Scientific Explanation* (The Free Press, New York, 1965).

physical laws are 'homonomic' but what mental generalizations that there are are 'heteronomic'; combining mental and physical terms in a single statement is like mixing 'grue' with 'emerald'; Quinean indeterminacy besets the mental but nothing analogous obtains for the physical; and so on. We are then tempted to ask: does Davidson expect us to infer from these dissimilarities and divergences that there can be no laws connecting the two systems? But how can he? No simple list of differences between the two domains will have any tendency to show that no laws can connect them. When two arbitrary domains are considered, there is no a priori obvious reason to think there are lawful connections between them; nor need there be any obvious reason to think there are none. We would of course expect that any argument designed to show that there are, or that there are not, correlation laws, will make use of some properties of the two particular domains involved. So differences between the mental and the physical must count; but noting them can only be a starting point. The substance of the argument must show why, given just *these* differences, there can be no correlation laws.[12]

To fix the general picture in mind, consider a domain U of objects and two sets, F and G, of properties. For example, think of U as a set of medium-sized material bodies, F as a set of colors, and G as a set of shapes. We may suppose that each object in U has exactly one color in F and one shape in G. Here we would not expect to find regular correlations between colors and shapes; an object of a given color could be of any shape, and vice versa. Thus, we would not expect true generalizations of the form:

(A) Every object in U with color C has shape S.

Or of the form:

(B) Every object in U with shape S has color C.

But this is not to say that, contrary to our justified expectations, we may not in fact find, say:

12 After reviewing the differences noted by Davidson between the mental and the physical, Honderich writes: 'Still, we are not given a reason for thinking that [Psychophysical Anomalism] follows from the description of the two domains. As others have asked, what reason is there for thinking that an item which falls in one domain, and whose description then depends on X, cannot be in a lawlike connection with an item in the other domain, whose description then depends on Y? There is no general truth to the effect that there cannot be lawlike connection between items whose descriptions have different necessary connections. . . . Davidson remarks that his argument is no proof. It must also be said, I think, that his argument is at least crucially incomplete' ('Psycho-

(C) Every red object in U is round.

If this should happen, though, we would surely think it was pure luck, the result of a fortuitous choice of U. Given what we know about colors and shapes, we would not take the truth of (C) as indicating a *lawlike* connection between being red and being round; the truth of (C) is a coincidence, not a matter of law. We are especially unlikely to take it as lawlike if it is the single isolated correlation between colors and shapes; if it were a law we would expect it to be part of a broader system of color–shape correlations.

Turning to the matter at hand, consider the domain to be the set of persons, and F and G to be, respectively, the set of psychological properties and the set of physical properties. Davidson's point is that even if we should find a true generalization of the form:

(D) All persons with mental property M have physical property P,

we will not, and should not, consider this a *law*. What then is a law? Davidson follows the standard philosophical usage: a law is distinguished from a 'mere generalization' by these two marks: (1) it can support counterfactuals and subjunctives, and (2) it is confirmable by observation of instances. Our (C) above, about all red things being round, meets neither of these criteria; it fails to back a counterfactual such as 'If bananas were red, they would be round', and the only way it could be confirmed is by an exhaustive examination of all objects in the domain, there being no instance-to-instance accretion of positive confirmation.

It will be important to keep in mind the crucial role that considerations of lawlikeness must play in Davidson's central argument; for the argument is designed to show, not that there can be no true psychophysical generalizations of the form (D), but that there can be no psychophysical laws. Davidson is quite explicit on this point.[13] And for good reason; brief reflection will show why this strategy is the only possible one: whether any generalization of the form (D) is true is a contingent empirical matter that can be known only through tedious observation, if at all. No armchair philosophical argument can insure that some statements of this form, by sheer luck or coincidence, will not turn out to be true; it surely cannot do this any more than it can show that a generalization like (C), that all

physical Lawlike Connections and Their Problem', pp. 292–3). This reaction is typical and understandable. What I intend to do is to help complete Davidson's argument.
13 'Mental Events', p. 216.

red things are round, is true, or that it is false. Moreover, whether something like (C) or (D) is true is of no philosophical interest; what is of interest is whether, if true, it would be a law. Davidson thinks we can show from the very idea of what it is to be psychological that no generalization of the form (D), whether true or false, can be lawlike. Its being lawlike is independent of its de facto truth or falsity, and hence can be established or refuted by a priori arguments. At least, that is Davidson's view.

These considerations suggest a clue to the structure of Davidson's argument: *the argument works, to the extent that it does, only with respect to psychophysical laws, and it should fail, more or less obviously, if 'true psychophysical generalization' is substituted for 'psychophysical law' throughout the argument.* What needs to be done, therefore, is to identify the features of the mental and those of the physical that, while tolerating true psychophysical generalizations, are inimical to these generalizations being lawlike. And if this is to be done, the argument must consciously exploit the special characteristics of laws that set them apart from de facto generalizations.

III

The leading idea of Davidson's argument as I see it can be introduced through an analogy. Most of us remember being told by politicians or political analysts that a democratic nation cannot, on pain of damaging its own integrity as a democracy, enter into a genuine treaty relationship with a totalitarian state. We can also imagine something like this said of two religions: the systems are so alien to each other that no regularized and stable relationship between them is possible. The hidden argument here may be something like this: two systems of government or religion are so fundamentally opposed to each other in their basic commitments that a stable and principled relationship cannot be maintained between them on pain of compromising the integrity of one or both of the systems involved. It might be that a democratic state, if it is to honor its treaty obligations to a totalitarian state, must of necessity violate its own commitment to democratic principles. A weaker relationship could be tolerated, but treaty relations are too strict and binding, imposing on the participants obligations that weaker relations do not impose.

Whatever merits the foregoing might have, the structure of Davidson's argument, I believe, is similar: *the mental realm is characterized by certain essential features which would be seriously compromised if there were connections as strong as laws, with their modal and subjunctive force, linking it with the physical realm, which has its own distinctive essential features incompatible with those of the mental.* These features of the mental are essential in that they are *constitutive* or *definitive* of the system of mental concepts; the mental realm cannot sustain their loss and still retain its identity as a mental system. Further, these features are *global* in the sense that they characterize the mental as a system, not primarily individual mental phenomena or concepts in isolation; and similarly for the essential features of the physical. The argument could be run the other way also: given its own commitment to certain constitutive principles not shared by the mental, the physical realm can no more readily tolerate nomological relationships with the mental, without endangering its identity as a physical system. Mere psychophysical generalizations, being weaker than laws, do no harm to either psychology or physics, but laws with their modal force would bring them too close together, leading to a clash of their incompatible natures.

This way of looking at Davidson's argument explains exactly why the argument is supposed to work for psychophysical laws but not for true psychophysical generalizations. True generalizations, unless they are lawlike, are merely accidental and do not signify any deep or intimate relationship between the two realms (recall the case of colors and shapes). But laws are different: nomic connections are strong enough to *transmit,* or *transfer,* the constitutive properties of the physical to the mental, and vice versa, thereby damaging the integrity of the recipient system. Mere generalizations, even if true, do not have this power of transmitting features of one system to the other. We shall try to fill out this preliminary sketch of the argument by giving concrete meaning to this idea of laws 'transmitting' certain features across systems, but a hint of how this can be understood is contained in the observation that laws, in virtue of their modal force, can underwrite certain inferences that mere de facto generalizations cannot sanction.

The skeletal structure of what I take to be Davidson's principal argument can, therefore, be exhibited as follows:

The mental system has a certain essential characteristic X and the physical system a certain essential characteristic Y, where X and Y are mutually incompatible. Laws linking the two systems, if they exist, would 'transmit' these characteristics from one system to the other, leading to incoherence. Therefore, there can be no laws connecting the mental with the physical so long as the two systems are to retain their distinctive identities.

It is worth pointing out that the argument as sketched has a general interest going beyond its application to the psychophysical case; if appropriate properties X and Y are identified, the argument would apply to any two domains and help establish the conclusion that there could not be lawlike connections between them. In any event, the proposed line of interpretation explains, and is supported by, the following remarks by Davidson: 'If the case of supposed laws linking the mental and the physical is different, it can only be because to allow the possibility of laws would amount to changing the subject. By changing the subject I mean here: deciding not to accept the criterion of the mental in terms of the vocabulary of the propositional attitudes.'[14] Davidson is saying that if there were psychophysical laws we would lose the mental ('change the subject') as characterized in terms of intentionality; such laws would compromise the essential intentionality of the mental.

Two things need to be done to flesh out the skeletal argument: (1) we need to identify one or more essential characteristics of the mental, and do the same for the physical, to play the role of X and Y, that is, to be transmitted, or be compromised, by the supposed laws between the mental with the physical, and (2) we must explain in what sense laws can 'transmit' these characteristics from one system to the other. Let us turn to the first task.

Davidson does not tell us in a general way what he means by 'intentional'; instead he simply tells us that the paradigmatic mental states he has in mind are *propositional attitudes,* that is, psychological states with *propositional content* typically expressed by that-clauses and gerunds (e.g., fearing that the pipes are frozen, being embarrassed about missing his appointment for the second time). What then are the crucial features of such states that can be used to fill out Davidson's argument? Consider the following remarks by Davidson:

> Any effort at increasing the accuracy and power of a theory of behavior forces us to bring more and more of the whole system of the agent's beliefs and motives directly into account. But in inferring this system from the evidence, we necessarily impose conditions of coherence, rationality, and consistency. These conditions have no echo in physical theory, which is why we can look for no more than rough correlations between psychological and physical phenomena.[15]

> Just as we cannot intelligibly assign a length to any object unless a comprehensive theory holds of objects of that sort, we cannot intelligibly attribute any propositional attitude to an agent except within the framework of a viable theory of his beliefs, desires, intentions, and decisions.

> There is no assigning beliefs to a person one by one on the basis of his verbal behavior, his choices, or other local signs no matter how plain and

14 Ibid., p. 216.
15 'Psychology as Philosophy', in *Essays on Actions and Events,* p. 231.

evident, for we make sense of particular beliefs only as they cohere with other beliefs, with preferences, with intentions, hopes, fears, expectations, and the rest. It is not merely, as with the measurement of length, that each case tests a theory and depends upon it, but that the content of a propositional attitude derives from its place in the pattern.[16]

These remarks vividly bring out Davidson's 'holism' of the mental: the mental is holistic in that the attribution of any single mental state to a person is strongly constrained by the requirement that the total system attributed to him of beliefs, desires, fears, hopes, and all the rest be *maximally coherent and rational*. This coherence or rationality maximization condition, on Davidson's view, is an essential feature of the intentional; without it we cannot make sense of ascription of contentful mental states. The holistic character of the mental, as embodied in the principle of rationality maximization, is constitutive of our conception of the mental as intentional; compromising this characteristic of the mental would be tantamount to 'changing the subject' – that is, as Davidson explains, abandoning the intentional conception of the mental. How does one maximize the coherence and rationality of a system of intentional states? This is an age-old issue of great importance to epistemology, moral philosophy, and philosophy of science, and we need not address it in a general way. What we need is a sense of what it is about. To begin, avoiding logical inconsistency and maximizing inductive rationality in one's belief system is obviously important; the internal coherence of the agent's system of preferences, e.g., that it satisfy the transitivity condition, is also a factor; we should also check whether the agent's decisions conform to his probabilities and preferences, and whether his feelings and emotions make sense in light of his wants and beliefs; and so on. Davidson's view is, to put it briefly and somewhat simplistically, that either the set of intentional states we attribute to a person satisfies certain minimal standards of rationality and coherence, or else there is no ground for attributing such a system to an agent; in fact, to consider an organism an *agent* is an expression of our willingness to consider it a rational psychological system, that is, to describe its behavior in terms appropriate for assessment in accordance with canons of rationality, and make sense of its decisions and actions as issuing in appropriate ways from its preferences and cognitions. We might add that the point of attributing intentional states to persons is to be able to formulate 'rationalizing explanations' of what they do, and that unless the system of intentional states so attributed is, in certain minimal ways, rational and coherent, no such

16 'Mental Events', p. 221.

explanations would be forthcoming. Davidson says that Quine's doctrine of translational indeterminacy is just another facet of this rationalistic holism of the mental; I shall make a few remarks later about how these two theses are related, but I believe we can construct an argument for Psychophysical Anomalism without an explicit reference to, or reliance on, the indeterminacy thesis.[17]

In point of being holistic, however, the mental is not unique; on Davidson's view, the physical, too, is holistic. Interdependence or seamlessness is common to both.[18] The holism of the physical lies in the fact that the physical, too, is characterized by certain 'synthetic a priori laws' which are *constitutive of* our conception of the physical, and which make possible the formulation of precise physical laws. Among them are principles that make physical measurement possible, such as the transitivity of 'longer than' or 'earlier than'.[19] Basic methodological rules governing theory construction and evidence, fundamental principles about space, time, and causality, and so on, may also qualify. Holism as such, therefore, is a side issue; what is crucial is the divergent constitutive principles from which the distinctive holism of each domain arises. As Davidson puts it, 'there are no strict psychophysical laws because of the disparate commitments of the mental and the physical schemes',[20] and 'there cannot be tight connections between the realms if each is to retain its allegiance to its proper source of evidence'.[21]

These two brief remarks by Davidson are especially revealing: the mental and physical are not able to 'keep allegiance' to their respective constitutive principles and at the same time enter into the kind of 'tight connection' signified by the presence of laws linking them. For the two sets of constitutive principles represent the 'disparate commitments' of the two systems, commitments they cannot disown if they are to preserve their identities. What we now need to understand is exactly how the presence of nomological links is inconsistent with each system's retaining its allegiance to its constitutive principles.

If rationality, therefore, is the essential characteristic of the mental in Davidson's argument, what is the essential feature of the physical that will clash with rationality? I believe we can simply take this as the absence of rationality as a constitutive element of the physical. As Davidson says in a passage already quoted, conditions of coherence, rationality, and consistency 'have no echo in physical theory'.

17 As Lycan emphasizes in 'Psychological Laws', p. 23.   18 'Mental Events', p. 222.
19 Ibid., pp. 220–1.   20 Ibid., p. 222.   21 Ibid., p. 222.

IV

My suggestion is that we try to understand the crucial step in Davidson's argument in terms of the greater inferential strength of laws, compared with de facto generalizations, on account of their modal force. I shall now formulate two specific arguments based on this idea.

Suppose that, on available evidence, the attribution to a person of either of the two mental states, m_1 or m_2, is warranted, and that the principle of rationality maximization enjoins the choice of m_1 over m_2 (we may suppose that the joint attribution of both states contravenes this principle). Suppose further that there are neural states, n_1 and n_2, which are *nomologically coextensive* with m_1 and m_2 respectively; that is, we have laws affirming that as a matter of law, n_1 occurs to an organism at a time just in case m_1 occurs to it at that time; similarly for n_2 and m_2. Now the neural states, n_1 and n_2, being theoretical states of physical theory, have *conditions of attribution,* that is, conditions under which their attribution to an organism is warranted. Such conditions are probably very complex and in some sense holistic; they are probably difficult to articulate, and we are not assuming that they must be observationally accessible. What matters is only that the ascertaining of whether they hold in a given situation is regulated by the constitutive rules and principles of physical theory, not by those of the mental. To say that C_1 is an attribution condition for n_1 must be more than to affirm a mere de facto coincidence of C_1 with n_1 (or with the warranted attribution of n_1); it is to commit oneself to a statement with modal force, which for simplicity we may express as follows:

(1) Necessarily, if C_1 obtains, n_1 occurs.

We also have the psychophysical law:

(2) Necessarily, m_1 occurs if and only if n_1 occurs,

whence:

(3) Necessarily, if C_1 obtains, m_1 occurs.

In the same way we have:

(4) Necessarily, if C_2 obtains, m_2 occurs,

where C_2 is an attribution condition of neural state n_2.

Consider the force of (3) and (4): they affirm that when a certain set of physical conditions holds, a specific mental state *necessarily* occurs, that we *must* attribute to an organism this mental state if those conditions are observed to obtain for it. And this means that the rationality maximization principle as an essential constraint on the attribution of mental states is in danger of being preempted, or seriously compromised, for the determination of whether these physical attribution conditions obtain is not subject to the constraint of this principle. Statements (3) and (4) would permit us to attribute intentional mental states independently of the rationality maximization rule; at least, they would force this rule to share its jurisdiction over mental attributions. In this way, these mental states threaten to escape the jurisdiction of the ruling constitutive principle of the mental, thereby losing their 'allegiance to [their] proper source of evidence'. By becoming so intimately associated with C_1 and C_2, which are under the jurisdiction of physical theory and its constitutive principles, they have in effect ceased to be mental states. For according to Davidson, being subject to the rule of rationality maximization is of the essence of intentional states; without this constraint the ascription of contentful intentional states would be unintelligible.

If something like this captures Davidson's argument, then we should not be able to run it without the assumption that the supposed psychophysical correlations are lawlike; this is the assumption (2) above. It is obvious that if the modality is removed from (2) we can no longer move from (1) to (3), although we could get the nonmodal analogue of (3) stating a de facto coincidence, 'if C_1 obtains, m_1 occurs'. But this is harmless; it exerts no pressure on the rationality maximization principle as a constraint on the attribution of m_1. A de facto conditional like this cannot be taken as stating an attribution condition of m_1 no matter how loosely we construe the notion of attribution condition.

Two points in this argument require further comments. The first concerns the assumption that mental states m_1 and m_2 have *coextensive* physical correlates. This assumption simplifies the argument and enables us to derive a salient and striking conclusion; but it can be weakened. Obvious further cases to consider would be, first, one where neural state n is only sufficient for mental state m and, second, one where n is only necessary for m. However, these do not exhaust all the possibilities, and it will be useful to consider this in a fully general setting. So let L(m,n) be an arbitrary law linking m and n. If this law is properly to be thought of as 'linking' m and n, then the logical form of L(m,n) must generate strong mutual constraints between the attribution of m and that of n. To assume m and n to be coextensive is to set these constraints at a maximum level; if n is only sufficient, or only necessary, for m, the constraint is weaker

206

but still quite strong. Now, the generalized argument for arbitrary $L(m,n)$ would be something like this: If $L(m,n)$ is to qualify as psychophysical law, the attribution of m to an organism must strongly constrain, and be strongly constrained by, the attribution of n to that organism, and to that extent the constitutive principles of one domain extend their regulative powers to the other domain, thereby infringing upon the latter's integrity and autonomy.

The second point concerns the modalities involved in the displayed statements (1)–(4); more specifically, a question can be raised whether the 'nomological modality' of (2) is the same as the modality involved in the statement of 'attribution condition' (1). This raises a host of complex issues which are best avoided here; a short and reasonable way to handle the point would be this: assume that the modality involved in (1) is that of unrestricted logical necessity, and that logical necessity entails nomological necessity. This would imply that the modality of (3) and (4) is at least as strong as the nomological modality of (2); the crucial step would be to argue that this is sufficient to make (3) and (4) a threat to the mentalistic identity of m_1 and m_2. If the likes of (3) and (4) were to hold, that would generate a strong pressure to integrate these affected mental states into physical theory.

We now turn to another way of filling out our skeletal argument. Let p be the statement 'Ypsilanti is within 10 miles of Ann Arbor' and q the statement 'Ypsilanti is within 20 miles of Ann Arbor'. The rule of rationality maximization presumably requires that whenever we attribute to a person the belief that p we must also attribute to him the belief that q. This much deductive closure seems required of any system of beliefs. Consider the following counterfactual:

(5) If S were to believe p, S would also believe q.

This dependence is *grounded in* the principle of rationality maximization; in fact, this principle may sanction a more specific principle enjoining us to attribute to a person all obvious logical consequences of beliefs already attributed to him. That (5) obtains is an important fact about the concept of belief, and is explainable in terms of the essential features of belief as an intentional state, that is, in terms of considerations of rationality and coherence of intentional systems. Suppose now that believing p and believing q have nomological coextensions, B_1 and B_2 respectively, in physical theory. We construe this to mean, or imply, the following:

(6) Necessarily, a person believes p if and only if he is in state B_1.
(7) Necessarily, a person believes q if and only if he is in state B_2.

Inferences involving counterfactuals are tricky; however, we may assume that (5), (6), and (7) together yield:

(8) If S were in state B_1, he would also be in state B_2.

Now, (8) is a *purely physical* counterfactual stating a dependency relation between two physical states; it might state a lawful dependency relation between two neurophysiological states involving discharges of large groups of neurons, or something of the sort. The fact that (6) and (7), the supposed psychophysical laws, would enable us to 'read off' a physical law from a psychological law is not the heart of the argument. We get closer to it when we ask: *What could possibly ground or explain this physical dependency?*

What then would explain or ground (8)? There are three possibilities to consider:

(a) The dependency expressed by (8) is physically fundamental – it is a basic law of physical theory requiring no explanation. This is highly implausible: we would expect fundamental physical laws to connect physical states a good deal simpler than neural correlates of beliefs.

(b) Statement (8) is explainable in terms of more fundamental physical laws. In this case, the same physical laws would yield, via (8), (6), and (7), a physical explanation of why the psychological dependency relation (5) holds, and this means that the role of the rationality maximization principle as a ground for (5) has been preempted, and that the concept of belief has effectively been removed from the jurisdiction of this principle. But the concept of belief that is outside the domain of rationality is no longer an intentional concept – not a concept of belief at all.

(c) The dependency relation (8), though not regarded as a basic physical law, has no physical explanation. But then we can explain it psychologically in terms of (5) via (6) and (7), as it was originally derived. But this is absurd: to ground a purely physical dependency in considerations of rationality of belief would have to be taken as an intolerable intrusion on the closedness and comprehensiveness of physical theory. Thus, none of the possibilities makes sense, and we must reject the supposed laws such as (6) and (7).

This concludes my attempt to flesh out Davidson's idea that psychophysical laws would bring too close together two systems with their 'disparate commitments'. There are no doubt other, perhaps more plausible, ways of doing so; however, what has been done here, I think, goes some way toward making Davidson's arguments more concrete and more palpable, and in my view not altogether implausible.

One might ask why we could not show, by the same argument, that there could not be laws connecting, say, biological and physical phenomena. The answer is that biology and physics are both physical theories sharing the same fundamental constitutive principles; they are governed not by 'disparate commitments' but one uniform set. I think this would be Davidson's response.[22] If, on the other hand, you believe in the uniqueness of 'vital phenomena' or 'entelechies', you could make up a Davidsonian argument to show the nomological irreducibility of the vital to the physical; your only problem would be to defend the relevant vitalistic premises.

There are some prominent considerations advanced by Davidson, especially in 'Mental Events', that have not been made use of in my interpretation. The distinction between 'homonomic' and 'heteronomic' laws is one example; another is his likening of psychophysical laws to the mixing of 'grue' and 'emerald'; I have already mentioned Davidson's approving references to translational indeterminacy. My view is that these do not, at least need not, play a crucial role in the argument. In 'Mental Events', the distinction between the two types of laws quickly leads into the discussion of synthetic a priori constitutive principles of physical theory, and this latter idea of course plays a role in my interpretation. I take the reference to 'grue'-like predicates as just a way of illustrating the incongruity that exists, in Davidson's eye, between mental and physical terms, an incongruity that, as we saw, is given a more precise meaning in terms of allegiance to disparate sets of constitutive principles.

V

I shall now briefly consider how Psychophysical Anomalism relates to the Anomalism of the Mental. In 'Mental Events', one gets a strong impression that Davidson intends to infer the latter from the former. The following is the crucial paragraph:

> It is not plausible that mental concepts alone can provide [a comprehensive framework for the description and law-based prediction and explanation of events], simply because the mental does not . . . constitute a closed system. Too much happens to affect the mental that is not itself a systematic

22 Actually what Davidson says about this is noncommittal: 'I do not want to say that analogous remarks may not hold for some other sciences, for example biology. But I do not know how to show that the concepts of biology are nomologically irreducible to the concepts of physics. What sets apart certain psychological concepts – their intentionality – does not apply to the concepts of biology' (in 'Comments and Replies' following 'Psychology as Philosophy', in *Essays on Actions and Events*, p. 241).

part of the mental. But if we combine this observation with the conclusion that no psychophysical statement is, or can be built into, a strict law we have the principle of the Anomalism of the Mental: there are no strict laws on the basis of which we can predict and explain mental phenomena.[23]

Davidson seems to be saying that we can infer the Anomalism of the Mental from the two premises: Psychophysical Anomalism and the statement that the mental, as distinguished from the physical, does not constitute a closed system. But how is the inference supposed to work?

I have no bright idea on interpreting this passage to yield a perspicuous and plausible argument. Instead I suggest another way of viewing the situation which, though possibly not Davidson's, is not altogether implausible and which seems to fit the large dialectic plan of 'Mental Events'. First, the Anomalism of the Mental can be thought of as being equivalent to the conjunction of Psychophysical Anomalism and the following thesis:

Psychological Anomalism:[24] There are no purely psychological laws, that is, laws connecting psychological events with other psychological events, which can be used to explain and predict these events.

If mental phenomena can be nomologically explained and predicted, then the required laws would have to be either psychophysical or purely psychological. Psychophysical Anomalism says laws of the first kind are not there; Psychological Anomalism says laws of the second kind are not there either. So there are no laws to explain and predict mental phenomena, and this is precisely the Anomalism of the Mental.

Thus, I see the Anomalism of the Mental simply as a conjunction of the two doctrines, Psychological Anomalism and Psychophysical Anomalism. This raises the question where Psychological Anomalism comes from. No readily identifiable argument for it can be found in 'Mental Events', although there is no question that Davidson is committed to it. Furthermore, there are passages in this paper that strongly suggest that the mental as an autonomous realm ought to have, or at least can have, its own laws. In particular, I have in mind Davidson's claim that the synthetic a priori constitutive principles of the physical domain are what makes 'homonomic' physical laws possible, and his explicit acknowledgement that the

23 'Mental Events', p. 224.
24 The term 'psychological anomalism' is not Davidson's. Davidson is clearly committed to this thesis; for example, his argument for anomalous monism cannot go through unless it is assumed that there are no purely psychological laws; it isn't enough merely to assume there are no psychophysical laws.

mental domain, too, has its own characteristic a priori constitutive principles. He says, too, that the attribution of propositional attitudes presupposes as a necessary condition a 'viable *theory* . . . of beliefs, desires, intention, and decisions'.[25] What is a theory made up of, if not laws? But how can this be reconciled with Psychological Anomalism, or indeed with the Anomalism of the Mental?

I suggest the following line of reconciliation: on Davidson's account the mental can, and does, have its own 'laws'; for example, 'laws' of rational decision making. The crucial point, though, is that these are *normative* rather than *predictive* laws. When Psychophysical Anomalism and Psychological Anomalism deny the existence of laws about the mental, the meaning of 'law' involved is one that is appropriate to physical theory, namely the concept of law that permits the formulation of nomological predictions and explanations on the basis of precisely characterized and empirically identifiable initial and boundary conditions. It may be recalled that the Anomalism of the Mental only denies the existence of (in Davidson's own words) 'strict laws on the basis of which behavior can be explained and predicted'. Thus, the existence of nonpredictive normative laws or principles is consistent with the Anomalism of the Mental and Psychological Anomalism. But what do these normative laws look like? I already mentioned principles of decision making; rules of deductive and inductive inference, appropriately phrased, should also be among the prominent examples; there may be principles that govern the coherence of emotions, both among themselves and in relation to other propositional attitudes such as beliefs and desires. These are the norms and rules that guide actions and decisions, and form the basis of rational evaluations of our motives, cognitions, and emotions. And I think there is a sense in which these principles serve as an essential basis for a certain special way in which actions and decisions can be understood and made intelligible.[26] The view of psychology that emerges from Davidson is one of a broad interpretative endeavor directed at human action, to understand its 'meaning' rather than search for law-based causal explanations that are readily convertible into predictions; psychology is portrayed as a hermeneutic inquiry rather than a predictive science.

In order to appreciate Davidson's overall aims and strategies in 'Mental Events', it is useful to attend to his initial stage-setting. His announced aim, which he likens to Kant's attempt to reconcile human freedom with

25 'Mental Events', p. 221 (emphasis added).
26 This is developed in somewhat greater detail in my 'Self-Understanding and Rationalizing Explanations', *Philosophia Naturalis,* 21 (1984): 309–20.

natural necessity, is to show how psychological anomaly is compatible with determinism. How is it possible for the mental to escape the nomological net of physical theory? How can this happen when mental phenomena apparently enter into intimate causal transactions with physical phenomena? In order to formulate this problem, something like Psychological Anomalism has to be *presupposed;* psychological anomaly is part of Davidson's starting point in 'Mental Events' rather than a conclusion to be proved. In the second paragraph of 'Mental Events' he says, 'I start from the assumption that both the causal dependence, and the anomalousness, of mental events are undeniable facts'. Thus, three elements are needed to generate the initial 'Kantian tension': psychological anomaly, the causal dependence of the mental upon the physical, and physical determinism. The tension consists in our need to answer this question: how can the mental be anomalous (i.e., escape physical determinism) when it is causally dependent on the physical domain governed by strict deterministic laws? How can we protect the anomalousness, and the autonomy, of mind?

As I see it, Davidson's resolution consists in pointing out, first, that the tension arises because psychophysical causal dependence is erroneously thought to require the existence of psychophysical laws, and then showing that there in fact can be no such laws to threaten mental anomaly. His argument for the first point leads to his celebrated defense of 'anomalous monism', a version of the so-called 'token-identity' theory; but from the viewpoint of the overall aims of 'Mental Events', anomalous monism is a side issue. In any event, it is assumed in all this that psychophysical laws would make the mental reducible to the physical, effectively destroying its autonomous character. Thus, Psychophysical Anomalism is what safeguards Psychological Anomalism, by insulating the mental from the full impact of physical determinism. This is why arguments for Psychophysical Anomalism occupy center stage in 'Mental Events', and why, on the other hand, there are no arguments for Psychological Anomalism. The former is the substance of what has to be established to answer the principal question of 'Mental Events'; the latter only a presupposition of that question.

Has Davidson ever offered an independent argument for Psychological Anomalism? I believe he has; his discussion of the problem of empirically confirming Ramsey-style decision theory in 'Psychology as Philosophy' can usefully be viewed as just such an argument. But a detailed discussion of this argument is outside the scope of this paper.

VI

In this concluding section I want to try to relate Davidson's views of the mental to a broader context. His initial Kantian tension can be redescribed (by replacing psychophysical causal dependence with psychophysical laws) to yield an inconsistent triad: (1) psychological anomaly, (2) physical determinism, and (3) lawlike linkages between the psychological and the physical. Faced with this triad, Davidson rejects (3), and that is his Psychophysical Anomalism. And the ultimate goal of this move is to insure the autonomy of the mental and the possibility of free agency.[27] It is instructive, I think, to compare Davidson's move with Quine's: Quine, too, would accept (2) and reject (3), where (3) of course is understood to concern the psychological conceived as the intentional. In fact, his doctrine of translational indeterminacy can be taken as the denial of the claim that the intentional psychological *supervenes* on the physical; on Quine's view, the fixing of the totality of physical fact does not suffice to fix the intentional. If there were a pervasive network of laws linking the intentional with the physical, then the intentional would supervene on the physical.[28] Davidson and Quine, however, part company in their reaction to this failure of supervenience: while Davidson takes it as insuring the autonomy of the mental, Quine takes it as showing the illegitimacy of the mental, as witness his well-known disparaging remarks about Brentano: 'One may accept the Brentano thesis [of the irreducibility of intentional terms] either as showing the indispensability of intentional idioms

27 Davidson writes, at the very end of 'Mental Events' (p. 225): 'The anomalism of the mental is thus a necessary condition for viewing action as autonomous.' It is no accident that he begins and ends his paper with quotations from Kant.

28 See Quine's reply to Noam Chomsky in *Words and Objections,* ed. D. Davidson and J. Hintikka (Reidel, Dordrecht, 1969), esp. p. 303, where he says: 'Consider, from this realistic point of view, the totality of truths of nature, known and unknown, observable and unobservable, past and future. The point about indeterminacy of translation is that it withstands even all this truth, the whole truth about nature.' I am aware that in 'Mental Events', p. 214, Davidson explicitly endorses supervenience of the mental upon the physical, in spite of the nonexistence of psychophysical laws. To make Davidson consistent, however, this supervenience must be taken in a fairly weak sense falling well short of full dependence or determination. I am here using the term 'supervenience' in a stronger sense in which what supervenes is wholly fixed when the supervenience base is fixed. The distinction between 'weak' and 'strong' supervenience and related matters are developed in detail in my 'Concepts of Supervenience', Essay 4 of this volume; a simpler and somewhat sketchier account is included in my 'Psychophysical Supervenience as a Mind–Body Theory', *Cognition and Brain Theory,* 5 (1982), and 'Supervenience and Supervenient Causation', *Southern Journal of Philosophy,* 12, supplement (1984), pp. 45–56.

and the importance of the autonomous science of intention, or as show-ing the baselessness of intentional idioms and the emptiness of a science of intention. My attitude, unlike Brentano's, is the second.'[29] For Quine, reducibility to an extensional physical base is an essential mark of legiti-macy. Davidson sees it as a threat to autonomy.

So there are two choices: the eliminativist physicalism of Quine and the dualism of Davidson. It undoubtedly will strike many readers as at best paradoxical to characterize Davidson as a dualist. I believe, however, that in spite of his anomalous monism, dualism in the form of a commit-ment to the mental as an autonomous domain is a nonnegotiable premise of Davidson's overall position in 'Mental Events'.

From this general perspective, we can also make sense of Davidson's somewhat cryptic remarks in 'Mental Events' linking Quine's thesis of translational indeterminacy with his Psychophysical Anomalism.[30] The essential function served by both doctrines is to pry apart the mental and the physical, and show the former to be irreducible, in a crucial way, to the latter. Where Davidson differs from Quine is in his attitude to this irreducibility. His attitude is strongly reminiscent of the dualism of Kant; it clearly is not Cartesian dualism – his anomalous monism is in effect the rejection of the interactionist dualism of the Cartesian variety.

One question remains: is there any reason for favoring this Kantian stance of mental autonomy over Quinean eliminativism? Alchemy and astrology are also irreducible to physical theory; we do not expect to find laws linking alchemical or astrological concepts with those of physics. But that hardly is any reason to champion an autonomous realm of alchemy or astrology! Here a Quinean response seems absolutely appropriate: so much the worse for alchemy and astrology! The irreducibility, nomologi-cal or conceptual, of these alleged inquiries to physical theory is conclu-sive evidence of the hollowness of their pretensions as serious theories of the world. Why should the case of the mental be different? This is a question of critical importance to the status of the mental in our scheme of things.

I think there is an answer, though this may not be Davidson's. The intentional psychological scheme – that is, the framework of belief, de-sire, and will – is one within which we deliberate about ends and means, and assess the rationality of actions and decisions. It is the framework that makes our normative and evaluative activities possible. No purely descriptive framework such as those of neurophysiology and physics, no

29 *Word and Object,* p. 221.   30 'Mental Events', p. 222.

matter how theoretically comprehensive and predictively powerful, can replace it. As long as we think of ourselves as reflective agents capable of deliberation and evaluation – that is, as long as we regard ourselves as agents capable of acting in accordance with a norm – we shall not be able to dispense with the intentional framework of beliefs, wants, and volitions. This again sounds Kantian: our commitment to the intentional framework is a reflection of our nature as rational agents, and our need for it arises out of the demands of practical reason, not those of theoretical reason.

12

What is "naturalized epistemology"?

1. EPISTEMOLOGY AS A NORMATIVE INQUIRY

Descartes' epistemological inquiry in the *Meditations* begins with this question: What propositions are worthy of belief? In the *First Meditation* Descartes canvasses beliefs of various kinds he had formerly held as true and finds himself forced to conclude that he ought to reject them, that he ought not to accept them as true. We can view Cartesian epistemology as consisting of the following two projects: to identify the criteria by which we ought to regulate acceptance and rejection of beliefs, and to determine what we may be said to know according to those criteria. Descartes' epistemological agenda has been the agenda of Western epistemology to this day. The twin problems of identifying the criteria of justified belief and coming to terms with the skeptical challenge to the possibility of knowledge have defined the central tasks of theory of knowledge since Descartes. This was as true of the empiricists, of Locke and Hume and Mill, as of those who more closely followed Descartes in the rationalist path.[1]

It is no wonder then that modern epistemology has been dominated by a single concept, that of *justification,* and two fundamental questions involving it: What conditions must a belief meet if we are justified in accepting it as true? and What beliefs are we in fact justified in accepting? Note that the first question does not ask for an "analysis" or "meaning"

An early version of this paper was read at a meeting of the Korean Society for Analytic Philosophy in 1984 in Seoul. An expanded version was presented at a symposium at the Western Division meetings of the American Philosophical Association in April, 1985, and at the epistemology conference at Brown University in honor of Roderick Chisholm in 1986. I am grateful to Richard Foley and Robert Audi who presented helpful comments at the APA session and the Chisholm Conference respectively. I am also indebted to Terence Horgan and Robert Meyers for helpful comments and suggestions.

1 In making these remarks I am only repeating the familiar textbook history of philosophy; however, what *our* textbooks say about the history of a philosophical concept has much to do with *our* understanding of that concept.

of the term "justified belief". And it is generally assumed, even if not always explicitly stated, that not just any statement of a necessary and sufficient condition for a belief to be justified will do. The implicit requirement has been that the stated conditions must constitute "criteria" of justified belief, and for this it is necessary that the conditions be stated *without the use of epistemic terms.* Thus, formulating conditions of justified belief in such terms as "adequate evidence", "sufficient ground", "good reason", "beyond a reasonable doubt", and so on, would be merely to issue a promissory note redeemable only when these epistemic terms are themselves explained in a way that accords with the requirement.[2]

This requirement, while it points in the right direction, does not go far enough. What is crucial is this: *the criteria of justified belief must be formulated on the basis of descriptive or naturalistic terms alone, without the use of any evaluative or normative ones, whether epistemic or of another kind.*[3] Thus, an analysis of justified belief that makes use of such terms as "intellectual requirement"[4] and "having a right to be sure"[5] would not satisfy this generalized condition; although such an analysis can be informative and enlightening about the interrelationships of these normative concepts, it will not, on the present conception, count as a statement of *criteria* of justified belief, unless of course these terms are themselves provided with nonnormative criteria. What is problematic, therefore, about the use of

2 Alvin Goldman explicitly states this requirement as a desideratum of his own analysis of justified belief in "What is Justified Belief?", in George S. Pappas (ed.), *Justification and Knowledge* (Dordrecht: Reidel, 1979), p. 1. Roderick M. Chisholm's definition of "being evident" in his *Theory of Knowledge,* 2nd ed. (Englewood Cliffs, N.J.: Prentice-Hall, 1977) does not satisfy this requirement as it rests ultimately on an unanalyzed epistemic concept of one belief being more reasonable than another. What does the real "criteriological" work for Chisholm is his "principles of evidence". See especially (A) on p. 73 of *Theory of Knowledge,* which can usefully be regarded as an attempt to provide nonnormative, descriptive conditions for certain types of justified beliefs.
3 The basic idea of this stronger requirement seems implicit in Roderick Firth's notion of "warrant-increasing property" in his "Coherence, Certainty, and Epistemic Priority", *Journal of Philosophy* 61 (1964): 545–57. It seems that William P. Alston has something similar in mind when he says, ". . . like any evaluative property, epistemic justification is a supervenient property, the application of which is based on more fundamental properties" (at this point Alston refers to Firth's paper cited above), in "Two Types of Foundationalism", *Journal of Philosophy* 73 (1976): 165–85 (the quoted remark occurs on p. 170). Although Alston doesn't further explain what he means by "more fundamental properties", the context makes it plausible to suppose that he has in mind nonnormative, descriptive properties. See section 7 below for further discussion.
4 See Chisholm, ibid., p. 14. Here Chisholm refers to a "person's responsibility or duty *qua* intellectual being".
5 This term was used by A. J. Ayer to characterize the difference between lucky guessing and knowing; see *The Problem of Knowledge* (New York & London: Penguin Books, 1956), p. 33.

217

epistemic terms in stating the criteria of justified belief is not its possible circularity in the usual sense; rather it is the fact that these epistemic terms are themselves essentially normative. We shall later discuss the rationale of this strengthened requirement.

As many philosophers have observed,[6] the two questions we have set forth, one about the criteria of justified belief and the other about what we can be said to know according to those criteria, constrain each other. Although some philosophers have been willing to swallow skepticism just because what we regard as the correct criteria of justified belief are seen to lead inexorably to the conclusion that none, or very few, of our beliefs are justified, the usual presumption is that our answer to the first question should leave our epistemic situation largely unchanged. That is to say, it is expected to turn out that according to the criteria of justified belief we come to accept, we know, or are justified in believing, pretty much what we reflectively think we know or are entitled to believe.

Whatever the exact history, it is evident that the concept of justification has come to take center stage in our reflections on the nature of knowledge. And apart from history, there is a simple reason for our preoccupation with justification: it is the only specifically epistemic component in the classic tripartite conception of knowledge. Neither belief nor truth is a specifically epistemic notion: belief is a psychological concept and truth a semantical-metaphysical one. These concepts may have an implicit epistemological dimension, but if they do, it is likely to be through their involvement with essentially normative epistemic notions like justification, evidence, and rationality. Moreover, justification is what makes knowledge itself a normative concept. On the surface at least, neither truth nor belief is normative or evaluative (I shall argue below, though, that belief does have an essential normative dimension). But justification manifestly is normative. If a belief is justified for us, then it is *permissible* and *reasonable*, from the epistemic point of view, for us to hold it, and it would be *epistemically irresponsible* to hold beliefs that contradict it. If we consider believing or accepting a proposition to be an "action" in an appropriate sense, belief justification would then be a special case of justification of action, which in its broadest terms is the central concern of normative ethics. Just as it is the business of normative ethics to delineate the conditions under which acts and decisions are justified from the moral point of view, so it is the business of epistemology to identify and analyze the conditions under which beliefs, and perhaps other propositional atti-

6 Notably by Chisholm in *Theory of Knowledge,* 1st ed., ch. 4.

218

tudes, are justified from the epistemological point of view. It probably is only a historical accident that we standardly speak of "normative ethics" but not of "normative epistemology". Epistemology is a normative discipline as much as, and in the same sense as, normative ethics.

We can summarize our discussion thus far in the following points: that justification is a central concept of our epistemological tradition, that justification, as it is understood in this tradition, is a normative concept, and in consequence that epistemology itself is a normative inquiry whose principal aim is a systematic study of the conditions of justified belief. I take it that these points are uncontroversial, although of course there could be disagreement about the details – for example, about what it means to say a concept or theory is "normative" or "evaluative".

2. THE FOUNDATIONALIST STRATEGY

In order to identify the target of the naturalistic critique – in particular, Quine's – it will be useful to take a brief look at the classic response to the epistemological program set forth by Descartes. Descartes' approach to the problem of justification is a familiar story, at least as the textbook tells it: it takes the form of what is now commonly called "foundationalism". The foundationalist strategy is to divide the task of explaining justification into two stages: first, to identify a set of beliefs that are "directly" justified in that they are justified without deriving their justified status from that of any other belief, and then to explain how other beliefs may be "indirectly" or "inferentially" justified by standing in an appropriate relation to those already justified. Directly justified beliefs, or "basic beliefs", are to constitute the foundation upon which the superstructure of "nonbasic" or "derived" beliefs is to rest. What beliefs then are directly justified, according to Descartes? Subtleties aside, he claimed that beliefs about our own present conscious states are among them. In what does their justification consist? What is it about these beliefs that makes them directly justified? Somewhat simplistically again, Descartes' answer is that they are justified because they are *indubitable,* that the attentive and reflective mind *cannot* but assent to them. How are nonbasic beliefs justified? By "deduction" – that is, by a series of inferential steps, or "intuitions", each of which is indubitable. If, therefore, we take Cartesian indubitability as a psychological notion, Descartes' epistemological theory can be said to meet the desideratum of providing nonepistemic, naturalistic criteria of justified belief.

Descartes' foundationalist program was inherited, in its essential outlines, by the empiricists. In particular, his "mentalism", that beliefs about one's own current mental state are epistemologically basic, went essentially unchallenged by the empiricists and positivists, until this century. Epistemologists have differed from one another chiefly in regard to two questions: first, what else belonged in our corpus of basic beliefs, and second, how the derivation of the nonbasic part of our knowledge was to proceed. Even the Logical Positivists were, by and large, foundationalists, although some of them came to renounce Cartesian mentalism in favor of a "physicalistic basis".[7] In fact, the Positivists were foundationalists twice over: for them "observation", whether phenomenological or physical, served not only as the foundation of knowledge but as the foundation of all "cognitive meaning" – that is, as both an epistemological and a semantic foundation.

3. QUINE'S ARGUMENTS

It has become customary for epistemologists who profess allegiance to a "naturalistic" conception of knowledge to pay homage to Quine as the chief contemporary provenance of their inspiration – especially to his influential paper "Epistemology Naturalized".[8] Quine's principal argument in this paper against traditional epistemology is based on the claim that the Cartesian foundationalist program has failed – that the Cartesian "quest for certainty" is "a lost cause". While this claim about the hopelessness of the Cartesian "quest for certainty" is nothing new, using it to discredit the very conception of normative epistemology is new, something that any serious student of epistemology must contend with.

Quine divides the classic epistemological program into two parts: *conceptual reduction* whereby physical terms, including those of theoretical science, are reduced, via definition, to terms referring to phenomenal features of sensory experience, and *doctrinal reduction* whereby truths about

---

7 See Rudolf Carnap, "Testability and Meaning", *Philosophy of Science* 3 (1936), and 4 (1937). We should also note the presence of a strong coherentist streak among some Positivists; see, e.g., Carl G. Hempel, "On the Logical Positivists' Theory of Truth", *Analysis* 2 (1935): 49–59, and "Some Remarks on 'Facts' and Propositions", *Analysis* 2 (1935): 93–96.

8 In W. V. Quine, *Ontological Relativity and Other Essays* (New York: Columbia University Press, 1969). Also see his *Word and Object* (Cambridge: MIT Press, 1969); *The Roots of Reference* (La Salle, Ill.: Open Court, 1973); (with Joseph Ullian) *The Web of Belief* (New York: Random House, 1970); and especially "The Nature of Natural Knowledge" in Samuel Guttenplan (ed.), *Mind and Language* (Oxford: Clarendon Press, 1975). See Frederick F. Schmitt's excellent bibliography on naturalistic epistemology in Hilary Kornblith (ed.), *Naturalizing Epistemology* (Cambridge: MIT/Bradford, 1985).

the physical world are appropriately obtained from truths about sensory experience. The "appropriateness" just alluded to refers to the requirement that the favored epistemic status ("certainty" for classic epistemologists, according to Quine) of our basic beliefs be transferred, essentially undiminished, to derived beliefs, a necessary requirement if the derivational process is to yield knowledge from knowledge. What derivational methods have this property of preserving epistemic status? Perhaps there are none, given our proneness to err in framing derivations as in anything else, not to mention the possibility of lapses of attention and memory in following lengthy proofs. But logical deduction comes as close to being one as any; it can at least be relied on to transmit truth, if not epistemic status. It could perhaps be argued that no method can preserve certainty unless it preserves (or is known to preserve) truth; and if this is so, logical deduction is the only method worth considering. I do not know whether this was the attitude of most classic epistemologists; but Quine assumes that if deduction doesn't fill their bill, nothing will.

Quine sees the project of conceptual reduction as culminating in Carnap's *Der Logische Aufbau der Welt*. As Quine sees it, Carnap "came nearest to executing" the conceptual half of the classic epistemological project. But coming close is not good enough. Because of the holistic manner in which empirical meaning is generated by experience, no reduction of the sort Carnap and others so eagerly sought could in principle be completed. For definitional reduction requires point-to-point meaning relations[9] between physical terms and phenomenal terms, something that Quine's holism tells us cannot be had. The second half of the program, doctrinal reduction, is in no better shape; in fact, it was the one to stumble first, for, according to Quine, its impossibility was decisively demonstrated, long before the *Aufbau,* by Hume in his celebrated discussion of induction. The "Humean predicament" shows that theory cannot be logically deduced from observation; there simply is no way of deriving theory from observation that will transmit the latter's epistemic status intact to the former.

I don't think anyone wants to disagree with Quine in these claims. It is not possible to "validate" science on the basis of sensory experience, if "validation" means justification through logical deduction. Quine of course does not deny that our theories depend on observation for evidential support; he has said that sensory evidence is the only evidence there is. To be sure, Quine's argument against the possibility of conceptual re-

---

9 Or confirmational relations, given the Positivists' verificationist theory of meaning.

duction has a new twist: the application of his "holism". But his conclusion is no surprise; "translational phenomenalism" has been moribund for many years.[10] And, as Quine himself notes, his argument against the doctrinal reduction, the "quest for certainty", is only a restatement of Hume's "skeptical" conclusions concerning induction: induction after all is not deduction. Most of us are inclined, I think, to view the situation Quine describes with no great alarm, and I rather doubt that these conclusions of Quine's came as news to most epistemologists when "Epistemology Naturalized" was first published. We are tempted to respond: of course we can't define physical concepts in terms of sense-data; of course observation "underdetermines" theory. That is why observation is observation and not theory.

So it is agreed on all hands that the classical epistemological project, conceived as one of deductively validating physical knowledge from indubitable sensory data, cannot succeed. But what is the moral of this failure? What should be its philosophical lesson to us? Having noted the failure of the Cartesian program, Quine goes on:[11]

> The stimulation of his sensory receptors is all the evidence anybody has had to go on, ultimately, in arriving at his picture of the world. Why not just see how this construction really proceeds? Why not settle for psychology? Such a surrender of the epistemological burden to psychology is a move that was disallowed in earlier times as circular reasoning. If the epistemologist's goal is validation of the grounds of empirical science, he defeats his purpose by using psychology or other empirical science in the validation. However, such scruples against circularity have little point once we have stopped dreaming of deducing science from observation. If we are out simply to understand the link between observation and science, we are well advised to use any available information, including that provided by the very science whose link with observation we are seeking to understand.

And Quine has the following to say about the failure of Carnap's reductive program in the *Aufbau:*[12]

> To relax the demand for definition, and settle for a kind of reduction that does not eliminate, is to renounce the last remaining advantage that we supposed rational reconstruction to have over straight psychology; namely, the advantage of translational reduction. If all we hope for is a reconstruction that links science to experience in explicit ways short of translation, then it would seem more sensible to settle for psychology. Better to discover how science is in fact developed and learned than to fabricate a fictitious structure to a similar effect.

10 I know of no serious defense of it since Ayer's *The Foundations of Empirical Knowledge* (London: Macmillan, 1940).
11 "Epistemology Naturalized", pp. 75–76. 12 Ibid., p. 78.

If a task is entirely hopeless, if we know it cannot be executed, no doubt it is rational to abandon it; we would be better off doing something else that has some hope of success. We can agree with Quine that the "validation" – that is, logical deduction – of science on the basis of observation cannot be had; so it is rational to abandon this particular epistemological program, if indeed it ever was a program that anyone seriously undertook. But Quine's recommendations go further. In particular, there are two aspects of Quine's proposals that are of special interest to us: first, he is not only advising us to quit the program of "validating science", but urging us to take up another specific project, an empirical psychological study of our cognitive processes; second, he is also claiming that this new program replaces the old, and that both programs are part of something appropriately called "epistemology". Naturalized epistemology is to be a kind of epistemology after all, a "successor subject" [13] to classical epistemology.

How should we react to Quine's urgings? What should be our response? The Cartesian project of validating science starting from the indubitable foundation of first-person psychological reports (perhaps with the help of certain indubitable first principles) is not the whole of classical epistemology – or so it would seem at first blush. In our characterization of classical epistemology, the Cartesian program was seen as one possible response to the problem of epistemic justification, the two-part project of identifying the criteria of epistemic justification and determining what beliefs are in fact justified according to those criteria. In urging "naturalized epistemology" on us, Quine is not suggesting that we give up the Cartesian foundationalist solution and explore others within the same framework[14] – perhaps, to adopt some sort of "coherentist" strategy, or to require of our basic beliefs only some degree of "initial credibility" rather than Cartesian certainty, or to permit some sort of probabilistic derivation in addition to deductive derivation of nonbasic knowledge, or to consider the use of special rules of evidence, like Chisholm's "principles of evidence",[15] or to give up the search for a derivational process that transmits undiminished certainty in favor of one that can transmit

13 To use an expression of Richard Rorty's in *Philosophy and the Mirror of Nature* (Princeton: Princeton University Press, 1979), p. 11.
14 Elliott Sober makes a similar point: "And on the question of whether the failure of a foundationalist programme shows that questions of justification cannot be answered, it is worth noting that Quine's advice 'Since Carnap's foundationalism failed, why not settle for psychology' carries weight only to the degree that Carnapian epistemology exhausts the possibilities of epistemology", in "Psychologism", *Journal of Theory of Social Behaviour* 8 (1978): 165–191.
15 See Chisholm, *Theory of Knowledge,* 2nd ed., ch. 4.

diminished but still useful degrees of justification. Quine's proposal is more radical than that. He is asking us to set aside the entire framework of justification-centered epistemology. That is what is new in Quine's proposals. Quine is asking us to put in its place a purely descriptive, causal-nomological science of human cognition.[16]

How should we characterize in general terms the difference between traditional epistemological programs, such as foundationalism and coherence theory on the one hand and Quine's program of naturalized epistemology on the other? Quine's stress is on the *factual* and *descriptive* character of his program; he says, "Why not see how [the construction of theory from observation] *actually proceeds?* Why not settle for psychology?";[17] again, "Better to *discover how science is in fact developed and learned than.* . . ."[18] We are given to understand that in contrast traditional epistemology is not a descriptive, factual inquiry. Rather, it is an attempt at a "validation" or "rational reconstruction" of science. Validation, according to Quine, proceeds via deduction, and rational reconstruction via definition. However, their *point* is justificatory – that is, to rationalize our sundry knowledge claims. So Quine is asking us to set aside what is "rational" in rational reconstruction.

Thus, it is normativity that Quine is asking us to repudiate. Although Quine does not explicitly characterize traditional epistemology as "normative" or "prescriptive", his meaning is unmistakable. Epistemology is to be "a chapter of psychology", a law-based predictive-explanatory theory, like any other theory within empirical science; its principal job is to see how human cognizers develop theories (their "picture of the world") from observation ("the stimulation of their sensory receptors"). Epistemology is to go out of the business of justification. We earlier characterized traditional epistemology as essentially normative; we see why Quine wants us to reject it. Quine is urging us to replace a normative theory of cognition with a descriptive science.

4. LOSING KNOWLEDGE FROM EPISTEMOLOGY

If justification drops out of epistemology, knowledge itself drops out of epistemology. For our concept of knowledge is inseparably tied to that of

16 "If we are seeking only the causal mechanism of our knowledge of the external world, and not a justification of that knowledge in terms prior to science. . . .", Quine, "Grades of Theoreticity", in L. Foster and J. W. Swanson (eds.), *Experience and Theory* (Amherst: University of Massachusetts Press, 1970), p. 2.
17 Ibid., p. 75. Emphasis added.   18 Ibid., p. 78. Emphasis added.

justification. As earlier noted, knowledge itself is a normative notion. Quine's nonnormative, naturalized epistemology has no room for our concept of knowledge. It is not surprising that, in describing naturalized epistemology, Quine seldom talks about knowledge; instead, he talks about "science" and "theories" and "representations". Quine would have us investigate how sensory stimulation "leads" to "theories" and "representations" of the world. I take it that within the traditional scheme these "theories" and "representations" correspond to beliefs, or systems of beliefs; thus, what Quine would have us do is to investigate how sensory stimulation leads to the formation of beliefs about the world.

But in what sense of "lead"? I take it that Quine has in mind a causal or nomological sense. He is urging us to develop a theory, an empirical theory, that uncovers lawful regularities governing the processes through which organisms come to develop beliefs about their environment as a causal result of having their sensory receptors stimulated in various ways. Quine says:[19]

> [Naturalized epistemology] studies a natural phenomenon, viz., a physical human subject. This human subject is accorded experimentally controlled input − certain patterns of irradiation in assorted frequencies, for instance − and in the fullness of time the subject delivers as output a description of the three-dimensional external world and its history. *The relation between the meager input and torrential output* is a relation that we are prompted to study for somewhat the same reasons that always prompted epistemology; namely, in order to see *how evidence relates to theory,* and in what ways one's theory of nature transcends any available evidence.

The relation Quine speaks of between "meager input" and "torrential output" is a causal relation; at least it is qua causal relation that the naturalized epistemologist investigates it. It is none of the naturalized epistemologist's business to assess whether, and to what degree, the input "justifies" the output, how a given irradiation of the subject's retinas makes it "reasonable" or "rational" for the subject to emit certain representational output. His interest is strictly causal and nomological: he wants us to look for patterns of lawlike dependencies characterizing the input–output relations for this particular organism and others of a like physical structure.

If this is right, it makes Quine's attempt to relate his naturalized epistemology to traditional epistemology look at best lame. For in what sense is the study of causal relationships between physical stimulation of sensory receptors and the resulting cognitive output a way of "seeing how evidence relates to theory" in an epistemologically relevant sense? The causal

19 Ibid., p. 83. Emphasis added.

relation between sensory input and cognitive output is a relation between "evidence" and "theory"; however, it is not an *evidential relation*. This can be seen from the following consideration: the nomological patterns that Quine urges us to look for are certain to vary from species to species, depending on the particular way each biological (and possibly nonbiological) species processes information, but the evidential relation in its proper normative sense must abstract from such factors and concern itself only with the degree to which evidence supports hypothesis.

In any event, the concept of evidence is inseparable from that of justification. When we talk of "evidence" in an epistemological sense we are talking about justification: one thing is "evidence" for another just in case the first tends to enhance the reasonableness or justification of the second. And such evidential relations hold in part because of the "contents" of the items involved, not merely because of the causal or nomological connections between them. A strictly nonnormative concept of evidence is not our concept of evidence; it is something that we do not understand.[20]

None of us, I think, would want to quarrel with Quine about the interest or importance of the psychological study of how our sensory input causes our epistemic output. This is only to say that the study of human (or other kinds of) cognition is of interest. That isn't our difficulty; our difficulty is whether, and in what sense, pursuing Quine's "epistemology" is a way of doing epistemology — that is, a way of studying "how evidence relates to theory". Perhaps, Quine's recommendation that we discard justification-centered epistemology is worth pondering; and his exhortation to take up the study of psychology perhaps deserves to be heeded also. What is mysterious is why this recommendation has to be coupled with the rejection of normative epistemology (if normative epistemology is not a possible inquiry, why shouldn't the would-be epistemologist turn to, say, hydrodynamics or ornithology rather than psychology?). But of course Quine is saying more; he is saying that an understandable, if misguided, motivation (that is, seeing "how evidence relates to theory") does underlie our proclivities for indulgence in normative epistemology, but that we would be better served by a scientific study of human cognition than normative epistemology.

20 But aren't there those who advocate a "causal theory" of evidence or justification? I want to make two brief points about this. First, the nomological or causal input–output relations are not in themselves evidential relations, whether these latter are understood causally or otherwise. Second, a causal theory of evidence attempts to state *criteria* for "e is evidence for h" in causal terms; even if this is successful, it does not necessarily give us a causal "definition" or "reduction" of the concept of evidence. For more details see section 6 below.

But it is difficult to see how an "epistemology" that has been purged of normativity, one that lacks an appropriate normative concept of justification or evidence, can have anything to do with the concerns of traditional epistemology. And unless naturalized epistemology and classical epistemology share some of their central concerns, it's difficult to see how one could *replace* the other, or be a way (a better way) of doing the other.[21] To be sure, they both investigate "how evidence relates to theory". But putting the matter this way can be misleading, and has perhaps misled Quine: the two disciplines do not investigate the same relation. As lately noted, normative epistemology is concerned with the evidential relation properly so-called – that is, the relation of justification – and Quine's naturalized epistemology is meant to study the causal-nomological relation. For epistemology to go out of the business of justification is for it to go out of business.

5. BELIEF ATTRIBUTION AND RATIONALITY

Perhaps we have said enough to persuade ourselves that Quine's naturalized epistemology, while it may be a legitimate scientific inquiry, is not a kind of epistemology, and, therefore, that the question whether it is a better kind of epistemology cannot arise. In reply, however, it might be said that there was a sense in which Quine's epistemology and traditional epistemology could be viewed as sharing a common subject matter, namely this: they both concern beliefs or "representations". The only difference is that the former investigates their causal histories and connections whereas the latter is concerned with their evidential or justificatory properties and relations. This difference, if Quine is right, leads to another (so continues the reply): the former is a feasible inquiry, the latter is not.

I now want to take my argument a step further: I shall argue that the concept of belief is itself an essentially normative one, and in consequence that if normativity is wholly excluded from naturalized epistemology it cannot even be thought of as being about beliefs. That is, if naturalized epistemology is to be a science of beliefs properly so called, it must presuppose a normative concept of belief.

Briefly, the argument is this. In order to implement Quine's program of naturalized epistemology, we shall need to identify, and individuate, the input and output of cognizers. The input, for Quine, consists of phys-

21 I am not saying that Quine is under any illusion on this point. My remarks are directed rather at those who endorse Quine without, it seems, a clear appreciation of what is involved.

ical events ("the stimulation of sensory receptors") and the output is said to be a "theory" or "picture of the world" – that is, a set of "representations" of the cognizer's environment. Let us focus on the output. In order to study the sensory input–cognitive output relations for the given cognizer, therefore, we must find out what "representations" he has formed as a result of the particular stimulations that have been applied to his sensory transducers. Setting aside the jargon, what we need to be able to do is to attribute *beliefs,* and other contentful intentional states, to the cognizer. But belief attribution ultimately requires a "radical interpretation" of the cognizer, of his speech and intentional states; that is, we must construct an "interpretive theory" that simultaneously assigns meanings to his utterances and attributes to him beliefs and other propositional attitudes.[22]

Even a cursory consideration indicates that such an interpretation cannot begin – we cannot get a foothold in our subject's realm of meanings and intentional states – unless we assume his total system of beliefs and other propositional attitudes to be largely and essentially rational and coherent. As Davidson has emphasized, a given belief has the content it has in part because of its location in a network of other beliefs and propositional attitudes; and what at bottom grounds this network is the evidential relation, a relation that regulates what is reasonable to believe given other beliefs one holds. That is, unless our cognizer is a "rational being", a being whose cognitive "output" is regulated and constrained by norms of rationality – typically, these norms holistically constrain his propositional attitudes in virtue of their contents – we cannot intelligibly interpret his "output" as consisting of beliefs. Conversely, if we are unable to interpret our subject's meanings and propositional attitudes in a way that satisfies a minimal standard of rationality, there is little reason to regard him as a "cognizer", a being that forms representations and constructs theories. This means that there is a sense of "rational" in which the expression "rational belief" is redundant; every belief must be rational in certain minimal ways. It is not important for the purposes of the present argument what these minimal standards of rationality are; the only point that matters is that unless the output of our cognizer is subject to evaluation in accordance with norms of rationality, that output cannot be considered as consisting of beliefs and hence cannot be the object of an epistemological inquiry, whether plain or naturalized.

We can separate the core of these considerations from controversial

---

22 Here I am drawing chiefly on Donald Davidson's writings on radical interpretation. See Essays 9, 10, and 11 in his *Inquiries into Truth and Interpretation* (Oxford: Clarendon Press, 1984). See also David Lewis, "Radical Interpretation", *Synthese* 27 (1974): 331–44.

issues involving the so-called "principle of charity", minimal rationality, and other matters in the theory of radical interpretation. What is crucial is this: for the interpretation and attribution of beliefs to be possible, not only must we assume the overall rationality of cognizers, but also we must continually evaluate and re-evaluate the putative beliefs of a cognizer in their evidential relationship to one another and other propositional attitudes. It is not merely that belief attribution requires the umbrella assumption about the overall rationality of cognizers. Rather, the point is that *belief attribution requires belief evaluation,* in accordance with normative standards of evidence and justification. If this is correct, rationality in its broad and fundamental sense is not an optional property of beliefs, a virtue that some beliefs may enjoy and others lack; it is a precondition of the attribution and individuation of belief – that is, a property without which the concept of belief would be unintelligible and pointless.

Two objections might be raised to counter these considerations. First, one might argue that at best they show only that the normativity of belief is an epistemological assumption – that we need to assume the rationality and coherence of belief systems when we are trying to *find out* what beliefs to attribute to a cognizer. It does not follow from this epistemological point, the objection continues, that the concept of belief is itself normative.[23] In replying to this objection, we can by-pass the entire issue of whether the rationality assumption concerns only the epistemology of belief attribution. Even if this premise (which I think is incorrect) is granted, the point has already been made. For it is an essential part of the business of naturalized epistemology, as a theory of how beliefs are formed as a result of sensory stimulation, to *find out* what particular beliefs the given cognizers have formed. But this is precisely what cannot be done, if our considerations show anything at all, unless the would-be naturalized epistemologist continually evaluates the putative beliefs of his subjects in regard to their rationality and coherence, subject to the overall constraint of the assumption that the cognizers are largely rational. The naturalized epistemologist cannot dispense with normative concepts or disengage himself from valuational activities.

Second, it might be thought that we could simply avoid these considerations stemming from belief attribution by refusing to think of cognitive output as consisting of "beliefs", namely as states having propositional contents. The "representations" Quine speaks of should be taken as appropriate neural states, and this means that all we need is to be able to

23 Robert Audi suggested this as a possible objection.

discern neural states of organisms. This requires only neurophysiology and the like, not the normative theory of rational belief. My reply takes the form of a dilemma: either the "appropriate" neural states are identified by seeing how they correlate with beliefs,[24] in which case we still need to contend with the problem of radical interpretation, or beliefs are entirely by-passed. In the latter case, belief, along with justification, drops out of Quinean epistemology, and it is unclear in what sense we are left with an inquiry that has anything to do with knowledge.[25]

6. THE "PSYCHOLOGISTIC" APPROACH TO EPISTEMOLOGY

Many philosophers now working in theory of knowledge have stressed the importance of systematic psychology to philosophical epistemology. Reasons proffered for this are various, and so are the conceptions of the proper relationship between psychology and epistemology.[26] But they are virtually unanimous in their rejection of what they take to be the epistemological tradition of Descartes and its modern embodiments in philosophers like Russell, C. I. Lewis, Roderick Chisholm, and A. J. Ayer; and they are united in their endorsement of the naturalistic approach of Quine we have been considering. Traditional epistemology is often condemned as "aprioristic", and as having lost sight of human knowledge as a product of natural causal processes and its function in the survival of the organism and the species. Sometimes, the adherents of the traditional approach are taken to task for their implicit antiscientific bias or indifference to the new developments in psychology and related disciplines. Their own approach in contrast is hailed as "naturalistic" and "scientific", better attuned to significant advances in the relevant scientific fields such as "cognitive science" and "neuroscience", promising philosophical returns far richer than what the aprioristic method of traditional epistemology has been able to deliver. We shall here briefly consider how this new naturalism in epistemology is to be understood in relation to the classic epistemological program and Quine's naturalized epistemology.

Let us see how one articulate proponent of the new approach explains

24 For some considerations tending to show that these correlations cannot be lawlike see my "Psychophysical Laws", Essay 11 of this volume.
25 For a more sympathetic account of Quine than mine, see Hilary Kornblith's introductory essay, "What is Naturalistic Epistemology?", in Kornblith (ed.), *Naturalizing Epistemology*.
26 For more details see Alvin I. Goldman, *Epistemology and Cognition* (Cambridge: Harvard University Press, 1986).

the distinctiveness of his position vis-à-vis that of the traditional epistemologists. According to Philip Kitcher, the approach he rejects is characterized by an "apsychologistic" attitude that takes the difference between
knowledge and true belief – that is, justification – to consist in "ways
which are independent of the causal antecedents of a subject's states".[27]
Kitcher writes:[28]

> . . . we can present the heart of [the apsychologistic approach] by consider-
> ing the way in which it would tackle the question of whether a person's
> true belief that p counts as knowledge that p. The idea would be to disre-
> gard the psychological life of the subject, looking just at the various propo-
> sitions she believes. If p is 'connected in the right way' to other proposi-
> tions which are believed, then we count the subject as knowing that p. Of
> course, apsychologistic epistemology will have to supply a criterion for
> propositions to be 'connected in the right way' . . . but proponents of this
> view of knowledge will emphasize that the criterion is to be given in *logical*
> terms. We are concerned with logical relations among propositions, not
> with psychological relations among mental states.

On the other hand, the psychologistic approach considers the crucial
difference between knowledge and true belief – that is, epistemic justification – to turn on "the factors which produced the belief", focusing on
"processes which produce belief, processes which will always contain, at
their latter end, psychological events".[29]

It is not entirely clear from this characterization whether a psychologistic theory of justification is to be *prohibited* from making *any* reference
to logical relations among belief contents (it is difficult to believe how a
theory of justification respecting such a blanket prohibition could succeed); nor is it clear whether, conversely, an apsychologistic theory will
be permitted to refer at all to beliefs qua psychological states, or exactly
what it is for a theory to do so. But such points of detail are unimportant
here; it is clear enough, for example, that Goldman's proposal to explicate
justified belief as belief generated by a reliable belief-forming process[30]
nicely fits Kitcher's characterization of the psychologistic approach. This

27 *The Nature of Mathematical Knowledge* (New York: Oxford University Press, 1983), p. 14.
28 Ibid.
29 Ibid., p. 13. I should note that Kitcher considers the apsychologistic approach to be an
   aberration of the twentieth century epistemology, as represented by philosophers like
   Russell, Moore, C. I. Lewis, and Chisholm, rather than a historical characteristic of the
   Cartesian tradition. In "The Psychological Turn", *Australasian Journal of Philosophy* 60
   (1982): 238–53, Hilary Kornblith gives an analogous characterization of the two approaches to justification; he associates "justification-conferring processes" with the psychologistic approach and "epistemic rules" with the apsychologistic approach.
30 See Goldman, "What is Justified Belief?".

account, one form of the so-called "reliability theory" of justification, probably was what Kitcher had in mind when he was formulating his general characterization of epistemological naturalism. However, another influential form of the reliability theory does not qualify under Kitcher's characterization. This is Armstrong's proposal to explain the difference between knowledge and true belief, at least for noninferential knowledge, in terms of "a *law-like connection* between the state of affairs [of a subject's believing that p] and the state of affairs that makes 'p' true such that, given the state of affairs [of the subject's believing that p], it must be the case that p."[31] There is here no reference to the causal *antecedents* of beliefs, something that Kitcher requires of psychologistic theories.

Perhaps, Kitcher's preliminary characterization needs to be broadened and sharpened. However, a salient characteristic of the naturalistic approach has already emerged, which we can put as follows: justification is to be characterized in terms of causal or nomological connections involving beliefs as psychological states or processes, and not in terms of the logical properties or relations pertaining to the contents of these beliefs.[32]

If we understand current epistemological naturalism in this way, how closely is it related to Quine's conception of naturalized epistemology? The answer, I think, is obvious: not very closely at all. In fact, it seems a good deal closer to the Cartesian tradition than to Quine. For, as we saw, the difference that matters between Quine's epistemological program and the traditional program is the former's total renouncement of the latter's normativity, its rejection of epistemology as normative inquiry. The talk of "replacing" epistemology with psychology is irrelevant and at best misleading, though it could give us a momentary relief from a sense of deprivation. When one abandons justification and other valuational concepts, one abandons the entire framework of normative epistemology. What remains is a descriptive empirical theory of human cognition which, if Quine has his way, will be entirely devoid of the notion of justification or any other evaluative concept.

As I take it, this is not what most advocates of epistemological naturalism are aiming at. By and large they are not Quinean eliminativists in regard to justification, and justification in its full-fledged normative sense

31 David M. Armstrong, *Truth, Belief and Knowledge* (London: Cambridge University Press, 1973), p. 166.
32 The aptness of this characterization of the "apsychologistic" approach for philosophers like Russell, Chisholm, Keith Lehrer, John Pollock, etc., can be debated. Also, there is the issue of "internalism" vs. "externalism" concerning justification, which I believe must be distinguished from the psychologistic vs. apsychologistic division.

continues to play a central role in their epistemological reflections. Where they differ from their nonnaturalist adversaries is the specific way in which the criteria of justification are to be formulated. Naturalists and nonnaturalists ("apsychologists") can agree that these criteria must be stated in descriptive terms – that is, without the use of epistemic or any other kind of normative terms. According to Kitcher, an apsychologistic theory of justification would state them primarily in terms of *logical* properties and relations holding for propositional contents of beliefs, whereas the psychologistic approach advocates the exclusive use of *causal* properties and relations holding for beliefs as events or states. Many traditional epistemologists may prefer criteria that confer upon a cognizer a position of special privilege and responsibility with regard to the epistemic status of his beliefs, whereas most self-avowed naturalists prefer "objective" or "externalist" criteria with no such special privileges for the cognizer. But these differences are among those that arise within the familiar normative framework, and are consistent with the exclusion of normative terms in the statement of the criteria of justification.

Normative ethics can serve as a useful model here. To claim that basic ethical terms, like "good" and "right", are definable on the basis of descriptive or naturalistic terms is one thing; to insist that it is the business of normative ethics to provide *conditions* or *criteria* for "good" and "right" in descriptive or naturalistic terms is another. One may properly reject the former, the so-called "ethical naturalism", as many moral philosophers have done, and hold the latter; there is no obvious inconsistency here. G. E. Moore is a philosopher who did just that. As is well known, he was a powerful critic of ethical naturalism, holding that goodness is a "simple" and "nonnatural" property. At the same time, he held that a thing's being good "follows" from its possessing certain naturalistic properties. He wrote:[33]

> I should never have thought of suggesting that goodness was 'non-natural',
> unless I had supposed that it was 'derivative' in the sense that, whenever a
> thing is good (in the sense in question) its goodness ... 'depends on the
> presence of certain non-ethical characteristics' possessed by the thing in
> question: I have always supposed that it did so 'depend', in the sense that,
> if a thing is good (in my sense), then that it is so *follows* from the fact that
> it possesses certain natural intrinsic properties. ...

It makes sense to think of these "natural intrinsic properties" from which a thing's being good is thought to follow as constituting naturalistic crite-

33 Moore, "A Reply to My Critics", in P. A. Schilpp (ed.), *The Philosophy of G. E. Moore* (Chicago & Evanston: Open Court, 1942), p. 588.

ria of goodness, or at least pointing to the existence of such criteria. One can reject ethical naturalism, the doctrine that ethical concepts are definitionally eliminable in favor of naturalistic terms, and at the same time hold that ethical properties, or the ascription of ethical terms, must be governed by naturalistic criteria. It is clear, then, that we are here using "naturalism" ambiguously in "epistemological naturalism" and "ethical naturalism". In our present usage, epistemological naturalism does not include (nor does it necessarily exclude) the claim that epistemic terms are definitionally reducible to naturalistic terms. (Quine's naturalism is eliminative, though it is not a definitional eliminativism.)

If, therefore, we locate the split between Quine and traditional epistemology at the descriptive vs. normative divide, then currently influential naturalism in epistemology is not likely to fall on Quine's side. On this descriptive vs. normative issue, one can side with Quine in one of two ways: first, one rejects, with Quine, the entire justification-based epistemological program; or second, like ethical naturalists but unlike Quine, one believes that epistemic concepts are naturalistically definable. I doubt that very many epistemological naturalists will embrace either of these alternatives.[34]

7. EPISTEMIC SUPERVENIENCE – OR WHY NORMATIVE EPISTEMOLOGY IS POSSIBLE

But why should we think that there *must* be naturalistic criteria of justified belief and other terms of epistemic appraisal? If we take the discovery and systematization of such criteria to be the central task of normative epistemology, is there any reason to think that this task can be fruitfully pursued, that normative epistemology is a possible field of inquiry? Quine's point is that it is not. We have already noted the limitation of Quine's negative arguments in "Epistemology Naturalized", but is there a positive reason for thinking that normative epistemology is a viable program? One could consider a similar question about the possibility of normative ethics.

34 Richard Rorty's claim, which plays a prominent role in his arguments against traditional epistemology in *Philosophy and the Mirror of Nature,* that Locke and other modern epistemologists conflated the normative concept of justification with causal-mechanical concepts is based, I believe, on a conflation of just the kind I am describing here. See Rorty, ibid., pp. 139ff. Again, the critical conflation consists in not seeing that the view, which I believe is correct, that epistemic justification, like any other normative concept, must have factual, naturalistic criteria, is entirely consistent with the rejection of the doctrine, which I think is incorrect, that justification itself *is,* or is *reducible* to, a naturalistic-nonnormative concept.

I think there is a short and plausible initial answer, although a detailed defense of it would involve complex general issues about norms and values. The short answer is this: we believe in the supervenience of epistemic properties on naturalistic ones, and more generally, in the supervenience of all valuational and normative properties on naturalistic conditions. This comes out in various ways. We think, with R. M. Hare,[35] that if two persons or acts coincide in all descriptive or naturalistic details, they cannot differ in respect of being good or right, or any other valuational aspects. We also think that if something is "good" – a "good car", "good drop shot", "good argument" – then that must be so "in virtue of" its being a "certain way", that is, its having certain "factual properties". Being a good car, say, cannot be a brute and ultimate fact: a car is good because it has a certain contextually indicated set of properties having to do with performance, reliability, comfort, styling, economy, etc. The same goes for justified belief: if a belief is justified, that must be so because it has certain factual, nonepistemic properties, such as perhaps that it is "indubitable", that it is seen to be entailed by another belief that is independently justified, that it is appropriately caused by perceptual experience, or whatever. That it is a justified belief cannot be a brute fundamental fact unrelated to the kind of belief it is. There must be a *reason* for it, and this reason must be grounded in the factual descriptive properties of that particular belief. Something like this, I think, is what we believe.

Two important themes underlie these convictions: first, values, though perhaps not reducible to facts, must be "consistent" with them in that objects that are indiscernible in regard to fact must be indiscernible in regard to value; second, there must be nonvaluational "reasons" or "grounds" for the attribution of values, and these "reasons" or "grounds" must be *generalizable* – that is, they are covered by *rules* or *norms*. These two ideas correspond to "weak supervenience" and "strong supervenience", which I have discussed elsewhere.[36] Belief in the supervenience of value upon fact, arguably, is fundamental to the very concepts of value and valuation.[37] Any valuational concept, to be significant, must be governed by a set of criteria, and these criteria must ultimately rest on factual

35 *The Language of Morals* (London: Oxford University Press, 1952), p. 145.
36 See "Concepts of Supervenience", Essay 4 of this volume.
37 Ernest Sosa, too, considers epistemological supervenience as a special case of the supervenience of valuational properties on naturalistic conditions, in "The Foundation of Foundationalism", *Noûs* 14 (1980): 547–64, especially p. 551. See also James Van Cleve's instructive discussion in his "Epistemic Supervenience and the Circle of Belief", *The Monist* 68 (1985): 90–104, especially pp. 97–99.

characteristics and relationships of objects and events being evaluated. There is something deeply incoherent about the idea of an infinitely descending series of valuational concepts, each depending on the one below it as its criterion of application.[38]

It seems to me, therefore, that epistemological supervenience is what underlies our belief in the possibility of normative epistemology, and that we do not need new inspirations from the sciences to acknowledge the existence of naturalistic criteria for epistemic and other valuational concepts. The case of normative ethics is entirely parallel: belief in the possibility of normative ethics is rooted in the belief that moral properties and relations are supervenient upon nonmoral ones. Unless we are prepared to disown normative ethics as a viable philosophical inquiry, we had better recognize normative epistemology as one, too.[39] We should note, too, that epistemology is likely to parallel normative ethics in regard to the degree to which scientific results are relevant or useful to its development.[40] Saying this of course leaves large room for disagreement concerning how relevant and useful, if at all, empirical psychology of human motivation and action can be to the development and confirmation of normative ethical theories.[41] In any event, once the normativity of epistemology is clearly taken note of, it is no surprise that epistemology and normative ethics share the same metaphilosophical fate. Naturalized epistemology makes no more, and no less, sense than naturalized normative ethics.

38 Perhaps one could avoid this kind of criteriological regress by embracing directly apprehended valuational properties (as in ethical intuitionism) on the basis of which criteria for other valuational properties could be formulated. The denial of the supervenience of valuational concepts on factual characteristics, however, would sever the essential connection between value and fact on which, it seems, the whole point of our valuational activities depends. In the absence of such supervenience, the very notion of valuation would lose its significance and relevance. The elaboration of these points, however, would have to wait for another occasion; but see Van Cleve's paper cited in the preceding note for more details.

39 Quine will not disagree with this: he will "naturalize" them both. For his views on values see "The Nature of Moral Values" in Alvin I. Goldman and Jaegwon Kim (eds.), *Values and Morals* (Dordrecht: Reidel, 1978). For a discussion of the relationship between epistemic and ethical concepts see Roderick Firth, "Are Epistemic Concepts Reducible to Ethical Concepts?" in the same volume.

40 For discussions of this and related issues see Goldman, *Epistemology and Cognition*.

41 For a detailed development of a normative ethical theory that exemplifies the view that it is crucially relevant, see Richard B. Brandt, *A Theory of the Good and the Right* (Oxford: Clarendon Press, 1979).

13

Mechanism, purpose, and explanatory exclusion

I want to reopen the question whether the same bit of behavior, say an action we perform such as climbing a ladder, can be given both a "mechanistic" explanation, in terms of physiological processes and laws, and a "purposive" explanation, in terms of "reasons" (e.g., goals and beliefs). In a paper published in 1968,[1] Norman Malcolm defended a negative answer. He argued that once an action has been explained by setting forth its physiological causal antecedents it is no longer open to us to explain it by citing the agent's reasons, that is, his beliefs, desires, intentions, and the like. Alvin Goldman immediately replied to Malcolm,[2] arguing that mechanistic and purposive explanations are indeed compatible, that we can in fact characterize a type of situation in which one and the same behavior can be seen to be explainable both physiologically and rationally.

I want to reopen this debate not only because there is more to be said on this issue but also, and more importantly, because the issue has significant implications for some problems of much current interest in the philosophy of mind. A proper appreciation of the broader methodological issues and options involved will, I believe, help us to get clearer about some matters of current controversy. As we shall see, the question of explanatory compatibility leads us to more general questions about the pos-

My thanks to David Benfield, John Biro, Brian McLaughlin, Joseph Mendola, and Michael Resnik for helpful comments.
1 "The Conceivability of Mechanism", *Philosophical Review* 77 (1968): 45–72. Reprinted in Gary Watson (ed.), *Free Will* (Oxford: Oxford University Press, 1982). Page references to this article are to the reprinted version in Watson. For an earlier defense of a position similar to Malcolm's see Alasdair C. MacIntyre, "Determinism", *Mind* 66 (1957): 28–41.
2 "The Compatibility of Mechanism and Purpose", *Philosophical Review* 78 (1969): 468–82; also in his *A Theory of Human Action* (Englewood Cliffs, N.J.: Prentice-Hall, 1970), pp. 157–65. For another defense of the compatibility position and a critique of MacIntyre, see Daniel C. Dennett, "Mechanism and Responsibility", in Dennett, *Brainstorms* (Montpelier, Vt.: Bradford Books, 1981). G. H. von Wright defends a "two explanandum solution" in *Explanation and Understanding* (Ithaca: Cornell University Press, 1971), pp. 118–31.

sibility of *multiple explanations of a single explanandum,* and the relationship between two distinct explanatory theories covering overlapping domains of phenomena. Ultimately, these issues will be seen to arise from some basic assumptions about the epistemology and the metaphysics of explanation, and, in particular, the question of "realism" about explanations.

What Malcolm calls a "purposive explanation" of an action is one that conforms to the familiar "belief-desire" pattern of action explanation. Such an explanation explains an action by specifying the "reason for which" the agent did what he did, that is, by indicating what he wanted to accomplish and what he took to be an optimal way of realizing his want. We shall refer to such explanations as "rationalizing explanations"; these explanations provide us with the agent's considerations, explicit or implicit, that rationalize the actions to be explained. We need not think of belief-desire explanations as the only kind of rationalizing explanations ("I hit him because he insulted my wife"); nor need we think of rationalizations as the only mode of action explanation in vernacular psychology. However, belief-desire explanations seem to have a central place in our common everyday understanding of what we, and our fellow humans, do, and one could rightly claim, I think, that they constitute the basic mode of understanding actions in intentional psychology. Moreover, the question whether or not such explanations can coexist with physiological explanations of behavior is certain to generalize to other modes of intentional explanations, and how we answer this question will have direct implications for the current debate concerning the relationship between vernacular ("folk") psychology and the systematic science of human behavior, whether the latter is taken to be a relatively high-level "cognitive science" or a lower-level "neuroscience".[3]

But this problem of the relationship between vernacular and systematic psychology can itself be further generalized: What is the relationship between two explanatory theories (especially, two successive theories) of the same phenomena? Can the same phenomena be correctly explained by two different theories? Can we accept two such theories, each purporting to provide independent explanations of the same data? Suppose we accept either the compatibility thesis, or the incompatibility thesis, regarding the two types of action explanation. Could either position be generalized? Is it *in general* the case that an event can be given more than

3 See, e.g., Paul Churchland, *Scientific Realism and the Plasticity of Mind* (Cambridge: Cambridge University Press, 1979); Stephen P. Stich, *From Folk Psychology to Cognitive Science* (Cambridge: MIT Press, 1983); Terence Horgan and James Woodward, "Folk Psychology is Here To Stay", *Philosophical Review* 94 (1985): 197–226.

one explanation – or more than one type of explanation? Or is it the case that *in general* no event (perhaps, nothing) can be given more than one explanation? Are there general conditions under which explanations *exclude* each other?

I shall now place my cards on the table. On the question of the compatibility of action explanations, I think Malcolm is fundamentally right, although, as we shall see, this does not necessarily show Goldman to be wrong. I shall argue that the criticisms that have been raised against Malcolm, while they point to some interesting possibilities and need to be reckoned with, do not refute what I take to be the heart of Malcolm's arguments, and that on the special auxiliary assumptions Malcolm appears to accept, rationalizing explanations and physiological explanations do exclude each other. My central considerations will not depend on any special features of reasons and causes, or of mind and matter, but involve instead some broad reflections on the nature of explanation and causation – in particular, kinds of situation in which explanations with mutually consistent explanantia can yet compete against each other. This will lead me to formulate what I shall call "the principle of explanatory exclusion", something that many will, I am afraid, consider absurdly strong and unacceptable. Roughly, this principle says this: No event can be given more than one *complete* and *independent* explanation. What "complete" and "independent" may mean in this context is obviously important, and my discussion will be sensitive to the need of making these notions clearer; I should say right now, though, that I shall not be offering general definitions of these notions, but depend rather on the discussion of specific cases to generate reasonably cohesive senses for these terms. My strategy will be this: I shall argue my case principally for *causal explanations,* advancing at the same time some general considerations that will, I hope, make the exclusion principle seem a plausible constraint on explanations in general.

1. MALCOLM'S ARGUMENT

Although the exact form of physiological explanation of behavior, and also exactly how we view the structure of rationalizing explanation, are ultimately unimportant (as they should be if our results are to be of general interest), it will be useful to have some fixed points of reference. For this purpose we may simply turn to Malcolm's own view of the matter. He takes a physiological explanation of behavior to have the familiar form of a Hempelian "covering-law" or "deductive-nomological" ("D–N") argument:

(N) Whenever an organism of structure S is in neurophysiological state q it will emit movement m. Organism O of structure S was in neurophysiological state q.
Therefore, O emitted m.

A rationalizing explanation for Malcolm has the following, again familiar, form:

(R) Whenever an organism has goal G and believes that behavior B is required to bring about G, O will emit B. O had G and believed B was required for G.
Therefore, O emitted B.

Whether (R), too, is a D–N argument (Malcolm argues it is not) will play no role in the discussion to follow, although we need to assume, with Malcolm, that (R) represents the goal-belief complex as a "cause" or "condition" of the occurrence of the behavior. This is important: as will become clear, the incompatibility between these explanations stands out in the starkest way when they are both construed as causal explanations – as attempts to provide causal conditions from which the action or behavior issued.[4]

Before presenting his incompatibility argument, Malcolm tries to exclude the possibility that a rationalizing explanation of the form (R) is "less basic than" and "dependent on"[5] physiological explanations. I think that Malcolm's attempt is unsuccessful, for various reasons.[6] But whether or not Malcolm is successful here is less interesting for our purposes than why he makes the attempt. Recall that the provisional formulation of the explanatory exclusion principle I gave earlier only prohibits more than one *complete* and *independent* explanation for a given phenomenon. Although Malcolm does not say why he takes up the question of explana-

---

4 This means that one way in which one might try to eliminate the incompatibility is to interpret rationalizing explanation as a fundamentally *noncausal* mode of understanding actions. I believe that this is an approach well worth exploring: a rationalizing explanation is to be viewed as a *normative assessment* of an action in the context of the agent's relevant intentional states. For some elaboration on this idea see my "Self-Understanding and Rationalizing Explanations", *Philosophia Naturalis* 21 (1984): 309–20.

5 Malcolm, "The Conceivability of Mechanism", p. 131.

6 For one, the notion of "dependence" used is too narrow and seems at best to characterize a special subcase: for another, his argument makes use of special assumptions needing justification and exploits what appears to be local features of the particular case on hand. For a discussion of Malcolm's argument see William L. Rowe, "Neurophysiological Laws and Purposive Principles", *Philosophical Review* 81 (1971): 502–508.

tory dependence at this point, a rationale is not far to seek: if the rational-izing explanation is *dependent* on the physiological explanation in an appropriate sense (e.g., by being *reducible* to it), then in truth there is only one explanation here, and the question of explanatory compatibility does not arise. The two explanations could peacefully coexist, but the peace is purchased at a price: they are no longer independent explanations. The explanatory efficacy of one would have been shown to derive from the other, and ultimately the physiological explanation would have to be taken as telling a deeper and more inclusive story of how the behavior came about.

What then is "the exact logical relationship between neural and pur-posive explanations of behaviour",[7] as Malcolm puts it? He asks: "Can explanations of both types be true of the same bit of behaviour on one and the same occasion?".[8] This is the problem of explanatory compatibil-ity. But you will have noticed that the two explanatory schemes, (N) and (R), do not, strictly speaking, have the same explanandum; their explanatory conclusions are different, one speaking of the "emission of (bodily movement) m" and the other of the "emission of (behavior) B". Given this apparent difference in the explananda, it might appear that the question of compatibility could not arise. Malcolm is aware of this "dual explanandum solution" (as we might call it), and responds as follows:[9]

> Take the example of the man climbing a ladder in order to retrieve his hat from the roof. This explanation relates his climbing to his intention. A neurophysiological explanation of his climbing would say nothing about his intention but would connect his movements on the ladder with chemi-cal changes in body tissues or with the firing of neurons. Do the two ac-counts interfere with one another?
> I believe there *would* be a collision between the two accounts if they were offered as explanations of one and the same occurrence of a man's climbing a ladder.

Although exactly how this is a response to the dual explanandum problem is somewhat uncertain, Malcolm seems to think that there is some con-crete event here, the man's movement up the ladder, represented by the two conclusions, which serves as the shared explanandum of the explana-tions. In our discussion we will assume this is the case (Goldman does not dispute this assumption); if we do not, the problem of explanatory incompatibility could be restated, though this would bring in complica-

7 Malcolm, "The Conceivability of Mechanism", p. 132.   8 Ibid.   9 Ibid., p. 133.

tions.[10] We may simply note here that although the two explanandum statements are not equivalent or synonymous, there is an evident sense in which they "describe" one and the same event, the same concrete happening, and that we could consider the compatibility problem stated with respect to this event however described. For now it will not matter exactly what this shared explanandum is, as long as it exists.

Malcolm's argument for the claim that not both explanations can hold seems to make use of the following assumption:[11]

(I) If event C is nomologically sufficient for the occurrence of event E, then no event wholly distinct from C is necessary for E.

Using this principle, Malcolm appears to argue as follows: Suppose there is a physiological explanation of a man's ladder climbing conforming to schema (N) above. This explanation shows a certain physiological event ("neurophysiological state q") to be nomologically sufficient for the behavior. If this physiological event is indeed *sufficient* for the climbing, the climbing should occur whether or not any *other* event (such as beliefs and desires) occurred. That is, no other event should be necessary for the occurrence of the climbing, and the physiological explanation in itself should be deemed complete and sufficient as an explanation of the behavior. Once we know the physiological condition is present, we can be wholly confident that the ladder climbing will occur; it isn't necessary to verify whether other events, such as beliefs and intentions, are also present.[12] That the climbing would have occurred whether or not the rationalizing belief and desire occurred surely demonstrates the causal and explanatory irrelevance of the belief and desire.[13] For an explanatory connection can hold only if a dependency relation of some sort is present; perhaps, the condition that explains why an event occurred must at least be necessary in the circumstances for the occurrence of the event. Notice, by the way, that, as thus formulated, this is a general argument entirely

---

10 I believe there is much to be said in favor of the "two explananda" approach in the case of action explanations (see my "Self-Understanding and Rationalizing Explanation"). I am being somewhat cavalier about this issue here because our two disputants do not raise it and my real focus is on the general question of explanatory compatibility. For an interesting recent instance of this dual explanandum approach see Fred Dretske, *Explaining Behavior: Reasons in a World of Causes* (Cambridge: MIT Press, 1988).

11 As spelled out by Goldman (with minor changes of wording).

12 This assumes, as Malcolm is aware, that beliefs and desires are not identical with physiological events – namely, that the so-called identity thesis about the mental is false. If the identity holds, we do not have two *independent* explanations. More on this later.

13 Unless, perhaps, the behavior is overdetermined by the neurophysiological event and the belief-desire pair. This possibility is discussed below.

independent of the subject matters of the two explanations; it makes no use of the fact that one of the explanations deals in psychological states and the other in neurophysiology, or the fact that the explanandum concerns human action or behavior. This is clear from the fact that (I) is wholly general and topic-neutral.

The crucial principle (I) as stated is obviously implausible if we consider causal conditions obtaining at different times:[14] e.g., let C be nomologically sufficient for E, and E for C*, where C occurs before E, and E before C*. Then C* is nomologically necessary for E. But seemingly there is no incoherence here. Or suppose C is sufficient for C*, which occurs later, and C* in turn is necessary for E, where E is later than C*. Again, there is no evident incoherence. Following Goldman, therefore, one might revise the principle like this:

(II) If C is sufficient for a later event E, then no event occurring at the same time as C and wholly distinct from it is necessary for E.

And it is this weaker principle that Goldman tries to undermine in his discussion of Malcolm's incompatibility argument.[15]

Goldman's objection to (II) is this: Suppose that two events, C and C*, are "simultaneous nomic equivalents"[16] in the sense that as a matter of law, C occurs (to an object) at a time if and only if C* occurs at the same time. Then if C is sufficient for E, then C*, too, is sufficient for E. If C is necessary for E then so is C*, and we may suppose C to be both necessary and sufficient for the subsequent event E. This means two distinct events, C and C*, are such that C is sufficient, and C* is necessary, for E.

There are various complex issues here involving the interrelations among necessity, sufficiency, cause, explanation, and the like. But fortunately we can largely ignore them, for what is crucial to the issue of explanatory compatibility is just this claim: *if C and C* are simultaneous*

14 Goldman, *A Theory of Human Action,* pp. 160–61.
15 Malcolm would be ill advised to rest his argument on this revised principle (although the principle may be valid). For he would be powerless to show the incompatibility between a rationalizing explanation and a physiological explanation which makes use of physiological initial conditions occurring a little later or earlier than the belief and desire invoked in the rationalizing explanation. What is crucial is not that the two conditions for E occur at the same time; it's rather that they belong in distinct, independent causal chains (or chains of conditions).
16 So we are treating C and C*, and also E, as "event types" or "generic events". In fact, talk of "necessity" and "sufficiency" seems to make clear sense only for generic events. But our discussion can be taken to concern individual events if we take these latter to be instantiations of generic events. See my "Events as Property Exemplifications", Essay 3 of this volume. However, no particular views concerning the nature of events are presupposed in the present discussion.

nomic equivalents, in the sense explained, then one constitutes an explanation for a given event if and only if the other does. If this claim is correct, the existence of physiological correlates for beliefs and desires would guarantee the possibility of both a rationalizing and a physiological explanation of an action. If all mental events have nomic equivalents in physiological states and processes (we may call this "the psychophysical correlation thesis"), every rationalizing explanation would have a physiological counterpart with the same explanandum.

2. NOMIC EQUIVALENTS AND DEPENDENT EXPLANATIONS

The claim just mentioned, to the effect that if C and C* are simultaneous nomic equivalents, one is an explanation of a given event just in case the other is, holds on the Hempelian account of explanation. But this unrestricted claim is surely dubious: it could be that although the situation is as described, C* is only an "epiphenomenon" of C, and, although C* is nomologically sufficient (and perhaps also necessary) for E, it does not explain why E occurs.[17] Thus, C could be the underlying pathological state of some disease, C* a simultaneous symptom of this state, and E a later stage of the disease. A case like this, therefore, is not one in which there are two explanations for one explanandum; for epiphenomena do not explain.

But let us not dwell on this possibility (although, as will be seen, it foreshadows others to be considered below), assuming instead something like the Hempelian nomic sufficiency account as our working model of explanation (this is what both Malcolm and Goldman do). The explanatory compatibilist may be willing to concede the possibility of epiphenomena just mentioned; for all he needs to refute Malcolm's claim is just one case in which each of two simultaneous nomic equivalents constitutes an explanans for the same event; surely, he may reason, not every case in which we have simultaneous nomic equivalents is one in which one of them is an epiphenomenon of the other. In any case, on the Hempelian model, if C and C* are nomic equivalents, the two explanations making use of them are "nomically equivalent explanations" in a straightforward sense; also, under the nomic-subsumptive account of causal relations, C and C* may be called "nomically equivalent causes". For it would be a matter of law that one is an explanation of a given event if and only if the

17 On epiphenomena see, e.g., David Lewis, "Causation", *Journal of Philosophy* 70 (1973): 556–67.

other is, and that C is a cause of a given event if and only if C* is also its cause. Thus, if beliefs and desires have nomological coextensions in physiological states, for every rationalizing explanation of an action there is a nomologically equivalent physiological explanation (which we could formulate if we had sufficient knowledge of psychophysiological correlating laws). The fact that these explanations are nomically equivalent in this sense should alert us to the possibility that here we do not have two *independent* explanations of the same action. As I said, as a matter of nomological necessity, one is an explanation of that action just in case the other is.

Thus, our interim conclusion appears to be this: In the sort of situation Goldman asks us to consider, either one of the two nomically equivalent states is an epiphenomenon of the other so that we do not have two explanations of the same event, or else we have two explanations that are not nomologically independent. But what is wrong with nomologically dependent or equivalent explanations in this sense? Aren't they sufficient to show the possibility of giving two distinct explanations of one and the same event? And if the psychophysical correlation thesis holds, aren't we assured of the general possibility of explaining behavior both rationally and physiologically?

And there seem to be instances of just this sort in other areas of science. For example, we might explain the behavior of some substance subjected to certain conditions by an appeal to its gross physical dispositional properties (ductility, conductivity, viscosity, etc.) on the one hand, and on the other by formulating a more theoretical account by invoking the microstructures that underlie these dispositions as their "nomic equivalents". Don't we in such cases have exactly the kind of example that fits Goldman's argument? Such examples seem legion: we often deepen and enrich our understanding of natural phenomena by moving away from their observable features and the rough "phenomenological laws" that govern them, to their underlying micro-structures, and by invoking more systematic "theoretical laws" appropriate to these states. (At least, that is the textbook account of progress in scientific theorizing.) Perhaps, rationalizing explanations are related to physiological explanations in just this way – that is, as macro- to underlying micro-explanations – via a pervasive system of correlation laws providing for each psychological state a physiological "simultaneous nomic equivalent".

Whether such correlation laws exist, especially for contentful intentional states ("propositional attitudes") such as belief, desire, and intention, is a controversial question on which much has been written in the past two decades. I think that a preponderance of philosophical evidence is now on the side of "psychophysical anomalism", the thesis that there are not, and cannot be, precise laws connecting intentional states with physiological states of the brain (or any physical states).[18] If we have no confidence in the existence of such correlating laws, whether the correlations are species- or structure-specific, or uniform across all organisms and structures, the solution in terms of "nomic equivalents" would only be an idle possibility. But I do not want to pursue this issue of psychophysical laws here; for the general question still remains whether the existence of nomologically equivalent states opens for us the possibility of having multiple explanations of a single event. That is, we want to know how things would stand if there were psychophysical correlations.

What I want to claim is this: the kind of situation Goldman describes, namely one in which two events C and C* are seen to be nomologically necessary and sufficient for each other, and in which each of them is thought to constitute an explanans for one and the same event E, is an *inherently unstable situation*. This is so especially when C and C* are each a member of a system of events (or concepts) such that the two systems to which they respectively belong show the kind of systematic nomological connections Goldman envisages for the psychological and the physiological. The instability of the situation generates a strong pressure to find an acceptable *account* of the relationship between C and C*, and, by extension, that between the two systems to which they belong; the instability is dissipated and a cognitive equilibrium restored when we come to see a more specific relationship between the two explanations. As we shall see, in cases of interest, the specific relationship replacing equivalence will be either identity or some asymmetric dependency relation.

Another way of putting my point would be this: a certain instability exists in a situation in which two distinct events are claimed to be nomologically *equivalent* causes or explanations of the same phenomenon; stability is restored when *equivalence is replaced by identity or some asymmetric relation of dependence*. That is, either two explanations (or causes) in effect collapse into one or, if there indeed are two distinct explanations (or causes) here, we must see one of them as dependent on, or derivative from, the other – or, what is the same, one of them as gaining explanatory or causal dominance over the other.

The tension in this situation that gives rise to the instability can be seen

---

18 Perhaps the most influential argument for psychophysical anomalism is one defended by Donald Davidson in "Mental Events", reprinted in his *Essays on Actions and Events* (New York: Oxford University Press, 1980). See my "Psychophysical Laws", Essay 11 of this volume, for an exegesis and discussion of Davidson's argument and additional references.

in various ways. First, if C and C* are each a sufficient cause of the event E, then why isn't E *overdetermined?* It is at best extremely odd to think that each and every bit of action we perform is overdetermined in virtue of having two distinct sufficient causes.[19] To be sure, this differs from the standard case of overdetermination in which the two overdetermining causes are not nomologically connected. But why does the supposed no-mological relationship between C and C* void the claim that this is a case of causal overdetermination? Notice the trade-off here: the closer this is to a standard case of overdetermination, the less dependent are the two explanations in relation to each other, and, correlatively, the more one stresses the point that this is not a case of standard overdetermination because of the nomic equivalence between the explanations, the less plausible is one's claim that we have here two distinct and independent explanations.

Second, if C and C* are nomic equivalents, they co-occur as a matter of law – that is, it is nomologically impossible to have one of these occur without the other. Why then do they not form a *single jointly sufficient* cause of E rather than two individually sufficient causes? How do we know that each of C and C* is not just a partial cause of E? Why, that is, should we not regard C and C* as forming a *single complete* explanation of E rather than two separately sufficient explanations of it? How do we decide one way or the other?

When we reflect on the special case of psychophysical causation, where C, let's say, is a psychological event, C* is its physiological correlate, and E is some bodily movement associated with an action, it would be highly implausible to regard C as directly acting on the body to bring about E (e.g., my belief and desire telekinetically acting on the muscles in my arm and shoulder and making them contract, thereby causing my arm to go up); it would be more credible to think that if the belief-desire pair is to cause the movement of my arm, it must "work through" the physical causal chain starting from C*, some neural event in the brain, culminating in a muscle contraction. If this is right, we cannot regard C and C* as constituting *independent* explanations of E. We must think of the causal efficacy of C in bringing about E as dependent on that of its physical correlate C*.[20]

19 Goldman is aware of this point but does not follow up its implications; in fact, he, like Malcolm, considers the possibility that beliefs and desires are neural states. See below for this "identity solution".
20 I believe this picture can be generalized; see my "Epiphenomenal and Supervenient Causation", Essay 6 of this volume.

I believe that these perplexities are removed only when we have an account of the relation between C and C*, the two supposed causes of a single action, and that, as I shall argue, an account that is adequate to this task will show that C and C* could not each constitute a *complete* and *independent* explanation of the action.

A case that nicely illustrates this is the identity solution: by saying that C and C* are in fact one and the same event, we can neatly resolve the situation. Malcolm is clearly aware of this (as is Goldman); for in the course of his incompatibility argument he explicitly rejects the psycho-physical identity thesis.[21] On the identity view, there is here one cause of E, not two whose mutual relationship we need to give an account of. As for explanation, at least in an objective sense, there is one explanation here, and not two. The two explanations differ only in the linguistic apparatus used in referring to, or picking out, the conditions and events that do the explaining; they are only descriptive variants of one another. They perhaps give causal information about E in different ways, each appropriate in a particular explanatory context; but they both point to one objective causal connection, and are grounded in this single causal fact.[22]

What are other possible accounts of the relation between C and C*? The standard model of theory reduction has it that for a theory to be "reduced to" another, the primitive theoretical predicates of the target theory must be connected via "bridge laws" with predicates, presumably complex ones, of the base theory to which it is reduced, in such a fashion as to enable the derivation of the laws of the target theory from those of the reducer.[23] It is clear that if a bridge law of the biconditional form were available for each primitive predicate of the theory to be reduced, its reducibility is assured. For all we need to do is to rewrite the basic laws of the target theory in the vocabulary of the reducer by the use of the biconditonal laws, and add these rewrites, as needed, to the axioms of the reducer. In any event, the point is that if each psychological event has a simultaneous physiological nomic equivalent, all the conditions nec-

21 Malcolm, "The Conceivability of Mechanism", p. 134.
22 An identity account in the present context would be a form of the so-called "type identity" theory (talk of "nomic equivalence" between C and C*, for example, implies that these represent "generic events" or event types, not concrete events); however, the point applies to the "token identity" theory as well. For example, Donald Davidson's causal theory of action is one example: reasons (e.g., beliefs and desires) are causes of action, but they are redescribable in physical (presumably, physiological) terms and hence *are* physical events; and it is under their physical descriptions that reasons and actions are subsumed under law. Thus, for Davidson, the duality of explanation vanishes (whether this is Davidson's intended result is another question, however).
23 See Ernest Nagel, *The Structure of Science* (New York: Harcourt, 1961).

essary for the reduction of psychology to physiology, in the currently standard sense of reduction, are satisfied. Our intentional psychology, with all its rationalizations, would be ripe for reductive absorption into physiology and associated sciences, and rationalizing explanations would cease to be *independent* explanations of actions.[24] The relation between a rationalizing explanation and the physiological explanation to which it is reduced would indeed be like that between a macro-explanation of – to resort again to a stock example – some thermal phenomenon (the expansion of a gas upon being heated) and its underlying micro-explanation (in terms of the increasing kinetic energies of the gas molecules). Here we are not dealing with two independent stories about the phenomenon; the main difference between them is that one tells a more detailed, more revealing, and theoretically more fecund story than the other. The sort of tension that Malcolm tries to exploit when we have both a rationalizing and a physiological explanation of an action no longer exists. The reason is that the two explanations are no longer independent – one is reducible to the other.

The supposed existence of psychophysical nomic coextensions, therefore, does not show that rationalizing explanations and physiological explanations could coexist as independent explanations of actions; on the contrary, it would show that explanations of one type are reductively dependent on those of the other type. For it would place us precisely in a situation tailor-made for the physiological reduction of psychology, namely one in which rationalizing explanation will be deprived of its status as an independent mode of understanding actions, a situation that, as we saw, Malcolm wanted to exclude. If such reducibility should obtain, the claim that rationalizing explanation provides us with a distinctive mode of understanding human action would be undermined. What explanatory efficacy rationalizing explanation possesses would derive from that of the underlying physiological explanation – at least in this sense: we would be able to give a physiology-based explanation of why, and

24 So, on the present construal, both Malcolm and Goldman come out right about the two types of explanation. For we are construing Malcolm to be saying that rationalizing and mechanistic explanations are not compatible as *independent* explanations; and Goldman does *not* claim that the two types of explanations are independent in our sense. In "Mechanism and Responsibility" Daniel C. Dennett, too, addresses the compatibility issue; however, his focus is different. His main aim is to show that the behavior of finite mechanisms, "tropistic systems", can be explained from "the intentional stance". Even if Dennett's conclusion is accepted, our problem remains: What is the relationship between "intentional-stance explanations" and "physical-stance explanations"? Are the two types of explanations compatible when they concern the same bit of behavior?

how, it is that reasons explain actions, and if we take a causal view of the situation, then precisely how, and by what mechanism, reasons cause actions.

3. CAUSAL EXPLANATIONS AND EXPLANATORY EXCLUSION

The general principle of explanatory exclusion states that two or more complete and independent explanations of the same event or phenomenon cannot coexist. The meanings of "complete" and "independent" are obviously crucial. I shall not be offering definitions of these terms; rather I shall focus on some specific cases falling under the intended distinctions, with the hope that, in the course of my discussion, reasonably determinate core meanings will emerge that will give the exclusion principle clear and substantial enough content. A thorough examination of explanatory exclusion will inevitably spill over into the long-standing debate over the nature of explanation, a topic on which nothing like a consensus now exists. The discussion to follow will inevitably rest on certain intuitive assumptions about how explanations, especially causal explanations, work; however, I hope that the discussion will succeed in showing that whatever model of explanation you accept, unless you take a wholly fictionalist or instrumentalist view of explanation, the principle of explanatory exclusion is a plausible general constraint.

It seems to me that the case for explanatory exclusion is most persuasively made for causal explanations of individual events. Suppose then that we are offered two such explanations of a single event:

> Explanation A cites C as a cause of E.
> Explanation B cites C^* as a cause of E.

What are we to think of such a situation? Various possibilities can be distinguished:

Case 1. We find that $C = C^*$. That is, there is one cause here, not two. We saw how this works for the case of psychophysical causation under the mind–body identity theory.[25] This, when available, is the simplest and perhaps the most satisfying way of relieving the tension created by the

---

25 The precise formulation here would be affected somewhat by whether one takes the "token identity" or the "type identity" theory, and what view of the nature of events is adopted. However, the general point should apply regardless of the positions taken on these matters.

existence of the two explanations. Such identities are often found in a reductive context where one of the explanations specifies the cause by a deeper, and more theoretical and systematic, description.

Case 2. C is distinct from C*, but is in some clear sense "reducible" to, or "supervenient" on, C*. This sort of situation will arise in a reductive context of the sort just considered provided that for whatever reason we stop short of *identifying* the reductively related events or states. Thus, the psychophysical case considered earlier would be an instance of this kind if we believed in the nomological reducibility of psychological states to physical states, without, however, wishing to identify psychological states with their physical correlates; or if we believed in the "supervenience" in an appropriate sense of the psychological upon the physical, without identifying a supervenient psychological state with its physical base. In such a situation it is possible to treat causal relations involving psychological events and states as themselves supervenient upon, or reducible to, more fundamental physical causal processes. I have discussed "supervenient causation" extensively elsewhere.[26] In any event we do not have in cases of this kind two *independent* causal explanations of the same event. The two explanations can coexist because one of them is dependent, reductively or by supervenience, on the other.

Case 3. Neither C nor C* is in itself a "sufficient cause" of E, though each is an indispensable component of a sufficient cause. As has often been observed, when we are called on to provide a cause or an explanation for an event we usually select a causal factor that, for various epistemological or pragmatic reasons, is believed to be the most appropriate to the situation. A stock example goes like this: we might explain why an automobile accident occurred by citing, say, the congested traffic, or the icy road, or the faulty brakes, or the driver's inexperience, etc., depending on the explanatory context, even though each of these conditions played an essential role in causing the accident. If C and C* are related in this way we do not have two *complete* explanations – in one sense of "complete explanation", namely one in which a complete explanation specifies a sufficient set of causal conditions for the explanandum. It is clear that two

26 In "Causality, Identity, and Supervenience in the Mind–Body Problem", *Midwest Studies in Philosophy* 4 (1979): 31–49; and "Epiphenomenal and Supervenient Causation", Essay 6 of this volume. See also Ernest Sosa, "Mind–Body Interaction and Supervenient Causation", *Midwest Studies in Philosophy* 9 (1984): 271–81. For a general discussion of supervenience see my "Concepts of Supervenience", Essay 4 of this volume.

incomplete explanations, in this sense, of the same event can coexist. The explanatory exclusion principle only bans more than one complete and independent explanation of the same event.

Case 3a.[27] C is a proper part of C*. If so, C as an explanation of E is neither complete in itself nor independent of C*.

Case 4. C and C* are different links in the same causal chain leading, say, from C to C* and then to E. In this case again we do not have two *independent* causal explanations; the explanans of one, C*, is causally dependent on the explanans of the other, C.

Case 5. C and C* are distinct and each a sufficient cause of E. We may think of them as belonging to two distinct and independent causal chains. This then is a case of *causal overdetermination:* E would have occurred even if either C or C* had not occurred, or had not caused it; the other would have been sufficient to bring it about. Thus, a man is shot dead by two assassins whose bullets hit him at the same time; or a building catches fire because of a short circuit in the faulty wiring and a bolt of lightning that hits the building at the same instant. It isn't obvious in cases like these just how we should formulate an explanation of why or how the overdetermined event came about; however, it is not implausible to think that failing to mention either of the overdetermining causes gives a misleading and incomplete picture of what happened, and that both causes should figure in any *complete* explanation of the event. If this is right, the present case is not one in which two complete and independent explanations are possible for one event.

Thus I disagree with Hempel when he says that when we have a case of "explanatory overdetermination", in which we have two or more complete D–N arguments with the same explanandum statement (e.g., "The length of this metallic rod increased"), then either argument *singly* can be considered as "complete" (one of them might explain it by invoking the fact that the rod was heated, and another might explain it by citing the fact that it was subjected to longitudinal stress).[28] Given Hempel's overriding concern with the inferential-predictive dimension of explanation, his position on this issue is not surprising. For as a predictive inference either D–N argument is wholly complete and sufficient. How-

27 I own this case to Karl Pfeifer.
28 Carl G. Hempel, *Aspects of Scientific Explanation* (New York: The Free Press, 1965), p. 419.

252

ever, when it is a causal explanation of the lengthening of the rod that we are looking for, when we want to know *why* the rod's length increased, the situation seems radically altered: our understanding of why the event occurred is at best incomplete, and perhaps flawed, if we were unaware of one or the other "explanation".

The sense of "completeness" of an explanation I have just invoked is different from that used in characterizing the case of "partial cause" (Case 3 above), although this does not preclude a broader sense covering both. However, exactly how we deal with cases of causal overdetermination is not crucial to my general claims about explanatory exclusion; for it is unlikely that those who want to allow for multiple explanations of a single event would be willing to restrict them to instances of causal overdetermination. The exclusion principle would retain substantial content even if cases of overdetermination were exempted. In any event, the important point to note is this: that we have a case of causal overdetermination on hand is one way in which a satisfactory account of the relation between C and C* can go, removing the perplexities generated by the claim that each is a cause of some single event.

These considerations suggest the following simple argument for explanatory exclusion for causal explanations: Suppose that C and C* are invoked as each giving a complete explanation of E. Consider the two questions: (1) Would E have occurred if C had not occurred? and (2) Would E have occurred if C* had not occurred? If the answer is a "yes" to both questions, this is a classic case of overdetermination, and, as was discussed in preceding paragraphs, we can treat this case as one in which either explanation taken alone is incomplete, or else exempt all overdeterminative cases from the requirement of explanatory exclusion. If the answer is a "no" to at least one of the questions, say the first, that must be because if C had not occurred, C* would not have either. And this means that C and C* are not independent, and hence that the two explanations are not independent explanations of E.

The foregoing discussion of the subcases is useful as a way of making clearer what could be meant by the "completeness" and "independence" of explanations. When we examine the particular possibilities that seem to permit two distinct explanations of one event, we seem to be able to find – and we seem compelled to look for – reasons for saying that either they are not independent or at least one of them is not complete. Two explanations of one event create a certain epistemic tension, a tension that is dissipated only when we have an account of how they, or the two causes they indicate, are related to each other. Finding out which of the cases canvassed holds for the given case is what is needed to relieve the tension.

4. REMARKS ON THE EPISTEMOLOGY AND METAPHYSICS OF EXPLANATION

When we look for an explanation of an event, we are typically in a state of puzzlement, a kind of epistemic predicament.[29] A successful explanation will get us out of this state. If our discussion is not too far off target, what it shows is that *too many explanations will put us right back into a similar epistemic predicament,* which can be relieved only when we have an explanation of how the explanations are related to one another.

Perhaps there is the following account of why this is so. Some writers have emphasized the unifying or simplifying role of explanation and tried to connect this with understanding.[30] It makes sense to think that multiple explanations of a single explanandum are presumptively counterproductive in regard to the goal of simplification and unification. When two distinct explanations are produced to account for a single phenomenon, we seem to be headed in a direction exactly opposite to the maxim of explanatory simplification "Explain as much as you can with the fewest explanatory premises". Unity is achieved through the promotion of interconnections among items of knowledge, and simplicity is enhanced when these interconnections are seen or interpreted as dependency relations. For the main role of dependency relations in a system is that they help reduce the number of required independent assumptions or primitives. If simplicity and unity of theory is our aim when we seek explanations, multiple explanations of a single phenomenon are self-defeating – unless, that is, we are able to determine that their explanatory premises are related to one another in appropriate ways. It is clear that showing that the explanatory premises of one explanation are dependent on those of the other, in any of the senses of dependence distinguished in the preceding section in connection with causal explanations, is in effect an attempt to reduce the number of independent explanatory premises – that is, a move toward restoring the simplifying and unifying role of explanations.

29 Sylvain Bromberger calls it a "p-predicament" or "b-predicament" in his "An Approach to Explanation" in R. J. Butler (ed.), *Analytic Philosophy,* 2nd series (Oxford: Basil Blackwell, 1965).

30 See, e.g., Michael Friedman, "Explanation and Scientific Understanding", *Journal of Philosophy* 71 (1974): 5–19; Philip Kitcher, "Explanation, Conjunction, and Unification", *Journal of Philosophy* 73 (1976): 207–12.

These reflections, though sketchy and programmatic, provide us with a clue to a possible way of understanding the concept of dependence for explanations, a notion that we have made a rather liberal use of without a general explanation. One theme that runs through the various different cases of "dependent explanations" we have surveyed seems to be this: if an explanation is dependent on a second, the two explanations taken together are committed to no more independent assumptions about the world than is the second explanation taken alone. This dovetails nicely with the view that explanations enhance understanding through simplification and unification. Here we would be trading in the notion of "independent explanation" for that of "independent assumption"; but that, I think, may well be progress.

These are general considerations not restricted to causal explanations. However, explanatory exclusion seems most obvious, and almost trivial, for causal explanations of individual events, and the reason seems to be this: we think of these explanations as directly tied to the actual causal histories of the events being explained, and their "correctness" as explanations is determined by the accuracy with which they depict the causal connections as they exist. When two such explanations of one event are on hand, we need to know how they are situated in relation to each other on the causal map of the event; one thing that cannot be allowed to happen, if our explanations are to be coherent, is that they tell two different stories about the same region of the causal map.[31] Explanatory exclusion may seem obvious for causal explanations, but this is not to say it is trivial: the above considerations at least assume "causal realism", the belief that there is a determinate objective fact of the matter about the causal history of any given event.[32] We must also assume certain metaphysical principles about causation, e.g. the principle (II) cited in section 1 above.

I take it that *explaining* is an epistemological activity, and that an *explanation,* in the sense of the "product" or "theoretical content" of such an activity,[33] is something about which we can have various cognitive attitudes (e.g., accepting, doubting, having evidence for, etc.). To be in need of an explanation is to be in an epistemically incomplete and imperfect

---

31 Cf. Peter Railton's notion of an "ideal explanatory text" in "Probability, Explanation, and Information", *Synthese* 48 (1981): 233–56; also, David Lewis, "Causal Explanation", in *Philosophical Papers* II (New York: Oxford University Press, 1986).

32 I discuss this and related topics in some detail in "Explanatory Realism, Causal Realism, and Explanatory Exclusion", *Midwest Studies in Philosophy* 12 (1988): 225–40.

33 For some of the basic terminological distinctions see Bromberger, "An Approach to Explanation"; and Peter Achinstein, *The Nature of Explanation* (New York and Oxford: Oxford University Press, 1983), esp. Introduction and ch. 1.

state, and to gain an explanation is to improve one's epistemic situation; it represents an epistemic gain. However, knowledge must involve the real world: to know that p requires the truth of p, and to have a causal explanation of an event requires that the event specified as its cause be, in reality, a cause of that event. Let us once again focus on causal explanations of individual events, and set aside other sorts of explanation (e.g., explanation of laws and regularities, of what a word means, of how to interpret a rule, of how a mathematical proof works, etc.). The kind of view I have just alluded to, namely that a causal explanation of E in terms of C is a "correct explanation" only if C is in reality a cause of E, can be called an "objectivist" or "realist" conception of explanation. And the view that explanations must be "real" or "objective" in this sense can be called *explanatory realism.*

More generally, a realist conception of explanation holds that such notions as "objective truth" or "correctness" or "accuracy" make sense for explanations, and do so in a more or less literal way, and that an explanation is correct or accurate *in virtue of* there obtaining "in the real world" a certain determinate relationship between the explanandum and what is adduced as an explanation of it. Further, it maintains that an explanation represents a real addition to knowledge only if it has this property of correctness or accuracy, and that an explanation is epistemically acceptable only if we have good reason to think that the explanatory relation it purports to portray in fact holds in this objective sense. In short, it holds that explanations are appropriately evaluated on the basis of such objective criteria as accuracy and truth. Saying all this is not to slight the epistemological dimension of explanation. On the contrary: just as knowledge that something is so is canceled if the thing is not so, an explanation of X in terms of Y is voided if either Y does not exist or an appropriate relationship between X and Y does not in reality obtain. And just as the claim to know that p is, and must be, withdrawn when there is reason to believe that p does not hold, an explanation of X in terms of Y must be withdrawn, on explanatory realism, if we have reason to think that the claimed relationship does not in fact obtain between X and Y. Such things as understanding, intellectual satisfaction, making things intelligible, dispelling puzzles and apparent inconsistencies, etc., are crucial; however, we do not believe these things are *properly earned* unless an explanation is correct in some objective sense. The case for explanatory realism is best made – at least, can be made most explicitly – with respect to causal explanations, for here the notion of an "objective correlate" of explanation has an acceptably clear sense, clear enough for explicit consideration.[34]

It is helpful to distinguish between two versions of the exclusion principle. Suppose, for some given event, you have an explanation and I have another, distinct explanation. It can be rational, from an epistemological point of view, for you to accept yours, and for me to accept mine. But can they both be "correct" or "true" explanations? The *metaphysical* principle of explanatory exclusion says this: *they can both be correct explanations only if either at least one of the two is incomplete or one is dependent on the other.*[35] There is a corresponding *epistemological* exclusion principle: *No one may accept both explanations unless one has an appropriate account of how they are related to each other.* What counts as an "appropriate account" of the relationship, in the case of causal explanations, is as illustrated in the preceding section: ideally we must know which of these cases holds, or at least be satisfied that one of these cases, though we may not know which, does.

I should add a few remarks about the individuation of explananda. Some believe that an explanandum is fixed only when a statement representing it is fixed, a view closely tied to the inferential view of explanation;[36] this is often allied with the view that it is not events as concrete occurrences but *aspects* of events (or why a given event has a certain property) that are the proper objects of explaining. Thus, we do not explain, say, the Japanese surrender to the Allied forces or Harry's accident, but rather such things as, say, why the Japanese surrender came as late as it did or how Hirohito was able to override the objections of the powerful military leaders, or why Harry's car ran off the road in broad daylight. These disputes, however, seem largely immaterial to my present concerns: if it is aspects of events, rather than events *simpliciter,* that are explained, then explanatory exclusion would apply to these event aspects.[37] If concrete occurrences are explainable, at least in the sense of explaining *why*

34 Some would want to *analyze* the very notion of causation in terms of explanation, but I believe that is a mistake. See, e.g., Michael Scriven, "Causation as Explanation", *Noûs* 9 (1975): 3–16; Kim, "Causes as Explanations: A Critique", *Theory and Decision* 13 (1981): 293–309.

35 It might be possible for the two explanations to be each dependent on a third, without one of them being dependent on the other. It seems that in such a situation both explanations could stand.

36 See Hempel, *Aspects of Scientific Explanation,* pp. 421–22.

37 These seem similar to what Fred Dretske has called "event allomorphs" in "Referring to Events", in Peter A. French et al. (eds.), *Contemporary Perspectives in the Philosophy of Language* (Minneapolis: University of Minnesota Press, 1977).

they occurred, then they, too, would be subject to explanatory exclusion. Matters here are somewhat complicated because there are different views about the proper construal of events in causal and explanatory contexts.[38] But trying to heed these complexities and subtleties would be a largely pointless exercise in philosophical precision for the purposes at hand.[39]

The metaphysical principle makes sense only if some form of explanatory realism is accepted – that is, only if it makes sense, literal sense, to speak of the "correctness", "accuracy", and "truth" of explanations. And the acceptance of the metaphysical principle will provide a ground for abiding by the epistemological rule of exclusion. I think, though, that the epistemological principle can hold even if explanatory realism is rejected. Even if we abandon the idea that there are objective explanatory relations in the world, we may still find something cognitively unsettling and dissonant about having to face, or accept, two or more independent explanations of the same phenomenon. The explanatory premises of one explanation need not logically contradict those of another, and there may be sufficient evidential warrant for thinking each set to be true. However, accepting the two sets of premises as constituting explanations of the same event (or any one thing), each complete in itself and independent of the other, may induce a sort of incoherence into our belief system. This may be one instance of epistemic incoherence that is not a case of logical (deductive or inductive) inconsistency or incoherence. I earlier tried to explain why this might be so on the basis of the view that the primary epistemic role of explanation is simplification and unification of our belief system. In connection with the coherence theory of justification, "explanatory coherence" is often prominently mentioned – how explanatory relations generate mutually supportive coherence in a system of beliefs. If our speculations here have a point, it can be summarized thus: *too many explanations can be a source of incoherence rather than increased coherence.*

It is interesting to contrast this situation with *predictions* or *proofs.* As I noted briefly above, it seems that, unlike explanatory overdetermination,

38 For a discussion of these matters and further references see my "Causation, Nomic Subsumption, and the Concept of Event", Essay 1 of this volume.
39 Robert Cummins has made an interesting distinction between explanation "by subsumption" (under a causal law) and explanation "by analysis" (into component parts). See his *The Nature of Psychological Explanation* (Cambridge: MIT Press, 1983), esp. chs. 1 and 2. Could one and the same explanandum be given explanations of these two types? According to Cummins, however, subsumptive explanation explains *changes* and analytical explanation explains *properties,* so that the explananda are different. It seems also possible to construe the two explanations as mutually complementary but each only a partial explanation of a single explanandum, under a coarse-grained individuation of explananda.

predictive overdetermination does not create any sort of epistemic tension, any need to look for an account of how two predictive arguments, both predicting the same phenomenon, are related. Predictive or inferential overdetermination is simply a matter of overabundance of evidence. I infer that Peggy is in, because I can hear her typing and also because her lights are on. We predict that this steel rod will get longer because we know it's being stretched, and also because we know it's being heated. There are no problems here.[40] It is when such inferences are invested with explanatory import that a need for an account of their mutual relationship arises. And this is so, it seems to me, because explanations make a claim about how things are connected in the world, a claim that is absent in mere proofs or inferences. If this is right, the fact of explanatory exclusion shows that explanations cannot be construed as mere proofs or arguments.[41]

As I said, explanatory realism seems to fit comfortably with explanatory exclusion, although it is not, I think, entailed by it. One interesting possibility is *not* to argue for explanatory exclusion on the basis of explanatory realism, but rather to go the opposite route, namely to give independent considerations favoring the epistemological version of explanatory exclusion and then advocate explanatory realism as the most natural account of it.

Before moving on to the final section I would like to deal with a possible objection: it might be said that there is no need to appeal to any special, and potentially controversial, epistemological or metaphysical views concerning explanation in order to justify something like the rule of explanatory exclusion, and that all we really need is Ockham's Razor, the familiar principle of simplicity, that enjoins us to get by with the fewest possible entities, hypotheses, theoretical principles, and, of course, explanations. In reply, I would first note that the general simplicity requirement is vague and its application requires a more precise interpretation of the situation to which it is to be applied. In particular, we need to determine exactly at what point the entities in question begin to be

40 Nor when we see that the same mathematical propositions can be given two different proofs. Some philosophers think, however, that certain proofs are more "explanatory" than others, in the sense that they seem to give us an explanation of "what makes the theorem hold". However, one could argue, I think, that the same principle of exclusion must apply to multiple *explanatory proofs* of the same mathematical proposition.

41 These remarks tie in with the standard discussion of "realism" vs. "instrumentalism" about scientific theories – especially, the common view that an instrumentalist conception of scientific theories, though viable as an account of their predictive utility, deprives them of explanatory significance.

multiplied "beyond necessity". In fact, determining where the excess baggage starts is the difficult part; the rest is trivial. The exclusion principle does the difficult work: it says that for any event more than one complete explanation is excess baggage. More, the principle helps us answer the following question: If, as is usually thought, explanations represent epistemic gains, why aren't two explanations better than one? It is not at all obvious that considerations of parsimony alone should mandate us to reject all but one explanation. We can indeed think of explanatory exclusion as a special case falling under the general simplicity requirement: it is a specific rule concerning one important way in which simplicity is to be gained in explanatory matters, and it explains why this form of simplicity is to be desired. That is, the explanatory exclusion principle provides a rationale for the application of Ockham's Razor to multiple explanations of a single explanandum.

5. APPLICATIONS

In this final section I want to describe two examples from recent philosophical discussions in which the explanatory exclusion principle seems to be employed in a tacit but crucial way. The examples I shall discuss are not intended to constitute an argument for the exclusion principle; rather, they are intended to show that the principle is often accepted or presupposed, if only implicitly. Alternatively, they can be thought of as "applications" of the explanatory exclusion principle. Evidence such as this shows that, even apart from general theoretical considerations, the principle does carry a degree of prima facie plausibility, and should not be rejected without good reason.

The account of theory reduction we earlier referred to, one that was formulated by Ernest Nagel, is a model of *conservative reduction*. For in a reduction of this kind the reduced theory survives the reduction, being conserved as a subtheory of the reducing theory. Its concepts are conserved by being tied, via the "bridge laws", to the concepts of the reducing theory, and its laws are reincarnated as derived laws of the more fundamental theory. For a theory to be reduced in this way to another theory whose legitimacy is not in question is for it to be vindicated and legitimatized.

There is another account of reduction, due to John Kemeny and Paul Oppenheim,[42] that is thought to give us an analysis of *eliminative* or *replace-*

42 "On Reduction", *Philosophical Studies* 7 (1956): 6–19.

ment reduction. A theory is reduced to another, on this model, just in case all the data explainable by the first theory are explainable by the second. In cases of interest, the second theory, that is, the reducer, will do a good deal better than the first, the reducee. There need be no direct conceptual or nomological connections between the theories themselves; their theoretical vocabularies may be wholly disjoint and there may be no "bridge laws" connecting them. Nor need there be a logical incompatibility, or a negative inductive or evidential relationship between them. It is just that one theory, the reducer, does its job better than (or at least as well as) the reducee, relative to their shared domain.

It is clear that any case of Nagelian reduction can be construed as a case of Kemeny-Oppenheim reduction, so that it is not strictly correct to characterize all cases of the latter as replacement or eliminative reductions. But it is also clear that any case of Kemeny-Oppenheim reduction that is not also a case of Nagel reduction is one that involves, or ought to involve, the elimination of the weaker reduced theory by the richer theory that reduces it. Thus, the phlogiston theory of combustion was reduced in the sense of Kemeny and Oppenheim to the oxidation theory, and was replaced by it. The impetus theory of motion was reduced, and eliminated, in the same sense, by modern dynamic theory of motion. And so on. A general principle like the following seems to be at work here: *If a theory is confronted by another that explains more, the only way it can survive is for it to be conservatively reduced to the latter.*

The question I want to raise is why this holds, or ought to hold. Why should we replace, and abandon, a Kemeny-Oppenheim reduced theory in favor of its reducer? Notice that the reducing theory does not in general *logically exclude* the reduced theory; there need be no logical incompatibility between them. Further, the reduced theory need not have been falsified; in fact, as far as direct evidence goes there may be good reason to think it is true. So why not keep them both? Notice the consequences of abandoning the reduced theory: its characteristic theoretical entities, properties, events, and states are no longer to be recognized as "real". They share the fate of the discarded theory: phlogiston had to go when the phlogiston theory was thrown out.

The reason I raise these points is that they help to give structure to the current debate concerning the future of vernacular psychology, the rich and motley collection of truisms and platitudes about our motives, desires, beliefs, hopes, actions, etc. It is in terms of such truisms that we explain, and predict at least in a limited way, the behavior of our fellow humans and ourselves. It strikes many of us as inconceivable that we can

261

entirely dispense with this framework of intentional psychology; it is not clear that our conception of ourselves as persons and agents could survive the loss of the vernacular psychological scheme.

However, many philosophers have raised doubts about the reality of vernacular psychology – and the reality of such states as belief, desire, and intention. The thought is that the rapidly developing and expanding "cognitive science" will likely supersede the vernacular so that at some point in the future the rational thing to conclude will be that there are no such things as beliefs and desires, and there never were. But in what sense of "supersede"? How should vernacular psychology be related to cognitive science if it is to survive, and if the states it recognizes, such as beliefs and desires, are to continue to be recognized as real?

Those who argue for the potential, and likely, elimination of vernacular psychology, and intentional psychological states that constitute its core, often point to two considerations: first, compared with systematic cognitive science the vernacular suffers from explanatory failure, and second there is no prospect of reducing it to a systematic scientific theory. For example, Paul Churchland, a forceful proponent of this position, writes:[43]

> As examples of central and important mental phenomena that remain largely or wholly mysterious within the framework of FP [folk psychology], consider the nature and dynamics of mental illness, the faculty of creative imagination . . . the nature and psychological functions of sleep . . . the common ability to catch an outfield fly ball on the run . . . the internal construction of a 3-D visual image . . . the rich variety of perceptual illusions . . . the miracle of memory . . . the nature of the learning process itself. . . .

There are phenomena, Churchland is saying, that can be adequately explained within cognitive science but are untouched by the vernacular. A further implicit assumption is that cognitive science can explain everything explained by vernacular psychology. The claim then is that the vernacular is Kemeny-Oppenheim reducible to systematic cognitive science.

Churchland is also skeptical about the conservative Nagel reducibility of vernacular psychology to cognitive science. He says: "A successful reduction cannot be ruled out, in my view, but FP's [folk psychology's] explanatory impotence and long stagnation inspire little faith that its categories will find themselves neatly reflected in the framework of neuroscience".[44] Here he is saying that a conservative reduction is unlikely because

43 "Eliminative Materialism and the Propositional Attitudes", *Journal of Philosophy* 78 (1981): 67–90. The quotation is from p. 73.
44 Ibid., p. 75.

there is little reason to believe in the existence of the bridge laws connecting vernacular psychological states with neurophysiological states. Thus the structure of Churchland's argument exemplifies the pattern we discerned earlier: vernacular psychology must be eliminated because it is Kemeny-Oppenheim reducible to cognitive neuroscience without being conservatively reducible to it.[45]

Thus, we are faced with the following question: granted that neuroscience has a wider explanatory range than vernacular psychology, why can't the two coexist anyway, without vernacular psychology being nomologically reduced to neuroscience? Why should we discard the vernacular and conclude that there aren't, and never have been, such things as beliefs, hopes, regrets, and wishes?

The explanatory exclusion principle provides a simple explanation of why the two theories, even if they do not logically or evidentially exclude each other, compete against each other and why their peaceful coexistence is an illusion. For vernacular psychology and neuroscience each claim to provide explanations for the same domain of phenomena, and because of the failure of reduction in either direction, the purported explanations must be considered independent. Hence, by the exclusion principle, one of them has to go.[46]

I think similar considerations can account for an otherwise puzzling aspect of Thomas Kuhn's celebrated theory of scientific "paradigms".[47] According to Kuhn, successive paradigms addressing the same range of phenomena are "incommensurable" with each other. They make use of different concepts, different methodologies, different criteria for generating problems and evaluating proposed solutions. As is well known, Kuhn says in various places that different paradigms do not, perhaps cannot, even share the same problems; nor can they, strictly speaking, share the

45 Churchland also intimates that laws of vernacular psychology have been falsified. This is a controversial point, and even if it is true, it would not force the *elimination* of vernacular psychology (at least, that of intentional psychology); all it would show is that the vernacular needs improvement. To argue for an outright elimination, some principle like explanatory exclusion seems essential; and if we have such a principle, we don't need the premise about the falsity of vernacular psychology.

46 The right way to save vernacular psychology, in my view, is to stop thinking of it as playing the same game that "cognitive science" is supposed to play – that is, stop thinking of it as a "theory" whose primary raison d'être is to generate law-based causal explanations and predictions. We will do better to focus on its normative role in the evaluation of actions and the formation of intentions and decisions. If vernacular psychology competes against cognitive science in the prediction game, it cannot win, and the best thing it can hope for is reductive absorption into its more systematic (and better funded) rival.

47 *The Structure of Scientific Revolutions* (Chicago: University of Chicago Press, 1962).

263

same data. But I am here assuming that Kuhn must allow a sense in which different successive paradigms can, and do, share an overlapping domain of subject matters. Otherwise much of his theory of paradigms makes little sense.

Now one might raise the following question about paradigms: If they are, as Kuhn says, mutually incommensurable, and hence cannot even contradict each other, why can't we accept them all? Why must we discard the old paradigm when we construct a new one? After all, no paradigm is ever literally falsified, according to Kuhn, and every paradigm serves useful explanatory and predictive purposes, making its unique scientific contributions. So why not accumulate paradigms? We could do this without fear of logical incoherence or inconsistency, for paradigms are mutually incommensurable and hence cannot contradict each other. We would have a "cumulative theory" of scientific progress through accumulation of paradigms instead of the usual cumulative theory of scientific knowledge which Kuhn rejects.

Again, an answer is forthcoming from the explanatory exclusion principle: Kuhn takes for granted the incompatibility of successive paradigms directed at the same phenomena because he tacitly accepts the explanatory exclusion principle, and we go along with him because we, too, do not question it. I take it that, for Kuhn, each paradigm purports to provide complete and independent explanations of the data within its domain – complete and independent relative to other competing paradigms. It follows from the explanatory exclusion principle: No more than one paradigm for a single domain.

14

The myth of nonreductive materialism

I

Reductionism of all sorts has been out of favor for many years. Few among us would now seriously entertain the possibility that ethical expressions are definable, or reducible in some broader sense, in terms of "descriptive" or "naturalistic" expressions. I am not sure how many of us can remember, in vivid enough detail, the question that was once vigorously debated as to whether so-called "physical-object statements" are translatable into statements about the phenomenal aspects of perceptual experience, whether these are conceived as "sense data" or as some manner of "being appeared to". You may recall the idea that concepts of scientific theories must be reduced, via "operational definitions", to intersubjectively performable procedures whose results can be ascertained through observation. This sounded good – properly tough-minded and hard-nosed – but it didn't take long for philosophers and scientists to realize that a restrictive constraint of this sort was neither enforceable nor necessary – not necessary to safeguard science from the threat of metaphysics and pseudo-science. These reductionisms are now nothing but museum pieces.

In philosophy of mind, too, we have gone through many reductionisms; some of these, such as logical behaviorism, have been defunct for many years; others, most notably, the psychoneural identity theory, have been repeatedly declared dead; and still others, such as versions of functionalism, are still hanging on, though with varying degrees of difficulty. Perhaps as a result of the singular lack of success with which our earlier reductionist efforts have been rewarded, a negative image seems to

My thanks to Richard Brandt, Sydney Shoemaker, and Ernest Sosa for helpful comments on earlier versions, and to David Benfield, Barry Loewer, and Brian McLaughlin for discussing with me some of the topics of this paper.

have emerged for reductionisms in general. Many of us have the feeling that there is something rigid and narrow-minded about reductionist strategies. Reductionisms, we tend to feel, attempt to impose on us a monolithic, strait-jacketed view of the subject matter, the kind of cleansed and tidy picture that appeals to those obsessed with orderliness and discipline. Perhaps, this impression has something to do with the reductionists' ritual incantations of slogans like "parsimony", "simplicity", "economy", and "unity", all of them virtues of a rather puritanical sort. Perhaps, too, reductionisms are out of step with the intellectual style of our times: we strive for patterns of life and thought that are rich in diversity and complexity and tolerant of disagreement and multiplicity. We are apt to think that the real world is a messy place and resists any simplistic drive, especially one carried on from the armchair, toward simplification and unification. In fact, the word "reductionism" seems by now to have acquired a negative, faintly disreputable flavor – at least in philosophy of mind. Being a reductionist is a bit like being a logical positivist or member of the Old Left – an aura of doctrinaire naiveté hangs over him.

At any rate, reductionism in the mind–body problem has been out of fashion for two decades; it has been about that long since the unexpectedly early demise of the psychoneural identity theory, a doctrine advertised by its proponents as the one that was in tune with a world view adequately informed by the best contemporary science. Surprisingly, the abandonment of psychoneural reductionism has not led to a resurgence of dualism. What is curious, at least in terms of the expectations set by the earlier mind–body debates, is the fact that those who renounced reductionism have stayed with physicalism. The distinctive feature of the mind–body theories that have sprung up in the wake of the identity theory is the belief, or hope, that one can be an honest-to-goodness physicalist without at the same time being a reductionist. In fact, a correct and realistic view of science as it is practiced will show us, the new physicalists assure us, that as an account of the "cross-level" relation between theories, classical reductionism is untenable everywhere, not just about the psychophysical relation. The leading idea in all this has been the thought that we can assuage our physicalist qualms by embracing "ontological physicalism",[1] the claim that all that exists in spacetime is physical, but,

---

1 Throughout I will be using "physicalism" and "materialism" (and their derivatives) interchangeably; similarly, "mental" and "psychological".

at the same time, accept "property dualism", a dualism about psychological and physical attributes, insisting that psychological concepts or properties form an irreducible, autonomous domain. The issue I want to explore here is whether or not a robust physicalist can, consistently and plausibly, swear off reductionism – that is, whether or not a substantial form of physicalism can be combined with the rejection of psychophysical reduction.

To lay my cards on the table, I will argue that a middle-of-the-road position of the sort just described is not available. More specifically, I will claim that a physicalist has only two genuine options, eliminativism and reductionism. That is, if you have already made your commitment to a version of physicalism worthy of the name, you must accept the reducibility of the psychological to the physical, or, failing that, you must consider the psychological as falling outside your physicalistically respectable ontology. Of course, you might decide to reconsider your commitment to physicalism; but I will not here consider what nonphysicalist alternatives there might be which are still live possibilities for us. So if I am right, the choices we face concerning the mind–body problem are rather stark: there are three – antiphysicalist dualism, reductionism, and eliminativism.

II

Pressures from two sources have been largely responsible, I believe, for the decline of reductionism in philosophy of mind, a decline that began in the late 1960s. One was Donald Davidson's "Anomalism of the Mental", the doctrine that there are no precise or strict laws about mental events.[2] According to Davidson, the mental is anomalous not only in that there are no laws relating mental events to other mental events but none relating them to physical events either. This meant that no nomological linkages between the mental and the physical are available to enable the reduction of the former to the latter. The second antireductionist pressure came from a line of argument based on the phenomenon of "multiple realizability" of mental states, which Hilary Putnam forcefully brought to philosophical attention, claiming that it directly refuted the reductive materialism of Smart and Feigl.[3] Jerry Fodor and others have developed

2 See Davidson, "Mental Events" in *Essays on Actions and Events* (Oxford: Oxford University Press,1980). This paper was first published in 1970.
3 See Putnam, "The Nature of Mental States" in *Mind, Language, and Reality: Philosophical Papers,* vol. II (Cambridge: Cambridge University Press, 1975). This article was first published in 1967.

this idea into a general antireductionist argument, advancing the claim that the "special sciences", such as psychology, sociology, and economics, are in general irreducible to physical theory, and that reductive materialism, or "type identity theory", is generally false as a theory about science.[4] Earlier physicalists would have regarded the irreducibility as evidence showing the mental to be beyond the pale of a scientifically respectable ontology; that is, they would have inferred eliminativism from the irreducibility. This in fact was Quine's response to the problem of intentionality.[5] But not for the latter-day physicalists: for them, the irreducibility only means that psychology, and other special sciences, are "autonomous", and that a physicalist can, in consistency and good conscience, accept the existence of these isolated autonomous domains within science.

Let us begin with Davidson. As noted, the Anomalism of the Mental can be thought of as the conjunction of two claims: first, the claim that there are no purely psychological laws, that is, laws connecting psychological events with other psychological events, and second, the claim that there are no laws connecting psychological events with physical events. The second claim, which we might call "Psychophysical Anomalism", is what underlies Davidson's argument against reductionism. The argument is simple and direct: the demise of analytical behaviorism scotched the idea that the mental could be definitionally reduced to the physical. Further, Psychophysical Anomalism shows that a nomological reduction of the mental isn't in the offing either. The implicit assumption about reduction in this argument is one that is widely shared: reduction of one theory to another requires the derivation of the laws of the reduced theory from those of the reducer, and for this to be possible, terms of the first theory must be appropriately connected, via "bridge principles", with those of the second. And the bridge principles must be either conceptually underwritten as definitions, or else express empirical lawlike correlations ("bridge laws" or "theoretical identities").[6]

This is all pretty straightforward. What was striking was the further

4 Jerry Fodor, "Special Sciences, or the Disunity of Science as a Working Hypothesis", *Synthese* 28 (1974): 97–115. See also Richard Boyd, "Materialism without Reductionism: What Physicalism Does Not Entail", in *Readings in Philosophy of Psychology*, ed. Ned Block (Cambridge: Harvard University Press, 1980).

5 As it is the response of some recent eliminativists; see, e.g., Paul Churchland, "Eliminative Materialism and the Propositional Attitudes", *Journal of Philosophy* 78 (1981): 67–90.

6 The classic source on reduction is Ernest Nagel, *The Structure of Science* (New York: Harcourt, Brace & World, 1961), ch. 11.

philosophical conclusions Davidson inferred from these considerations. Far from deriving some sort of dualism, he used them to argue for a materialist monism. His argument is well known, but it bears repeating. Mental events, Davidson observed, enter into causal relations with physical events.[7] But causal relations must be backed by laws; that is, causal relations between individual events must instantiate lawful regularities. Since there are no laws about the mental, either psychophysical or purely psychological, any causal relation involving a mental event must instantiate a physical law, from which it follows that the mental event has a physical description, or falls under a physical event kind. From this it further follows that the event is a physical event. For an event is physical (or mental) if it falls under a physical event kind (or a mental event kind).

It follows then that all events are physical events – on the assumption that every event enters into at least one causal relation. This assumption seems entirely unproblematic, for it only leaves out events that are both *causeless* and *effectless*. If there are any such events, it is difficult to see how their existence can be known to us; I believe we could safely ignore them. So imagine a Davidsonian universe of events: all these events are physical events, and some of them are also mental. That is to say, all events have physical properties, and some of them have mental properties as well. Such is Davidson's celebrated "anomalous monism".

Davidson's ontology recognizes individual events as spatiotemporal particulars. And the principal structure over these events is causal structure; the network of causal relations that interconnects events is what gives intelligible structure to this universe of events. What role does mentality play, on Davidson's anomalous monism, in shaping this structure? The answer: None whatever.

For anomalous monism entails this: *the very same network of causal relations would obtain in Davidson's world if you were to redistribute mental properties over its events any way you like; you would not disturb a single causal relation if you randomly and arbitrarily reassigned mental properties to events, or even removed mentality entirely from the world.* The fact is that under Davidson's anomalous monism, mentality does no causal work. Remember: on anomalous monism, events are causes or effects only as they instantiate physical laws, and this means that an event's mental properties make no causal differ-

7 Actually the argument can proceed with a weaker premise to the effect that mental events enter into causal relations, either with physical events or with other mental events.

ence. And to suppose that altering an event's mental properties would also alter its physical properties and thereby affect its causal relations is to suppose that Psychophysical Anomalism, a cardinal tenet of anomalous monism, is false.[8]

Anomalous monism, therefore, permits mental properties no causal role, not even in relation to other mental properties. What does no causal work does no explanatory work either; it may as well not be there – it's difficult to see how we could miss it if it weren't there at all. That there are in this world just these mental events with just these mental characteristics is something that makes no causal difference to anything. On anomalous monism, that an event falls under a given mental kind is a causally irrelevant fact; it is also something that is entirely inexplicable in causal terms. Given all this, it's difficult to see what point there is in recognizing mentality as a feature of the world. I believe that if we push anomalous monism this way, we will find that it is a doctrine virtually indistinguishable from outright eliminativism.

Thus, what we see is this: anomalous monism, rather than giving us a form of nonreductive physicalism, is essentially a form of eliminativism. Unlike eliminativism, it allows mentality to exist; but mentality is given no useful work and its occurrence is left wholly mysterious and causally inexplicable. This doesn't strike me as a form of existence worth having. In this respect, anomalous monism does rather poorly even in comparison with epiphenomenalism as a realism about the mental. Epiphenomenalism gives the mental a place in the causal network of events; the mind is given a well-defined place, if not an active role, in the causal structure of the world.

These observations highlight the importance of *properties;* for it is in terms of properties and their interrelations that we make sense of certain concepts that are crucial in this context, such as law, causality, explanation, and dependence. Thus, the anomalousness of mental properties has

---

8 Davidson says in "Mental Events" that he believes in the supervenience of the mental on the physical, and this does introduce a constraint on the distribution of physical properties when the distribution of mental properties is altered. This, however, does not detract substantively from the point being made here. For one, it is still true, on the notion of supervenience Davidson favors (which corresponds to "weak supervenience"; see his "Reply to Essays X–XII" in *Essays on Davidson: Actions and Events,* ed. Bruce Vermazen and Merrill B. Hintikka (Oxford: Oxford University Press, 1985)), that the removal of all mental properties from events of this world would have no consequence whatever on how the physical properties are distributed over them. For another, the supervenience of the mental is best regarded as an independent thesis, and my present remarks only concern the implications of anomalous monism. I consider the supervenience view below in section IV.

far-reaching consequences within Davidson's framework: within it, anomalous properties are causally and explanatorily impotent, and it is doubtful that they can have any useful role at all. The upshot is that we don't get in Davidson's anomalous monism a plausible form of nonreductive physicalism; his anomalous monism comes perilously close to outright eliminativism.[9]

III

Let us now turn to the multiple realizability (or "compositional plasticity") of psychological events and its implications for psychophysical reduction. In a passage that turned out to have a profound impact on the discussions of the mind–body problem, Putnam wrote:[10]

> Consider what the brain-state theorist has to do to make good his claims. He has to specify a physical-chemical state such that *any* organism (not just a mammal) is in pain if and only if (a) it possesses a brain of a suitable physical-chemical structure; and (b) its brain is in that physical-chemical state. This means that the physical-chemical state in question must be a possible state of a mammalian brain, a reptilian brain, a mollusc's brain (octopuses are mullusca, and certainly feel pain), etc. At the same time, it must *not* be a possible (physically possible) state of the brain of any physically possible creature that cannot feel pain. Even if such a state can be found, it must be nomologically certain that it will also be a state of the brain of any extraterrestrial life that may be found that will be capable of feeling pain before we can even entertain the supposition that it may *be* pain.

This paragraph helped bring on an unexpectedly early demise for the psychoneural identity theory of Smart and Feigl, and inspired a new theory of the mental, functionalism, which in spite of its assorted difficulties is still the most influential position on the nature of the mental[11] Putnam's

---

9 Davidson's overall views of the mental are richer and more complex than the present discussion might seem to indicate. I believe that they contain some distinctly dualistic elements; for a discussion of this aspect of Davidson, see my "Psychophysical Laws", Essay 11 of this volume. There have been some interesting recent attempts, which I cannot discuss here, to reconcile anomalous monism with the possibility of mental causation; see, e.g., Ernest LePore and Barry Loewer, "Mind Matters", *Journal of Philosophy* 84 (1987): 630–842; Brian McLaughlin, "Type Epiphenomenalism, Type Dualism, and the Causal Priority of the Physical", *Philosophical Perspectives* 3 (1989): 109–136; Terence Horgan, "Mental Quausation", *Philosophical Perspectives* 3 (1989): 47–76.

10 Putnam, "The Nature of Mental States".

11 Putnam himself has abandoned functionalism; see his *Representation and Reality* (Cambridge: MIT Press, 1988), chs. 5 and 6.

basic point is that any psychological event-type can be "physically realized" or "instantiated" or "implemented" in endlessly diverse ways, depending on the physical-biological nature of the organism or system involved, and that this makes it highly implausible to expect the event to correlate uniformly with, and thus be identifiable with, some "single" type of neural or physical state. This idea has been used by Fodor to formulate a general antireductionist argument, whose gist can be quickly summarized.

As we have seen, reduction of one theory to another is thought to require the derivation of the laws of the reduced theory from the laws of the reducer via "bridge laws". If a predicate of the theory being reduced has a nomologically coextensive predicate in the reducing theory, the universally quantified biconditional connecting the two predicates will be available for use as a bridge law.[12] Let us say that the vocabulary of the reduced theory is "strongly connected" with that of the reducing theory if such a biconditional bridge law correlates each predicate of the former with a predicate of the latter. It is clear that the condition of strong connectibility guarantees reduction (on the assumption that the theory being reduced is a true theory). For it would enable us to rewrite basic laws of the target theory in the vocabulary of the reducer, using these biconditional laws in effect as definitions. Either these rewrites are derivable from the laws of the reducing theory, or else they can be added as additional basic laws. In the latter case, the reducer theory has been expanded; but that does not diminish the ontological and conceptual import of the reductive procedure.

But what multiple realization puts in doubt, according to the antireductionist, is precisely the strong connectibility of mental predicates vis-à-vis physical-neural predicates. For any psychological property, there is in principle an endless sequence of nomologically possible physical states such that, though each of them "realizes" or "implements" it, none of them will by itself be coextensive with it. Why can't we take the *disjunction* of these physical states as the physical coextension of the mental property? Putnam somewhat disdainfully dismisses this move, saying only that "this does not have to be taken seriously".[13] I think there are some complex issues here about disjunctive predicates vs. disjunctive properties, complexity of predicates vs. that of properties, etc.; but these are likely

12 There are some complex logical and ontological details we are leaving out here. See, for details, Robert L. Causey, *Unity of Science* (Dordrecht: Reidel, 1977).
13 "The Nature of Mental States", p. 437.

to be contentious issues that can only distract us at present.[14] So let us go along with Putnam here and disregard the disjunctive solution to the multiple realization problem.

In rejecting the disjunction move, however, Putnam appears to be assuming this: *a physical state that realizes a mental event is at least nomologically sufficient for it.* For if this assumption were rejected, the disjunction move couldn't even get started. This generates laws of the form "$P_i \rightarrow M$", where M is a mental state and P_i is a physical state that realizes it. Thus, where there is multiple realization, there must be psychophysical laws, each specifying a physical state as nomologically sufficient for the given mental state. Moreover, Putnam's choice of examples in the quotation above, which are either biological species or determinate types of physical structures ("extraterrestrials"), and his talk of "species-specificity" and "species-independence"[15] suggest that he is thinking of laws of a somewhat stronger form, "$S_i \rightarrow (M \leftrightarrow P_i)$", which, *relative to species or structure* S_i, specifies a physical state, P_i, as *both necessary and sufficient* for the occurrence of mental state M. A law of this form states that any organism or system, belonging to a certain species, is such that it has the given mental property at a time if and only if it is in a certain specified physical state at that time. We may call laws of this form "species-specific bridge laws".

In order to generate laws of this kind, biological species may turn out to be too wide; individual differences in the localization of psychological functions in the brain are well known. Moreover, given the phenomena of learning and maturation, injuries to the brain, etc., the neural structure that subserves a psychological state or function may change for an individual over its lifetime. What is important is that these laws are relative to physical-biological structure-types, although for simplicity I will continue to put the matter in terms of species. The substantive theoretical assumption here is the belief that for each psychological state there are physical-biological structure-types, at a certain level of description or

14 Note also that derivational reduction does not *require* strong connectibility; any set of bridge laws, of whatever form and strength, will do as long as it enables the derivations. But this obviously depends on the strength of the two theories involved, and there seems to be little of interest that is sufficiently general to say about this. There are also philosophical considerations for thinking that biconditionals and attribute identities are important in reduction. Cf. Lawrence Sklar, "Types of Inter-Theoretic Reduction", *British Journal for the Philosophy of Science* 18 (1967): 109–124. For further discussion of multiple realization see Essay 16 of this volume.
15 "The Nature of Mental States", p. 437.

specification, that generate laws of this form. I think an assumption of this kind is made by most philosophers who speak of multiple realizations of psychological states, and it is in fact a plausible assumption for a physicalist to make.[16] Moreover, such an assumption seems essential to give meaning to the very idea of a physical realization; what else could "physical realization" mean?

So what I am saying is this: the multiple realization argument perhaps shows that the strong connectibility of mental properties vis-à-vis physical properties does not obtain; however, it *presupposes* that *species-specific strong connectibility* does hold. Merely to defeat the antireductionist argument, I need not make this second claim; all I need is the weaker claim that the phenomenon of multiple realization is *consistent* with the species-specific strong connectibility, and it seems to me that that is plainly true.

The point of all this is that the availability of species-specific biconditional laws linking the mental with the physical breathes new life into psychophysical reductionism. Unlike species-independent laws, these laws cannot buy us a *uniform* or *global* reduction of psychology, a reduction of every psychological state to a uniform physical-biological base across all actual and possible organisms; however, these laws will buy us a series of *species-specific* or *local* reductions. If we had a law of this form for each psychological state-type for a given species, say humans, we would have a physical reduction of human psychology; this reduction would tell us how human psychology is physically implemented, how the causal connections between our psychological events and processes work at the physical-biological level, what biological subsystems subserve our cognitive capacities and functions, and so forth. This is reduction in a full-blown sense, except that it is limited to individuals sharing a certain physical-biological structure. I believe "local reductions" of this sort are the rule rather than an exception in all of science, not just in psychology.[17] In any case, this is a plausible picture of what in fact goes on in neurobiology, physiological psychology, cognitive neuroscience, etc. And it seems to me that any robust physicalist must expect,

16 Ned Block says, "Most functionalists are willing to allow . . . that for each type of pain-feeling organism, there is (perhaps) a single type of physical state that realizes pain in that type of organism", in his "Introduction: What is Functionalism?" in Block, ed., *Readings in Philosophy of Psychology,* vol. 1 (Cambridge: Harvard University Press, 1980), p. 172. Such a law would have exactly the form under discussion.

17 On this point see Berent Enc, "In Defense of the Identity Theory", *Journal of Philosophy* 80 (1983): 279–298.

and demand, the possibility of local reductions of psychology just in this sense.[18]

Thus, the conclusion we must draw is that the multiple realizability of the mental has no antireductionist implications of great significance; on the contrary, it entails, or at least is consistent with, the local reducibility of psychology, local relative to species or physical structure-types. If psychological states are multiply realized, that only means that we shall have multiple local reductions of psychology. The multiple realization argument, if it works, shows that a global reduction is not in the offing; however, local reductions are reduction enough, by any reasonable scientific standards and in their philosophical implications.

IV

Some have looked to the idea of "supervenience" for a formulation of physicalism that is free of reductionist commitments. The promise of supervenience in this area appears to have been based, at least in part, on the historical circumstance that some prominent ethical theorists, such as G. E. Moore and R. M. Hare, who constructed classic arguments against naturalistic reductionism in ethics, at the same time held the view that moral properties are "supervenient" upon descriptive or naturalistic properties. So why not think of the relation between psychological and physical properties in analogy with the relation, as conceived by these ethical theorists, between moral and descriptive properties? In each instance, the supervenient properties are in some substantive sense dependent on, or determined by, their subvenient base properties and yet, it is hoped, they are not reducible to them. This was precisely the line of thinking that appears to have prompted Davidson, who was the first to inject supervenience into the discussion of the mind–body problem. He wrote:[19]

Although the position I describe denies there are psychophysical laws, it is consistent with the view that mental characteristics are in some sense dependent, or supervenient, on physical characteristics. Such supervenience might be taken to mean that there cannot be two events alike in all physical respects but differing in some mental respects, or that an object cannot alter in some mental respect without altering in some physical respect. Dependence or supervenience of this kind does not entail reducibil-

18 This point, and some related points, are elaborated in Essay 16 of this volume. See also "Postscripts on Mental Causation", section 2.
19 "Mental Events", in Davidson, *Essays on Actions and Events,* p. 214.

ity through law or definition: if it did, we could reduce moral properties to descriptive, and this there is good reason to *believe* cannot be done. . . .

Although Davidson himself did not pursue this idea further, many other philosophers have tried to work this suggestive idea into a viable form of nonreductive materialism.

The central problem in implementing Davidson's suggestion has been that of defining a supervenience relation that will fill the twin requirements he set forth: first, the relation must be *nonreductive;* that is, a given domain can be supervenient on another without being reducible to it. Second, the relation must be one of *dependence:* if a domain supervenes on another, there must be a sturdy sense in which the first is dependent on the second, or the second determines the first. But it has not been easy to find such a relation. The main difficulty has been this: if a relation is weak enough to be nonreductive, it tends to be too weak to serve as a dependence relation; conversely, when a relation is strong enough to give us dependence, it tends to be too strong – strong enough to imply reducibility.

I will not rehearse here the well-known arguments pro and con concerning various supervenience relations that have been proposed. I will instead focus on one supervenience relation that has seemed to several philosophers[20] to hold the most promise as a nonreductive dependency relation, viz., that of "global supervenience". The generic idea of supervenience is that things that are indiscernible in respect of the "base" (or "subvenient") properties cannot differ in respect of the supervenient properties. Global supervenience applies this consideration to "worlds", giving us the following formulation of psychophysical supervenience:

Worlds that are indiscernible in all physical respects are indiscernible in mental respects; in fact, physically indiscernible worlds are one and the same world.

Thus, any world that is just like this world in all physical details must be just like it in all psychological respects as well. This relation of supervenience is appropriately called "global" in that worlds rather than individu-

20 Including Terence Horgan in his "Supervenience and Microphysics", *Pacific Philosophical Quarterly* 63 (1982): 29–43; John Haugeland in "Weak Supervenience", *American Philosophical Quarterly* 19 (1982): 93–103; John Post in *The Faces of Existence* (Ithaca: Cornell University Press, 1987); and Bradford Petrie, "Global Supervenience and Reduction", *Philosophy and Phenomenological Research* 48 (1987): 119–130. The model-theoretic notion of determination worked out by Geoffrey Hellman and Frank Thompson, in "Physicalism: Ontology, Determination, and Reduction", *Journal of Philosophy* 72 (1975): 551–564, is closely related to global supervenience.

als within worlds are compared for discernibility or indiscernibility in regard to sets of properties. What is it for two worlds to be physically, or mentally, indiscernible? For simplicity let us assume that the same individuals exist in all the worlds:[21] we may then say that two worlds are indiscernible with respect to a set of properties just in case these properties are distributed over individuals in the same way in the two worlds.

It can be shown that, as hoped, the global supervenience of the mental on the physical does not entail the existence of psychophysical laws;[22] thus, global supervenience is consistent with the nomological irreducibility of the mental to the physical. The only question then is whether it yields an appropriate relation of dependency between the mental and the physical, one that is strong enough to qualify it as a physicalism. The answer, I will argue, is in the negative.

We may begin by observing that the global supervenience of the mental permits the following: Imagine a world that differs from the actual world in some minute physical detail (we may suppose that in that world one lone hydrogen atom somewhere in deep space is slightly displaced relative to its position in this world). This world with one wayward hydrogen atom could, consistently with the global supervenience of the mental, be as different as you please from the actual world in any mental respect (thus, in that world nothing manifests mentality, or mentality is radically redistributed in other ways). The existence of such a world and other similarly aberrant worlds does not violate the constraints of global supervenience; since they are not physically indiscernible from the actual world, they could, under global supervenience, differ radically from this world in psychological characteristics.[23]

If that doesn't convince you of the weakness of global supervenience as a determination or dependency relation, consider this: it is consistent with global supervenience for there to be two organisms in our actual world which, though wholly indiscernible physically, are radically different in mental respects (say, your molecule-for-molecule duplicate is to-

---

21 Even with this simplifying assumption certain complications arise; however, we may disregard them for the purposes of this paper. For further details see my "Supervenience for Multiple Domains", Essay 7 of this volume.

22 At least not in a straightforward way. See my "'Strong' and 'Global' Supervenience Revisited", Essay 5 of this volume. (Added 1993: This matter remains controversial; see "Postscripts on Supervenience", section 3, for further discussion.)

23 This particular difficulty can be largely met by formulating global supervenience in terms of *similarity* between worlds rather than indiscernibility. See my "'Strong' and 'Global' Supervenience Revisited."

tally lacking in mentality). This is consistent with global supervenience because there might be no other possible world that is just like this one physically and yet differs in some mental respect.[24]

It seems to me that indiscernibility considerations at the global level, involving whole worlds, are just too coarse to give us the kind of dependency relation we should demand if the mental is truly dependent on the physical. Like it or not, we treat individuals, and perhaps also aggregates of individuals smaller than total worlds, as psychological units, and it seems to me that if psychophysical determination or dependence means anything, it ought to mean that the psychological nature of each such unit is wholly determined by its physical nature. That is, dependency or determination must hold at the local as well as the global level.

Moreover, talk of whole worlds in this connection, unless it is anchored in determinative relations obtaining at the local level, has little verifiable content; it is difficult to see how there can be empirical evidence for the global supervenience thesis that is not based in evidence about specific psychophysical dependencies – evidence concerning dependencies and correlations between specific psychological and physical properties. In fact, it seems to me that we must look to local dependencies for an *explanation* of global supervenience as well as for its evidence. Why is it the case that no two worlds can exist that are indiscernible physically and yet discernible psychologically? Or why is it the case that "physical truths determine all the truths",[25] as some prefer to put it? I think this is a legitimate question to raise, and as far as I can see the only answer, other than the response that it is a brute, unexplainable metaphysical fact, is in terms of local correlations and dependencies between specific mental and physical properties. If the global supervenience of the mental on the physical were to be proposed as an unexplainable fact that we must accept on faith, I doubt that we need to take the proposal seriously. Specific psychophysical dependencies holding for individuals, and other proper parts of the world, are both evidence for, and an explanatory ground of, global supervenience.

The trouble is that once we begin talking about correlations and dependencies between specific psychological and physical properties, we are in effect talking about psychophysical laws, and these laws raise the specter of unwanted physical reductionism. Where there are psychophysical

24 This shows that global supervenience is consistent with the failure of "weak supervenience". See my "'Strong' and 'Global' Supervenience Revisited".
25 See Hellman and Thompson, "Physicalism: Ontology, Determination, and Reduction"; Post, *The Faces of Existence*.

laws, there is always the threat, or promise, of psychophysical reduction. We must conclude that supervenience is not going to deliver to us a viable form of nonreductive materialism.

V

So far I have reviewed three influential formulations of nonreductive materialism, Davidson's anomalous monism, the Putnam-Fodor doctrine of psychological autonomy, and supervenient physicalism, and found them wanting either as a materialism or as an antireductionism. In this final section, I want to advance a direct argument to show why the prospects for nonreductive physicalism are dim.

Let us first of all note that nonreductive physicalism is not to be a form of eliminativism; that is, it acknowledges the mental as a legitimate domain of entities. What sort of entities? Here let us, for convenience, make use of the Davidsonian scheme of individual events, thinking of mentality to be exhibited as properties of these events. Thus, as a noneliminativist, the nonreductive physicalist believes that there are events in her ontology that have mental properties (e.g., being a pain, being a belief that snow is cold, etc.). I argued earlier, in discussing Davidson's anomalous monism, that if your noneliminativism is to be more than a token gesture, you had better find some real causal work for your mental properties. The fact that a given event is a mental event of a certain kind must play some causal-explanatory role in what other events occur and what properties they have. Thus, I am supposing that a nonreductive physicalist is a mental realist, and that to be a mental realist, your mental properties must be *causal properties* – properties in virtue of which an event enters into causal relations it would otherwise not have entered into.

Let me now make a further assumption: psychophysical causation takes place – that is, some mental events cause physical events. For example, a sudden sharp pain felt in my hand causes a jerky withdrawal of the hand. It is true that in a Davidsonian domain, all events are physical; that is, every event has some physical property. But when I say that mental events cause physical events, something stronger is intended, namely that an event, *in virtue of its mental property,* causes another event to have a certain physical property. An argument could be constructed to the same effect, I believe, without this special assumption, but it would be longer and more involved. I believe that this assumption will be granted by most of us – it will be granted by anyone who believes that at least sometimes our

279

limbs move because we have certain desires and beliefs.[26] When I walk to the water fountain for a drink of water, my legs move in the way they do in part because of my desire for water and my belief that there is water to be had at the water fountain.

There is a further assumption that I believe any physicalist would grant, namely "the causal closure of the physical domain". Roughly, it says this: *any physical event that has a cause at time t has a physical cause at t.* This is the assumption that if we trace the causal ancestry of a physical event, we need never go outside the physical domain. To deny this assumption is to accept the Cartesian idea that some physical events need nonphysical causes, and if this is true there can in principle be no complete and self-sufficient physical theory of the physical domain. If the causal closure failed, our physics would need to refer in an essential way to nonphysical causal agents, perhaps Cartesian souls and their psychic properties, if it is to give a complete account of the physical world. I think most physicalists would find that picture unacceptable.

Now we are ready to derive some consequences from these assumptions. Suppose that a certain event, in virtue of its mental property, causes a physical event. The causal closure of the physical domain says that this physical event must also have a physical cause. We may assume that this physical cause, in virtue of its physical property, causes the physical event. The following question arises: *What is the relationship between these two causes, one mental and the other physical?* Each is claimed to be a cause of the physical effect. There are two initial possibilities that we can consider.

First, when we are faced with two purported causes of a single event, we could entertain the possibility that each is only a *partial cause,* the two together making up a full or sufficient cause, as when a car crash is said to be caused by the driver's careless braking and the icy condition of the road. Applied to our case, it says that the mental cause and the physical cause are each only a partial cause, and that they *together* make up one sufficient cause. This surely is an absurd thing to say, and in any case it violates the causal closure principle in that it regards the mental event as a necessary constituent of a full cause of a physical event; thus, on this view, a full causal story of how this physical event occurs must, at least partially, go outside the physical domain.

Could it be that the mental cause and the physical cause are each an *independent sufficient* cause of the physical effect? The suggestion then is

---

26 For a forceful statement of this point see Fred Dretske, *Explaining Behavior: Reasons in a World of Causes* (Cambridge: MIT Press, 1988).

that the physical effect is *overdetermined*. So if the physical cause hadn't occurred, the mental cause by itself would have caused the effect. This picture is again absurd: from what we know about the physiology of limb movement, we must believe that if the pain sensation causes my hand to withdraw, the causal chain from the pain to the limb motion must somehow make use of the causal chain from an appropriate central neural event to the muscle contraction; it makes no sense to think that there might be an independent, perhaps telekinetic, causal path from the pain to the limb movement. Moreover, the overdetermination idea violates the causal closure principle as well: in the counterfactual situation in which the physical cause does not occur, the closure principle is violated. For the idea that the mental and the physical cause are each an independent sufficient cause involves the acceptance of the counterfactual that if the physical cause had not occurred, the mental cause would have occurred and caused the physical effect. This is in violation of the causal closure principle.

These two ways of looking at the situation are obvious nonstarters. We need a more plausible answer to the question, how are the mental cause and the physical cause of the single physical effect related to each other? Given that any physical event has a physical cause, how is a mental cause *also* possible? This I call "the problem of causal-explanatory exclusion", for the problem seems to arise from the fact that a cause, or causal explanation, of an event, when it is regarded as a full, sufficient cause or explanation, appears to *exclude* other *independent* purported causes or causal explanations of it.[27]

At this point, you might want to protest: why all this beating around the bush? Why not just say the mental cause and the physical cause are one and the same? Identification simplifies ontology and gets rid of unwanted puzzles. Consider saying that there are in this glass two distinct substances, H_2O and water; that is, consider saying that water and H_2O co-occur everywhere as a matter of law but that they are distinct substances nonetheless. This would invite a host of unwanted and unnecessary puzzles: given that what is in the glass weighs a total of ten ounces, how much of the weight is to be attributed to the water and how much to the H_2O? By dropping a lighted match in the glass, I extinguish it. What caused it? Was it the water or the H_2O? Were they each only a partial cause, or was the extinguishing of the match overdetermined? The identification of the water with the H_2O puts all these questions to rest

27 This idea is developed in greater detail in my "Mechanism, Purpose, and Explanatory Exclusion", Essay 13 of this volume.

in a single stroke: there is here one thing, not two. The identity solution can work similar magic in our present case: the pain *is* a neural state – here there is one cause, not two. The limb motion was caused by the pain, that is to say, by a neural state. The unwanted puzzles vanish.

All this is correct. But what does the identity solution involve? Remember that what is for us at issue is the causal efficacy of *mental properties* of events vis-à-vis their physical properties. Thus, the items that need to be identified are properties – that is, we would need to identify mental properties with physical properties. If this could be done, that would be an excellent way of vindicating the causal powers of mentality.

But this is precisely the route that is barred to our nonreductivist friends. The identification of mental properties with physical properties is the heart of reductionist "type physicalism". These property identities would serve as bridge laws par excellence, enabling a derivational reduction of psychology to physical theory. The identities entail psychophysical correlations of biconditional form, stable over possible, or nomologically possible, worlds, and this, we have been told, is excluded by Davidson's mental anomalism and Putnam's multiple realization argument. So the identity solution is out of the question for the nonreductive materialist. Is there any other way to respond to the causal exclusion problem, a way that falls short of identifying mental with physical attributes?

There is one, but it isn't something that would be palatable to the nonreductivist. I believe that the only way other than the identity solution is to give a general account of causal relations involving macro-events as "supervenient causal relations", causal relations that are supervenient on micro-causal processes. You put a kettle of water on the stove and turn on the burner; and soon the water starts to boil. Heating the water caused it to boil. That is a causal relation at the macro-level. It is natural to think of this causal relation as a supervenient on certain underlying causal processes at the micro-level. The heating of water supervenes on the increasing kinetic energy of water molecules, and when their mean kinetic energy reaches a certain level, water molecules begin to move in turbulence, some of them being ejected into the air. Boiling is a macro-state that supervenes on just these micro-processes. A sharp pain causes an anxiety attack five seconds later. What's going on? Again, it is tempting, and natural, to think thus: the pain is supervenient on a certain underlying neural activity, and this neural event causes another neural event to occur. The anxiety attack occurs because it is supervenient on this second neural event.

The general model of supervenient causation applied to macro-causal relations is this: macro-event m is a cause or effect of event E in virtue of the fact that m is supervenient on some micro-event, n, which is a cause or effect of event E.[28] The suggestion then is that we use this model to explain mental causation: a mental event is a cause, or an effect, of another event in virtue of the fact that it is supervenient on some physical event standing in an appropriate causal relation to this event. Thus, mental properties are seen as deriving their causal potential from the physical properties on which they supervene. That is the main idea.

But what sort of supervenience relation is involved in this picture? Global supervenience obviously will not do; it does not give us a way of speaking of supervenience of specific mental properties on specific physical properties, since it only refers to indiscernibility holding for worlds. Supervenient causation in my sense requires talk of specific mental properties supervening on specific physical base properties, and this is possible only if there are laws correlating psychological properties with physical properties. This is what I have called elsewhere "strong supervenience", and it can be argued plausibly that supervenience of this strength entails the possibility of reducing the supervenient to the subvenient.[29] I will spare you the details here, but the fact that this form of supervenience directly involves psychophysical laws would be enough to give pause to any would-be nonreductive physicalist. I am not entirely certain that this supervenience solution will suffice; that is, I am not certain that anything short of the identity solution will resolve the exclusion problem.[30] However, I believe that it is the only alternative to explore if, for whatever reason, you are unwilling or unable to go for psychophysical

28 For critical discussions of this model, see Brian McLaughlin, "Event Supervenience and Supervenient Causation", *Southern Journal of Philosophy* 22, *The Spindel Conference Supplement on Supervenience* (1984): 71–91; Peter Menzies, "Against Causal Reductionism," *Mind* 97 (1988): 560–574.

29 I am putting the point somewhat tentatively here because it involves several currently contentious issues. For a general argument for this point, see my "Concepts of Supervenience", Essay 4 of this volume, especially section III; and "Supervenience as a Philosophical Concept", Essay 8 of this volume. However, this argument makes use of infinite disjunctions and conjunctions (actually, infinite disjunctions are all one needs; see "Supervenience as a Philosophical Concept"). If the argument is found objectionable because of this feature, it could be supplemented with an argument modeled on my argument in section III above against the Putnam-Fodor antireductionist thesis. This means that the supervenience relation needed for the model of supervenient causation sketched here must require that each supervenient property have a *nomologically coextensive base property relative to the given physical structure*. There are, I believe, plausible considerations in favor of this stronger supervenience relation as a basis for the concept of supervenient causation (or the reduction of causal relations); however, I cannot go into the details here. (Added 1993: Some of these issues are discussed further in Essay 16 of this volume.)

30 (Added 1993.) See "Postscripts on Mental Causation", section 1, in this volume.

attribute identities. But I doubt that this solution will be found acceptable by the nonreductivist any more than the identity solution.

If nonreductive physicalists accept the causal closure of the physical domain, therefore, they have no visible way of accounting for the possibility of psychophysical causation. This means that they must either give up their antireductionism or else reject the possibility of psychophysical causal relations. The denial of psychophysical causation can come about in two ways: first, you make such a denial because you don't believe there are mental events; or second, you keep faith with mental events even though you acknowledge that they never enter into causal transactions with physical processes, constituting their own autonomous causal world. So either you have espoused eliminativism, or else you are moving further in the direction of dualism, a dualism that posits a realm of the mental in total causal isolation from the physical realm. This doesn't look to me much like materialism.

Our conclusion, therefore, has to be this: nonreductive materialism is not a stable position. There are pressures of various sorts that push it either in the direction of outright eliminativism or in the direction of an explicit form of dualism.

15

Dretske on how reasons explain behavior

In a series of papers[1] and a recent book,[2] Fred Dretske has been working out an innovative account of how reasons explain behavior. His starting point is what we may call "the causal thesis", often associated with Davidson,[3] that reasons rationalize behavior by being its *cause*. With Davidson, therefore, Dretske takes rationalizing explanations to be a species of causal explanation, explanations that specify the causal antecedents of their explananda. Reasons are beliefs, desires, and other assorted "content-bearing" states, and these are among the paradigmatic instances of intentional mental states. Thus, the problem of explaining how reasons *rationalize* (that is, explain by providing reasons) is, for Dretske, the problem of giving an account of how intentional states can be causes, that is, the problem of *intentional* or *rational causation*. If we further assume, with Dretske, that the behavior to be rationalized is, or often involves, bodily events and processes, our problem is seen as a special case of the problem of *psychophysical causation,* that of understanding how mental events or states can enter into causal relations with physical events, as their causes or their effects. There is of course an even broader problem of *mental causation,* the problem of explaining how mental events can enter into any sort of causal relation, either as causes or as effects, whether with physical events or with other mental events.

The reality of the mental is closely tied to the possibility of mental causation, and anyone who takes a realist attitude toward the mental must

My thanks to Ernest Sosa for helpful discussion.
1 "Machines and the Mental", *Proceedings and Addresses of the American Philosophical Associations* 59 (1985), pp. 23–33; "The Explanatory Role of Content" and "Reply to Cummins", in Robert Grimm and Daniel Merrill, eds., *Contents of Thought* (University of Arizona Press, Tucson, 1988); "Reason as Causes", "Putting Information to Work", "The Causal Role of Content", presented at various conferences and lectures.
2 *Explaining Behavior: Reasons in a World of Causes* (MIT Press, Cambridge, 1988).
3 Donald Davidson, "Actions, Reasons, and Causes", reprinted in Davidson, *Essays on Actions and Events* (Oxford University Press, Oxford, 1980).

be prepared with an account of how mental causation is possible. Dretske is a realist about the mental and takes the problem of rational causation seriously. And the project he sets for himself strikes one as just right: he wants to show how reasons, *in virtue of their content,* can be causes of physical behavior. In explaining how reasons can be causes, he does not want to call on the supposed neurobiological properties of beliefs and desires; rather, he wants to vindicate the causal relevance of their representational or semantic properties, the properties that make them the beliefs and desires that they are. To solve the problem of rational causation we must show, Dretske believes, how beliefs and desires – in virtue of their representational content, *not* their neural-physical properties – can cause, and causally explain, behavior and action.

What is more ambitious, it is part of Dretske's program to show that intentional psychology, that is, psychological theory that invokes contentful inner states ("propositional attitudes"), has a special role in the explanation of behavior, over and beyond what neurobiology and other physical theories can provide. He is convinced that "content has an essential and ineliminable role to play in the explanation of behavior", and that this is so not because "we are too ignorant of neurobiology to know what is really in there making the limbs move".[4]

Many interesting questions arise regarding various aspects of Dretske's suggestive proposals. In this paper, however, I will largely confine myself to some broadly metaphysical issues concerning Dretske's program; in particular, I will suggest another way of formulating a Dretskean account that seems better able to handle certain problems. I begin with a review of some current issues concerning mental causation.

1. THREE PROBLEMS OF MENTAL CAUSATION

To begin with, why is mental causation thought to be a "problem"? As we would expect, the answer is that there are certain assumptions, which we take to have a legitimate claim on our respect, that make mental causation prima facie problematic. One possible response of course is to deny that mental causation ever takes place. However, that cannot be our initial response: mental causation seems like an everyday phenomenon with which all of us are only too familiar. A bee sting causes a sharp pain (physical-to-mental causation), and the pain in turn makes me wince (mental-to-physical causation). The lingering pain leads me to think that

---

4 "The Explanatory Role of Content", p. 32.

I had better call the doctor (mental-to-mental causation), and I go into the kitchen for the telephone (mental-to-physical causation). And so forth. But these everyday instances are not all; there are also seemingly compelling theoretical reasons.

We standardly explain actions by rationalizing them – that is, by providing "reasons for which" we did what we did; and as Davidson has emphasized, it is difficult to evade the conclusion that the explanatory efficacy of reasons derives crucially from their causal efficacy. For there seems in the offing no satisfactory noncausal account of the critical distinction between something merely being a *reason for* an action and its being a *motivating reason;* and only motivating reasons, it seems, can explain why an agent did what was done. If this is right, the vindication of the rationalizing mode of understanding human action requires an account of how reasons can cause actions. To drive this home, the point can be contraposed: if we cannot make sense of mental causation, or its subspecies, rational causation, we would be forced to scrap rationalizing explanations as a way of understanding human behavior; and this pretty much is to scrap the whole framework of intentional psychology. All this seems unavoidable under the causal thesis. Whether we should ultimately adhere to the causal interpretation of rationalization is a question we cannot take up here. However, we can say this much in its favor: If it can be made to work, that would be an excellent way of accounting for the explanatory efficacy of rationalizations. And, in general, there is good reason for thinking that mental realism and the possibility of mental causation stand or fall together: what possible good could causeless and effectless entities do for us?

What then are the assumptions that prompt us to vindicate mental causation? I believe there are three such assumptions currently on the scene each of which makes apparent trouble for mental causation. Two of these are well known; the third is less widely discussed but equally crucial. One is "the anomalism of the mental" ("mental anomalism" hereafter) made famous by Davidson.[5] Another is what I will call "syntacticalism".[6] The third I call "causal-explanatory exclusion". Each of these generates a distinct problem of mental causation, though the problems are to some extent interconnected. A comprehensive theory of mental causation must

5 Davidson, "Mental Events", in *Essays on Actions and Events*.
6 After Stephen P. Stich's "syntactic theory of the mind" in *From Folk Psychology to Cognitive Science* (MIT Press, Cambridge, 1983). This doctrine is related to what Jerry Fodor calls "methodological solipsism"; see his "Methodological Solipsism Considered as a Research Strategy in Cognitive Science", in *Representations* (MIT Press, Cambridge, 1981).

provide a solution to each problem, a solution that simultaneously satisfies the constraints of all three problems.

Why does mental anomalism pose a difficulty for mental causation? The initial difficulty, as set forth by Davidson, arises when mental anomalism is combined with the widely accepted nomological requirement on causal relations,[7] the condition that events standing in a causal relation must instantiate a causal law. But this seems to make mental causation impossible: mental causation requires mental events to instantiate laws, but mental anomalism says there are no laws about mental events. Davidson's solution to this difficulty is again well known: his "anomalous monism". True, says Davidson, mental events in causal relations must instantiate laws; since there aren't any psychological laws, that could only mean that they instantiate physical laws. This shows that mental events fall under physical event kinds (or have true physical descriptions), from which it further follows, argues Davidson, that they are physical events.

But this elegantly simple solution has not satisfied everyone. On the contrary, there has been a virtual unanimity among Davidson's commentators on just why anomalous monism is less than fully satisfying as an account of mental causation.[8] Take any mental event, m, that stands in a causal relation, say as a cause of event e. According to Davidson, this causal relation obtains in virtue of the fact that m and e instantiate a physical law. Thus, m has a certain physical (presumably, neural) property N, and e has a physical property P, such that an appropriate causal law relates events of kind N with events of kind P. But this shows that the fact that m is a mental event – that it is the kind of mental event it is – is given no role whatever in determining what causal relations it enters into; it seems that what causal relations hold for m are fixed, wholly and exclusively, by the totality of m's physical properties; and there appears in this picture no causal work that m's mental properties can do, or need to do. This seems to consign mental properties to the status of epiphenomena.[9] Thus, the problem of mental causation arising out of mental anomalism is to answer

7 Not as widely accepted as it used to be; but all known alternatives have their own difficulties, and it seems fair to say that the nomological conception of causation, in its many variants, is still "the received view".
8 See, e.g., Frederick Stoutland, "Oblique Causation and Reasons for Action", *Synthese* 43 (1980), pp. 351–367; Ted Honderich, "The Argument for Anomalous Monism", *Analysis* 42 (1982), pp. 59–64; Ernest Sosa, "Mind–Body Interaction and Supervenient Causation", *Midwest Studies in Philosophy* 9 (1984), pp. 271–282; Kim, "Self-Understanding and Rationalizing Explanations", *Philosophia Naturalis* 21 (1984), pp. 309–320.
9 Brian McLaughlin calls this "type epiphenomenalism" in "Type Epiphenomenalism, Type Dualism, and the Causal Priority of the Physical", *Philosophical Perspectives* 3 (1989), pp. 109–136.

this question: *How can anomalous properties be causal properties?* A solution to this problem would have to show either that, contrary to Davidson, mental properties are not in reality anomalous, or that being anomalous in Davidson's sense is no barrier to having causal relevance or entering into causal relations.

Although Dretske sometimes motivates his project by reference to Davidson, the problem of anomalous mental properties is not his main worry about mental causation. Rather, his primary concern appears to stem from syntacticalism, and his theory is best viewed as a response to this problem. By "syntacticalism" I mean the doctrine that only "syntactic" properties of internal states, not their "semantic" (or "content" or "representational") properties, are psychologically relevant – in particular, to behavior causation. Given the further assumption that the intentionality of mental states consists in their semantic or representational character (some will take this as a conceptual truth), syntacticalism appears to entail that intentional properties of mental states, those properties in which their mentality consists, are causally irrelevant. But what persuades us to take syntacticalism seriously?

Many people seem to find the following line of consideration plausible, at least at first blush: the internal cause of physical behavior must be supervenient on the total internal physical state of the agent or organism at the time.[10] For it seems a highly plausible assumption that if two organisms are in an identical total internal physical state, they will emit identical motor output. However, semantical properties of internal states are not in general supervenient on their synchronous intrinsic physical properties, for they as a rule involve facts about the organism's history and ecological conditions.[11] Thus, two organisms whose total states at a given time have identical intrinsic physical properties can differ in respect of the semantical properties they instantiate; they can differ in the contents of their beliefs and desires, the extensions of their expressions, etc. Thus, what semantical properties are instantiated by the internal states of an organism is a *relational* fact, a fact that essentially involves the organism's relationship to various environmental and historical factors. This makes semantical

10 For a more detailed statement of this argument see Stephen P. Stich, "Autonomous Psychology and the Belief-Desire Thesis", *The Monist* 61 (1978), pp. 573–591.

11 There are well-known considerations supporting this view; see, e.g., Hilary Putnam, "The Meaning of 'Meaning'", in *Philosophical Papers*, Vol. II: *Mind, Language, and Reality* (Cambridge University Press, Cambridge, 1975); Tyler Burge, "Individualism and the Mental", *Midwest Studies in Philosophy* 4 (1979), pp. 73–121; Stich, "Autonomous Psychology and the Belief-Desire Thesis"; Kim, "Psychophysical Supervenience", Essay 10 of this volume.

properties relational, or extrinsic, whereas we expect causative properties involved in behavior production to be nonrelational, or intrinsic, properties of the organism. If inner states are implicated in behavior causation, it seems that all the causal work is done by their "syntactic" properties,[12] leaving their semantic properties causally idle. The problem of mental causation generated by syntacticalism, therefore, is to answer the following question: *How can extrinsic, relational properties be causally efficacious in behavior production?*

This problem of relational properties stands out vividly in the context of Dretske's informational theory of content.[13] On this theory, what it is for a state s_i to have content F depends ultimately, though in complex ways, on there being a causal-nomological relationship between the occurrence of s_i and the presence of F in the organism's environment. If the same organism had been placed in a different environment, a state that is identical with s_i in intrinsic physical properties (or s_i itself) might have content G rather than F, or no content at all. But the causal potential of s_i for the production of physical behavior must be the same as long as the state retains the same internal physical-physiological properties – or so it seems. So how could the fact that an internal state has content F, rather than content G, make a causal difference to the organism's behavior?

That is the second problem of mental causation, a central problem of Dretske's recent work on intentionality and the explanation of behavior. Let us now turn to our third and final problem: suppose then that we have somehow put together an account of how mental events can be causes of physical events. But these events, qua physical events, must have physical causes; it surely would be an anachronistic retrogression to Cartesian interactionism to think that there are physical events that have *only nonphysical* causes. To countenance such events would amount to the rejection of the causal-explanatory closure of the physical domain, a principle that seems minimally required of any serious form of physicalism. Thus, if a belief-desire pair, m, causes bodily movement b, it is highly plausible for a physicalist to suppose that the total physical state of the

12 We may take "syntactic properties" to be physical properties of inner states in terms of which psycho-computational processes are to be defined. This presupposes the computational view of mental processes; if that view is set aside, we may simply talk of physical properties of inner states to generate the second problem of mental causation. It is important to see that what I call the problem of syntacticalism arises even if the computational view is rejected.

13 Dretske's principal work in this vein is *Knowledge and the Flow of Information* (MIT Press, Cambridge, 1981); it is continued in *Explaining Behavior.*

agent at the time contains a full cause of b. So mental event m causes behavior b; and also a physical event, p, causes b. *What is the relationship between m and p?* If m and p are each countenanced as an independent sufficient cause of b, we would have to conclude that b is *overdetermined,* which seems absurd. Nor does it make sense to say that m and b are each only a *partial cause* and that they *together* make up a sufficient cause of b. Unquestionably, the simplest and most satisfying solution is *identity:* if we could say that m and p are one and the same event, the problem would vanish. That is the classic solution offered by identity materialism: m just is p, and here there is one cause of b, not two.

The identity solution is undoubtedly attractive, and perhaps feasible, when m and p are "token" events or states; however, its availability is in serious doubt if we are worried about the causal powers of mental *properties.* And the causal relevance of mental properties is precisely the problem we are at present concerned with, as may be recalled from our discussion of mental anomalism and syntacticalism. The difficulty is that mental anomalism apparently rules out the identity solution; for the property identity "m = p" entails that the two properties precisely correlate over all possible worlds. And even those who reject Davidson's arguments for mental anomalism, or mental anomalism itself, are likely to view mental-physical property identities as too strong and unwarranted.[14] Acceptance of such identities is often associated these days with mind–body theories commonly thought outmoded and discredited, such as reductionism and type-identity theory. Thus, the solution that m = p is not a real option for most of us; we need to know how the relation between m and p, each as a cause of behavior b, is to be understood.[15]

The foregoing I call the problem of "causal-explanatory exclusion". For the considerations of the sort we have just seen, when generalized, seem to show that there can be *at most* one complete and independent causal explanation, or one fully sufficient cause, for any single event.[16] It is clear that the phenomenon of causal-explanatory exclusion presents a special problem for mental causation, especially for mental-to-physical causation, if we assume, with most recent writers on mental causation, a

14 For example, most of those who take the multiple realizability of mental events seriously would reject psychophysical attribute identities.
15 Here I have developed this problem in terms of cause; it can be developed in a parallel way for causal explanations. See my "Mechanism, Purpose, and Explanatory Exclusion", Essay 13 of this volume.
16 For details see my "Mechanism, Purpose, and Explanatory Exclusion".

broadly physicalist framework. Thus, the core of the exclusion problem is to answer this question: *Given that every physical event has a physical cause, how is a mental cause also possible?*

Any theory of mental causation, even if it is primarily geared to either or both of the first two problems, must be responsive to the problem of exclusion. Having shown that mental properties, in spite of their anomalousness and extrinsicness, can be causal properties, one must further show how they find a place in an essentially physical world, a world whose causal structure is supposed to be defined at bottom by the causal-nomological relations among physical properties.

2. DRETSKE'S DUAL-EXPLANANDUM STRATEGY

Among the recent writers on mental causation, Dretske seems alone in being sensitive to the problem of exclusion, although he does not explicitly formulate it. He writes:[17]

> One doesn't hear anything about beliefs and desires in the neurobiological explanation of the origin, pattern or propagation of those electrical pulses that bring about muscle contractions and, hence, finger and arm movements. Hence, if it were muscle contractions, finger and arm movements, we were trying to explain, it would be hard to see, from *this* standpoint, what role content was supposed to play in this explanatory game. Unless, of course, one is prepared to say, as I am not, that neurobiologists systematically overlook an important causal factor in their explanatory efforts.

The relationship between an intentional and a neurobiological explanation of behavior is just a special case of the exclusion problem. It seems that here Dretske is accepting the essential point of this problem set forth in the preceding section. He is saying that if we take neurobiology to provide a complete causal account of muscle contractions and other bodily movements, it would be difficult to find a causal role for beliefs and desires with respect to these bodily happenings. That is, neurobiological explanations of bodily happenings would exclude these events' being *also* explained by rationalizing causes. Of course, if beliefs and desires were *reducible* to, or *reductively identifiable* with, neural states of the agent or organism, the two types of explanation could stand together, for rationalizations would then be reducible to biological explanations. If that should be the case, intentional states would be implicitly preserved in neurobiology, whether or not we "hear anything about beliefs and desires" in this sci-

17 "The Explanatory Role of Content", pp. 33–34.

ence, just as thermodynamic properties are implicitly preserved in statistical mechanics.

It seems that Dretske rejects the reduction option because he thinks it is incompatible with his commitment to a relational theory of content; as we saw, content properties on his view are relational properties essentially involving conditions external to the organism, and hence cannot be reduced to, or reductively identified with, internal neurobiological states of the organism. In a revealing passage, he writes:[18]

> I'm a realist about content, and my realism stems from a conviction that content has an essential and ineliminable role to play in the explanation of behavior. We don't describe one another as believing this and desiring that because it is, as it is with certain machines, merely a useful predictive strategy. Nor do we do it because we are too ignorant of neurobiology to know what is really in there making the limbs move. We describe each other in this way because our inner states actually have a content and it is this content that explains why we do what we do.

Here Dretske is doing a number of things: first, he is expressing his realism about the mental and mental causation; second, he sets his project as a defense of an "essential and ineliminable" causal-explanatory role for intentional properties; and third, and this is a related point, he is here apparently ruling out the possibility of reducing beliefs and desires to neurobiological states or processes. He seems to be saying that even if we knew all about the neurobiology of behavior production, there would still be something we would be missing, something concerning the causal fact of the matter, unless we also had a rationalizing explanation of it. It should be obvious that a solution to the exclusion problem that saves all of these claims would be hard to come by.

What then is Dretske's solution to the exclusion problem? The general approach he adopts can be called "the dual-explanandum strategy": Resolve the explanatory rivalry by holding that the two explanations do not in reality share the same explanandum. Since the explanations address different explananda, the potential for conflict vanishes. The same strategy has been used before: it has been held that rationalizations explain actions in a full-fledged intentional and teleological sense whereas physiological explanations explain "mere" bodily motion such as muscle contractions and limb movements.[19]

Dretske's implementation of the dual-explanandum approach is

18 Ibid., p. 32.
19 See Georg von Wright's discussion in *Explanation and Understanding* (Cornell University Press, Ithaca, 1971), ch. 3.

different and more sophisticated. His point is that rationalizations explain *behavior,* that is, what we *do,* not bodily movements, while these bodily happenings are just what neurobiology and other physical theory explain. Thus, the distinction between behavior, or doings, and bodily movements such as muscle contractions ("motor output") is crucial to Dretske's overall account. And Dretske does not disappoint: an elegant account of behavior is developed in the first two chapters of *Explaining Behavior.* Briefly, Dretske's concept of behavior is, in his own words, that of "endogenously produced movement, movement that has its causal origin *within* the system whose parts are moving".[20] Let M be some bodily movement of organism S and C its cause: for this to be an instance of behavior, it must be the case that C is an internal state of S. Thus, for Wilbur to raise his arm, it must be the case that his arm rises as an effect of some state *within* Wilbur. This contrasts with the case in which his arm rises, as an effect of someone else's grasping the hand and pulling it up. In the latter case, the cause of the motor output is not internal to Wilbur, and this is why it does not count as his *doing* something: there is here no action or behavior on his part.

We must be careful, Dretske tells us, to identify behavior not with motor output M which, as it happens, has an internal cause C, but rather with the relational structure, *C's causing M.* What Wilbur did is to cause his arm to rise, and the behavior consists in *some internal state C of Wilbur causing M.* Thus, to explain what Wilbur did in this case, according to Dretske, is to explain why some internal C in Wilbur caused M. In brief, behaviors are *causings,* and explanations of behavior must explain these causings by providing *causes of causings.* Neurobiology has M, the "product" or "result" of behavior, as its proper explanandum; it can also explain *how,* that is, through what sequence of intervening states, C led to the production of M. However, it is the proper job of rationalizations to explain *why C caused M,* and in order to do this, they must specify events or states that cause C to cause M.

How successful is the dual-explanandum approach in resolving the exclusion issue? Before we examine Dretske's version of this approach, there is an important general point to notice about this strategy: *a successful execution of the strategy requires commitment to dualism.* For the sundering of the explanandum is only the first step; there still is the second, crucial step that must be taken if the exclusion problem is to be solved. This is so because we need yet to rule out the possibility that one or the other of

20 *Explaining Behavior,* p. 2.

the two explananda that have been distinguished is amenable to both a rationalizing and a physical explanation (where is Dretske's argument to show that behavior as he conceives it isn't also neurobiologically explainable?). As long as this possibility is alive, the exclusion issue remains. To resolve it, friends of this approach must claim, for each of the two explananda, that it is not explainable both rationally and physically. To hold that neither is explainable rationally defeats the whole enterprise of vindicating the causal-explanatory powers of reasons; so that is not an option for the friends of dual explananda. There is only one other choice: to claim that one of the explananda, namely one that is rationally explainable, is not explainable physically. So this leaves us with phenomena in the world which cannot be explained physically; or, to speak in terms of causes, there are phenomena in the world that have nonphysical causes. These things are either physical or nonphysical; if they are nonphysical, we have a dualism of entities, and dual systems of causes and explanations; if they are physical, some physical things have only nonphysical causes, a form of Cartesian causal dualism and a violation of the causal closure of the physical. Either way, we seem stuck with a robust form of mind–body dualism.

Dretske wants to give intentional psychology a special and ineliminable causal-explanatory job to do. The job he assigns to it is to explain a special set of explananda, relational structures of the form *C's causing M*, where C is some internal state of a behaving system S and M is S's motor output. If the explanatory job is to be a genuine and substantive one, which it must be if it is to vindicate intentional psychology, these causings must be regarded as full-fledged entities in our ontology. Are they then physical things or nonphysical things? M is motor output, and Dretske takes C, its cause, as an inner physical state; so it is likely that Dretske would consider these relational structures as physical as well. In any case, if they are nonphysical, we have a dualism of entities; if they are part of the physical domain, Dretske is stuck with mental causes of physical phenomena.

Is this a violation of the causal closure of the physical? As we saw, once we recognize a nonphysical cause of a physical event, the closure principle requires us to recognize a physical cause of it as well; and once we have these two causes of a single event, the only way to make sense of the situation is some form of identity or reduction option. Dretske is a naturalist and physicalist; and we can be confident that he would not tolerate violation of the physical causal closure. So this only leaves the reduction-identity option for him. But isn't this option ruled out by something we noted earlier, namely his apparent rejection of the reductive resolution of the exclusion problem for rationalizing and biological explanations of behavior? And it may seem also inconsistent with something that Dretske clearly holds, namely that content properties are not reducible to biological properties.

The apparent inconsistency can be seen to vanish if we note that different reduction bases may be involved here. Dretske can hold his non-reductive thesis concerning content in relation to the *internal biology* of the organism as the reduction base, while endorsing at the same time the reducibility of content properties to a wider physical base. This wider reduction base would be an appropriate spatiotemporal stretch of physical environment around the organism; it would include all the physical facts and conditions, past and present, upon which the content properties of the organism supervene.

But if this reductive option is accepted, how plausible is it to claim an essential and ineliminable causal role for content properties of intentional states? What our considerations make plain is that if you accept a broadly physicalist framework, there really can be no independent causal job for mental items – that is, independent of, and ineliminable with respect to, physical items. To insist on an irreducible causal role for the mental is destined to lead to forms of dualism. Dretske's project of finding an ineliminable causal role for content properties makes sense only if the ineliminability is understood in relation to the *internal* biology of the behaving organism. We should note that "ineliminable" is not synonymous with "irreducible" or "independent": one could plausibly argue that to be reduced is to be conserved, not to be eliminated. If the ineliminability Dretske has in mind for the causal role of reasons is consistent with its reducibility, I have no complaint whatever. The only point I want to make is this: if the causal role of reasons is to be preserved within a physicalist framework, the exclusion problem tells us that it must be physically reduced.

Contentful psychological states, for Dretske, are essentially relational, involving as they do ecological and historical conditions external to the organism. Thus, a psychological explanation invoking such a state necessarily involves a *relational explanans,* which the *internal* biological theory of the organism is unable to supply. Thus, the point is not that these psychological explanantia are nonbiological or nonphysical, but rather that they are relational and hence noninternal biological and noninternal physical. The contrast between psychology and biology, therefore, comes to this: biology, being conceived by Dretske to concern only the internal biological-physical properties of the organism, can explain motor outputs

296

of the organism, but is incapable of explaining why internal state C causes a given motor output M (we don't as yet have an argument for this latter claim). To explain this causal-relational structure, we must resort to facts concerning the organism's relationship to its environment, and this is where intentional psychology, in virtue of its representational and semantic character, can have a role.

Our discussion has shown, I believe, that Dretske's distinction between doings and things done, or between behavior and motor output, does not in itself solve the exclusion problem. The reason is that given his commitment to naturalism and physicalism, he cannot go the full distance with the dual-explanandum approach. In fact, the dual-explanandum approach is not the crucial element in his resolution of the exclusion problem; what has the crucial role here is his *reductive account of content*, the program of his *Knowledge and the Flow of Information* and subsequent works. So I am construing Dretske as a reductionist about content: the reduction-identity option is his way out of the exclusion problem. As we saw, however, that option comes into apparent conflict with mental anomalism, and Dretske would have to contend with the usual arguments in support of anomalism and antireductionism. Dretske describes his program on content as the "naturalization" of content; to resolve the exclusion problem, however, naturalization must be understood in the sense of "physicalization", not in the narrower sense which only requires expulsion of the supernatural, the theological, and the essentially normative-evaluative. I will have more to say about the issue of reduction and supervenience in our discussion of the substance of Dretske's proposals.

3. DRETSKE'S ACCOUNT OF HOW REASONS EXPLAIN

The explanandum of a rationalization, according to Dretske, has the following form: *some internal state C of organism S causes motor output M*. Two aspects of this explanandum can be objects of explanation: *how* does C cause M? and *why* does C cause M? On Dretske's account, neurobiology is concerned with the how-question; intentional psychology with the why-question. But the second explanatory question can be further subdivided, for it can be construed as asking either: (a) why does C cause M *at this time rather than another*? or (b) why does C cause *output M rather than M**? If we are asking (a), we are asking for a "triggering cause", Dretske says, and it can be answered by providing a specific event that triggered the causal process (C → M) by causing C. (E.g., "Why did the thermostat

297

turn on the furnace now? Because the room temperature dropped below 70 degrees just now".) Question (b), however, asks for a "structuring cause": to answer it, we must show how C got "hooked up" with the agent's motor output system so that C causes output of type M rather than another kind. (E.g., "Why did the thermostat turn on the furnace rather than the dishwasher? Because its bimetallic element is wired to the furnace, not the dishwasher, in such a way that it functions as a switch for it".) The causal-explanatory job of reasons, according to Dretske, is to serve as the structuring cause of motor output.

Let's look at how this is supposed to work. What needs to be explained is how some internal state of the system, in virtue of its content property, explains why C got hooked up with M. As I understand it, Dretske's story goes like this: Suppose that for some reason it is advantageous to system S to emit motor output M when, and only when, property F is instantiated in its vicinity. How can a reliable connection between F and the production of M be secured? Obviously, S must be equipped with an F-detector or indicator, an appropriate sensory receptor, that registers F just when F is present in its vicinity. When F is detected, the F-detector, we may assume, goes into a certain determinate state. So far we have not been clear as to whether internal state C is a "token" or "type"; we hereby declare C to be a token state.[21] We will think of C as a token state of the F-detector caused by F's presence in S's vicinity at the time; thus the F-detector registers the presence of F by going into state C. But this happens only because C has a certain neurobiological property, N, and *in general* the F-detector registers the presence of F by entering a state with property N. Thus, the registering at t of F by the F-detector consists in the detector's going into a token state with property N at t. Thus, the problem of securing a reliable connection between the presence of F and the emission of motor output M is now reduced to that of securing a reliable connection between occurrences of an internal state with N and emissions of M. Dretske's point is that when the emission of M in the presence of F is advantageous to the organism (e.g., it satisfies some needs of the organism; the organism is rewarded when it emits M in the presence of F, punished when it fails to do so), the N $\rightarrow$ M connection will often develop, although the biology of how this happens may still be largely unknown. This is nothing other than the process of learning; so

---

21 It seems that in *Explaining Behavior*, Dretske uses the letter "C" ambiguously, sometimes to stand for a token state and sometimes for a state type (similarly, "Si" in "The Explanatory Role of Content"). I have disambiguated "C", using "C" for token states and "N" for types (properties) of states.

Dretske's point is just that familiar associative learning of this kind takes place.

Thus, the fact that property N registers F plays an essential role in N's being causally hooked up with M in system S, so that whenever the organism (or its F-detector) goes into a state of kind N, motor output of kind M is produced. On Dretske's informational account of content, the nomic correlation between F and N implies that token state C carries *informational content* F; and C does this in virtue of being an instance of N, that is, an N-state. And when certain further conditions are met, we may say that C *represents* F, or has the *content property of representing* F; and C comes to have F (or that F is present in the vicinity) as its intentional content. As Dretske emphasizes, the fact that N is "recruited" or "promoted" as a cause of M is essential to the representational character of N itself; it is in virtue of this fact that N acquires the *function of* indicating F, beyond merely de facto indicating F. It is this acquisition of function that makes possible *misrepresentation:* if the organism, or its F-detector, goes into an N-state, when no F is present, the organism (or its state) still represents F, although this is a case of misrepresentation. On Dretske's view, an internal state like this, that is, a representational state capable of misrepresentation, exhibits the sort of intentionality appropriate to beliefs.

But where does desire come in? Dretske associates desire with the possibility of learning through reinforcement. The N → M causal hookup can develop only if the organism has a structure of preferences and aversions that make reinforcement possible; this is the assumption we made above when we assumed that the emission of M in the presence of F is "advantageous" to the organism. So both belief and desire play a causal role in the establishment of the N → M causal connection.

This in brief is Dretske's account. He will be the first to admit that the account as summarized here is only a prototypic model that is not capable, without much refinement and enrichment, of handling more complex cases of behavior causation in which intentional states with more complex and abstract content interanimate each other to generate decisions and actions. For example, it isn't obvious how the model will handle even the basic mode of rationalization that proceeds by way of means–end practical reasoning.[22] He will say, though, that the simple model at least shows the possibility of how intentional states, in virtue of their content, can cause, and provide causal understanding of, our behavior.

22 See, however, ch. 6 ("The Interactive Nature of Reasons") of *Explaining Behavior.*

Dretske's is an original and suggestive account, one that takes the representational character of intentional states seriously; it is in many ways more direct and straightforward as a response to syntacticalism than other available responses, such as what we may call the "narrow explanans" strategy (e.g., Fodor[23]), which attempts to find nonrelational, "narrow" content properties to do the necessary causal-explanatory work, and the diametrically opposite approach, what may be called the "wide explanandum" strategy (e.g., Burge[24]), which externalizes the explananda of rationalizations to match their wide, relational explanantia. Unlike the former, Dretske's approach continues to work with wide content properties; unlike the latter, it does not externalize the explananda, although it does construe them relationally.

4. A PUZZLE

I want to begin by considering exactly how Dretske's account is an account of the explanatory role of reasons in behavior causation. As may be recalled, what we want is an account of how question (i) below is, or can be, correctly answered by (ii).

(i) Why did agent (or system) S do A at t?
(ii) Because S had reason R at t.

For S to have reason R, we may suppose, is for S to be in some internal state with content property R (the property of representing, say, that F is present). Given this and Dretske's analysis of behavior or "doings", our problem is to explain how (b) below is an answer to (a):

(a) Why did some internal state C of S cause M at t?
(b) Because S was in an internal state C at t, and C had content property R.

It will be convenient to use locutions of the form "state C's having property R at t", and think of causal relations, causal relevance, etc., as holding between items denoted by such expressions. This will facilitate talk of the causal relevance of properties of token events and states. Thus, the expression "C's having R at t caused M" is to mean the same as our earlier expression "C, in virtue of having R, caused M". (M itself can be similarly expressed, but that won't be necessary.) The use of this locution does not prevent us from taking token states or events also as causes: for

23 See J. A. Fodor, *Psychosemantics* (MIT Press, Cambridge, 1987).
24 See Tyler Burge, "Individualism and Psychology", *Philosophical Review* 95 (1986), pp. 3–45, especially section I.

C to cause M is for there to be some property P such that C's having P causes M. This shows that the adoption of the locution is not a mere linguistic decision; it reflects the view that causal relations between token events hold in virtue of the properties these events have, and that it makes sense to speak of causal relations between properties.[25]

In any event, Dretske's project is to give an account of how (b) can be a correct explanation in response to (a). Now, the heart of his account, as sketched in the preceding section, is that content properties of inner states discharge their causal-explanatory role by explaining how the appropriate hookups between these internal states and motor output were established. Property R, being a representational property, is a relational property, and when token state C with R occurs, this is in virtue of C's having a nonrelational, intrinsic neural property N. N corresponds to things like a specific degree of the thermometric property of a given thermometer (e.g., a specific height of the mercury column) and the specific degree of curvature of the bimetallic element of a thermostat. We may call such an N "an internal indicating property" for the given content property. And it is C's having N at t that causes the occurrence of M at the time (after the N → M structure has been established). Dretske does not explicitly advert to such internal properties with the indicated causal role, but I believe this is because he uses "C", at least sometimes, to denote an event type rather than a token (as we do), so that for him C plays the role of our N; in any case, properties like N must exist.

I think we can think of Dretske's account as proceeding in the following way. First, consider inserting the following between (a) and (b):

(1) Because internal state C of S had N at t, where N is an internal indicating property of R, and N is properly hooked up with M in system S.

We can think of (1) as having the role of bridging the gap between (b) and (a); that is, (b) correctly explains (a) because (b) explains (1), which in turn explains (a). I think we can accept (1) as an explanation of (a). But how, or why, does (b) explain (1), or its crucial component, that N is hooked up with M in S? The reason why this component is crucial should be obvious: for Dretske, rationalizations must account for why M, rather than another type of motor output M*, is produced when S goes into a state with R, and the part of (1) that helps do this is precisely the clause that the N → M causal hookup now exists in S. As I understand it, it is the heart of Dretske's account that content property R figures in a causal

25 This is not a new assumption; it underlies the criticism of anomalous monism we saw earlier, and is a presupposition of the first two problems of mental causation.

explanation of how the N → M causal structure through a process of conditioning and learning came to be established in S. So our question is this: exactly how does the fact that C has content property R explain this?

What puzzles me is this. C is a token state that occurs at t,[26] whereas the N → M structure that is present in S at t and is causally responsible for the production of M on this occasion has been there all along, having been emplaced before t, perhaps much before t. So how could C, or C's having R *at t,* causally explain why or how the N → M structure came to be in S? On Dretske's theory, the fact that N is an internal indicator property corresponding to content property R is a causally crucial factor in N's being "recruited" as a cause of M. But what explains this recruitment is the past history of instantiations of these properties (i.e., the particular history of reinforcements), along with the general nomic correlation between N and F. So, again, how can C's having R at t bring it about that C's having N at t causes M?[27]

This difficulty can be somewhat mitigated, I believe, if the story is put, more explicitly and consciously, in terms of explanation rather than causation. For we can imagine saying something like this:

> Look at it this way. In trying to explain why C caused M, we invoke the fact that C has content property R, the property of representing F. And C represents F in virtue of having neural property N. Of course, C occurs now, and it now has property R. So I am not saying that C, or C's now having R, caused the N → M hookup in the organism. It's rather this: when we say that C has R, or represents F, we are saying a lot more than what's happening now. For the organism has the capacity now to represent F because it has had a certain history of learning and conditioning, a history of interactions with its environment and of internal changes caused by such interactions. In particular, the organism is now in a state that represents F because it has in the past exercised its capacity to indicate F and learned to associate F-indications (instances of N) with a certain motor output M. It is this historical background of the organism's capacity to represent F that grounds the explanatory power of C's now having R in explaining why C causes M.

26 The reader may recall that we earlier chose to take C to be a token state, whereas there is some ambiguity as to whether Dretske takes C as a token or type. If C is taken as a state type, the question being raised here can of course be stated in terms of an *instance* of C, that is, a token C-state.

27 This seems related to, but not identical with, a complaint that Robert Cummins makes against Dretske in his commentary on "The Explanatory Role of Content" in *Contents of Thought,* p. 51. Cummins says that Dretske changes the subject by moving from his original project of explaining why C, in virtue of having content property R, causes M to one of explaining how the C → M causal structure was acquired by the system. I am assuming that an explanation of the acquisition of the C → M structure can be a part of an explanation of the original explanandum.

This strikes me not altogether implausible as a way of telling the story Dretske wants to tell about content. In the next section, I will present a modified Dretskean account that resolves my puzzle and serves as a framework for the explanatory story just told.

5. A MODIFIED DRETSKEAN ACCOUNT

Consider a system S in which the N → M (Dretske's C → M) causal structure has already been established in the required way. In particular, the system is now able to represent (not merely indicate) the presence of F in its vicinity. As we saw, this means that the system represents F at t just in case it enters at t into an N-state. Having acquired the capacity to represent F, the system is also capable of *misrepresenting* F: it misrepresents that F is present just in case it represents that F is present when F is not present. How does the system manage to represent F when F is not there? By entering an N-state, of course: S misrepresents F just in case S enters an N-state in the absence of F. Whether S, or an internal state of S, has at t the content property of representing F does not depend on the presence at t of F in S's vicinity, nor on any other external condition at t; it is solely a matter of the occurrence of an N-state in S.

Given this, it is natural and plausible to think of S's representing F at t, or S's being at t in a state that represents F, as supervenient on S's internal N-state at t. (This isn't to say that the property of representing F supervenes on N *in general*, for all systems; we are here talking about S with its particular history and ecology.) Considerations of misrepresentation make this plausible: even if F is not present at t outside S, S will represent that F is present (and hence misrepresent F) as long as an N-state is realized in S.[28] True, there is a dependence on the history of learning and conditioning: on Dretske's account, the relationship between the occurrence of N in S and S's representing F depends on S's learning history that has entrenched the N → M causal structure. But the existence *now* in S of this causal structure is exactly the present repository, so to speak, of the causal powers of S's representing F. The causal role in S of state N consists of two essential components: (1) it is typically caused by the presence of F in S's vicinity, and (2) it causes S to emit motor output M.

It seems to me that the foregoing is consistent with the main components of Dretske's account. Notice, though, that our story makes the content property of representing F supervenient on neural property N. To

---

28 Although in time the N-state may acquire a new indicator function and come to underlie S's capacity to represent a property other than F.

repeat, I am not saying that this content property in general, in all organisms and systems, supervenes on N, but only that for system S as it now exists, with its history of learning and with the N → M structure already in place, the supervenience holds. Given that the occurrence of this content property supervenes on N, it is appealing to think of the causal role of this content property as itself supervenient on the causal powers of the subvenient property N. Thus, whatever causes a given token N-state also causes it to be a token R-state, and whatever is caused by this state's having R is caused by its having N. In S, the causal powers of R are supervenient on the causal powers of N.

This greatly simplifies the picture: the causal powers of the content state lie in the neural state on which the content state supervenes. We now have a solution to the exclusion problem: content properties have no independent causal powers of their own; their causal powers (hence their explanatory powers) depend wholly on those of the underlying neural properties. As a response to the problem of syntacticalism, our modified account says this: although content properties are relational properties in the sense that an organism's capacity to instantiate them depends on its past history and relationship to external events, the causal power of a given instance of a content property lies wholly in the causal power of the neural state on which it supervenes. The relationality of the content property plays no role in behavior causation; thus, the account is consistent with the supervenience condition stressed by syntacticalism, the requirement that the proximate cause of physical behavior must supervene on the synchronous internal physical state of the organism. However, the account need not be committed to a broader supervenience principle for content properties in general, to the effect that what content properties a given organism instantiates at a time must supervene solely on the concurrent internal physical properties it instantiates; for physically identical organisms with different histories can differ in respect of their capacity for having content properties.[29]

Let us see how this modified account stands in relation to Dretske's. The crucial difference between them is that in the revised picture content states supervene on the synchronous neural states of the system, whereas Dretske thinks of content states as essentially relational and hence nonsu-

29 These remarks by no means settle all the issues raised by syntacticalism; for one thing, the account being sketched needs to be worked out in much greater detail, taking into account the diverse ways in which content can involve external factors. Its relationship to the "narrow content" strategy must be thought through as well.

pervenient. I am suggesting that if we push Dretske's account in a certain way it is in fact natural, perhaps inevitable, to think of them as supervenient.[30] But what happens to Dretske's carefully worked-out story about the learning and conditioning and its bearing on the establishment of the N → M structure? In the new picture, the story plays a similar role but its "location" is different: its new role is to explain how system S came to have the capacity to represent F, and do so by entering an inner state with N. This in effect is an explanation of how in S the content property of representing F came to supervene on N. The history of learning and conditioning whereby the N → M structure came to be entrenched in S is of course a crucial part of this explanatory story. But the present causal power of this content state is wholly and exclusively dependent on the causal powers of underlying N; it has nothing directly to do with the history of the system – in particular, nothing to do with the entrenchment of the N → M structure in the system. A given instantiation of the content property causes something in virtue of the fact that the instance of N on which it supervenes causes it. This solves "the puzzle" of the preceding section.

Let me conclude with the following summary. In Dretske's account, C's having content property R explains why S emits M (rather than M*) by explaining how an N → M structure (rather than an N → M* structure) came to be present in S. Our puzzle was how C's now having R can explain the emplacement of the N → M structure or its present existence in S. The modified account represents the situation in two stages:

Stage 1: Why does C's having R at t cause M?
Because C's having R at t supervenes on C's having N at t, and at t there exists in S an N → M causal structure.

Stage 2: But why is the N → M structure present in S? How did content property R (i.e., the property of representing F) come to supervene on N in S? And how did S acquire the capacity to represent F?
Because, in S, N is the internal indicator property of F, and through a process of conditioning and learning the N → M causal structure was established in S; this means also that in S, R came to supervene on N. In the process, N has acquired the function of indicating F, and this is how S came to have the capacity to represent F.

30 I want to note that I am not myself advocating this form of supervenience thesis for intentional states. A supervenience thesis of this form is committed to physical reductionism concerning intentionality (I earlier argued that Dretske is committed to content reductionism). My claim is conditional: if we want to make sense of intentional causation of physical behavior, the only viable way seems to involve supervenience of intentional states on physical processes.

The Stage 2 explanation may seem to have three distinct explananda, but that is only an appearance; for Dretske they are interrelated and interdependent components of a single story. The fact that Dretske's original account is broken down into two explanations, each with its own explanandum, is important. This is precisely what allows us to dispel the puzzle; it does this by separating the question of how an intentional state, with the causal power it has, can cause a certain motor output from the question of how it came to have that causal power and how the organism came to have the capacity to be in that intentional state.

6. VARIETIES OF INTENTIONAL CAUSATION

Consider cases in which one intentional state (say, a belief) causes another intentional state (say, another belief). There surely are such cases, but it is not at all clear how Dretske's model of intentional causation, with its essential involvement of motor output, can be adapted for them. However, the idea that underlies our modified account yields the following simple and natural account: Belief b_1 causes belief b_2 in virtue of the fact that b_1 supervenes on N_1, b_2 supervenes on N_2, and N_1 stands in an appropriate causal relation with N_2. This model of "supervenient causation",[31] in which mental causation is treated as "supervenient causation" dependent on underlying physical-biological causal processes, is applicable to mental causal relations in general, not just to cases involving intentional states and behavior or actions. It applies to cases in which a physical event causes an intentional state (e.g., causation of perceptual beliefs): a physical event causes an intentional state in virtue of its causing another physical state upon which the intentional state supervenes. What I have called "the modified Dretskean account" is simply an application of this model of supervenient causation in a Dretskean environment.

There is another class of intentional causation seemingly untouched by Dretske's account, cases in which an intentional state, *in virtue of its content property,* causes a bodily event which is not motor output in the familiar sense, and, more importantly, which is *not rationalized* by the content property. The thought that your airplane is about to take off makes your muscles tense and your mouth go dry. Certain thoughts, in virtue of their content, can cause all sorts of bodily changes not standardly thought of as doings or actions; your muscles grow tense and your pulse quickens, you blush and perspire, facial tics are set off, tears well up in your eyes, etc. If

31 For more details on supervenient causation see "Epiphenomenal and Supervenient Causation", Essay 6 of this volume, and "Postscripts on Mental Causation", section 1.

you insist on calling these responses "behavior", I have no objection; the main point is that there is no obvious or natural way to fit such cases to Dretske's model of learning and reinforcement. These cases are interesting because they are cases in which content properties serve as causal properties, but not as rationalizing properties; it is because my thought is a thought that p that it causes me to blush, but my blushing is not rationalized by the thought. Moreover, such "nonrationalizing intentional causation", as we might call it, can occur, it seems, in instances of mental-to-mental causation as well. Because of the "wiring" in your brain, the thought that p can cause the thought that q, even if p and q have no significant logical or conceptual relationship, and the thought that q is not in any sense rationalized by the thought that p; we know psychological associations occur in all sorts of ways. We are also familiar with cases in which phenomenal mental events ("qualia") cause intentional states (recall Proust's madeleines).

Such cases are handled, routinely and uniformly, by the model of supervenient causation: the thought that p supervenes on a certain neural state, which causes the blushing, the muscle tensing, etc. The model applies uniformly to all cases of mental causation, including causal relations involving nonintentional, phenomenal mental states. In contrast, Dretske's account is expressly constructed to explain a limited subclass of intentional causation, cases in which intentional states are rationalizing causes of bodily behavior, and there seems no obvious or natural way to generalize it. We can also see the attraction of the two-stage account stated at the end of the preceding section. The explanation in Stage 1 applies to mental causation in general; the explanation in Stage 2 concerns one particular way in which a content property can come to supervene on a neurobiological property. We can think of Dretske's interesting theory chiefly as a contribution to Stage 2: it elaborates one important way in which that often comes about – learning and conditioning. But perhaps that need not be the only way. Such supervenience relations might hold because of the genes; and there seems no difficulty in imagining a surgical construction or implantation of the $N \to M$ structure in an organism (Dretske would claim that in such cases the organism lacks the capacity to represent F). The point I want to stress is that the provenance of these structures makes no difference to the Stage 1 explanations. Dretske allows only learning to generate structures appropriate for rational causation; that might be true – this can certainly be debated. No matter how this debate is resolved, the separation of the two explanatory stages makes us see that questions about how organisms come to have contentful intentional states can be discussed independently of questions about how the metaphysics of mental causation is to be explained.

Crucial to the model of supervenient causation as applied here to intentional causation is the claim that in spite of their relationality with respect to external conditions, content properties can be thought of as supervenient on the internal neural-physical properties of organisms, organisms with certain histories and related in appropriate ways to environmental conditions. The main trick is to isolate these noninternal, relational properties as specifications of the class of systems and organisms to which the supervenience claim is to apply. Thus, we can think of these relational properties as "parameters" that fix a context within which supervenience claims can be formulated rather than as part of such claims. (We may call such supervenience relations "parametric supervenience".) Even if we hold, with Dretske, that content properties, as representational properties, do not in general supervene on the synchronic internal physical properties of organisms, that need not rule out a supervenience thesis restricted by a specified set of historical and ecological parameters. But I must leave this idea in the form of a programmatic proposal here; a general account of this concept of supervenience and its application to mental causation needs to be worked out.

16

Multiple realization and the metaphysics of reduction

I. INTRODUCTION

It is part of today's conventional wisdom in philosophy of mind that psychological states are "multiply realizable", and are in fact so realized, in a variety of structures and organisms. We are constantly reminded that any mental state, say pain, is capable of "realization", "instantiation", or "implementation" in widely diverse neural-biological structures in humans, felines, reptiles, mollusks, and perhaps other organisms further removed from us. Sometimes we are asked to contemplate the possibility that extraterrestrial creatures with a biochemistry radically different from the earthlings', or even electro-mechanical devices, can "realize the same psychology" that characterizes humans. This claim, to be called hereafter "the Multiple Realization Thesis" ("MR",[1] for short), is widely accepted by philosophers, especially those who are inclined to favor the functionalist line on mentality. I will not here dispute the truth of MR, although what I will say may prompt a reassessment of the considerations that have led to its nearly universal acceptance.

And there is an influential and virtually uncontested view about the philosophical significance of MR. This is the belief that MR refutes psychophysical reductionism once and for all. In particular, the classic psychoneural identity theory of Feigl and Smart, the so-called "type physicalism", is standardly thought to have been definitively dispatched by MR to the heap of obsolete philosophical theories of mind. At any rate, it is this claim, that MR proves the physical irreducibility of the mental, that will be the starting point of my discussion.

This paper is descended from an unpublished paper, "The Disunity of Psychology as a Working Hypothesis?", which was circulated in the early 1980s. I am indebted to the following persons, among others, for helpful comments: Fred Feldman, Hilary Kornblith, Barry Loewer, Brian McLaughlin, Joe Mendola, Marcelo Sabates, and James Van Cleve.
1 On occasion, "MR" will refer to the *phenomenon* of multiple realization rather than the *claim* that such a phenomenon exists; there should be no danger of confusion.

Evidently, the current popularity of antireductionist physicalism is owed, for the most part, to the influence of the MR-based antireductionist argument originally developed by Hilary Putnam and elaborated further by Jerry Fodor[2] – rather more so than to the "anomalist" argument associated with Donald Davidson.[3] For example, in their elegant paper on nonreductive physicalism,[4] Geoffrey Hellman and Frank Thompson motivate their project in the following way:

> Traditionally, physicalism has taken the form of reductionism – roughly, that all scientific terms can be given explicit definitions in physical terms. Of late there has been growing awareness, however, that reductionism is an unreasonably strong claim.

But why is reductionism "unreasonably strong"? In a footnote Hellman and Thompson explain, citing Fodor's "Special Sciences":

> Doubts have arisen especially in connection with functional explanation in the higher-level sciences (psychology, linguistics, social theory, etc.). Functional predicates may be physically realizable in heterogeneous ways, so as to elude physical definition.

And Ernest LePore and Barry Loewer tell us this:[5]

> It is practically received wisdom among philosophers of mind that psychological properties (including content properties) are not identical to neurophysiological or other physical properties. The relationship between psychological and neurophysiological properties is that the latter *realize* the former. Furthermore, a single psychological property might (in the sense of conceptual possibility) be realized by a large number, perhaps an infinitely many, of different physical properties and even by non-physical properties.

They then go on to sketch the reason why MR, on their view, leads to the rejection of mind–body reduction:[6]

> If there are infinitely many physical (and perhaps nonphysical) properties which can realize F then F will not be reducible to a basic physical prop-

2 Jerry Fodor, "Special Sciences, or the Disunity of Sciences as a Working Hypothesis" (hereafter, "Special Sciences"), *Synthese* 28 (1974): 97–115; reprinted in *Representations* (Cambridge: MIT Press, 1981), and as the introductory chapter in Fodor, *The Language of Thought* (New York: Crowell, 1975).
3 Donald Davidson, "Mental Events", reprinted in *Essays on Actions and Events* (Oxford: Oxford University Press, 1980).
4 "Physicalism: Ontology, Determination, and Reduction", *Journal of Philosophy* 72 (1975): 551–64. The two quotations below are from p. 551.
5 "More on Making Mind Matter", *Philosophical Topics* 17 (1989): 175–92. The quotation is from p. 179.
6 "More on Making Mind Matter", p. 180.

erty. Even if F can only be realized by finitely many basic physical properties it might not be reducible to a basic physical property since the disjunction of these properties might not itself be a basic physical property (i.e., occur in a fundamental physical law). We will understand 'multiple realizability' as involving such irreducibility.

This antireductionist reading of MR continues to this day; in a recent paper, Ned Block writes:[7]

> Whatever the merits of physiological reductionism, it is not available to the cognitive science point of view assumed here. According to cognitive science, the essence of the mental is computational, and any computational state is "multiply realizable" by physiological or electronic states that are not identical with one another, and so content cannot be identified with any one of them.

Considerations of these sorts have succeeded in persuading a large majority of philosophers of mind[8] to reject reductionism and type physicalism. The upshot of all this has been impressive: MR has not only ushered in "nonreductive physicalism" as the new orthodoxy on the mind–body problem, but in the process has put the very word "reductionism" in disrepute, making reductionisms of all stripes an easy target of disdain and curt dismissals.

I believe a reappraisal of MR is overdue. There is something right and instructive in the antireductionist claim based on MR and the basic argument in its support, but I believe that we have failed to follow out the implications of MR far enough, and have as a result failed to appreciate its full significance. One specific point that I will argue is this: the popular view that psychology constitutes an *autonomous special science,* a doctrine heavily promoted in the wake of the MR-inspired antireductionist dialectic, may in fact be inconsistent with the real implications of MR. Our discussion will show that MR, when combined with certain plausible metaphysical and methodological assumptions, leads to some surprising conclusions about the status of the mental and the nature of psychology as a science. I hope it will become clear that the fate of type physicalism is not among the more interesting consequences of MR.

7 In "Can the Mind Change the World?", in *Meaning and Method: Essays in Honor of Hilary Putnam,* ed. George Boolos (Cambridge: Cambridge University Press, 1990), p. 146.
8 They include Richard Boyd, "Materialism Without Reductionism: What Physicalism Does Not Entail", in Block, *Readings in Philosophy of Psychology,* vol. 1; Block, in "Introduction: What is Functionalism?" in his anthology just cited, pp. 178–79; John Post, *The Faces of Existence* (Ithaca: Cornell University Press, 1987); Derk Pereboom and Hilary Kornblith, "The Metaphysics of Irreducibility", *Philosophical Studies* 63 1991): 125–45. One philosopher who is not impressed by the received view of MR is David Lewis; see his "Review of Putnam", in Block, *Readings in Philosophy of Psychology,* vol. 1.

II. MULTIPLE REALIZATION

It was Putnam, in a paper published in 1967,[9] who first injected MR into debates on the mind–body problem. According to him, the classic reductive theories of mind presupposed the following naive picture of how psychological kinds (properties, event and state types, etc.) are correlated with physical kinds:

For each psychological kind *M* there is a unique physical (presumably, neurobiological) kind *P* that is *nomologically coextensive* with it (i.e., as a matter of law, any system instantiates *M* at *t* iff that system instantiates *P* at *t*).

(We may call this "the Correlation Thesis".) So take pain: the Correlation Thesis has it that pain as an event kind has a neural substrate, perhaps as yet not fully and precisely identified, that, as a matter of law, always cooccurs with it in all pain-capable organisms and structures. Here there is no mention of species or types of organisms or structures: the neural correlate of pain is invariant across biological species and structure types. In his 1967 paper, Putnam pointed out something that, in retrospect, seems all too obvious:[10]

Consider what the brain-state theorist has to do to make good his claims. He has to specify a physical-chemical state such that any organism (not just a mammal) is in pain if and only if (a) it possesses a brain of a suitable physical-chemical structure; and (b) its brain is in that physical-chemical state. This means that the physical-chemical state in question must be a possible state of a mammalian brain, a reptilian brain, a mollusc's brain (octopuses are mollusca, and certainly feel pain), etc. At the same time, it must not be a possible brain of any physically possible creature that cannot feel pain.

Putnam went on to argue that the Correlation Thesis was *empirically false*. Later writers, however, have stressed the multiple realizability of the mental as a *conceptual* point: it is an a priori, conceptual fact about psychological properties that they are "second-order" physical properties, and that their specification does not include constraints on the manner of their

---

9 Hilary Putnam, "Psychological Predicates", in W. H. Capitan and D. D. Merrill, eds., *Art, Mind, and Religion* (Pittsburgh: University of Pittsburgh, 1967); reprinted with a new title, "The Nature of Mental States," in Ned Block, ed., *Readings in Philosophy of Psychology*, vol. 1 (Cambridge: Harvard University Press, 1980).
10 "The Nature of Mental States", p. 228 (in the Block volume).

physical implementation.[11] Many proponents of the functionalist account of psychological terms and properties hold such a view.

Thus, on the new, improved picture, the relationship between psychological and physical kinds is something like this: there is no single neural kind N that "realizes" pain, across all types of organisms or physical systems; rather, there is a multiplicity of neural-physical kinds, N_h, N_r, N_m, . . . such that N_h realizes pain in humans, N_r realizes pain in reptiles, N_m realizes pain in Martians, etc. Perhaps, biological species as standardly understood are too broad to yield unique physical-biological realization bases; the neural basis of pain could perhaps change even in a single organism over time. But the main point is clear: any system capable of psychological states (that is, any system that "has a psychology") falls under some structure type T such that systems with structure T share the same physical base for each mental state-kind that they are capable of instantiating (we should regard this as relativized with respect to time to allow for the possibility that an individual may fall under different structure types at different times). Thus physical realization bases for mental states must be relativized to species or, better, physical structure types. We thus have the following thesis:

If anything has mental property M at time t, there is some physical structure type T and physical property P such that it is a system of type T at t and has P at t, and it holds as a matter of law that all systems of type T have M at a time just in case they have P at the same time.

We may call this "the Structure-Restricted Correlation Thesis" (or "the Restricted Correlation Thesis" for short).

It may have been noticed that neither this nor the correlation thesis speaks of "realization".[12] The talk of "realization" is not metaphysically neutral: the idea that mental properties are "realized" or "implemented" by physical properties carries with it a certain ontological picture of mental properties as derivative and dependent. There is the suggestion that when we look at concrete reality there is nothing over and beyond instantiations of physical properties and relations, and that the instantiation on a given occasion of an appropriate physical property in the right contextual (often causal) setting simply *counts as*, or *constitutes*, an instantiation of

11 Thus, Post says, "Functional and intentional states are defined without regard to their physical or other realizations", *The Faces of Existence*, p. 161. Also compare the earlier quotation from Block.

12 As far as I know, the term "realization" was first used in something like its present sense by Hilary Putnam in "Minds and Machines", in Sydney Hook, ed., *Dimensions of Mind* (New York: New York University Press, 1960).

a mental property on that occasion. An idea like this is evident in the functionalist conception of a mental property as *extrinsically* characterized in terms of its "causal role", where what fills this role is a physical (or, at any rate, nonmental) property (the latter property will then be said to "realize" the mental property in question). The same idea can be seen in the related functionalist proposal to construe a mental property as a "second-order property" consisting in the having of a physical property satisfying certain extrinsic specifications. We will recur to this topic later; however, we should note that someone who accepts either of the two correlation theses need not espouse the "realization" idiom. That is, it is prima facie a coherent position to think of mental properties as "first-order properties" in their own right, characterized by their intrinsic natures (e.g., phenomenal feel), which, as it happens, turn out to have nomological correlates in neural properties. (In fact, anyone interested in defending a serious dualist position on the mental should eschew the realization talk altogether and consider mental properties as first-order properties on a par with physical properties.) The main point of MR that is relevant to the antireductionist argument it has generated is just this: *mental properties do not have nomically coextensive physical properties, when the latter are appropriately individuated.* It may be that properties that are candidates for reduction must be thought of as being realized, or implemented, by properties in the prospective reduction base;[13] that is, if we think of certain properties as having their own intrinsic characterizations that are entirely independent of another set of properties, there is no hope of *reducing* the former to the latter. But this point needs to be argued, and will, in any case, not play a role in what follows.

Assume that property M is realized by property P. How are M and P related to each other and, in particular, how do they covary with each other? LePore and Loewer say this:[14]

> The usual conception is that e's being P realizes e's being F iff e is P and there is a strong connection of some sort between P and F. We propose to understand this connection as a necessary connection which is *explanatory.* The existence of an explanatory connection between two properties is stronger than the claim that $P \rightarrow F$ is physically necessary since not every physically necessary connection is explanatory.

13 On this point see Robert Van Gulick, "Nonreductive Materialism and Intertheoretic Constraints", in *Emergence or Reduction?*, ed. Ansgar Beckermann, Hans Flohr, and Jaegwon Kim (Berlin: De Gruyter, 1992).
14 "More on Making Mind Matter", p. 179.

Thus, LePore and Loewer require only that the realization base of M be *sufficient* for M, not both necessary and sufficient. This presumably is in response to MR: if pain is multiply realized in three ways as above, each of N_h, N_r, and N_m will be sufficient for pain, and none necessary for it. This I believe is not a correct response, however; the correct response is not to weaken the joint necessity and sufficiency of the physical base, but rather to *relativize* it, as in the Restricted Correlation Thesis, with respect to species or structure types. For suppose we are designing a physical system that will instantiate a certain psychology, and let $M_1, \ldots, M_n$ be the psychological properties required by this psychology. The design process must involve the specification of an n-tuple of physical properties, $P_1, \ldots, P_n$, all of them instantiable by the system, such that for each i, P_i constitutes a *necessary and sufficient* condition *in this system* (and others of relevantly similar physical structure), not merely a sufficient one, for the occurrence of M_i. (Each such n-tuple of physical properties can be called a "physical realization" of the psychology in question.[15]) That is, for each psychological state we must design into the system a nomologically coextensive physical state. We must do this *if we are to control both the occurrence and nonoccurrence of the psychological states involved,* and control of this kind is necessary if we are to ensure that the physical device will properly instantiate the psychology. (This is especially clear if we think of building a computer; computer analogies loom large in our thoughts about "realization".)

But isn't it possible for multiple realization to occur "locally" as well? That is, we may want to avail ourselves of the flexibility of allowing a psychological state, or function, to be instantiated by alternative mechanisms within a single system. This means that P_i can be a *disjunction* of physical properties; thus, M_i is instantiated in the system in question at a time if and only if at least one of the disjuncts of P_i is instantiated at that time. The upshot of all this is that LePore and Loewer's condition that $P \to M$ holds as a matter of law needs to be upgraded to the condition that, *relative to the species or structure type in question (and allowing P to be disjunctive), $P \leftrightarrow M$* holds as a matter of law.[16]

15 Cf. Hartry Field, "Mental Representation", in Block, *Readings in Philosophy of Psychology* (Cambridge: Harvard University Press, 1981), vol. 2.
16 What of LePore and Loewer's condition (ii), the requirement that the realization basis "explain" the realized property? Something like this explanatory relation may well be entailed by the realization relation; however, I do not believe it should be part of the definition of "realization"; that such an explanatory relation holds should be a consequence of the realization relation, not constitutive of it.

For simplicity let us suppose that pain is realized in three ways as above, by N_h in humans, N_r in reptiles, and N_m in Martians. The finitude assumption is not essential to any of my arguments: if the list is not finite, we will have an infinite disjunction rather than a finite one (alternatively, we can talk in terms of "sets" of such properties instead of their disjunctions). If the list is "open-ended", that's all right, too; it will not affect the metaphysics of the situation. We allowed above the possibility of a realization base of a psychological property itself being disjunctive; to get the discussion going, though, we will assume that these Ns, the three imagined physical realization bases of pain, are not themselves disjunctive – or, at any rate, that their status as properties is not in dispute. The propriety and significance of "disjunctive properties" is precisely one of the principal issues we will be dealing with below, and it will make little difference just at what stage this issue is faced.

III. DISJUNCTIVE PROPERTIES AND FODOR'S ARGUMENT

An obvious initial response to the MR-based argument against reducibility is "the disjunction move": Why not take the disjunction, $N_h \lor N_r \lor N_m$, as the single physical substrate of pain? In his 1967 paper, Putnam considers such a move but dismisses it out of hand: "Granted, in such a case the brain-state theorist can save himself by ad hoc assumptions (e.g., defining the disjunction of two states to be a single 'physical-chemical state'), but this does not have to be taken seriously".[17] Putnam gives no hint as to why he thinks the disjunction strategy does not merit serious consideration.

If there is something deeply wrong with disjunctions of the sort involved here, that surely isn't obvious; we need to go beyond a sense of unease with such disjunctions and develop an intelligible rationale for banning them. Here is where Fodor steps in, for he appears to have an argument for disallowing disjunctions. As I see it, Fodor's argument in "Special Sciences" depends crucially on the following two assumptions:

(1) To reduce a special-science theory T_M to physical theory T_P, each "kind" in T_M (presumably, represented by a basic predicate of T_M) must have a nomologically coextensive "kind" in T_P;

(2) A disjunction of heterogeneous kinds is not itself a kind.

17 "The Nature of Mental States", p. 228 (in the Block volume).

316

Point (1) is apparently prompted by the derivational model of intertheoretic reduction due to Ernest Nagel:[18] the reduction of T_2 to T_1 consists
in the derivation of laws of T_2 from the laws of T_1, in conjunction with
"bridge" laws or principles connecting T_2-terms with T_1-terms. Although this characterization does not in general require that each T_2-
term be correlated with a *coextensive* T_1-term, the natural thought is that
the existence of T_1-coextensions for T_2-terms would in effect give us
definitions of T_2-terms in T_1-terms, enabling us to rewrite T_2-laws exclusively in the vocabulary of T_1; we could then derive these rewrites of T_2-
laws from the laws of T_1 (if they cannot be so derived, we can add them
as additional T_1-laws – assuming both theories to be true).

Another thought that again leads us to look for T_1-coextensions for
T_2-terms is this: for genuine reduction, the bridge laws must be construed
as *property identities*, not mere *property correlations* – namely, we must be in
a position to identify the property expressed by a given T_2-term (say,
water-solubility) with a property expressed by a term in the reduction
base (say, having a certain molecular structure). This of course requires
that each T_2-term have a nomic (or otherwise suitably modalized) coextension in the vocabulary of the reduction base. To put it another way,
ontologically significant reduction requires the reduction of higher-level
properties, and this in turn requires (unless one takes an eliminativist
stance) that they be identified with complexes of lower-level properties.
Identity of properties of course requires, at a minimum, an appropriately
modalized coextensivity.[19]

So assume M is a psychological kind, and let us agree that to reduce M,
or to reduce the psychological theory containing M, we need a physical
coextension, P, for M. But why should we suppose that P must be a
physical "kind"? But what is a "kind", anyway? Fodor explains this notion in terms of *law*, saying that a given predicate P is a "kind predicate"
of a science just in case the science contains a law with P as its antecedent
or consequent.[20] There are various problems with Fodor's characterization, but we don't need to take its exact wording seriously; the main idea

18 *The Structure of Science* (New York: Harcourt, Brace & World, 1961), chap. 11.
19 My remarks here and in the preceding paragraph assume that the higher-level theory
   requires no "correction" in relation to the base theory. With appropriate caveats and
   qualifications, they should apply to models of reduction that allow such corrections, or
   models that only require the deduction of a suitable analogue, or "image", in the reduction base – as long as the departures are not so extreme as to warrant talk of replacement
   or elimination rather than reduction. Cf. Patricia Churchland, *Neurophilosophy* (Cambridge: MIT Press, 1986), chap. 7.
20 See "Special Sciences", pp. 132–33 (in *Representations*).

317

is that kinds, or kind predicates, of a science are those that figure in the laws of that science.

To return to our question, why should "bridge laws" connect kinds to kinds, in this special sense of "kind"? To say that bridge laws are "laws" and that, by definition, only kind predicates can occur in laws is not much of an answer. For that only invites the further question why "bridge laws" ought to be "laws" – what would be lacking in a reductive derivation if bridge laws were replaced by "bridge principles" which do not necessarily connect kinds to kinds.[21] But what of the consideration that these principles must represent property identities? Does this force on us the requirement that each reduced kind must find a coextensive kind in the reduction base? No; for it isn't obvious why it isn't perfectly proper to reduce kinds by identifying them with properties expressed by non-kind (disjunctive) predicates in the reduction base.

There is the following possible argument for insisting on kinds: if M is identified with non-kind Q (or M is reduced via a biconditional bridge principle "$M \leftrightarrow Q$", where Q is a non-kind), M could no longer figure in special science laws; e.g., the law, "$M \rightarrow R$", would in effect reduce to "$Q \rightarrow R$", and therefore lose its status as a law on account of containing Q, a non-kind.

I think this is a plausible response – at least, the beginning of one. As it stands, though, it smacks of circularity: "$Q \rightarrow R$" is not a law because a non-kind, Q, occurs in it, and Q is a non-kind because it cannot occur in a law and "$Q \rightarrow R$", in particular, is not a law. What we need is an *independent* reason for the claim that the sort of Q we are dealing with under MR, namely a badly heterogeneous disjunction, is unsuited for laws.

This means that point (1) really reduces to point (2) above. For, given Fodor's notion of a kind, (2) comes to this: disjunctions of heterogeneous kinds are unfit for laws. What we now need is an *argument* for this claim; to dismiss such disjunctions as "wildly disjunctive" or "heterogeneous and unsystematic" is to label a problem, not to offer a diagnosis of it.[22] In the sections to follow, I hope to take some steps toward such a diagnosis and

---

21 Fodor appears to assume that the requirement that bridge laws must connect "kinds" to "kinds" is part of the classic positivist conception of reduction. I don't believe there is any warrant for this assumption, however.

22 See Pereboom and Kornblith, "The Metaphysics of Irreducibility", in which it is suggested that laws with disjunctive predicates are not "explanatory". I think, though, that this suggestion is not fully developed there.

draw some implications which I believe are significant for the status of mentality.

IV. JADE, JADEITE, AND NEPHRITE

Let me begin with an analogy that will guide us in our thinking about multiply realizable kinds.

Consider *jade:* we are told that jade, as it turns out, is not a mineral kind, contrary to what was once believed; rather, jade comprises two distinct minerals with dissimilar molecular structures, *jadeite* and *nephrite*. Consider the following generalization:

(L) Jade is green

We may have thought, before the discovery of the dual nature of jade, that (L) was a law, a law about jade; and we may have thought, with reason, that (L) had been strongly confirmed by all the millions of jade samples that had been observed to be green (and none that had been observed not to be green). We now know better: (L) is really a conjunction of these two laws:

(L₁) Jadeite is green
(L₂) Nephrite is green

But (L) itself might still be a law as well; is that possible? It has the standard basic form of a law, and it apparently has the power to support counterfactuals: if anything were jade – that is, if anything were a sample of jadeite or of nephrite – then, in either case, it would follow, by law, that it was green. No problem here.

But there is another standard mark of lawlikeness that is often cited, and this is "projectibility", the ability to be confirmed by observation of "positive instances". Any generalized conditional of the form "All *Fs* are *G*" can be confirmed by the *exhaustion* of the class of *Fs* – that is, by eliminating all of its potential falsifiers. It is in this sense that we can verify such generalizations as "All the coins in my pockets are copper" and "Everyone in this room is either first-born or an only child". Lawlike generalizations, however, are thought to have the following further property: observation of positive instances, *Fs* that are *Gs*, can strengthen our credence in the next *F*'s being *G*. It is this kind of instance-to-instance accretion of confirmation that is supposed to be the hallmark of lawlikeness; it is what explains the possibility of confirming a generalization about an

319

indefinitely large class of items on the basis of a finite number of favorable observations. This rough characterization of projectibility should suffice for our purposes.

Does (L), "Jade is green", pass the projectibility test? Here we seem to have a problem.[23] For we can imagine this: on re-examining the records of past observations, we find, to our dismay, that all the positive instances of (L), that is, all the millions of observed samples of green jade, turn out to have been samples of jadeite, and none of nephrite! If this should happen, we clearly would not, and should not, continue to think of (L) as well confirmed. All we have is evidence strongly confirming (L_1), and none having anything to do with (L_2). (L) is merely a conjunction of two laws, one well confirmed and the other with its epistemic status wholly up in the air. But all the millions of green jadeite samples *are* positive instances of (L): they satisfy both the antecedent and the consequent of (L). As we have just seen, however, (L) is not confirmed by them, at least not in the standard way we expect. And the reason, I suggest, is that jade is a true disjunctive kind, a disjunction of two heterogeneous nomic kinds which, however, is not itself a nomic kind.[24]

That disjunction is implicated in this failure of projectibility can be seen in the following way: inductive projection of generalizations like (L) with disjunctive antecedents would sanction a cheap, and illegitimate, confirmation procedure. For assume that "All *F*s are *G*" is a law that has been confirmed by the observation of appropriately numerous positive instances, things that are both *F* and *G*. But these are also positive instances of the generalization "All things that are *F or H* are *G*", for any *H* you please. So, if you in general permit projection of generalizations with a disjunctive antecedent, this latter generalization will also be well confirmed. But "All things that are *F or H* are *G*" logically implies "All *H*s are *G*". Any statement implied by a well-confirmed statement must itself be well confirmed.[25] So "All *H*s are *G*" is well confirmed – in fact, it is confirmed by the observation of *F*s that are *G*s!

23 The points to follow concerning disjunctive predicates were developed about a decade ago; however, I have just come across some related and, in some respects similar, points in David Owens's interesting paper "Disjunctive Laws", *Analysis* 49 (1989): 197–202. See also William Seager, "Disjunctive Laws and Supervenience", *Analysis* 51 (1991): 93–98.

24 This can be taken to define one useful sense of kind heterogeneity: two kinds are heterogeneous with respect to each other just in case their disjunction is not a kind.

25 Note: this doesn't say that for any *e*, if *e* is "positive evidence" for *h* and *h* logically implies *j*, then *e* is positive evidence for *j*. About the latter principle there is some dispute; see Carl G. Hempel,"Studies in the Logic of Confirmation", reprinted in Hempel, *Aspects of Scientific Explanation* (New York: The Free Press, 1965), especially pp.

One might protest: "Look, the very same strategy can be applied to something that is a genuine law. We can think of any nomic kind – say, being an emerald – as a disjunction, being an African emerald or a non-African emerald. This would make 'All emeralds are green' a conjunction of two laws, 'All African emeralds are green' and 'All non-African emeralds are green'. But surely this doesn't show there is anything wrong with the lawlikeness of 'All emeralds are green'". Our reply is obvious: the disjunction, "being an African emerald or non-African emerald", does not denote some heterogeneously disjunctive, nonnomic kind; it denotes a perfectly well-behaved nomic kind, that of being an emerald! There is nothing wrong with disjunctive predicates as such; the trouble arises when the kinds denoted by the disjoined predicates are heterogeneous, "wildly disjunctive", so that instances falling under them do not show the kind of "similarity", or unity, that we expect of instances falling under a single kind.

The phenomenon under discussion, therefore, is related to the simple maxim sometimes claimed to underlie inductive inference: "similar things behave in similar ways", "same cause, same effect", and so on. The source of the trouble we saw with instantial confirmation of "All jade is green" is the fact, or belief, that samples of jadeite and samples of nephrite do not exhibit an appropriate "similarity" with respect to each other to warrant inductive projections from the observed samples of jadeite to unobserved samples of nephrite. But similarity of the required sort presumably holds for African emeralds and non-African emeralds – at least, that is what we believe, and that is what makes the "disjunctive kind", being an African emerald or a non-African emerald, a single nomic kind. More generally, the phenomenon is related to the point often made about disjunctive properties: disjunctive properties, unlike conjunctive properties, do not guarantee similarity for instances falling under them. And similarity, it is said, is the core of our idea of a property. If that is your idea of a property, you will believe that there are no such things as disjunctive properties (or "negative properties"). More precisely, though, we should remember that properties are not inherently disjunctive or conjunctive any more than classes are inherently unions or intersections, and that any property can be expressed by a disjunctive predicate. Properties of course can be conjunctions, or disjunctions, *of* other properties. The point about disjunctive properties is best put as a closure condition on properties: the class of

30–35; Rudolf Carnap, *Logical Foundations of Probability* (Chicago: University of Chicago Press, 1950), pp. 471–76.

properties is not closed under disjunction (presumably, nor under negation). Thus, there may well be properties P and Q such that P or Q is also a property, but its being so doesn't follow from the mere fact that P and Q are properties.[26]

V. JADE AND PAIN

Let us now return to pain and its multiple realization bases, N_h, N_r, and N_m. I believe the situation here is instructively parallel to the case of jade in relation to jadeite and nephrite. It seems that we think of jadeite and nephrite as distinct kinds (and of jade not as a kind) because they are different chemical kinds. But why is their being distinct as chemical kinds relevant here? Because many important properties of minerals, we think, are supervenient on, and explainable in terms of, their microstructure, and chemical kinds constitute a microstructural taxonomy that is explanatorily rich and powerful. Microstructure is important, in short, because macrophysical properties of substances are determined by microstructure. These ideas make up our "metaphysics" of microdetermination for properties of minerals and other substances, a background of partly empirical and partly metaphysical assumptions that regulate our inductive and explanatory practices.

The parallel metaphysical underpinnings for pain, and other mental states in general, are, first, the belief, expressed by the Restricted Correlation Thesis, that pain, or any other mental state, occurs in a system when, and only when, appropriate physical conditions are present in the system, and, second, the corollary belief that significant properties of mental states, in particular nomic relationships amongst them, are due to, and explainable in terms of, the properties and causal-nomic connections among their physical "substrates". I will call the conjunction of these two beliefs "the Physical Realization Thesis".[27] Whether or not the microexplanation of the sort indicated in the second half of the thesis amounts to a "reduction" is a question we will take up later. Apart from this question,

26 On issues concerning properties, kinds, similarity, and lawlikeness, see W. V. Quine, "Natural Kinds", in *Ontological Relativity and Other Essays* (New York: Columbia University Press, 1969); David Lewis, "New Work for a Theory of Universals", *Australasian Journal of Philosophy* 61 (1983): 347–77; D. M. Armstrong, *Universals* (Boulder, Colo.: Westview Press, 1989).

27 This term is a little misleading since the two subtheses have been stated without the term "realization" and may be acceptable to those who would reject the "realization" idiom in connection with the mental. I use the term since we are chiefly addressing philosophers (mainly functionalists) who construe the psychophysical relation in terms of realization, rather than, say, emergence or brute correlation.

though, the Physical Realization Thesis is widely accepted by philosophers who talk of "physical realization", and this includes most functionalists; it is all but explicit in LePore and Loewer, for example, and in Fodor.[28]

Define a property, N, by disjoining N_h, N_r, and N_m; that is, N has a disjunctive definition, $N_h \vee N_r \vee N_m$. If we assume, with those who endorse the MR-based antireductionist argument, that N_h, N_r, and N_m are a heterogeneous lot, we cannot make the heterogeneity go away merely by introducing a simpler expression, "N"; if there is a problem with certain disjunctive properties, it is not a *linguistic* problem about the form of expressions used to refer to them.

Now, we put the following question to Fodor and like-minded philosophers: If pain is nomically equivalent to N, the property claimed to be wildly disjunctive and obviously nonnomic, *why isn't pain itself equally heterogeneous and nonnomic as a kind?* Why isn't pain's relationship to its realization bases, N_h, N_r, and N_m, analogous to jade's relationship to jadeite and nephrite? If jade turns out to be nonnomic on account of its dual "realizations" in distinct microstructures, why doesn't the same fate befall pain? After all, the group of actual and nomologically possible realizations of pain, as they are described by the MR enthusiasts with such imagination, is far more motley than the two chemical kinds comprising jade.

I believe we should insist on answers to these questions from those functionalists who view mental properties as "second-order" properties, i.e., properties that consist in having a property with a certain functional specification.[29] Thus, pain is said to be a second-order property in that it is the *property of having some property with a certain specification* in terms of its typical causes and effects and its relation to other mental properties; call this "specification H". The point of MR, on this view, is that there is more than one property that meets specification H – in fact, an open-ended set of such properties, it will be said. But pain itself, it is argued, is a more abstract but well-behaved property at a higher level, namely the property of having one of these properties meeting specification H. It should be clear why a position like this is vulnerable to the questions that have been raised. For the property of having property P is exactly identical with P, and the property of having *one* of the properties, P_1, P_2, . . . , P_n, is exactly identical with the disjunctive property, $P_1 \vee P_2 \vee \ldots \vee P_n$. On the assumption that N_h, N_r, and N_m are all the properties satisfying

28 See "Special Sciences", and "Making Mind Matter More", *Philosophical Topics* 17 (1989): 59–79.
29 See, e.g., Block, "Can the Mind Change the World?", p. 155.

specification H, the property of having a property with H, namely pain, is none other than the property of having either N_h or N_r or $N_m{}^{30}$ – namely, the *disjunctive* property, $N_h \vee N_r \vee N_m$! We cannot hide the disjunctive character of pain behind the second-order *expression*, "the property of having a property with specification H". Thus, on the construal of mental properties as second-order properties, mental properties will in general turn out to be disjunctions of their physical realization bases. It is difficult to see how one could have it both ways – that is, to castigate $N_h \vee N_r \vee N_m$ as unacceptably disjunctive while insisting on the integrity of pain as a scientific kind.

Moreover, when we think about making projections over pain, very much the same worry should arise about their propriety as did for jade. Consider a possible law: "Sharp pains administered at random intervals cause anxiety reactions". Suppose this generalization has been well confirmed for humans. Should we expect *on that basis* that it will hold also for Martians whose psychology is implemented (we assume) by a vastly different physical mechanism? Not if we accept the Physical Realization Thesis, fundamental to functionalism, that psychological regularities hold, to the extent that they do, in virtue of the causal-nomological regularities at the physical implementation level. The reason the law is true for humans is due to the way the human brain is "wired"; the Martians have a brain with a different wiring plan, and we certainly should not expect the regularity to hold for them just because it does for humans.[31] "Pains cause anxiety reactions" may turn out to possess no more unity as a scientific law than does "Jade is green".

Suppose that in spite of all this Fodor insists on defending pain as a nomic kind. It isn't clear that that would be a viable strategy. For he would then owe us an explanation of why the "wildly disjunctive" N, which after all is equivalent to pain, is not a nomic kind. If a predicate is nomically equivalent to a well-behaved predicate, why isn't that enough to show that it, too, is well behaved, and expresses a well-behaved property? To say, as Fodor does,[32] that "it is a law that . . ." is "intensional" and does not permit substitution of equivalent expressions ("equivalent" in various

---

30 We might keep in mind the close relationship between disjunction and the existential quantifier standardly noted in logic textbooks.

31 It may be a complicated affair to formulate this argument within certain functionalist schemes; if, for example, mental properties are functionally defined by Ramseyfying a total psychological theory, it will turn out that humans and Martians cannot share any psychological state unless the same total psychology (including the putative law in question) is true (or held to be true) for both.

32 "Special Sciences", p. 140 (in *Representations*).

appropriate senses) is merely to locate a potential problem, not to resolve it.

Thus, the nomicity of pain may lead to the nomicity of N; but this isn't very interesting. For given the Physical Realization Thesis, and the priority of the physical implicit in it, our earlier line of argument, leading from the nonnomicity of N to the nonnomicity of pain, is more compelling. We must, I think, take seriously the reasoning leading to the conclusion that pain, and other mental states, might turn out to be nonnomic. If this turns out to be the case, it puts in serious jeopardy Fodor's contention that its physical irreducibility renders psychology an autonomous special science. If pain fails to be nomic, it is not the sort of property in terms of which laws can be formulated; and "pain" is not a predicate that can enter into a scientific theory that seeks to formulate causal laws and causal explanations. And the same goes for all multiply realizable psychological kinds – which, according to MR, means *all* psychological kinds. There are no scientific theories of jade, and we don't need any; if you insist on having one, you can help yourself with the *conjunction* of the theory of jadeite and the theory of nephrite. In the same way, there will be theories about human pains (instances of N_h), reptilian pains (instances of N_r), and so on; but there will be no unified, integrated theory encompassing all pains in all pain-capable organisms, only a conjunction of pain theories for appropriately individuated biological species and physical structure types. Scientific psychology, like the theory of jade, gives way to a conjunction of structure-specific theories. If this is right, the correct conclusion to be drawn from the MR-inspired antireductionist argument is not the claim that psychology is an irreducible and autonomous science, but something that contradicts it, namely that it cannot be a science with a unified subject matter. This is the picture that is beginning to emerge from MR when combined with the Physical Realization Thesis.

These reflections have been prompted by the analogy with the case of jade; it is a strong and instructive analogy, I think, and suggests the possibility of a general argument. In the following section I will develop a direct argument, with explicit premises and assumptions.

VI. CAUSAL POWERS AND MENTAL KINDS

One crucial premise we need for a direct argument is a constraint on concept formation, or kind individuation, in science that has been around for many years; it has lately been resurrected by Fodor in connection with content externalism.[33] A precise statement of the constraint may be difficult and controversial, but its main idea can be put as follows:

[Principle of Causal Individuation of Kinds] Kinds in science are individuated on the basis of causal powers; that is, objects and events fall under a kind, or share in a property, insofar as they have similar causal powers.

I believe this is a plausible principle, and it is, in any case, widely accepted.

We can see that this principle enables us to give a specific interpretation to the claim that N_h, N_r, and N_m are *heterogeneous* as kinds: the claim must mean that they are *heterogeneous as causal powers* – that is, they are diverse as causal powers and enter into diverse causal laws. This must mean, given the Physical Realization Thesis, that pain itself can show no more unity as a causal power than the disjunction, $N_h \vee N_r \vee N_m$. This becomes especially clear if we set forth the following principle, which arguably is implied by the Physical Realization Thesis (but we need not make an issue of this here):

[The Causal Inheritance Principle] If mental property M is realized in a system at t in virtue of physical realization base P, the causal powers of *this instance of M* are identical with the causal powers of P.[34]

It is important to bear in mind that this principle only concerns the causal powers of *individual instances of M;* it does not identify the causal powers of mental property M *in general* with the causal powers of some physical property P; such identification is precluded by the multiple physical realizability of M.

Why should we accept this principle? Let us just note that to deny it would be to accept *emergent* causal powers: causal powers that magically emerge at a higher level and of which there is no accounting in terms of lower-level properties and their causal powers and nomic connections. This leads to the notorious problem of "downward causation" and the

33 See, e.g., Carl G. Hempel, *Fundamentals of Concept Formation in Empirical Science* (Chicago: University of Chicago Press, 1952); W. V. Quine, "Natural Kinds". Fodor gives it an explicit statement in *Psychosemantics* (Cambridge: MIT Press, 1988), chap. 2. A principle like this is often invoked in the current externalism/internalism debate about content; most principal participants in this debate seem to accept it.

34 A principle like this is sometimes put in terms of "supervenience" and "supervenience base" rather than "realization" and "realization base". See my "Epiphenomenal and Supervenient Causation", Essay 6 of this volume. Fodor appears to accept just such a principle of supervenient causation for mental properties in chap. 2 of his *Psychosemantics*. In "The Metaphysics of Irreducibility" Pereboom and Kornblith appear to reject it.

attendant violation of the causal closure of the physical domain.[35] I believe that a serious physicalist would find these consequences intolerable.

It is clear that the Causal Inheritance Principle, in conjunction with the Physical Realization Thesis, has the consequence that mental kinds cannot satisfy the Causal Individuation Principle, and this effectively rules out mental kinds as scientific kinds. The reasoning is simple: instances of M that are realized by the same physical base must be grouped under one kind, since *ex hypothesi* the physical base is a causal kind; and instances of M with different realization bases must be grouped under distinct kinds, since, again *ex hypothesi,* these realization bases are distinct as causal kinds. Given that mental kinds are realized by diverse physical causal kinds, therefore, it follows that mental kinds are not causal kinds, and hence are disqualified as proper scientific kinds. Each mental kind is sundered into as many kinds as there are physical realization bases for it, and psychology as a science with disciplinary unity turns out to be an impossible project.

What is the relationship between this argument and the argument adumbrated in our reflections based on the jade analogy? At first blush, the two arguments might seem unrelated: the earlier argument depended chiefly on epistemological considerations, considerations on inductive projectibility of certain predicates, whereas the crucial premise of the second argument is the Causal Individuation Principle, a broadly metaphysical and methodological principle about science. I think, though, that the two arguments are closely related, and the key to seeing the relationship is this: causal powers involve laws, and laws are regularities that are projectible. Thus, if pain (or jade) is not a kind over which inductive projections can be made, it cannot enter into laws, and therefore cannot qualify as a causal kind; and this disqualifies it as a scientific kind. If this is right, the jade-inspired reflections provide a possible rationale for the Causal Individuation Principle. Fleshing out this rough chain of reasoning in precise terms, however, goes beyond what I can attempt in this paper.

VII. THE STATUS OF PSYCHOLOGY: LOCAL REDUCTIONS

Our conclusion at this point, therefore, is this: If MR is true, psychological kinds are not scientific kinds. What does this imply about the status

---

35 For more details see my "'Downward Causation' in Emergentism and Nonreductive Physicalism", in *Emergence or Reduction?,* ed. Beckermann, Flohr, and Kim, and "The Nonreductivist's Troubles with Mental Causation", Essay 17 of this volume.

of psychology as a science? Do our considerations show that psychology is a pseudo-science like astrology and alchemy? Of course not. The crucial difference, from the metaphysical point of view, is that psychology has physical realizations, but alchemy does not. To have a physical realization is to be physically grounded and explainable in terms of the processes at an underlying level. In fact, if each of the psychological kinds posited in a psychological theory has a physical realization for a fixed species, the theory can be "locally reduced" to the physical theory of that species, in the following sense. Let S be the species involved; for each law L_m of psychological theory T_m, $S \to L_m$ (the proposition that L_m holds for members of S) is the "S-restricted" version of L_m; and $S \to T_m$ is the S-restricted version of T_m, the set of all S-restricted laws of T_m. We can then say that T_m is "locally reduced" for species S to an underlying theory, T_p, just in case $S \to T_m$ is reduced to T_p. And the latter obtains just in case each S-restricted law of T_m, $S \to L_m$,[36] is derivable from the laws of the reducing theory T_p, taken together with bridge laws. What bridge laws suffice to guarantee the derivation? Obviously, an array of S-restricted bridge laws of the form, $S \to (M_i \leftrightarrow P_j)$, for each mental kind M_i. Just as unrestricted psychophysical bridge laws can underwrite a "global" or "uniform" reduction of psychology, species- or structure-restricted bridge laws sanction its "local" reduction.

If the same psychological theory is true of humans, reptiles, and Martians, the psychological kinds posited by that theory must have realizations in human, reptilian, and Martian physiologies. This implies that the theory is locally reducible in three ways, for humans, reptiles, and Martians. If the dependence of the mental on the physical means anything, it must mean that the regularities posited by this common psychology must have divergent physical explanations for the three species. The very idea of physical realization involves the possibility of physically explaining psychological properties and regularities, and the supposition of multiple such realizations, namely MR, involves a commitment to the possibility of multiple explanatory reductions of psychology.[37] The important moral of MR we need to keep in mind is this: *if psychological*

36 Or an appropriately corrected version thereof (this qualification applies to the bridge laws as well).

37 In "Special Sciences" and "Making Mind Matter More" Fodor appears to accept the local reducibility of psychology and other special sciences. But he uses the terminology of local *explanation,* rather than reduction, of psychological regularities in terms of underlying microstructure. I think this is because his preoccupation with Nagelian uniform reduction prevents him from seeing that this is a form of inter-theoretic reduction if anything is.

properties are multiply realized, so is psychology itself. If physical realizations of psychological properties are a "wildly heterogeneous" and "unsystematic" lot, psychological theory itself must be realized by an equally heterogeneous and unsystematic lot of physical theories.

I am inclined to think that multiple local reductions, rather than global reductions, are the rule, even in areas in which we standardly suppose reductions are possible. I will now deal with a possible objection to the idea of local reduction, at least as it is applied to psychology. The objection goes like this: given what we know about the differences among members of a single species, even species are too wide to yield determinate realization bases for psychological states, and given what we know about the phenomena of maturation and development, brain injuries, and the like, the physical bases of mentality may change even for a single individual. This throws into serious doubt, continues the objection, the availability of species-restricted bridge laws needed for local reductions.

The point of this objection may well be correct as a matter of empirical fact. Two points can be made in reply, however. First, neurophysiological research goes on because there is a shared, and probably well-grounded, belief among the workers that there are not huge individual differences within a species in the way psychological kinds are realized. Conspecifics must show important physical-physiological similarities, and there probably is good reason for thinking that they share physical realization bases to a sufficient degree to make search for species-wide neural substrates for mental states feasible and rewarding. Researchers in this area evidently aim for neurobiological explanations of psychological capacities and processes that are generalizable over all or most ("normal") members of a given species.

Second, even if there are huge individual differences among conspecifics as to how their psychology is realized, that does not touch the metaphysical point: as long as you believe in the Physical Realization Thesis, you must believe that every organism or system with mentality falls under a physical structure type such that its mental states are realized by determinate physical states of organisms with that structure. It may be that these structures are so finely individuated and so few *actual* individuals fall under them that research into the neural bases of mental states in these structures is no longer worthwhile, theoretically or practically. What we need to recognize here is that the scientific possibility of, say, human psychology is a contingent fact (assuming it is a fact); it depends on the fortunate fact that individual humans do not show huge physiological-biological differences that are psychologically relevant. But if they did, that would not change the metaphysics of the situation one bit; it would remain true that the psychology of each of us was determined by, and locally reducible to, his neurobiology.

Realistically, there are going to be psychological differences among individual humans: it is a commonsense platitude that no two persons are exactly alike – either physically or psychologically. And individual differences may be manifested not only in particular psychological facts but in psychological regularities. If we believe in the Physical Realization Thesis, we must believe that our psychological differences are rooted in, and explainable by, our physical differences, just as we expect our psychological similarities to be so explainable. Humans probably are less alike among themselves than, say, tokens of a Chevrolet model.[38] And psychological laws for humans, at a certain level of specificity, must be expected to be statistical in character, not deterministic – or, if you prefer, "ceteris paribus laws" rather than "strict laws". But this is nothing peculiar to psychology; these remarks surely apply to human physiology and anatomy as much as human psychology. In any case, none of this affects the metaphysical point being argued here concerning microdetermination and microreductive explanation.

VIII. METAPHYSICAL IMPLICATIONS

But does local reduction have any interesting philosophical significance, especially in regard to the status of mental properties? If a psychological property has been multiply locally reduced, does that mean that the property itself has been reduced? Ned Block has raised just such a point, arguing that species-restricted reductionism (or species-restricted type physicalism) "sidesteps the main metaphysical question: 'What is common to the pains of dogs and people (and all other species) in virtue of which they are pains?'".[39]

Pereboom and Kornblith elaborate on Block's point as follows:

> . . . even if there is a single type of physical state that normally realizes pain in each type of organism, or in each structure type, this does not show that pain, *as a type of mental state,* is reducible to physical states. Reduction,

38 Compare J. J. C. Smart's instructive analogy between biological organisms and superheterodyne radios, in *Philosophy and Scientific Realism* (London: Routledge & Kegan Paul, 1963), pp. 56–57. Smart's conception of the relation between physics and the special sciences, such as biology and psychology, is similar in some respects to the position I am defending here.

39 "Introduction: What is Functionalism?" in *Readings in Philosophy of Psychology,* pp. 178–79.

in the present debate, must be understood as reduction of types, since the primary object of reductive strategies is explanations and theories, and explanations and theories quantify over types. . . . The suggestion that there are species-specific reductions of pain results in the claim that pains in different species have nothing in common. But this is just a form of eliminativism.[40]

There are several related but separable issues raised here. But first we should ask: Must all pains have "something in common" in virtue of which they are pains?

According to the phenomenological conception of pain, all pains do have something in common: they all *hurt*. But as I take it, those who hold this view of pain would reject any reductionist program, independently of the issues presently on hand. Even if there were a species-invariant uniform bridge law correlating pains with a single physical substrate across all species and structures, they would claim that the correlation holds as a brute, unexplainable matter of fact, and that pain as a qualitative event, a "raw feel", would remain irreducibly distinct from its neural substrate. Many emergentists apparently held a view of this kind.

I presume that Block, and Pereboom and Kornblith, are speaking not from a phenomenological viewpoint of this kind but from a broadly functionalist one. But from a functionalist perspective, it is by no means clear how we should understand the question "What do all pains have in common in virtue of which they are all pains?" Why should all pains have "something in common"? As I understand it, at the core of the functionalist program is the attempt to explain the meanings of mental terms *relationally*, in terms of inputs, outputs, and connections with other mental states. And on the view, discussed briefly earlier, that mental properties are second-order properties, pain is the property of having a property with a certain functional specification H (in terms of inputs, outputs, etc.). This yields a short answer to Block's question: what all pains have in common is the pattern of connections as specified by H. The local reductionist is entitled to that answer as much as the functionalist is. Compare two pains, an instance of N_h and one of N_m; what they have in common is that each is an instance of a property that realizes pain – that is, they exhibit the same pattern of input-output-other internal state connections, namely the pattern specified by H.

40 In their "The Metaphysics of Irreducibility". See also Ronald Endicott, "On Physical Multiple Realization", *Pacific Philosophical Quarterly* 70 (1989): 212–24. In personal correspondence Earl Conee and Joe Mendola have raised similar points. There is a useful discussion of various metaphysical issues relating to MR in Cynthia Macdonald, *Mind–Body Identity Theories* (London and New York: Routledge, 1989).

But some will say: "But *H* is only an *extrinsic* characterization; what do these instances of pain have in common that is *intrinsic* to them?" The local reductionist must grant that on his view there is nothing intrinsic that all pains have in common in virtue of which they are pains (assuming that N_h, N_r, and N_m "have nothing intrinsic in common"). But that is also precisely the consequence of the functionalist view. That, one might say, is the whole point of functionalism: the functionalist, especially one who believes in MR, would not, and should not, look for something common to all pains over and above *H* (the heart of functionalism, one might say, is the belief that mental states have no "intrinsic essence").

But there is a further question raised by Block et al.: What happens to properties that have been locally reduced? Are they still with us, distinct and separate from the underlying physical-biological properties? Granted: human pain is reduced to N_h, Martian pain to N_m, and so forth, but what of *pain itself*? It remains unreduced. Are we still stuck with the dualism of mental and physical properties?

I will sketch two possible ways of meeting this challenge. First, recall my earlier remarks about the functionalist conception of mental properties as second-order properties: pain is *the property of having a property with specification H*, and, given that N_h, N_r, and N_m are the properties meeting *H*, pain turns out to be the disjunctive property, $N_h \vee N_r \vee N_m$. If you hold the second-order property view of mental properties, pain has been reduced to, and survives as, this disjunctive physical kind. Quite apart from considerations of local reduction, the very conception of pain you hold commits you to the conclusion that pain is a disjunctive kind, and if you accept any form of respectable physicalism (in particular, the Physical Realization Thesis), it is a disjunctive *physical* kind. And even if you don't accept the view of mental properties as second-order properties, as long as you are comfortable with disjunctive kinds and properties, you can, in the aftermath of local reduction, identify pain with the disjunction of its realization bases. On this approach, then, you have another, more direct, answer to Block's question: what all pains have in common is that they all fall under the disjunctive kind, $N_h \vee N_r \vee N_m$.

If you are averse to disjunctive kinds, there is another more radical, and in some ways more satisfying, approach. The starting point of this approach is the frank acknowledgement that MR leads to the conclusion that pain as a property or kind must go. Local reduction after all is reduction, and to be reduced is to be eliminated as an *independent* entity. You might say: global reduction is different in that it is also *conservative* – if pain is globally reduced to physical property *P*, pain survives as *P*. But it is also true that under local reduction, pain survives as N_h in humans, as N_r in reptiles, and so on. It must be admitted, however, that pain as a kind does not survive multiple local reduction. But is this so bad?

Let us return to jade once again. Is jade a *kind*? We know it is not a mineral kind; but is it any kind of a kind? That of course depends on what we mean by "kind". There are certain shared criteria, largely based on observable macroproperties of mineral samples (e.g., hardness, color, etc.), that determine whether something is a sample of jade, or whether the predicate "is jade" is correctly applicable to it. What all samples of jade have in common is just these observable macrophysical properties that define the applicability of the predicate "is jade". In this sense, speakers of English who have "jade" in their repertoire associate the same *concept* with "jade"; and we can recognize the existence of the concept of jade and at the same time acknowledge that the concept does not pick out, or answer to, a property or kind in the natural world.

I think we can say something similar about pain and "pain": there are shared criteria for the application of the predicate "pain" or "is in pain", and these criteria may well be for the most part functionalist ones. These criteria generate for us a *concept of pain,* a concept whose clarity and determinacy depend, we may assume, on certain characteristics (such as explicitness, coherence, and completeness) of the criteria governing the application of "pain". But the concept of pain, on this construal, need not pick out an objective kind any more than the concept of jade does.

All this presupposes a distinction between concepts and properties (or kinds). Do we have such a distinction? I believe we do. Roughly, concepts are in the same ball park as predicates, meanings (perhaps, something like Fregean *Sinnen*), ideas, and the like; Putnam has suggested that concepts be identified with "synonymy classes of predicates",[41] and that comes close enough to what I have in mind. Properties and relations, on the other hand, are "out there in the world"; they are features and characteristics of things and events in the world. They include fundamental physical magnitudes and quantities, like mass, energy, size, and shape, and are part of the causal structure of the world. The property of being water is arguably identical with the property of being H_2O, but evidently the concept of water is distinct from the concept of H_2O (Socrates had the former but not the latter). Most of us would agree that ethical predicates are meaningful, and that we have the concepts of "good", "right", etc.; however, it is a debatable issue, and has lately been much debated, whether

41 In "The Nature of Mental States".

there are such properties as goodness and rightness.[42] If you find that most of these remarks make sense, you understand the concept–property distinction that I have in mind. Admittedly, this is all a little vague and programmatic, and we clearly need a better-articulated theory of properties and concepts; but the distinction is there, supported by an impressively systematic set of intuitions and philosophical requirements.[43]

But is this second approach a form of mental eliminativism? In a sense it is: as I said, on this approach no properties in the world answer to general, species-unrestricted mental concepts. But remember: there still are pains, and we sometimes are in pain, just as there still are samples of jade. We must also keep in mind that the present approach is not, in its ontological implications, a form of the standard mental eliminativism currently on the scene.[44] Without elaborating on what the differences are, let us just note a few important points. First, the present view does not take away species-restricted mental properties, e.g., human pain, Martian pain, canine pain, and the rest, although it takes away "pain as such". Second, while the standard eliminativism consigns mentality to the same ontological limbo to which phlogiston, witches, and magnetic effluvia, have been dispatched, the position I have been sketching views it on a par with jade, tables, and adding machines. To see jade as a non-kind is not to question the existence of jade, or the legitimacy and utility of the concept of jade. Tables do not constitute a scientific kind; there are no laws about tables as such, and being a table is not a causal-explanatory kind. But that must be sharply distinguished from the false claim that there are no tables. The same goes for pains. These points suggest the following difference in regard to the status of psychology: the present view allows, and in fact encourages, "species-specific psychologies", but the standard eliminativism would do away with all things psychological – species-specific psychologies as well as global psychology.

To summarize, then, the two metaphysical schemes I have sketched offer these choices: either we allow disjunctive kinds and construe pain and other mental properties as such kinds, or else we must acknowledge that

---

42 I of course have in mind the controversy concerning moral realism; see essays in Geoffrey Sayre-McCord, ed., *Essays on Moral Realism* (Ithaca: Cornell University Press, 1988).

43 On concepts and properties, see, e.g., Hilary Putnam, "On Properties", in *Mathematics, Matter and Method* (Cambridge: Cambridge University Press, 1975); Mark Wilson, "Predicate Meets Property", *Philosophical Review* 91 (1982): 549–90, especially section III.

44 Such as the versions favored by W. V. Quine, Stephen Stich, and Paul Churchland.

our general mental terms and concepts do not pick out properties and kinds in the world (we may call this "mental property irrealism"). I should add that I am not interested in promoting either disjunctive kinds or mental irrealism, a troubling set of choices to most of us. Rather, my main interest has been to follow out the consequences of MR and try to come to terms with them within a reasonable metaphysical scheme.

I have already commented on the status of psychology as a science under MR. As I argued, MR seriously compromises the disciplinary unity and autonomy of psychology as a science. But that does not have to be taken as a negative message. In particular, the claim does not imply that a scientific study of psychological phenomena is not possible or useful; on the contrary, MR says that psychological processes have a foundation in the biological and physical processes and regularities, and it opens the possibility of enlightening explanations of psychological processes at a more basic level. It is only that at a deeper level, psychology becomes sundered by being multiply locally reduced. However, species-specific psychologies, e.g., human psychology, Martian psychology, etc., can all flourish as scientific theories. Psychology remains *scientific,* though perhaps not a *science.* If you insist on having a global psychology valid for all species and structures, you can help yourself with that, too; but you must think of it as a *conjunction* of species-restricted psychologies and be careful, above all, with your inductions.

17

The nonreductivist's troubles with mental causation

I. A BIFURCATED WORLD OR A LAYERED ONE?

Mind–body dualism in the classic Cartesian style envisages two nonoverlapping domains of particulars ("substances") that are, by and large, equal in ontological standing. Mental items are thought to share a certain defining property ("thinking" or "consciousness," according to Descartes) that excludes the defining property shared by the items on the physical side ("extension," according to Descartes). And associated with each domain is a distinct family of properties, mental properties for one and physical properties for the other, in terms of which the particulars within that domain can be exhaustively characterized. We are thus presented with a *bifurcated* picture of reality: the world consists of two metaphysically independent spheres existing side by side.

But not everyone who accepts a picture like this thinks that the two domains are entirely unrelated; although there are notable exceptions, such as Leibniz and Malebranche, many substantival dualists, including of course Descartes, have held that, in spite of their separateness and independence, the domains are *causally* connected: mental events can be, and sometimes are, causes and effects of physical events, and changes in a mind can be causes or effects of changes in a body. This means that events of both kinds can occur *as links in the same causal chain:* if you pick a physical event and trace its causal ancestry or posterity, you may run into mental events, and similarly if you start off with a mental event. It follows then that under Cartesian causal dualism there can be *no complete physical theory of physical phenomena.* For it allows physical occurrences that cannot be causally explained by invoking physical antecedents and laws alone. Any comprehensive theory of the physical world must, on Cartesian interactionism, include references to nonphysical causal agents and laws governing their behavior. We can say then that *Cartesian interactionism violates the causal closure of the physical domain.* Of course, it violates the causal

336

closure of the mental domain as well; Cartesianism implies that no scientific theory could hope to achieve complete coverage unless it encompassed both the physical and mental realms – unless, that is, we had a *unified theory* of both mental and physical phenomena.

The ontological picture that has dominated contemporary thinking on the mind–body problem is strikingly different from the Cartesian picture. The Cartesian model of a *bifurcated* world has been replaced by that of a *layered* world, a hierarchically stratified structure of "levels" or "orders" of entities and their characteristic properties. It is generally thought that there is a bottom level, one consisting of whatever microphysics is going to tell us are the most basic physical particles out of which all matter is composed (electrons, neutrons, quarks, or whatever). And these objects, whatever they are, are characterized by certain fundamental physical properties and relations (mass, spin, charm, or whatever). As we ascend to higher levels, we find structures that are made up of entities belonging to the lower levels, and, moreover, the entities at any given level are thought to be characterized by a set of properties distinctive to that level. Thus, at a certain level, we will find lumps of H_2O molecules, with such properties as transparency, power to dissolve sugar and salt, their characteristic density and viscosity, and so on. At still higher levels we will find cells and organisms with their "vital" properties, and farther up organisms with consciousness and intentionality. Beyond them, there are social groups of organisms, and perhaps groups consisting of such groups.[1] Sometimes, one speaks in terms of "levels of description," "levels of analysis," or "levels of language"; the layered model is often implicit in such talk.

Thus, the world as portrayed in the new picture consists of an array of levels, each level consisting of two components: a set of *entities* constituting the domain of particulars for that level and a set of *properties* defined over this domain. What gives this array structure is the mereological relation of *being part of*: entities belonging to a given layer are mereologically composed of entities belonging to the lower levels, and this relation generates a hierarchical ordering of the levels. As earlier noted, this multitiered picture usually carries the assumption that there is a bottom tier, a layer of entities that have no physically significant parts.

The characterization thus far of the layered model leaves one important

---

1 For a useful and informative presentation of this layered picture, see Paul Oppenheim and Hilary Putnam, "Unity of Science as a Working Hypothesis," in *Minnesota Studies in the Philosophy of Science,* vol. 2, eds. Herbert Feigl, Michael Scriven, and Grover Maxwell (Minneapolis: University of Minnesota Press, 1958).

question unanswered: How are the *properties* characteristic of entities at a given level related to those that characterize entities of its adjacent levels? Given that entities at distinct levels are ordered by the part–whole relation, is it the case that properties associated with different levels are also ordered by some distinctive and significant relationship?[2]

That is the crucial question answers to which have defined various currently contested positions on certain metaphysical and methodological issues including, most notably, the mind–body problem. The classic positivist answer is that the distinctive properties of entities at a given level are *reducible to,* or *reductively explainable in terms of,* the properties and relations characterizing entities at lower levels. That is *reductionism.* But reductionism has had a rough time of it for the past few decades, and has been eclipsed by its major rivals, *eliminativism* and *nonreductivism.* These positions agree in their claim that higher-level properties are in general not reducible to lower-level ones, but differ on the status of irreducible higher properties. Nonreductivism maintains that they can be real and genuine properties of objects and events of this world, constituting an ineliminable part of its true ontology. Eliminativism, on the other hand, holds that they are useless danglers that must be expunged from the correct picture of reality. Thus, the split between nonreductivism and eliminativism hinges on the significance of reducibility: the former, unlike the latter, rejects reducibility as a test of legitimacy for higher-level properties, and holds that such properties can form an autonomous domain, a domain for an independent "special science" that is irreducible to the sciences about lower-level phenomena. *Emergentism,* which was influential during the first half of this century, was the first systematic articulation of this nonreductivist approach.

At first blush, the layered model may appear to hold promise as an elegant way of averting violation of the causal closure of the physical: causal interactions could perhaps be confined within each level, in a way that respected the autonomy and closedness of the causal processes at the fundamental physical level. In particular, on the nonreductivist version of the layered model, it may be possible to view causal chains at a given level, like the properties distinctive of that level, as forming an autonomous and self-contained realm immune to causal intrusions from neighboring levels. Moreover, this picture may not preclude the assignment of some special status to physical causation: in spite of the causal–nomological auton-

2 When the layered model is described in terms of "levels of description" or "levels of language," there is a corresponding question about how the descriptive apparatus (predicates, concepts, sentences, etc.) of one level is related to that of another.

omy at each level, causal relations at higher levels may in some sense depend, or supervene, on the causal-nomological processes occurring at the lower levels[3] – just as, on the nonreductivist view, the irreducibility of higher-level properties is thought to be consistent with their supervenience on the lower-level properties and relations.

Let us narrow our focus on the mind–body problem. *Nonreductive physicalism,* a position that can deservedly be called "the received view" of today, is nonreductivism applied to the mind–body case. It consists of the two characteristic theses of nonreductivism: its ontology is physical monism, the thesis that physical entities and their mereological aggregates are all that there is; but its "ideology" is antireductionist and dualist, consisting in the claim that psychological properties are irreducibly distinct from the underlying physical and biological properties. Its dualism is reflected in the belief that, though physically irreducible, psychological properties are genuine properties nonetheless, as real as underlying physical-biological properties. And there is a corollary about psychology: psychology is an autonomous special science independent of the physical and biological sciences in its methodology and in the concepts and explanations it generates.[4]

As we saw, Cartesian interactionism involves violation of the causal closure of the physical, and that was one cause of its downfall. I shall argue that nonreductive physicalism, and its more generalized companion, emergentism, are vulnerable to similar difficulties; in particular, it will be seen that the physical causal closure remains very much a problem within the stratified ontology of nonreductivism. Nonreductive physicalism, like Cartesianism, founders on the rocks of mental causation.

II. NONREDUCTIVE PHYSICALISM AND "PHYSICAL REALIZATION"

The basic ontological thesis of nonreductive physicalism confers on the physical a certain kind of primacy: all concrete existents are physical –

3 Brian McLaughlin, "Type Epiphenomenalism, Type Dualism, and the Causal Priority of the Physical," *Philosophical Perspectives* 3 (1989): 109–136; J. A. Fodor, "Making Mind Matter More," *Philosophical Topics* 17 (1989): 59–79.

4 There is also the position of Donald Davidson in his "Mental Events," reprinted in Davidson, *Essays on Actions and Events* (Oxford: Oxford University Press, 1980), which accepts both physical ontological monism (usually formulated as a thesis about individual *events*) and property dualism of nonreductive physicalism as characterized here, while rejecting the corollary about the scientific status of psychology. Davidson's views on psychology are hinted at by the title of one of his papers on this issue, "Psychology as Philosophy," in *Essays on Actions and Events.*

there are no nonphysical particulars, no souls, no Cartesian mental substances, and no "vital principles" or "entelechies." Stated as a thesis about properties, physical primacy in this sense comes to this: all mental properties are instantiated in physical particulars. Thus, although there can be, and presumably are, objects and events that have only physical properties, there can be none with mental properties alone; mentality must be instantiated in physical systems.

There appears to be no generally accepted account of exactly what it means to say that something is "physical." Minimally perhaps a physical entity must have a determinate location in space and time; but that may not be enough. Perhaps an entity is physical just in case it has some physical property or other. But what makes a property a physical property? Perhaps, the best answer we could muster is what Hellman and Thompson have offered: explain "physical" by reference to current theoretical physics.[5] This strategy can be extended to higher-level sciences, chemistry and biology; when we reach psychological properties, however, the question as to what should be regarded as our reference scientific theories is itself an unsettled philosophical issue centrally involved in the debates about reductionism and mental causation. For mental properties, then, we must look to vernacular psychology and its characteristic intentional idioms of belief, desire, and the rest, and their intentional analogues in systematic psychology. Nothing in the discussion to follow will depend on precise general definitions of "physical" and "mental."

In any case, many physicalists, including most nonreductive physicalists, are not willing to rest with the ontological primacy of the physical in the sense explained, just as many substantival dualists are not content merely to posit two separate and independent domains. Most nonreductive physicalists want to go beyond the claim that mental properties are had by physical systems; they want to defend a thesis of *primacy, or basicness, for physical properties in relation to mental properties.* The main idea here is that, in spite of their irreducibility, mental properties are in some robust sense *dependent on* or *determined by* physical-biological properties. This means that the property dualism of nonreductive physicalism is an attenuated dualism: it is a dualism with dependency relations between the two domains, just as Cartesian dualism is a dualism with causal connections between its two domains. For many nonreductive physicalists, therefore, irreducibility is not the last word on the mind–body relation-

5 In their "Physicalism: Ontology, Determination, and Reduction," *Journal of Philosophy* 72 (1975): 551–564.

ship. The irreducibility claim is a negative thesis; nonreductive physicalists want a positive account of the relationship between the two sets of properties. Here, the catchwords are "dependence" and "determination." Hellman and Thompson, who have proposed an elegant form of nonreductive physicalism, describe their project as follows:

> Of late there has been a growing awareness, however, that reductionism is an unreasonably strong claim. Along with this has come recognition that reductionism is to be distinguished from a purely ontological thesis concerning the sorts of entities of which the world is constituted. . . . Although a purely ontological thesis is a necessary component of physicalism it is insufficient in that it makes no appeal to the power of physical law. . . . we seek to develop principles of *physical determination* that spell out rather precisely the underlying physicalist intuition that the physical facts determine all the facts.[6]

Hellman and Thompson speak of physical *facts* as determining all the *facts;* presumably, that happens only because what objects have which *physical properties* (including relations) determines what *mental properties* these objects have.

But how do we capture this relation of determination, or dependence, in a way that escapes the threat of reductionism? Answering this question has been one of the principal projects of nonreductive physicalists in the past two decades. Two ideas have been prominent: "supervenience" and "physical realization." Hellman and Thompson themselves gave an account of the determination relation that is very close to what is now commonly known as "global supervenience": once the physical character of a world is fixed, its entire character is thereby fixed.[7] The idea that mental states are "physically realized" (or "instantiated" or "implemented") gained currency, in the late 1960s,[8] chiefly through an argument ("the multiple realization argument") that helped to defeat reductive physicalism and install nonreductivism in its current influential position. The reputed trouble for reductionism was that the realization is

---

6 "Physicalism: Ontology, Determination, and Reduction," pp. 551–552.

7 For a survey of supervenience relations see Essay 8 of this volume.

8 As far as I know, Hilary Putnam first introduced the idea of "physical realization," in the early 1960s, to describe the relationship between "logical" and "structural" states of computing machines, extending it by analogy to the mental–physical case; see his "Minds and Machines," in *Dimensions of Mind,* ed. Sydney Hook (New York: New York University Press, 1960). I believe that the idea really began catching on, in discussions of the mind–body problem, when it was used to formulate the influential "multiple realization argument" in Putnam's seminal paper "Psychological Predicates" (later reprinted under the title "The Nature of Mental States"), in *Art, Mind and Religion,* eds. W. H. Capitan and D. D. Merrill (Pittsburgh: University of Pittsburgh Press, 1967).

"multiple," namely that any given mental state is realizable in a variety of widely diverse physical structures, and that this makes its reductive identification with any single physical property hopeless. The two approaches, one based on "supervenience" and the other on "physical realization," are not mutually exclusive: as we shall see, on reasonable readings of the terms involved the claim that mental states are physically realized arguably entails the claim that they are physically supervenient. Whether the converse entailment holds is a question that depends, among other things, on the strength of the supervenience relation involved.

Many nonreductive physicalists avail themselves of both supervenience and realization, and some do so explicitly; for example, LePore and Loewer characterize nonreductive physicalism by three principles, one of which is "global supervenience," the thesis that "If two nomologically possible worlds are exactly alike with respect to fundamental physical facts . . . then they are exactly alike with respect to all other facts."[9] But they go on to say: "The relationship between psychological and neurophysiological properties is that the latter *realize* the former." What is it for a property to "realize" another? LePore and Loewer explain:

> Exactly what is it for one of an event's properties to *realize* another? The usual conception is that e's being P realizes e's being F iff e is P and e is F and there is a strong connection of some sort between P and F. We propose to understand this connection as a necessary connection which is *explanatory*. The existence of an explanatory connection between two properties is stronger than the claim that P → M is physically necessary since not every physically necessary connection is explanatory.[10]

It is clear that if all mental properties are realized in this sense by physical properties, the global supervenience of the mental on the physical is assured. In fact, their Physical Realization Thesis, as we might call it, entails a stronger form of supervenience, the "strong supervenience" of mental properties on physical ones.[11]

For the purposes of my arguments in this paper I wish to focus on those versions of nonreductive physicalism that make use of "physical realization" to explain the psychophysical property relationship. This for two reasons: first, there are a variety of nonequivalent supervenience relations, and this makes it difficult to formulate a reasonably uniform and perspicuous argument concerning supervenience-based versions; and, second, many philosophers have been converted to nonreductive physi-

---

9 Ernest LePore and Barry Loewer, "More on Making Mind Matter," *Philosophical Topics* 17 (1989): 175–191. The quotation is from pp. 177–178.
10 "More on Making Mind Matter," p. 179.   11 See Essay 4 of this volume.

calism by "the multiple realization argument" briefly alluded to earlier. In consequence, for many nonreductive physicalists, the Physical Realization Thesis is one of their early and basic commitments. It is often a sound expository strategy to formulate an argument in a stark and perspicuous fashion even if this involves making use of fairly strong premises, and then worry about how the argument might be qualified and finetuned to accommodate weaker assumptions. It may well be that there are versions of nonreductive physicalism to which my considerations do not apply, at least not directly;[12] I believe, though, that they are relevant to many of the more popular and influential versions of it.

Let us return to the concept of realization. LePore and Loewer, as we saw above, explain "realization" for properties of *events;* however, there is no need to confine the relation to events, and we will assume that the realization relation, without substantive changes, applies to properties of objects ("substances") as well to those of events. In any case, according to LePore and Loewer, P realizes M just in case (1) $P \rightarrow M$ holds with nomological necessity (LePore and Loewer say "physical necessity") and (2) P "explains" M. I think LePore and Loewer are correct in suggesting these two *kinds* of conditions; however, their specific conditions need improvement. Consider first their explanatory requirement: I believe the idea behind this requirement is correct, but we should look for an objective metaphysical relation between P and M, not an essentially epistemic relation like explanation; that is, we should view the explanatory relation between the two properties as being supported by a metaphysical realization relation. Here I am taking a realist attitude about explanation: if P explains M, that is so because some objective metaphysical relation holds between P and M. That P explains M cannot be a brute, fundamental fact about P and M. In causal explanations the required relation of course is the causal relation. In the case of realization, the key concepts, I suggest, are those of *causal mechanism* and *microstructure.* When P is said to "realize" M in system s, P must specify a microstructural property of s that provides a causal mechanism for the implementation of M in s; moreover, in interesting cases – in fact, if we are to speak meaningfully of "implementation" of M – P will be a member of a family of physical properties forming a network of nomologically connected microstructural states that provides a microcausal mechanism, in systems appropriately like s, for the nomo-

---

12 In particular, Davidson's "anomalous monism" *sans* a supervenience thesis will be largely immune to my argument. But there are other difficulties with such a position; in particular, an account of the causal powers of mental properties appears hopeless under anomalous monism. See Essay 14 of this volume.

logical connections among a broad system of mental properties of which M is an element. These underlying microstates will form an explanatory basis for the higher properties and the nomic relations among them; but the realization relation itself must be distinguished from the explanatory relation. Thus, my difference with LePore and Loewer in regard to their condition (2) is quite small: I agree that something like their explanatory condition should in general hold for the realization relation; however, it should not be regarded as constitutive of it.

What of the condition (1), to the effect that $P \rightarrow M$ be nomically necessary? I believe this condition is acceptable with the following proviso: in each system s in which M is physically realized, there must be a determinate set, finite or infinite, of physical properties, $P_1, P_2, \ldots$, each of which realizes M in the sense explained, so that we may consider the disjunctive property, $P_1 \vee P_2 \vee \ldots$, as a *nomic coextension* of M. Since I will not be making use of this requirement in this paper, I will not offer an argument for it here.[13]

III. NONREDUCTIVE PHYSICALISM AS EMERGENTISM

The nonreductive physicalism I have in mind, therefore, consists of the following theses:

1. [Physical Monism] All concrete particulars are physical.
2. [Antireductionism] Mental properties are not reducible to physical properties.
3. [The Physical Realization Thesis] All mental properties are physically realized; that is, whenever an organism or system instantiates a mental property M, it has some physical property P such that P realizes M in organisms of its kind.

And we must add a further thesis that is implicit in the above three and is usually taken for granted:

4. [Mental Realism] Mental properties are real properties of objects and events; they are not merely useful aids in making predictions or fictitious manners of speech.

I believe that these four basic tenets of nonreductive physicalism bring the position very close to "emergentism" – so close, in fact, that nonreductive physicalism of this variety is best viewed as a form of emergentism. I shall briefly explain why this is so.[14]

13 For reasons for requiring this see Essay 16 of this volume.
14 For details see Kim, "'Downward Causation' in Emergentism and Nonreductive Physicalism," in *Emergence or Reduction?*, eds. Ansgar Beckermann, Hans Flohr, and Jaegwon Kim (Berlin: De Gruyter, 1992).

Emergentists in general accepted a purely materialist ontology of concrete physical objects and events. For example, Samuel Alexander, one of the principal theoreticians of the emergence school, argues that there are no mental events over and above neural processes:

> We thus become aware, partly by experience, partly by reflection, that a process with the distinctive quality of mind or consciousness is in the same place and time with a neural process, that is, with a highly differentiated and complex process of our living body. We are forced, therefore, to go beyond the mere correlation of the mental with these neural processes and to identify them. There is but one process which, being of a specific complexity, has the quality of consciousness. . . . It has then to be accepted as an empirical fact that a neural process of a certain level of development possesses the quality of consciousness and is thereby a mental process; and, alternately, a mental process is *also* a vital one of a certain order.[15]

This is, almost word for word, just what is claimed by "token physicalism" or "the token-identity thesis," a form of nonreductive physicalism. It is no surprise then that Alexander calls his position a version of "the identity doctrine of mind and body."

Both the "layered" structure of the emergentist ontology and its fundamentally physicalist character are evident in the following passage from C. Lloyd Morgan, another leader of the movement:

> In the foregoing lecture the notion of a pyramid with ascending levels was put forward. Near its base is a swarm of atoms with relational structure and the quality we may call atomicity. Above this level, atoms combine to form new units, the distinguishing quality of which is molecularity; higher up, on one line of advance, are, let us say, crystals wherein atoms and molecules are grouped in new relations of which the expression is crystalline form; on another line of advance are organisms with a different kind of natural relations which give the quality of vitality; yet higher, a new kind of natural relatedness supervenes and to its expression the word "mentality" may . . . be applied. Vital*ism* and anim*ism* are excluded if they imply the insertion of Entelechy.[16]

Atoms and their mereological aggregates exhaust all of concrete existence; no "entelechies," or any other physically alien entities, are to be "inserted" at any point in the hierarchy of levels of existence, although new properties emerge to characterize more complex structures of basic entities. There is no room in this picture for any concrete existent not fully decomposable into atoms and other basic physical particulars.

15 *Space, Time, and Deity* (London: Macmillan, 1927), vol. 2, pp. 5–6.
16 *Emergent Evolution* (London: Williams and Norgate, 1923), p. 35.

The emergentist doctrine that "emergent" properties are irreducible to the "basal conditions" out of which they emerge is familiar; to most of us, this irreducibility claim is constitutive of the emergentist metaphysical worldview. Although the emergentists' idea of reduction or reductive explanation diverges from the model of reduction implicit in current antireductionist arguments,[17] the philosophical significance of the denial of reducibility between two property levels is the same: the higher-level properties, being irreducible, are genuine new additions to the ontology of the world. Alexander, for example, says this:

> Out of certain physiological conditions nature has framed a new quality mind, which is therefore not itself physiological though it lives and moves and has its being in physiological conditions. Hence it is that there can be and is an independent science of psychology. . . . No physiological constellation explains for us why it should be mind.[18]

This idea of irreducible higher properties lies at the basis of some recent versions of emergentism such as one promoted by the noted neurophysiologist Roger Sperry, who writes:

> First, conscious awareness . . . is interpreted to be a dynamic emergent property of cerebral excitation. As such conscious experience becomes inseparably tied to the material brain process with all its structural and physiological constraints. At the same time the conscious properties of brain excitation are conceived to be something distinct and special in their own right.[19]
>
> Among other implications of the current view for brain research is the conclusion that a full explanation of the brain process at the conscious level will not be possible solely in terms of the biochemical and physiological data. . . . [20]

For both emergentism and nonreductive physicalism, then, the doctrine of irreducible higher-level properties is the centerpiece of their respective positions; and their proponents take it to be what makes their positions distinctive and important. As net additions to the world, the emergent higher-level properties cannot be reduced or explained away; and as irreducible new features of the world, they form an autonomous domain, and, as Alexander says, make "an independent science of psy-

---

17 For more details see Kim, "'Downward Causation' in Emergentism and Nonreductive Physicalism."
18 *Space, Time, and Deity*, p. 8.
19 "A Modified Concept of Consciousness," *Psychological Review* 76 (1969): 532–536. The quotation is from p. 533.
20 "A Modified Concept of Consciousness," p. 535.

chology" possible. This is exactly what current nonreductive physicalists have been urging for over two decades: the "special sciences" are autonomous and independent from the underlying physical and biological sciences.[21]

Let us now turn to the third basic tenet of nonreductive physicalism, the Physical Realization Thesis. This involves the claim that for a mental property to be instantiated in a system, that system must instantiate an appropriate physical property, and further that whenever any system instantiates this physical property, the mental property must of necessity be instantiated by it as well. Mental events and states require physical bases, and when required physical bases are present, they must occur. A precisely parallel thesis was part of the emergentist doctrine: the emergence of higher-level properties requires appropriate "basal conditions," and when these basal conditions are present, they must of necessity emerge. For both the nonreductive physicalist and the emergentist, physical bases are *by themselves* sufficient for the appearance of the higher-level properties; as Morgan says, "no insertion of Entelechy," or any other nonphysical agent, is required for the emergence of higher properties:

> Since it is pretty sure to be said that to speak of an emergent quality of life savours of vitalism, one should here parenthetically say, with due emphasis, that if vitalism connotes anything of the nature of Entelechy or Elan – any insertion into physicochemical evolution of an alien influence which must be invoked to explain the phenomenon of life – then, so far from this being implied, it is explicitly rejected under the concept of emergent evolution.[22]

And Morgan goes on to stress the necessity of physical bases for all higher-level phenomena:

> Thus, for emergent evolution, conscious events at level C (mind) involves specific physiological events at level B (life), and these involve specific physico-chemical events at level A (matter). No C without B, and

21 In spite of all this, there is an apparent difference between emergentism and nonreductive physicalism concerning the relationship between properties belonging to adjacent levels. As may be recalled, LePore and Loewer require that the physical ("realization") base must *explain* the mental property it realizes. However, emergentists will deny that the "basal conditions" can ever constitute an explanatory basis for any property emergent from them. Much of the difference can be traced, I believe, to differing conceptions of explanation and reduction involved; for further details see Kim, "'Downward Causation' in Emergentism and Nonreductive Physicalism." This difference, whether real or only apparent, will not affect the applicability of the main argument of this paper to both emergentism and nonreductive physicalism.

22 *Emergent Evolution*, p. 12.

no B without A. No mind without life; and no life without "a physical basis." [23]

There is little doubt, I think, that on these three crucial tenets there is a broad agreement between emergentism and nonreductive physicalism, and that it is fair, and illuminating, to view nonreductive physicalism as a form of emergentism. It isn't for nothing that nonreductive physicalists sometimes speak of higher-level properties as "emergent." [24]

As for the fourth thesis of nonreductive physicalism, that is, Mental Realism, it is clear that the quotations from the emergentists that we have seen are shot through with realism about mentality. To the emergentist, emergent evolution is a historical fact of paramount importance; through the process of emergent evolution, the world has reached its present state – more complex, richer, and fuller. Most physicalists who reject reductionism also reject mental eliminativism; this realist attitude is implicit in what we have called the Physical Realization Thesis (assuming realism about the physical). And it is all but explicit in the claim, accepted by both emergentists and many nonreductivists, that psychology is a legitimate special science (unless one adopts a universal antirealism about all science); as such it must investigate a domain of real phenomena and systematize them by discovering laws and causal connections governing them.

IV. MENTAL REALISM AND MENTAL CAUSATION

But just what does the commitment to the reality of mental properties amount to? What is the significance of saying of anything that it is "real"? Alexander supplies an apt answer in a marvelous paragraph in which he curtly dismisses epiphenomenalism:

[Epiphenomenalism] supposes something to exist in nature which has nothing to do, no purpose to serve, a species of *noblesse* which depends on the work of its inferiors, but is kept for show and might as well, and undoubtedly would in time be abolished. [25]

This we may call "Alexander's dictum": *To be real is to have causal powers.* I believe this principle, as applied to concrete existents and their properties, will be accepted by most nonreductive physicalists.

23 *Emergent Evolution*, p. 15.
24 E.g., Hellman and Thompson say this: "what may be called 'emergence' of higher-order phenomena is allowed for without departing from the physical ontology," in "Physicalism: Ontology, Determination, and Reduction," p. 555.
25 *Space, Time, and Deity*, vol. 2, p. 8.

Emphasis on the causal role of emergent properties is pervasive in the emergentist literature. Here is a pair of revealing quotations:

> Just as the holistic properties of the organism have causal effects that determine the course and fate of its constituent cells and molecules, so in the same way, the conscious properties of cerebral activity are conceived to have analogous causal effects in brain function that control subset events in the flow pattern of neural excitation. In this holistic sense the present proposal may be said to place mind over matter, but not as any disembodied or supernatural agent.[26]

> But when some new kind of relatedness is supervenient (say at the level of life), the way in which the physical events which are involved run their course is different in virtue of its presence – different from what it would have been if life had been absent.[27]

What is striking about these paragraphs is the reference to "downward causation": both Morgan and Sperry seem to be saying that mentality, having emerged from physical-biological processes, takes on a causal life of its own and begins to *exercise causal influence "downward" to affect what goes on in the underlying physical-biological processes.* Whether the idea of such causation makes sense is one of the main questions I want to discuss in the balance of this paper. But let us first note what the nonreductive physicalist has to say about mental causation.

There is no question that the typical nonreductive physicalist has a strong commitment to the reality of mental causation. As we saw, our nonreductivist is not an eliminativist: why bother with mental properties unless you think that they are good for some causal work and can play a role in causal explanations? Fodor puts the point this way:

> I'm not really convinced that it matters very much whether the mental is the physical; still less that it matters very much whether we can prove it. Whereas, if it isn't literally true that my wanting is causally responsible for my reaching, and my itching is causally responsible for my scratching, and my believing is causally responsible for my saying, . . . if none of that is literally true, then practically everything I believe about anything is false and it's the end of the world.[28]

One could hardly declare one's yearnings for mental causation with more feeling than this! Nonreductive physicalists in general regard mental causation seriously; they have expended much energy and ingenuity trying

26 Sperry, "A Modified Concept of Consciousness," p. 533.
27 Morgan, *Emergent Evolution,* p. 16. 28 "Making Mind Matter More."

to show they are entitled to mental causation.[29] I don't think that they can have what they want, and that will be my main burden in the remainder of this paper. My argument, if correct, will also show that Fodor is wrong in feeling that he could have his wishes fulfilled without having to worry about the mind–body problem – about "whether the mental is the physical."

Here is my plan for the remainder of this paper: I shall first show that both emergentism and nonreductive physicalism are committed to downward causation – that is, mental-to-physical causation for the mind–body case. This should be no news to the emergentist: for in a sense downward causation is much of the point of the emergentist program. What I shall show would still be of interest, even for emergentism, since the argument will make clear that downward causation is *entailed* by the basic tenets of emergentism, and of nonphysical reductionism. I shall then argue that the idea of downward causation is highly problematic, and perhaps incoherent, given the basic physicalist commitments.

V. NONREDUCTIVE PHYSICALISM IS COMMITTED TO DOWNWARD CAUSATION

It is easy to see just how downward causation follows from the basic principles of emergentism and nonreductive physicalism. First, as we have observed, the emergentist and the nonreductive physicalist are mental realists, and Mental Realism, via Alexander's dictum, entails causal powers for mental properties. In fact, whether or not they accept Alexander's dictum, most of them will want causal powers for mental properties. Now, mental properties, on both positions, are irreducible net additions to the world. And this must mean, on Alexander's dictum, that mental properties bring with them *new causal powers, powers that no underlying physical-biological properties can deliver.* For unless mentality made causal contributions that are genuinely novel, the claim that it is a distinct and irreducible phenomenon over and beyond physical-biological phenomena would be hollow and empty. To be real, Alexander has said, is to have causal powers; *to be real, new, and irreducible, therefore, must be to have new, irreducible causal powers.*

This fits in well with the autonomy thesis, alluded to earlier, concern-

29 See, e.g., LePore and Loewer, "Mind Matters," *Journal of Philosophy* 93 (1987): 630–642, and "More on Making Mind Matter"; Fodor, "Making Mind Matter More"; Davidson, "Thinking Causes," in *Mental Causation,* eds. John Heil and Alfred Mele (Oxford: Clarendon Press, 1993).

ing the science of psychology: as an empirical science, psychology must generate causal explanations of phenomena in its domain; and as an irreducible, autonomous science, the causal explanations it delivers must themselves be irreducible, representing causal connections in the world not captured by the underlying sciences. The autonomy thesis, therefore, makes sense only if causal relations involving mental events are novel and irreducible – that is, mental properties are endowed with genuinely new causal powers irreducible to those of underlying physical-biological properties.

If M is a mental property, therefore, M must have some new causal powers. This must mean, let us suppose, that M manifests its causal powers by being causally efficacious with respect to another property, N; that is, a given instance of M can cause N to be instantiated on that occasion. We shall assume here a broadly nomological conception of causality, roughly in the following sense: an instance of M causes an instance of N just in case there is an appropriate causal law that invokes the instantiation of M as a sufficient condition for the instantiation of N. There are three cases to be distinguished: (i) the property N for which M is a cause is a mental property; (ii) N is a physical property; (iii) N is a higher-level property in relation to M. Case (i) is mental-to-mental causation ("same-level causation"); case (ii) is mental-to-physical causation (that is, "downward causation"); and case (iii) is a possibility if there are properties, perhaps social properties, that emerge from, or are realized by, mental properties ("upward causation").

My argument will show that case (i) is possible only if case (ii) is possible; namely, that mental-to-mental causation presupposes mental-to-physical causation. It will be clear that the same argument shows case (iii) presupposes case (ii), and therefore case (i). So suppose M is causally efficacious with respect to some mental property M^*, and in particular that a given instance of M causes an instance of M^*. But M^*, qua mental property, is physically realized; let P^* be its physical realization base. Now we seem to have two distinct and independent answers to the question, Why is this instance of M^* present? *Ex hypothesi*, it is there because an instance of M caused it; that's why it's there. But there is another answer: it's there because P^* physically realizes M^* and P^* is instantiated on this occasion. I believe these two stories about the presence of M^* on this occasion create a tension and must be reconciled.[30]

30 This is essentially identical to the situation we face when we are given two distinct independent causes for one and the same event, each claimed to be a sufficient cause. For further details see Essay 13 of this volume.

Is it plausible to suppose that the *joint* presence of M and P^* is responsible for the instantiation of M^*? No; because that contradicts the claim that M^* is physically realized by P^*. As we saw, this claim implies that P^* alone is sufficient to bring about M^*, whether or not any other condition, earlier or later or at the same time, obtained (unless it is somehow connected with the occurrence of P^* itself – we shall recur to this possibility below). And the supposition is also inconsistent with our initial assumption that the given instance of M was a sufficient condition for that instance of M^*. Nor is it plausible to suppose that the occurrence of M^* on this occasion was somehow *overdetermined* in that it has two distinct and independent origins in M and P^*. For this, too, conflicts with the assumption that M^* is a property that requires a physical realization base in order to be instantiated, and that this instance of M^* is there because it is realized by P^*. In the absence of P^*, we must suppose that M^* could not have been there – unless an alternate realization base had been present. In either case, every instance of M^* must have some physical base that is by itself sufficient for M^*; and this threatens to preempt M's claim to be the cause of this instance of M^*.

I believe the only coherent story we can tell here is to suppose that the M-instance caused M^* to be instantiated *by causing P^*, M^*'s physical realization base, to be instantiated*. This of course is downward causation, from M to P^*, a case of mental-to-physical causation. I believe the argument goes through with "physical realization" replaced with "emergence."[31] The gist of my argument is encapsulated in the following principle, which I believe will be accepted by most nonreductive physicalists: ›

[The causal realization principle] If a given instance of S occurs by being realized by Q, then any cause of this instance of S must be a cause of this instance of Q (and of course any cause of this instance of Q is a cause of this instance of S).

A parallel principle stated for emergence will be accepted by many, if not all, emergentists. In any case, I think we apply this principle constantly in daily life: for example, we treat pain by intervening with bodily processes, and we communicate by creating vibrations in the air or making marks on paper. (Direct mental-to-mental causation between different individuals is generally considered disreputable and unscientific: it goes by such names as "ESP," "telepathy," and "mind reading.")

But couldn't we avoid this commitment to downward causation by

31 See my "'Downward Causation' in Emergentism and Nonreductive Physicalism."

exploiting the fact that M, as a mental property, has its own physical realization base, say P? Why not say then that M's causation of P^* comes to merely this: M is physically realized by P, and P causes P^*. The more basic causal relation obtains between the two physical properties, P and P^*, and M's causation of M^* is ultimately grounded in the causal relation between their respective physical realization bases. I think this is a highly appealing picture,[32] but it is not something that our nonreductivists can avail themselves of. For the picture reduces the causal powers of M to those of its realization base P: P is doing all the causal work, and M's causation of P^*, or of M^*, turns out to be derivative from P's causal powers. Thus, M has no causal powers over and beyond those of P, and this is contrary to Alexander's dictum and the assumption that M is an irreducible property. I shall take up this point again in the next section.

What these reflections show is that within the stratified world of nonreductive physicalism and emergentism, "same-level" causation can occur only if "cross-level" causation can occur. It will not be possible to isolate and confine causal chains within levels; there will be inevitable leakage of causal influence from level to level.

VI. WHAT'S WRONG WITH DOWNWARD
CAUSATION?

So does downward causation make sense – that is, within the scheme of nonreductive physicalism? I think there are some severe problems. As we shall see, the tension arises out of an attempt to combine "upward determination" with "downward causation." The nonreductive physicalist wants both: mentality is determined by, and dependent on, the physical, and yet minds are to have causal powers, novel causal powers that can be exercised, if my argument is correct, only by causally affecting physical-biological processes in novel ways.

Suppose then that mental property M is causally efficacious with respect to physical property P^*, and in particular that a given instance of M causes a given instance of P^*. Given the Physical Realization Thesis, this instance of M is there because it is realized by a physical property, say P.

---

32 This is similar to the model of "supervenient causation" I have suggested in earlier papers of mine, e.g., Essay 6 of this volume. It has been called "causal reductionism" by Peter Menzies in "Against Causal Reductionism," *Mind* 97 (1988): 551–574. Also see LePore and Loewer, "More on Making Mind Matter," and Gabriel Segal and Elliott Sober, "The Causal Efficacy of Content," *Philosophical Studies* 63 (1991): 1–30.

Since P is a realization base for M, it is sufficient for M, and it follows that P is sufficient, as a matter of law, for P^*. Now, the question that must be faced is this: What reason is there for not taking P as the cause of P^*, bypassing M and treating it as an epiphenomenon?[33]

I believe this epiphenomenalist solution with regard to M cannot easily be set aside: we are looking for a causal explanation of why P^* is instantiated at this time. We see that M was instantiated and we can invoke a law connecting M-instances with P^*-instances. But we also see that P was instantiated at the same time, and there is an appropriate law connecting P-instances with P^*-instances. So the situation is this: P appears to have at least as strong a claim as M as a direct cause of P^* (that is, without M as an intervening link). Is there any reason for invoking M as a cause of P^* at all? The question is not whether or not P should be considered a cause of P^*; on anyone's account, it should be. Rather, the question is whether M should be given a distinct causal role in this situation. I believe there are some persuasive reasons for refusing to do so.

First, there is the good old principle of simplicity: we can make do with P as P^*'s cause, so why bother with M? Notice that given the simultaneity of the instances of M and P respectively, it is not possible to think of the M-instance as a temporally intermediate link in the causal chain from P to P^*. Moreover, if we insist on M as a cause of P^*, we run afoul of another serious difficulty, "the problem of causal-explanatory exclusion."[34] For we would be allowing two distinct sufficient causes, simultaneous with each other, of a single event. This makes the situation look like one of causal overdetermination, which is absurd. And *ex hypothesi*, it is not possible to regard M and P as forming a single jointly sufficient cause, each being individually necessary but insufficient. And given the assumed irreducibility of M, we cannot regard M as identical with P, or as a part of it. The exclusion problem, then, is this: Given that P is a sufficient physical cause of P^*, how could M *also* be a cause, a sufficient one at that, of P^*? What causal work is left over for M, or any other mental property, to do? M's claim as a cause of P^* will be weakened especially if, as we would expect in real-life neurobiological research,

---

33 To be precise, we should put this in terms of *instances* of these properties rather than the properties themselves. In what follows, liberties of this form are sometimes taken to avoid verbosity.

34 For more details see Essay 13 in this volume, and my "Explanatory Exclusion and the Problem of Mental Causation," in *Information, Semantics, and Epistemology*, ed. Enrique Villanueva (Oxford: Basil Blackwell, 1990).

there is a continuous causal chain, a mechanism, connecting P with P^*. It is clear that the exclusion problem cannot be resolved within the framework of nonreductive physicalism.

All these considerations, I want to suggest, point to something like the following as the natural picture for the layered physicalist world: all causal relations are implemented at the physical level, and the causal relations we impute to higher-level processes are derivative from and grounded in the fundamental nomic processes at the physical level.[35] This goes perhaps a bit, but not much, beyond what is directly implied by the supervenience thesis most nonreductive physicalists accept: if, as the supervenience thesis claims, all the facts are determined by physical facts, then all causal relations involving mental events must be determined by physical facts (presumably including facts about physical causation).

Consider, then, a somewhat bald way of stating this idea:

[The Causal Inheritance Principle] If M is instantiated on a given occasion by being realized by P, then the causal powers of *this instance of M* are identical with (perhaps, a subset of) the causal powers of P.

In other words, higher states are to inherit their causal powers from the underlying states that realize them. Nonreductivists must reject this principle; they will say that higher-level causal powers are "determined by," but not identical with (or reducible to), the lower-level causal powers. What our considerations have made clear is that if "determined but not identical" means that these higher-causal powers are genuinely novel powers, then nonreductivists are caught in a web of seemingly insurmountable difficulties. And I challenge these nonreductivists who would reject this principle to state an alternative principle on just how the causal powers of a realized property are connected with those of its realization base; or explain, if no such connections are envisioned, the significance of the talk of realization.

The implications of the Causal Inheritance Principle are devastating to nonreductive physicalism: if the causal powers of M are identical with those of its realization bases, then M in effect contributes nothing new causally, and M's claim to be a new, irreducible property is put in jeopardy. And if, as suggested, M is treated as an epiphenomenal dangler from its physical realization base, with no causal work of its own to do, the next step of the argument, as mandated by Alexander's dictum, will be that

35 There is a strong indication that Fodor, for example, accepts this sort of principle in his "Making Mind Matter More."

355

M ought to be "abolished." All this seems like an inescapable lesson of Alexander's dictum.

The case for skepticism about downward causation is strengthened when we see that, as in the case of Cartesian interactionist dualism, it breaches the causal closure of the physical domain. What is worse, when we see that *P*, *M*'s realization base, is there to serve as a full cause of *P** – and this will always be the case whenever a mental cause is invoked – the violation isn't even as well motivated as it is with Cartesian interactionism.

Most emergentists will have no problem with the failure of the physical causal closure; although they may have to tinker with their doctrines somewhere to ensure the overall consistency of their position, they are not likely to shed any tears over the fate of the closure principle. For many emergentists that precisely was the intended consequence of their position. I doubt, however, that contemporary nonreductive physicalists can afford to be so cavalier about the problem of causal closure: to give up this principle is to acknowledge that there can in principle be no complete physical theory of physical phenomena, that theoretical physics, insofar as it aspires to be a complete theory, must cease to be pure physics and invoke irreducibly nonphysical causal powers – vital principles, entelechies, psychic energies, élan vital, or whatnot. If that is what you are willing to embrace, why call yourself a "physicalist"? Your basic theory of the world will have to be a mixed one, a combined physical-mental theory, just as it would be under Cartesian interactionism. And all this may put the layered view of the world itself in jeopardy; it is likely to require some serious rethinking.

At this juncture it seems highly plausible that the only solution to the exclusion problem and the problem of the physical causal closure lies in some form of reductionism that will permit us to discard, or at least moderate, the claim that mental properties are distinct from their underlying physical properties. It is this claim that forced us to posit for mentality novel and distinct causal powers, thereby leading us to the present predicament. To identify the causal powers of mentality with those of its underlying physical base is, in effect, to deny it a distinct ontological status, and consider it reduced.

But a question must leap to your mind at this point, if you are at all familiar with current wisdom in philosophy of mind: Doesn't the Physical Realization Thesis itself, given the phenomenon of "multiple realizability," rule out any form of reductionism? Hasn't "the multiple realization argument" refuted reductionism once and for all?[36] The entrenched, almost automatic, response is "yes" to both questions. I believe the correct answer is a qualified but firm "no." But defending that answer is something I must leave for another time.[37]

36 See Putnam, "Psychological Predicates," and J. A. Fodor, "Special Sciences, or the Disunity of Science as a Working Hypothesis," *Synthese* 28 (1974): 97–115.

37 See Essay 16 of this volume for further details; for further development see "Postscripts on Mental Causation," section 2.

18

Postscripts on mental causation

1. MENTAL CAUSATION AS SUPERVENIENT CAUSATION

The account of mental causation defended in various essays in Part II views mental causation as "supervenient causation." The idea, roughly, is that for an instance of mental property M to cause, or be caused by, event e (let's assume e is a physical event), the following conditions must hold: there is a physical-biological property P such that (1) M supervenes on P; (2) P is instantiated on the occasion of M's instantiation; and (3) this instance of P causes e, or is caused by e (on your favorite account of physical causation). I still find something like this account, and a similar one for the case of mental–mental causation, attractive and appealing in many ways, but I believe that the account is faced with some difficulties that have yet to be resolved.

Some specific objections and criticisms have been voiced by philosophers including Brian McLaughlin, Peter Menzies, and Gabriel Segal and Elliott Sober.[1] Although the points made by them are by and large valid and need to be taken seriously, I do not think that they strike at the heart of the account; I think they are reasons for refining the account rather than reasons for abandoning the approach. (In fact, Segal and Sober helpfully offer an improved version of the account.) The approach has much intuitive plausibility as well as a potential to satisfy various philosophical requirements, and for that reason it may well be worth saving. The basic idea was a simple one: causal relations among macroevents and macroproperties must hold in virtue of (and therefore be explicable in terms of) causal relations holding for events and properties at a more basic level.

1 Brian McLaughlin, "Event Supervenience and Supervenient Causation," *Southern Journal of Philosophy* 22 (1984), the Spindel Conference Supplement: 71–92. Peter Menzies, "Against Causal Reductionism," *Mind* 97 (1988): 551–574. Gabriel Segal and Elliott Sober, "The Causal Efficacy of Content," *Philosophical Studies* 63 (1991): 1–30.

This is only a special case of the general thesis that all the facts about the world supervene on microphysical facts. But can this basic idea be developed into a viable philosophical account? I want to discuss here two potential difficulties with the model of supervenient causation, presented in Essay 4 and elsewhere, as a way of implementing this basic idea.

The first issue concerns how we should deal with the epiphenomenalist. He believes the following things: (1) mental events never cause anything, and mental properties are causally inert; (2) every mental event is caused by some physical event. The epiphenomenalist, therefore, believes that once all the physical facts are fixed, that fixes all the mental facts. That is, he accepts mind–body supervenience. The supervenience claim just stated has the form of "global supervenience"; but the epiphenomenalist, we can be sure, will be comfortable with the local supervenience of the mental on the physical – the thesis that the physical-biological states of an organism wholly determine its conscious states. But the epiphenomenalist also accepts (1), the claim that the mental is causally inert. And to all appearances epiphenomenalism is a consistent position. If this is the case, the model of supervenient causation cannot, it seems, be the whole story. For the epiphenomenalist is willing to accept that M_1 is supervenient on P_1 and that an instance of P_1 causes P_2 to be instantiated, but he rejects the causal efficacy of M_1 with respect to P_2. So the question is this: If "supervenient causation" is something that even the epiphenomenalist can live with, might it not be "causation" in name only? Is it a robust enough relation to vindicate the causal efficacy of the mental?[2]

True, on epiphenomenalism, the relation of M_1 to P_1 is not, strictly speaking, one of supervenience, but causation: P_1 *causes* M_1 to be instantiated, and, unlike mind–body supervenience as standardly understood, this may involve a time lapse between an instance of P_1 and the instance of M_1 it causes. In Essay 6, I attempt to exploit this difference, but offer no convincing explanation of why this difference should make a difference. I am now uncertain whether it is anything more than a mere technical difference; the epiphenomenalist would have been happy, I think, to use terms like "supervenience" or "supervenient determination" rather than

2 Among those who have raised worries of this sort are Cynthia and Graham Macdonald, "Mental Causes and Explanation of Action," in *Mind, Causation and Action*, eds. Leslie Stevenson, Roger Squires, and John Haldane (Oxford: Blackwell, 1986), p. 37; Peter Bieri, "Trying Out Epiphenomenalism," *Erkenntnis* 36 (1992): 283–310; and John R. Searle, *The Rediscovery of the Mind* (Cambridge, Mass.: The MIT Press, 1992), p. 125.

"causation" if they had been available. Whether the psychophysical relation is characterized as "causal determination" or "supervenient determination" might have made little difference to the epiphenomenalist.

One possible way of meeting this difficulty is this: we turn the table around and say that these considerations show after all that there are versions of epiphenomenalism that are not as implausible as epiphenomenalism is often thought to be, usually without a close consideration.[3] To be more exact, it may be arguable that the considerations that have led, or misled, the epiphenomenalist to his deflationary conclusions about the mind's causal powers in truth show only that mental causation is an instance of supervenient causation, and that this means (Essay 6) that *mental causation is as robust and respectable as any other kind of causal relation involving macroproperties and events.* In any case, there may only be a very fine line between epiphenomenalism about a class of (apparent) causal relations and the view that these causal relations are not among the fundamental causal processes of the world but are only supervenient or dependent on them. (This is similar to the fine line that separates an eliminativism about a class of entities and a reductionism about them.) In any case, physicalism must respect the basicness and priority of the physical, and this must include respect for the basicness of physical causation. If physical facts determine all the facts, it must be the case that physical facts, including causal facts about physical events and states, must determine all the facts about mental causation. For this reason, any "physicalistically correct" account of mental causation must inevitably make mental causation dependent on, and derivative from, physical causation, thereby exposing itself to the charge of epiphenomenalism.

As I argue in Essays 14, 15, and 17, one of the problems that must be addressed by any theory of mental causation is that of "causal exclusion." The problem, briefly, arises from the assumption, which is widely accepted by physicalists, that the physical domain is causally closed – that is, if a physical event has a cause at *t*, it has a physical cause at *t*. Given this assumption, it is difficult to see how mental properties can have any role in the causation of physical events – unless, that is, they are reductively identifiable with physical properties. But this is reductionist type physicalism which few philosophers now accept. In general, a sufficient cause of an event excludes the claim of any other distinct synchronous event to be a cause of the same event (Essay 13) – unless the situation is one of genuine causal overdetermination, a possibility that may be disregarded. The

3 On this question see Peter Bieri, "Trying Out Epiphenomenalism."

physical causal closure, therefore, seems to leave no room for nonphysical causes of physical events (Essays 14, 15, 17): If a physical event has a sufficient physical cause, what causal work is left for an event consisting in the instantiation of some *nonphysical* mental property?

Can the model of supervenient causation provide a nonreductivist solution to this problem? The supervenience relation involved is strong supervenience; it's clear that neither weak nor global supervenience is appropriate for the job. Let's set aside the potential difficulty that strong mental–physical supervenience might entail mental–physical reducibility, with the result that supervenient causation turns out to be a reductionist solution. Assuming then that some nonreductive supervenience relation is available for supervenient causation, let us return to our question: Is supervenient causation a solution to the exclusion problem?

The answer, I believe, is that supervenient causation as developed in Essay 6 may not be a fully adequate solution, and here is why. *Ex hypothesi, M_1* is supervenient on, but distinct from, *P_1,* and *P_1* is a sufficient cause of *P_2* (for brevity I delete references to *instances* of these properties). But if *P_1* is a sufficient cause of *P_2,* what causal work is there for *M_1* to contribute in the causation of *P_2?* Granted that *M_1* is supervenient on, and dependent on, *P_1* and hence not an independent cause of *P_2:* so long as *M_1* remains a distinct property not identified with *P_1,* we must, it would seem, still contend with the two purported causes of a single event. Given the assumption implicit in this model that fundamental causal processes occur at the physical level, the causal role imputed to *M_1* in relation to an event at the physical level should strike us as something mysterious, and we should wonder what purpose could be served by this shadowy "supervenient cause" that accompanies the physical cause. (It is plain that this problem is closely related to the problem of epiphenomenalism discussed earlier.)

We must conclude then that the supervenience of M on P does not by itself remove M as a competitor of P as a cause, and the threat of its being excluded by P seems to remain. We already know that the reductive identification of M with P eliminates the causal competition, and thereby solves the exclusion problem. Are there M–P relations that are intermediate in strength between supervenience and identity that will do just as well?

In a recent paper,[4] Stephen Yablo makes an interesting suggestion which consists of two parts: first, that if M is related to P as *determinable*

---

4 "Mental Causation," *Philosophical Review* 101 (1992): 245–280.

to *determinate,* an instance of M need not compete with an instance of P for causal role; and, second, that the relationship between mental properties and their underlying physical properties is appropriately construed on the model of the determinable–determinate relation.

Segal and Sober have suggested that the mere supervenience of M on P is too weak to serve as a basis of explaining the causal efficacy of M in terms of that of P, and that what is required for the job is a special form of supervenience, "mereological supervenience," according to which properties of a whole supervene on the properties and relationships characterizing its mereological parts.

Both these proposals fall under the supervenience approach to mental causation, and they are worthy of close scrutiny in connection with the exclusion problem. In particular, we need to see just why M and P will not compete as causes if they are related in the ways specified. And we need to know whether the mental–physical relation can be correctly described on the model of the determinable–determinate relation or mereological supervenience (on the latter question, see "Postscripts on Supervenience," section 2).

There is another possible approach which may hold more promise. This approach attempts to make use of the relation of "physical realization." The proposition that the mental is physically realized is widely accepted (Essay 16); many philosophers would consider it obvious and philosophically innocuous (but see below). The main idea of this approach is this: if a given instance of M occurs in virtue of being realized by P, the M-instance and its P-realizer do not compete for causal role. This approach will be discussed in some detail in the next postscript.

2. PHYSICAL REALIZATION AND MENTAL CAUSATION

One of the more salient conclusions of Essay 16 is that mental properties are causally inhomogeneous in the sense that two instances of the same mental property may have quite diverse causal powers, and that the more diversely a mental property is realized, the greater its causal inhomogeneity. We are assuming here of course that mental properties are in general multiply realizable, and that the physical realizers of mental properties are nomic-causal kinds. In the same essay, I proposed a causal principle ("the Causal Inheritance Principle") about multiply realizable properties, which says this: if a multiply realizable property M is instantiated on a given occasion in virtue of the instantiation of one of its realizers, P_i, the causal powers of *this instance of* M are the same as the causal powers of P_i.

Thus, the causal powers of mental property M are sundered into causal powers of its many diverse realizers, P_1, P_2, ... When we speak of the causal powers of M as such, we are speaking disjunctively of the causal powers of the P_i's; and when we speak of the causal powers of a particular M-instance without knowing, or referring to, the specific P_i that realizes M on that occasion, we are again speaking disjunctively of the causal powers of M's many possible realizers. It might be, as some have observed, that almost any property could realize any mental property, depending on the system in which it is embedded. If that should be true, we would have to conclude that little information was conveyed by talk of the causal powers of a mental property outside a specific context. However, in most situations there are likely to be enough background assumptions and tacit information to circumscribe, at least broadly, the class of possible alternative realizers so that reference to the causal powers of a mental property can carry important and useful content. For example, we already know a good deal about the nomologically possible neural substrates of human pains, and this can serve as the basis of useful causal information about instances of human pain.

Are mental properties "causally efficacious" on this account? The answer is that a mental property is causally efficacious as long as, and to the extent that, each of its possible realizers is causally efficacious; and a particular instance of a mental property has exactly the causal efficacy of its realizer on that occasion. This confirms the causal efficacy of mental properties.

But what about the exclusion problem? Consider an instance of M, and the P-instance that realizes it. According to the foregoing account, they have the same causal powers; in fact, the M-instance "inherits" its causal powers from the P-instance. But they are both invoked as a cause of some identical effect. Doesn't this mean that we are back in our predicament, one in which we have two distinct causes of a single event, and unless we are willing to countenance this as a case of causal overdetermination, are we not forced to apply the exclusion principle here, with the predictable consequence, namely that the mental loses out to the physical?

To see that the exclusion problem can be resolved on the present account, we need to attend to the concept of "realization." As the term "realization" is typically used in discussions of the mind–body problem, it seems to carry something like the following metaphysical picture: for M to be instantiated on a given occasion *is* for an appropriate P to be instantiated on that occasion in an appropriate causal environment. There is no further fact of the matter, as one might say, to M's instantiation on this occasion beyond P_i's instantiation in the particular context involved. I think this is precisely where the concept of "physical realizer" or "physical realization base" differs from concepts like "physical correlate" or "neural substrate." A serious attribute dualist, an emergentist or epiphenomenalist, or even a Cartesian, could allow that mental properties have neural (and other types of physical) correlates, but he would insist that this is only a matter of *two distinct properties* lawfully covarying with one another (he might even allow the mental side to "depend" on the physical side). For such a theorist, the instantiation of a mental property is an important additional fact beyond the instantiation of its neural substrate. This is why the serious property dualist will, and should, take mental properties as genuine, "first-order" properties with their own distinctive intrinsic natures, whereas the functionalist – the idiom of "realization" is central to most versions of functionalism – considers mental properties as extrinsic and relational, or "second order," constituted by their "causal roles" and specified by "job descriptions."

Given this general picture, a simple solution to the exclusion problem suggests itself. Unless disjunctive types are countenanced – and there are reasons for not doing so (Essay 16) – the standard type physicalism is precluded; that is, we cannot identify mental properties or kinds with physical ones, and we cannot in general identify M-instances with P-instances, for some physical property P. However, any given M-instance must be either a P_1-instance or P_2-instance or . . . , where P_1, P_2, . . . are realizers of M, and the set of all M-instances is the union of all these P_i-instances.[5] In this sense, we may say that mental kind M is *disjunctively identified* with physical kinds P_1, P_2, ... Note that M is not identified with the *disjunction* of P_1, P_2, . . . ; nor is an M-instance identified with an instance of the disjunctive property $P_1 \vee P_2 \vee$ . . . . We may call this proposal "multiple-type physicalism."

It is easy to see how the exclusion problem is dealt with on this approach. An M-instance is identical with a P_i-instance, for some M-realizer P_i, and hence there is one event here, not two, and this dissipates the causal competition.

---

5 This may lead to a revision of the standard property-exemplification account of events (Essay 3) – especially if mental properties, in spite of their multiple physical realizability, are accepted as legitimate event-generating properties. For on the standard account two property instances count as distinct events if the properties instantiated are distinct. I believe, though, that this is a problem about properties, not one directly about

Finally, let us see how the present proposal differs from token physicalism – for example, Davidson's "anomalous monism." [6] On token physicalism, mental tokens – that is, individual mental events – are identical with physical tokens, but mental kinds or properties are distinct from physical kinds and properties. Thus, token physicalism amounts to the claim that if any individual event falls under a mental kind, or has a mental property, it also falls under a physical kind, although mental kinds are not physical kinds. What is so unsatisfying about this as an account of the mind–body relation is the fact that it says nothing about the relationship between mental and physical properties; the only positive thing it says about that relationship is that mental and physical properties are co-instantiated in objects and events. Since token physicalism is usually formulated within a framework of events taken as unstructured particulars (sometimes called "Davidsonian events"), a direct comparison of it with what I have called "multiple-type physicalism" is a bit awkward, since the latter has been formulated within the framework of events taken as property exemplifications (Essay 3). However, it is not difficult to see that multiple-type physicalism goes beyond token physicalism in saying something about how mental properties and kinds are related to physical kinds. It states that for an event, or object, to have a mental property is for it to have one or another of its realizing physical properties.

The multiple realizability of the mental has led too many philosophers to jump onto the bandwagon of token physicalism. But that is a mistake; for token physicalism is entirely silent on the important insight concerning psychophysical type–type relations that is contained in the multiple realization thesis. Something like multiple-type physicalism seems to me nearer the correct ontology of mind for those who take multiple realization seriously.

What about mind–body reductionism? Again, token physicalism is unsatisfying here because it flatly denies any reductive relationship between the mental and the physical. But what the multiple physical realizability of the mental tells us is that we can reduce, and reductively explain, each and every instance of mental property M, even though we cannot reduce all M-instances at once. Unless disjunctive physical kinds are embraced, we cannot reduce M to some P; that much is entailed by the multiple realizability of the mental. But that is far from the whole story about

events. Considerations advanced in Essay 16 concerning disjunctive properties may be reason enough for excluding mental properties as constitutive properties of events.
6 Donald Davidson, "Mental Events," reprinted in *Essays on Actions and Events* (Oxford: Oxford University Press, 1980).

reduction; that each mental token event is physically reducible is a highly significant fact about the mind–body relationship. It may well be that something like multiple-type physicalism is what most proponents of token physicalism, especially those who have been moved to embrace it by considerations on multiple realization, have had in mind (although Davidson is not among them).

All this assumes that the mental is "physically realized." Is that true? Should we think of the psychophysical type–type relationship in terms of "realization"? Various issues arise here: one concerns "wide-content" states; another concerns the question whether all mental states – in particular, phenomenal states with qualitative content – are correctly viewed as realized by their neural substrates. As earlier noted, the fact (assuming that it is a fact) that mental properties have neural correlates does not imply that they are "realized" by the latter. This is the case even if we add the further assumption that mental properties depend on their neural correlates. The idiom of "realization" carries with it an implicit commitment to a view of mentality that has been closely associated with functionalism, something that not everyone will accept. As we saw, the emergentists, for example, will happily acknowledge, as one of their central claims, the thesis that all higher properties, including consciousness and mentality, have lower-level correlates ("basal conditions") on which they depend, but they will insist that mental properties, although they arise out of and depend on biological processes, remain irreducibly distinct from them as robust properties in their own right, with their own intrinsic characters. The instantiation of a mental property does not, on their view, *consist in* the instantiation of some lower-level property in an appropriate causal context, as the functionalist maintains. The intuition that militates against the functionalist position and its attendant "realization" idiom is the same intuition that makes the functionalist account of qualia and consciousness so unsatisfying to many people.

Ultimately, we are likely to face the following choice: either embrace the realization view and save mental causation, or insist on the unique and distinctive status of mental properties, especially the qualia, but be prepared to give them up as causal powers.[7] The paradoxical thing about this is that the choice offered may only be an illusion of a choice, for the two options may in the end collapse into one. If you choose the former, you may lose what makes the mental distinctively mental; and what good

7 Compare Frank Jackson, "Epiphenomenal Qualia," *Philosophical Quarterly* 32 (1982): 127–136. See also Terence Horgan, "Supervenient Qualia," *Philosophical Review* 96 (1987): 491–520.

is it, one might ask, if you save mental causation but end up losing mentality in the process? (The Vietnam metaphor of saving a village by destroying it comes to mind.) If you choose the latter, again you may lose the mental, for what good is something that is causally impotent? Why should we bother to save belief and desire, or qualia, if their presence or absence makes no difference to anything else and we can't use them to explain anything? Being real and having causal powers go hand in hand (Essay 17). We therefore seem to be up against a dead end. Perhaps, that is what's really so intractable about the problem of the mind.

Index

supervenience as a type of, 54, 165–169
See also Cambridge change, dependence,
    event; determination; superve-
    nience
Descartes, Rene, 216, 219, 230, 336
determination, 22, 26–32, 53–54, 60, 76
    holistic, 114
    micro-macro, 101–102, 322, 330
    physical, 341
    See also dependence, dependency
determinism
    causal, 76–77, 97, 102
    universal, 22, 30, 34
    See also microdeterminism
downward causation, 326, 349–356
Dreier, James 142n, 157n
Dretske, Fred, xiv, 257n, 280n, 285–308
dualism, 266–267, 284
    Cartesian, 336–337
    property dualism, 267, 332, 340
    substantival (substance), 336
Ducasse, C. J., 29, 33, 50

Edwards, Jonathan, 92–94, 102
Elgin, C. Z., 195n
eliminativism, 214, 234, 267–268, 270,
    279, 317, 334, 338, 348, 360
emergence, emergent property, 134–135,
    138, 158–160, 347
    irreducibility of, 346–347
emergentism, 134–135, 138, 158–160,
    338–339, 344–350
    See also downward causation
Enc, Berent, 274n
Endicott, Ronald, 331n
epiphenomenal causation, 92–108
epiphenomenalism, 94, 104–105, 158,
    348, 359–361
epiphenomenon, 94–95, 107, 244–245,
    288, 354
epistemology
    Cartesian, 216, 219
    naturalized, 216–236
    normative epistemology and normative
        ethics, 218–219, 232–234, 236
    normativity of, 216–219, 224–230
    possibility of epistemology, 234–236
event, 3–4, 8–12, 33–52
    composite event, 19, 30–31
    conjunctive event, 19
    constitutive object of, 9, 35–36, 41
    constitutive property (attribute) of, 9–12,
        17, 28, 35–38, 41, 43–45, 48, 52

    constitutive time of, 9, 35–36, 41
    Davidson's theory of, 38–42
    dyadic event, 10, 35
    elimination of, 36
    essential property of, 47–49
    event and action involving causal rela-
        tions, 49–52
    existence condition of, 9, 35–36
    generic, type of, 3, 12, 17, 35–38, 44–
        45, 48, 52
    identity condition of, 9–11, 35–36,
        38–39
    intrinsic description of, 42, 49
    location of, 4, 10, 18, 23, 40
    monadic event, 9–10, 35
    as ordered triple, 35–36
    proliferation of, 44–46
    as property exemplification, 8–12, 34ff.
    redescription of, 43–44
    sentential description of, 5–7
    supervenience of, 99
    See also Cambridge change, dependence,
        event
exclusion problem, *see* causal-explanatory
    exclusion; explanatory exclusion
explanation
    causal, 250–254
    dependent, 255
    explanatory overdetermination, 252
    Hempelian, 244
    independent and complete, 239,
        247–249
    multiple explanations of single explanan-
        dum, 237–243, 250ff.
    See also action: rationalizing explanation
        (rationalization) of
explanatory coherence, 258
explanatory compatibility, 237–238, 241
    See also explanatory exclusion
explanatory exclusion, 237–264
    application of, 260–264
    epistemological version, 257–259
    metaphysical version, 257–259
    and Ockham's Razor, 259–260
    principle of, 239–240, 250ff.
    See also causal–explanatory exclusion
explanatory realism, xii, 238, 256, 258–
    259, 343
Explanatory Thesis, 183, 188–190
extrinsic, *see* intrinsic/extrinsic

Fain, Haskell, 14n
Feigl, Herbert, 267, 271, 309

Montague, Richard, 9n
Moore, G. E., 54–55, 61, 62n, 74–75,
   136–137, 149–150, 157, 176–177,
   231n, 233, 275
moral supervenience, *see* normative (moral,
   ethical, valuational) supervenience
Morgan, C. Lloyd, 134, 138–139, 158–
   159, 345, 347–349n
Morton, Adam, 197n
multiple-domain supervenience, 112ff.
   epistemological issues of, 122
   for coordinated multiple domains, 123ff.
   metaphysical issues of, 123
   relationship with global supervenience,
      117–123
multiple realizability, 89, 98, 179–180,
   267, 271–275, 309ff., 365
   and psychophysical law, 273, 314–315,
      317–318
   and type physicalism, 309–310, 316ff.
   See also multiple realization argument;
      realization
multiple realization argument (against reductionism), 179–180, 267–268,
   271–275, 316ff., 341, 356–357
Multiple Realization Thesis (MR), 309
   See also multiple realizability

Nagel, Ernest, 134n, 150n, 248n, 260,
   268n, 317
naturalism, ethical, epistemological,
   233–234
nomic equivalent, simultaneous, 243–
   247
nomic subsumption, *see* subsumption
   under law
noninternal (state, property), *see* internal
   (state, property)
nonreducibility, 140
   See also reduction, reducibility
nonreductive physicalism (materialism),
   135, 144, 265–284, 310–311, 339ff.
   basic tenets of, 344
   and downward causation, 349–356
   as a form of emergentism, 344–348
   and mental causation, 349ff.
   and supervenience, 85–89, 275–279
nonreductivism, 338, 341
   See also nonreductive physicalism (mate-
      rialism)
normative (moral, ethical, valuational)
   supervenience, 54–56, 61–62, 77,
      109, 136–137, 141–142, 148–150,
      157, 166, 175–177, 235–236, 275

Oppenheim, Paul, 7n, 101n, 260–263,
   337n
Owens, David, 320n

pairing problem, 14–21
pairing relation, 14–15, 17, 21
Pap, Arthur, 5n
paradigm, scientific, 263–264
part–whole relation, *see* mereological
   relation
Paull, Cranston, 170
Pepper, Stephen C., 134n
Pereboom, Derk, 311n, 318n, 326n,
   330–331
Petrie, Bradford, 82n, 85n, 86, 88n, 154n,
   276n
Pfeifer, Karl, 252n
phenomenalism, translational, 128–129
physical realization, *see* realization
Physical Realization Thesis, 322–327,
   329–330, 332, 342, 344, 347–348,
   353, 356
physicalism, 96, 267
   multiple-type, 364–366
   ontological, 266
   and supervenience, 85–89, 275–279
   token, 345, 365
   type physicalism, 282, 309, 311, 360
   See also identity theory (mind–body, psy-
      chophysical, psychoneural); materi-
      alism; nonreductive physicalism
      (materialism)
Plantinga, Alvin, 130n
Pollock, John, 83n, 185n, 232n
Post, John, 152n, 157, 169n, 276n, 311n,
   313n
projectibility, 319–321, 327
property
   causal, 279
   closure under Boolean operations, 37,
      58, 73–74, 169–170, 321–322
   conjunctive, 153
   disjunctive, 152–153, 272, 316–318,
      320–321, 332, 334–335, 364
   distinguished from concept, 333–334
   distinguished from predicate, 72–73, 321
   extrinsic (noninternal), 88, 169–171,
      184–185, 289–290, 314, 332
   first-order, 314, 364

374

identity of, 43, 317–318
identity vs. correlation of, 317
infinite conjunction and disjunction of, 58–59, 72–73, 151–152
intrinsic (internal), 88, 162, 169–178, 183–185, 188–190, 314, 332
maximal, 58–59, 72–73, 115
negative, 153, 321
nomic, 321
nonrelational, 184
relational, 87–88, 163–165, 178, 184, 290
and resemblance (similarity), 153, 321
second-order, 312, 314, 323, 331–332, 364
semantic, 289–290
simplicity of, 72–73
syntactic, 289–290
property distribution, 113–117
individual-specific, 116
individuation of, 115–117
isomorphic, 116
structure-specific, 116
pseudoprocess, 93
psychological anomalism, 210–212
See also anomalism of the mental; psychophysical anomalism
psychological causation, *see* mental causation
psychological explanation, 188–191
psychology, status of, 194–197, 325, 327–330, 334–335
species-specific, 334–335
under nonreductive physicalism, 350–351
See also folk (vernacular) psychology
psychophysical anomalism, 139, 150, 196–197, 204, 209–213, 246, 268–270
See also anomalism of the mental; psychological anomalism
psychophysical causation, *see* mental causation
Psychophysical Correlation Thesis, 178–181
arguments against, 179–181
psychophysical law, 176, 178–181, 191, 194–215, 246
species-specific, 180, 273–274, 328–330
See also bridge laws (principles); psychophysical anomalism
psychophysical (mind–body) supervenience, 56–57, 63, 85, 107–109, 141–

142, 165, 167–169, 175–193, 270n, 275–279, 289, 341–342, 359
argument for, 191–193
for Cartesians, 112, 114, 121–123, 126
counterexamples against, 86–88, 181–183
evidence for, 86, 159, 178–181, 191–193
as minimal physicalism, 168–169
nonsupervenient psychological state, 86–88, 181–183
and physicalism, 176–177
of qualitative states, 193
Supervenience Thesis, 183, 185–186
as theory of the mind–body relation, 167–169
Putnam, Hilary, 86–88, 89n, 98n, 101n, 104n, 191n, 267, 271–273, 279, 282, 283n, 289n, 310, 312, 313n, 316, 333, 334n, 337n, 341n, 357n

Quine, W. V., 9n, 56n, 195, 198, 204, 213–214, 219–227, 229–230, 232, 236n, 268, 322n, 326n, 334n

Railton, Peter, 255n
rationality
as a characteristic of the mental, 203–204, 228–229
principle of rationality maximization, 203, 206–208
realization, 179–180, 272–274, 309–310, 313–316, 322, 341–344, 362–364, 366
and causal powers, 326, 362–363
concept of, 313–315, 342–344, 363–364, 366
and laws, 273, 313–315
of macroproperty, 98
physical realization of psychology, 179–180, 315, 329
realization base, 313, 315–316, 323, 326–327, 329
"realizer" vs. "correlate" or "substrate," 314, 331, 364, 366
and supervenience, 179–180, 342
See also multiple realizability; multiple realization argument (against reductionism)
reduction, reducibility, 97, 149ff., 248–249, 260–263, 268, 272, 309–311, 316–318

375